PICTORIAL HISTORY
OF MICHIGAN

PICTORIAL HISTORY OF MICHIGAN:

The Early Years

by

GEORGE S. MAY
Associate Professor of History
Eastern Michigan University

A John M. Munson Michigan History Fund Publication

MICHIGAN HISTORICAL COMMISSION
DEPARTMENT OF STATE

WILLIAM B. EERDMANS PUBLISHING COMPANY
GRAND RAPIDS, MICHIGAN

The Early Years
Copyright © 1967 by William B. Eerdmans Publishing Company

The Later Years
Copyright © 1969 by William B. Eerdmans Publishing Company

Printed in the United States of America

CONTENTS

FOREWORD

"I consider it important that the citizens of Michigan have adequate and correct knowledge of the history and functions of the state of Michigan and its institutions and that this should be taught to the young people in its schools and colleges." This was the judgment of Dr. John M. Munson when he established a trust fund for the publication of works dealing with Michigan history. A native of Pennsylvania and a graduate of Michigan State Normal College, Dr. Munson devoted his entire career to Michigan education. He served for a number of years in the State Department of Public Instruction, spent ten years as president of Northern State Teachers College (Marquette), and for a decade and a half was president of Michigan State Normal College (Ypsilanti). With a lifelong interest in the history of his adopted state, he established the John M. Munson Michigan History Fund and entrusted the Michigan Historical Commission with responsibility for the publication of such historical material.

The first book-length publication of the John M. Munson Michigan History Fund, F. Clever Bald's *Michigan in Four Centuries,* appeared in 1954 and almost immediately became the standard textbook treatment of Michigan history. Because of enthusiastic public response, the Michigan Historical Commission began the next year to gather material for a pictorial history that would serve as a companion volume to this scholarly book. The Commission Archivist, Dr. Philip Mason, now head of the Labor History Archives at Wayne State University, was the first director of the project, which was later carried through to completion by another staff member, Dr. George S. May. Early in 1966, Dr. May joined the staff of Eastern Michigan University, but he continued to work on the pictorial history. This volume is mainly the result of his dedicated efforts. His many other publications in the field of Michigan history, particularly those on Mackinac and the Civil War and his articles and reviews in regional historical quarterlies, give ample evidence of Dr. May's competence in this field.

The result of a dozen years of work by the Michigan Historical Commission, the *Pictorial History of Michigan: The Early Years* has been compiled with the hope of bringing to Michigan citizens a broader knowledge of the rich heritage of this region.

HUDSON MEAD, President 1966-67
Michigan Historical Commission

INTRODUCTION

In the world of the Twentieth Century, Michigan is generally distinguished from the other forty-nine members of the United States of America by its unique geographical outlines and by the fact of its association with the automobile industry and, to a secondary degree, with other manufacturing activities.

This has not always been the case. Although Michigan's geographical features have remained the same as long as mankind can remember, the products for which Michigan has been famous have changed greatly through the centuries. Before Michigan was a state, long before there was a United States, Michigan was known for its furs. Later, it became renowned for the fish that were found in the waters that separated its two great peninsulas, for the pine and other timber found in the vast forests that covered these peninsulas, for the rich soils that were found to the south, and for the equally rich mineral deposits in the northern reaches of the state.

For nearly three hundred years after Michigan first appears in the recorded annals of history, this area was part of the American West, a land of opportunity for anyone, be he fur trader, fisherman, lumberjack, miner, or farmer, who had the courage and the strength to wrest from this land the wealth nature had bestowed upon it. This book is an attempt to recreate, through pictures, that earlier Michigan which preceded the modern Michigan of the automobile and the freeway, the urbanized and industrialized state in America's Middle West which is famous, not for its natural resources, but for the products of its factories and laboratories.

The very term pictorial history is, to some extent, a misnomer, since any historical account must be based primarily on written records and no amount of pictures can provide the detailed knowledge and understanding that such documents provide. Yet historians who neglect the pictorial record do so at their own risk. One picture may or may not equal a thousand words, but the insight into the individuals who made history and into the conditions under which they lived that can be gained through a study of the pictures from a particular era is something that cannot be measured.

In an effort to approach the view of this earlier era in Michigan's history that was held by those who lived it, I have confined my selection, with only a very few exceptions, to illustrative material from the period or to photographs of physical objects that existed in those years. This means that the kind of re-creation of historical events by artists of a later generation that the reader may be accustomed to seeing in pictorial histories will not be found here. Although there are many paintings of this type that relate to topics included in this book and although their use would add considerable color, they have been excluded in the interests of historical authenticity. It is hoped that whatever may have been lost by this omission will be more than made up by the unusual variety of illustrative items of an original, historical character which I have been fortunate enough to locate and include in the pages that follow.

In any history, the historian must select the material he includes. This selectivity is probably most evident in a pictorial history. Many who are familiar with Michigan history will no doubt find that some of their favorite pictures have not been included or will think that certain topics deserve more attention than I have given to them. Space limitations, plus a desire to reproduce the pictures on as large a scale as possible, made it necessary to exclude much good material and to slight or leave out entirely some subjects. The decision as to what to include was made on the basis of my own personal, no doubt subjective, view of what was important as far as the present book is concerned.

In a work of this nature, many people and many organizations and institutions are involved. Elsewhere in the book I acknowledge the debt I owe to all those who aided in the collection of pictures. In addition, however, I should like to express my appreciation to several others without whose help and co-operation this history would never have been completed. I began this book when I was research archivist with the Michigan Historical Commission but I did the bulk of the work after joining the faculty of Eastern Michigan University. At all times the Commission staff was generous in its assistance while the expenses attending the collection and reproduction of pictures for the book were underwritten by the Commission's John M. Munson Michigan History Fund. To William B. Eerdmans, Jr., the publisher, is due the credit for suggesting the project in the first place and for his never-flagging desire to see that the physical appearance of the publication would be of the finest quality possible. Working with him and his staff, particularly Cornelius ("Casey") Lambregtse, who is responsible for the splendid design and layout of the book, was for me one of the most pleasant features of the entire project.

Finally, I am grateful for the support and encouragement of my wife during what must have seemed to her the interminable period that I worked on this book.

GEORGE S. MAY

Ann Arbor, Michigan

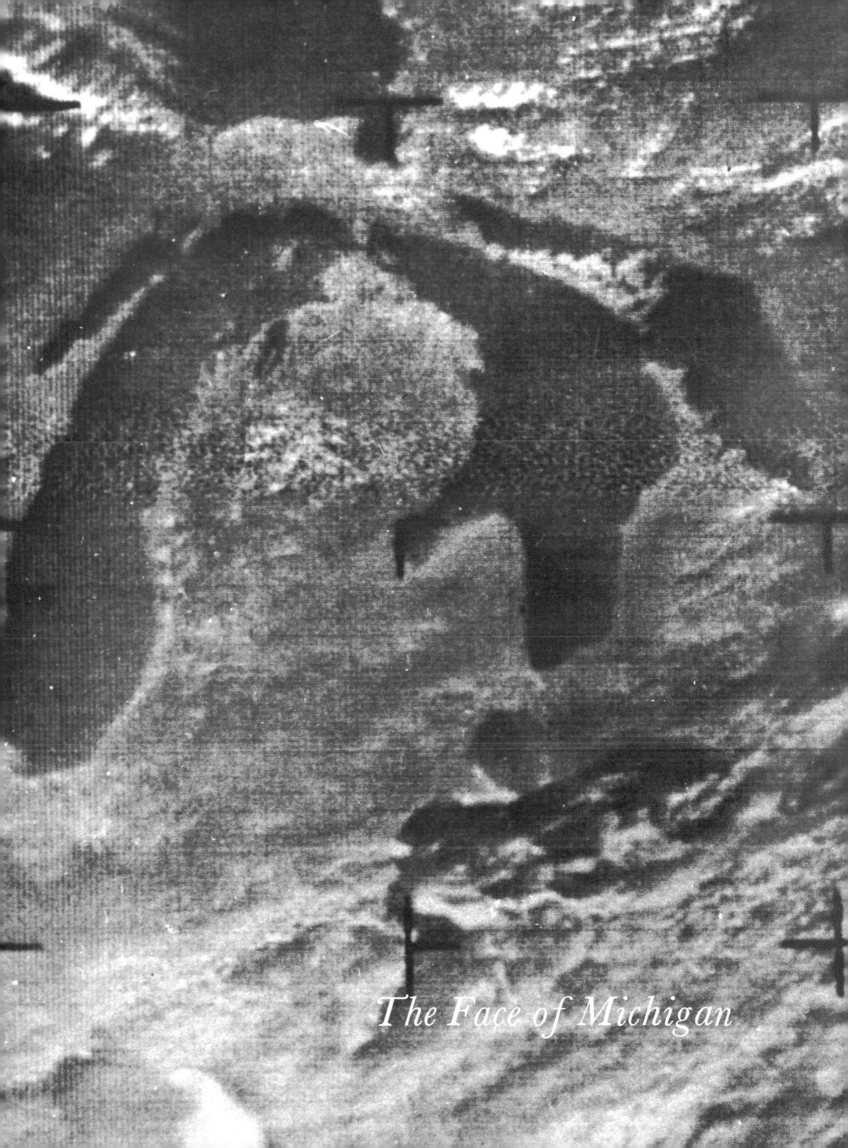

The Face of Michigan

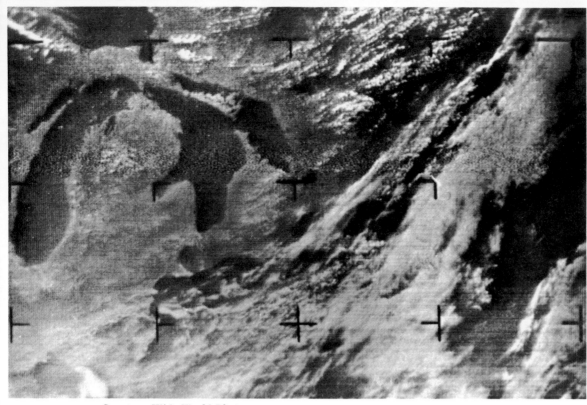

There could be no doubt about it. Through the clouds that obscured some areas to the east, the camera of NASA's weather satellite, Nimbus 1, had photographed the upper Great Lakes and the peninsulas that divide these vast bodies of fresh water. Even from five hundred miles above the earth's surface, the familiar outlines were clearly visible. The date was August 29, 1964. Michigan had had its picture taken.

Courtesy: Wide World Photos

Three centuries before the camera of Nimbus 1 recorded Michigan's image, the future state's distinctive geographical features were being gradually revealed to the civilized world of western Europe. The French, who had begun exploring the St. Lawrence River valley in the sixteenth century, probed ever deeper into the continent in the early decades of the 1600's. The extent of the knowledge which they gained was indicated by the French royal cartographer, Nicolas Sanson d'Abbeville, in this map of Canada or New France, published in 1656. All five Great Lakes are shown, although Sanson left Lake Superior and Lac de Puans (Lake Michigan) open-ended on the west, candidly admitting his ignorance of these interior regions. Although the shape of Michigan's two peninsulas was beginning to emerge on this map, Michigan as a geographical and political unit did not then exist, nor would it for another century and a half.

Courtesy: William L. Clements Library

The land which the French found and which is now called Michigan was then, as much of it still is today, a vast wilderness, covered with magnificent stands of timber, such as can be seen in Hartwick Pines State Park near Roscommon, timber that would later prove a source of seemingly unlimited wealth.

Courtesy: Michigan Department of Conservation

Although the green foliage that covered their surfaces imparted to Michigan's two peninsulas a certain sameness in appearance, the French soon discovered that there was actually a surprising variety in the topography of the area. There was a rugged character to the northern, or Upper Peninsula, as, for example, in the Porcupine Mountains in the west . . .

15

. . . or in its many waterfalls, especially the most majestic of them all, Tahquamenon Falls, near the peninsula's eastern end . . .

Courtesy: Michigan Tourist Council

. . . or in such spectacular phenomena as Miner's Castle, part of the Pictured Rocks, which, for all their beauty, are dwarfed by the cold majesty of Lake Superior, the world's largest non-saline lake, whose waters wash the entire northern shore of the Upper Peninsula, adding a certain harsh, yet appealing, feature to the peninsula's character.

16

A characteristic of lower Michigan is the rivers which flow to the east or to the west from a watershed running up through the center of the peninsula. Near the northern tip, a tortuous network of connecting lakes and rivers forms an inland waterway running from Lake Huron almost all the way across to Lake Michigan.

In the central part of the lower peninsula, Dead Stream Swamp, northwest of Houghton Lake, provides still another element of variety to Michigan's landscape. The Muskegon River, at the lower left, joins the Dead Stream, lower right, and the waterway then snakes its way down toward Reedsburg Dam.

17

On the lower peninsula's western shore, the prevailing winds sweeping in from Lake Michigan have brought about the formation of huge sand dunes such as this one, the giant, Sleeping Bear Dune. The winds, the lake, and the sands combined to provide the basis for a prosperous recreation industry and a climate that would foster the development of a bountiful fruit-growing agricultural economy.

Courtesy: Michigan Tourist Council

Northern Michigan's topography, the French found, contained much that was spectacular and strikingly beautiful, but it was the gently rolling, fertile lands of the southern third of the lower peninsula that would become home for the vast majority of the millions of people who came to reside in Michigan in the centuries after the French arrived. This characteristic of the terrain of southern Michigan also made the task of the twentieth-century road builder easier. This view is of the area around the I-96, US-27, and M-78 interchange, south of Lansing.

Courtesy: Michigan State Highway Department

The Prehistoric Indians

The French were not the first people in Michigan, for when they began arriving in the 1600's they were greeted by several thousand Indians, such as the Ottawas, one of whom was sketched by a Frenchman of somewhat primitive artistic talents.

The untrained eye sees little evidence of Indian life at the Spring Creek site, and, in fact, pitifully few remains are left of the people who inhabited Michigan for possibly ten thousand years before the first white inhabitants arrived. The best-known visible remains have been the mounds which these prehistoric Michiganians built for burial purposes and perhaps for other uses. The largest reported in Michigan was the great mound on the River Rouge, a half-mile from the Detroit River. It was seven to eight hundred feet long, four hundred feet wide, and at least forty feet high when viewed by Americans in the early nineteenth century. By the 1880's, when this sketch was published, it had been reduced to half its original size, and since that time it has been completely leveled.

Michigan's Indians, whose sole means of transportation was the canoe, were scattered over the two peninsulas, camping principally along the numerous waterways. One such campsite, located on high ground overlooking Spring Creek in Muskegon County, has been excavated by archaeologists, who determined that the site was occupied sometime around A.D. 1000.

Courtesy: Grand Rapids Press

The largest surviving group of authentic Indian mounds in Michigan are these, known as the Norton Mounds, located near the Grand River, west of Grand Rapids. They date from the time of Christ. The gravel pit in the foreground, dating from 1963, is a symbol of the forces of progress which erase the past in the name of the present.

Some of the Norton Mounds were excavated in 1963-64 by the University of Michigan and the Grand Rapids Public Museum. The archaeologists carefully dug down through the topsoil and into the mound itself, finally reaching the level at which bodies had been buried in a period in world history when France and England were mere outposts of the Roman Empire.

The skeletal remains found in one of the Norton Mounds are shown here, together with artifacts that were buried with these Indians.

Courtesy: University of Michigan Museum of Anthropology

Courtesy: University of Michigan Museum of Anthropology

Through a study of pottery, bone implements, and other artifacts found in the Norton Mounds, and by comparing them with artifacts found elsewhere, archaeologists are gradually able to piece together a picture of the cultural development of the prehistoric Indians.

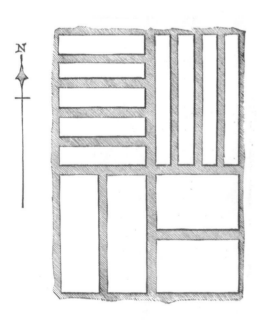

Courtesy: University of Michigan Museum of Anthropology

Long since obliterated by the white man's plow are the so-called Garden Beds which nineteenth-century settlers found in Kalamazoo County and a few other areas in the state. The exact purpose, whether ceremonial or utilitarian, that these ridges of earth, carefully laid out in geometric patterns, in some cases covering five acres, were intended to serve is a disputed subject. These, which were found in Kalamazoo County, are outlined in *Memorials of a Half-Century,* by Bela Hubbard, who declared that they were the most common type found by the pioneers. By the 1880's, when he wrote his book, however, Hubbard was unable to find scarcely a trace of any of the Garden Beds.

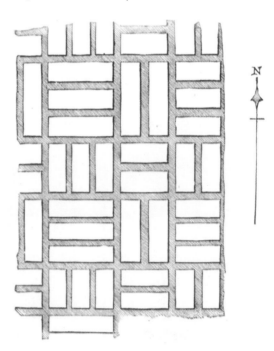

Indian rock carvings and paintings, which have furnished clues to the life of the prehistoric Indians elsewhere in the New World, are almost nonexistent in Michigan. One exception are the carvings on rock outcroppings near the confluence of the north and south forks of the Cass River in Sanilac County.

Time's weathering action has nearly erased these Sanilac Petroglyphs, as the engravings are called, but they are still visible, especially when the incisions are traced with chalk. What special meaning, if any, this figure and the geometric design held for the Indians who made the carvings can only be guessed.

Closely related in design to the Sanilac Petroglyphs are paintings, presumably of Indian origin, high above the water line of sheer rock cliffs known as Burnt Bluff, near Fayette on the southern shore of the Upper Peninsula.

But the best-known relics of Michigan's prehistoric Indians are the arrowheads and other stone implements which the farmer's plow and the amateur archaeologist's shovel have turned up by the thousands all over the state. Unless each such artifact is carefully identified as to where it was found, it is of little use to the anthropologist or professional archaeologist. Nevertheless, these simple, man-made weapons and tools can assist their finder in conjuring up a picture of the individuals who manufactured them, and who lived and died in Michigan over a period of years many times longer than the length of time that today's non-Indian inhabitants and their ancestors have resided in the same area.

The French advance into the interior of North America was led and directed by Samuel de Champlain. He reached the shores of Georgian Bay, the eastern arm of Lake Huron, in 1615, while others whom he sent out touched Michigan's shores by about 1620. No authentic portrait of Champlain exists, but there are several monuments, such as this one in Quebec, the city he founded in 1608, which honor Champlain as the "Father of New France." It was as a part of this colony that Michigan would first become acquainted with the white man and his ways.

In 1632 a map was published in Champlain's *Les Voyages de la Nouvelle France Occidentale* of which this is a section. Lake Huron (here called *Mer douce*) and Lake Superior (*Grand lac*) are shown, crudely to be sure, and they are connected by a series of rapids (*Sault*), to which the name Sault Ste. Marie would shortly be given.

Courtesy: William L. Clements Library

Courtesy: Public Archives of Canada

NOVVELLE FRANC

La Nation des Puans.

Isle ou il y a vne mine de cuiure.

grand lac.

Lieu ou les sauuages font secherie de framboise, et blues tous les ans.

Mer douce.
Descouuertures de ce grand lac, et de toutes ses terres depuis le sault St. Louis par le sr. de Champlain, es années 1614. et 1615. iusques en l'an 1618

ande riuiere qui vient du mi dy

Les gens de assistagueronons

Nation ou il y a quantité de beuffles

La nation neutre

Les gens de feu

Virginia

Lac des Biserenis.

Biserenis.

Chasse descaribous.

Cheueux releuez

Algommequin.

Gens de petun

Hurons.

Petite nation des Algommequins.

Lac St. Louis.

Lieu ou il y a forte Cerf.

Hiroçois.

Antouoronons.

Carantouan nou

Lac de Champlain.

Sain tonge.

Habitation de sauuages manganaticouoit.

C. Charles.

C. Henry.

Isle de l'Ascension.

Baye de nostre Da

Rhuière de C.

Carte de la nouuelle france, augmentee depuis la derniere, seruant a la nauigation faicte en son vray Meridien par le sr. de Champlain Capitaine pour le Roy en la Marine, lequel depuis l'an 1603 iusques en l'annee 1629, a descouuert plusieurs costes, terres, lacs, riueres, et Nations de sauuages, par cy deuant incogneus, comme il se voit en ses relations qu'il a faict Imprimer en 1632. ou il se voit cette marque I° ce sont habitations qu'ont faict les françois.

During the course of his explorations, Champlain became involved in an Indian war, taking the side of Canadian tribesmen against the Iroquois Indians south of the St. Lawrence River in New York. With their guns, a weapon then unknown to the Iroquois, the few Frenchmen easily won the day for their allies, as shown in this contemporary sketch of the event. The skirmish had important consequences for Michigan, since it made the fierce Iroquois the implacable enemies of France. Rather than following the St. Lawrence-Great Lakes waterway system, which ran through Iroquois country, the French would move westward through central Ontario. Thus it was that northern Michigan, which lies directly west of the route through Ontario, became the first part of the state to be reached by the white man.

In 1641, two Jesuit missionaries, Father Isaac Jogues, shown here in a rare contemporary portrait, and Father Charles Raymbault, went from their Huron Indian mission at the head of Georgian Bay to the river that links Lakes Superior and Huron. Here, at the rapids which they named Sault de Sainte Marie, the Jesuit fathers met with the Indians of the area and conducted the first Christian services ever held on Michigan soil.

Shortly after returning to their Huron mission, Father Jogues, Father Raymbault, and their colleagues and Indian converts were attacked by the Iroquois. In one of these attacks Father Jogues, who would be sainted by his church, was killed, an event depicted in a contemporary painting. It is appropriate that one of the Catholic churches in Sault Ste. Marie today honors with its name this Jesuit martyr.

The Huron Indians who survived the Iroquois onslaught fled westward to the distant shores of Lake Superior. An artist who illustrated Champlain's account of his explorations from 1615 through 1618 depicted members of this tribe in a rather romantic manner.

Eventually, when peace among the Iroquois and the French was temporarily restored, the Jesuits went west, seeking the remnants of the Christian Hurons. In the late 1600's, Father Jacques Marquette, shown here in a twentieth-century reconstruction of a faded painting on wood that is believed to be the only authentic surviving portrait of Marquette, served with these Indians near what is now Ashland, Wisconsin, as well as founding a mission at Sault Ste. Marie in 1668, which is the basis for the Soo's claim to being Michigan's oldest white settlement.

When the Huron Indians in the early 1670's again moved, this time east to the Straits of Mackinac, the Jesuits established a mission at this strategic point connecting Lakes Huron and Michigan. It was first located briefly on Mackinac Island in a bark chapel, similar to this one now seen on the island, a recent reconstruction based on seventeenth-century descriptions of such buildings.

Since the Indians helped the missionaries to build their missions, it was only natural that Indian building styles prevailed in these early mission structures. There are obvious similarities between the missionary's bark chapel and the bark- or skin-covered lodges of Michigan's Chippewa Indians, shown here in a sketch made in the nineteenth century by Lieutenant J. C. Tidball of the United States Army.

29

The first Jesuit known to have gone through the Straits of Mackinac to the west, however, was not Marquette but Father Claude Allouez who, for a quarter of a century before his death in 1689, carried on missionary work among the Indians throughout virtually the entire upper Great Lakes region. He lies buried at Niles, Michigan, where a Jesuit mission existed from the late 1680's to the 1760's. The traditional site of the grave of Allouez was marked by a wooden cross, as shown here in 1905. Later, in 1918, a local women's club erected a larger granite cross.

In 1671, Father Marquette established a permanent mission on the mainland of the Upper Peninsula opposite Mackinac Island. He named the mission after the founder of the Jesuit order, St. Ignatius of Loyola, and the modern city of St. Ignace, which grew up on this site, keeps this memory alive. Marquette Park, quiet and small, located just beyond the business section of St. Ignace, preserves what is thought to be the site of Marquette's mission. In the park, a few feet from the waters of the Straits of Mackinac, the avenue through which Marquette and his colleagues passed to seek out the lands and the Indians to the west, a modest monument, erected in 1882, marks the supposed spot where Marquette's bones were reburied in 1677, two years after he died somewhere along lower Michigan's western shore on his return from the Illinois country.

In addition to bringing the Christian religion to the Indians, the Jesuits in the course of their travels acquired a knowledge of the region which enabled them to make a major contribution to a better understanding of Michigan's geography. The best-known example is this Jesuit map of Lake Superior, published in 1672, which was the most accurate map of any of the Great Lakes until the nineteenth century.

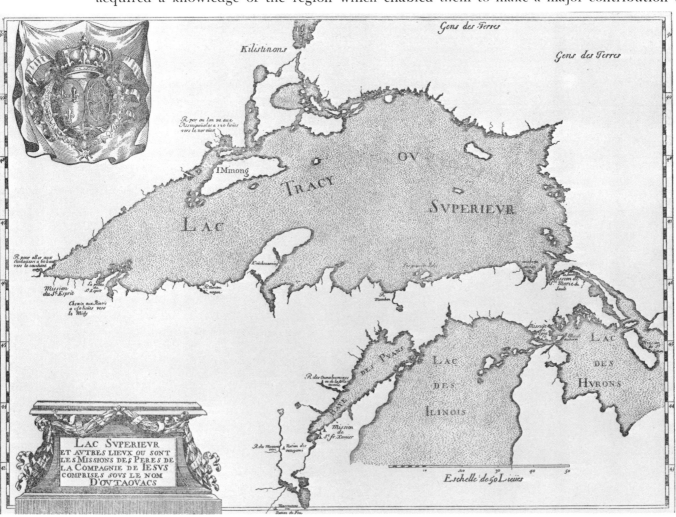

French exploration of Michigan and the Great Lakes was not confined to the Jesuits. Great names of lay explorers abound. Men like Louis Jolliet, who in 1673 went out from St. Ignace with Marquette on a journey of discovery to the Mississippi, and whose manuscript maps, such as this one, which Jolliet prepared upon his return, influenced European cartographers for many years.

A rival of Jolliet, and one of the most famous and controversial figures in the history of North American exploration, was René Robert Cavelier, the Sieur de la Salle. His exploits later would result in a statue of him ornamenting the exterior of the old Detroit City Hall for some ninety years. After the building was demolished in 1961, La Salle's statue (second from left), which was not an accurate representation since no authentic portrait of La Salle has been found, was stored away, along with statues of his fellow Frenchmen—Marquette, Father Gabriel Richard, and Cadillac— forgotten relics of an almost forgotten past.

31

Courtesy: William L. Clements Library

As part of his grandiose plans to establish French outposts in the west, La Salle built the *Griffin*, the first sailing vessel on the upper Great Lakes, an event depicted by a contemporary European artist who illustrated the travel narrative of Father Louis Hennepin, who sailed westward with La Salle on the *Griffin* in 1679. The disappearance of the vessel in or near Michigan waters on its return voyage is one of the most intriguing mysteries in Great Lakes history.

Courtesy: Minnesota Historical Society

Father Hennepin, shown here in a 1694 portrait, was a Recollect priest. The reliability of his narrative, particularly that dealing with what he claimed to have seen and done farther west, is debatable, but what he had to say about those parts of Michigan that he visited is both factual and interesting. Of the area that would become Detroit, he wrote: "Those who will one day have the happiness to possess this fertile and pleasant strait will be much obliged to those who have shown them the way."

On a bluff overlooking Lake Michigan at the mouth of the river that later became known as the St. Joseph, where he had come after leaving the *Griffin* in Green Bay, La Salle erected a fort as a temporary base for his explorations to the west. It was the first French establishment of this type in lower Michigan. Like most other sites of French activity in Michigan, nothing remains today save a marker erected nearly three centuries later by the Michigan Historical Commission. Without it, the visitor to the old Whitcomb Hotel in St. Joseph, located across the street from the plaque, would scarcely guess that the land upon which the hotel stands was once occupied by a band of French adventurers.

The attraction for most Frenchmen who came to Michigan, however, was not adventure or geographical curiosity or missionary zeal. The prime magnet was a relatively small fur-bearing animal which, with a few other animals, was greatly valued in Europe for its pelt. The beaver, which is still found and hunted in Michigan today, thus became the first of Michigan's natural resources to be exploited by the white man.

Despite the dominant role of the beaver in Michigan's economy for some two centuries, it is one of history's ironies that Michigan has come to be associated not with that patient, hard-working animal, but with the wolverine, an ill-tempered beast whose habits have made his name synonymous with glutton, facts which help explain the fun which the *Davy Crockett Almanac* had with the subject in 1845. Actually, there is little evidence that wolverines have ever lived in

A WOLVERINE,

The chaps from the Wolverine state, are the all-greediest, ugliest, an sourest characters on all Uncle Sam's twenty-six farms, they are, in thar natur, like their wolfish namesakes, always so etarnal hungry that they bite at the air, and hang their underlips, and show the harrow teeth of their mouths, as if they'd jump right into you, an swaller you hull, without salt. They are, in fact, half wolf, half man, and 'tother half saw mill. I met a wolverine one day in the forest, who had just swallowed a buck, an that war only enough to start his appetite, an make him al ravenous; he turned up his eyes at me, an opened his earthquake jaws as if he war goin to chop off my head without

A WOLVERINE.

axin. I chucked a lamb or two at him, but it war no more use than a hoss-fly to a buzzard. "Mr. Wolverine," says I, "you stare at me with a reg'lar cannibal grin, but darn me, if you mustn't fight before you can bite; my name's Crockett, an I'm an airthquake, and if the critter didn't draw up his under-lip, and fall to eaten off the bark of a tree, while his eyes watered along with his mouth, then take my whiskers for wolf skins.

Michigan, outside of zoos. Certainly, the value of wolverine pelts, wherever they came from, which were shipped from Michigan fur-trading posts was totally insignificant in the over-all picture.

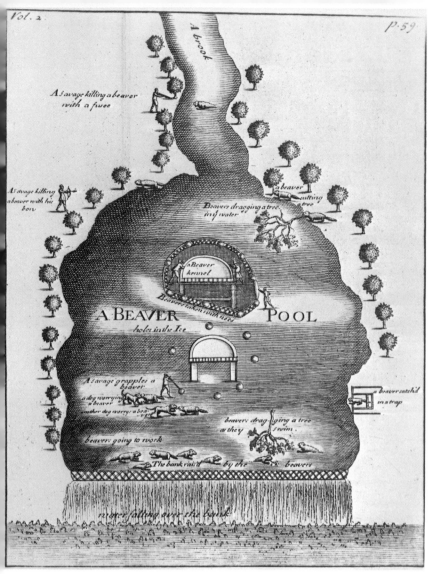

An early eighteenth-century artist, illustrating the Baron de Lahontan's account of his travels in New France, including what is now Michigan, drew this rather fanciful picture of beavers industriously at work and Indians, on whose efforts the fur trader depended for his supply of furs, just as industriously killing and trapping the animals.

Courtesy: William L. Clements Library

Lahontan, who was at the Straits of Mackinac in 1688, has left us a plan of this area, which was at that time the headquarters of the fur trade in the entire region of the upper Great Lakes. This copy of the plan, which appeared in the 1703 English edition of Lahontan's narrative, locates the mission at St. Ignace, the nearby settlement where the fur traders lived, and the villages of the Huron and Ottawa Indians. At the right-hand edge of the map is the tip of the lower peninsula, south of the straits connecting Lake Huron and what we now call Lake Michigan, but which was then commonly called the Lake of the Illinois. A few months after Lahontan left the straits, a fort was built at St. Ignace, although French soldiers had been sent there from time to time prior to the building of the post.

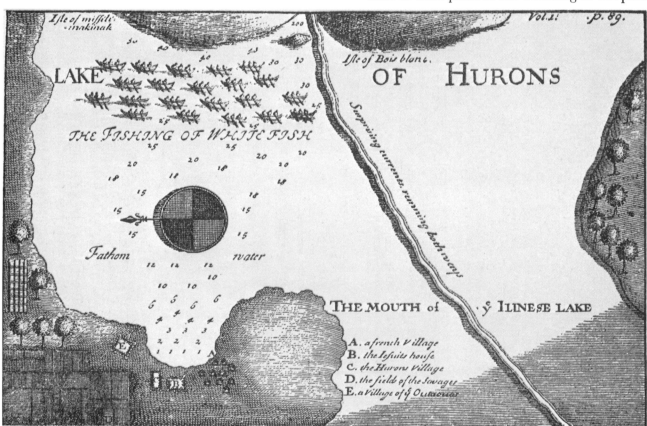

34

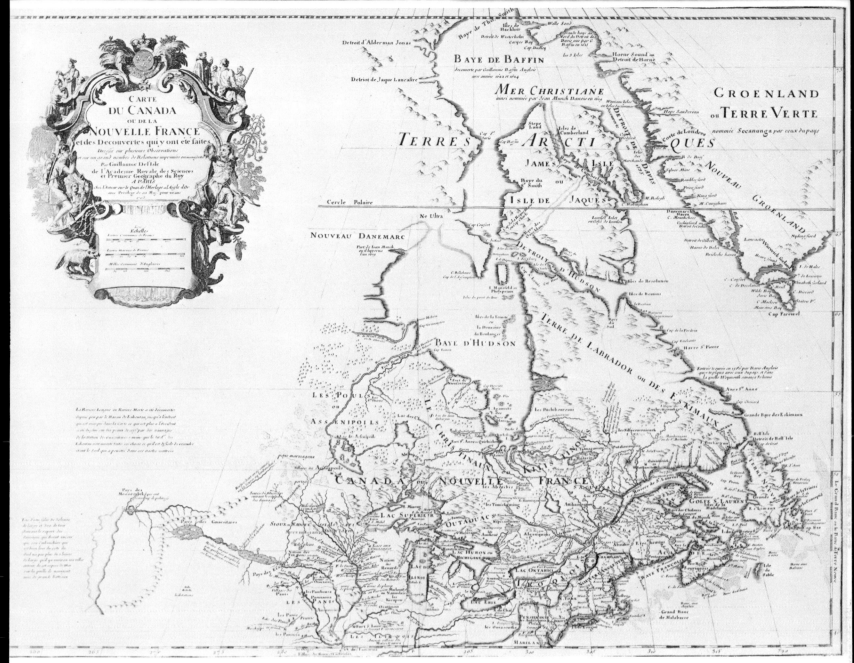

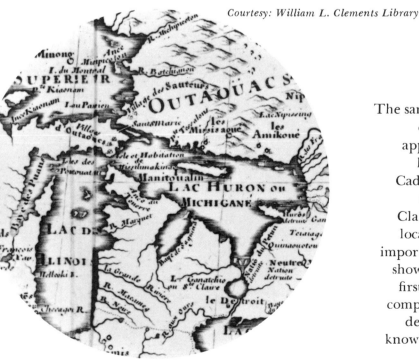

The same year, 1703, that Lahontan's map of the Straits of Mackinac appeared, a new name, Detroit, first appeared on a printed map. Michigan's largest city had its origin in 1701 when Antoine de la Mothe Cadillac established a settlement on the waterway or straits (*detroit*) linking Lake Erie with Lake St. Clair and ultimately with Lake Huron. Its strategic location made Detroit at once a post of pre-eminent importance in the fur trade. The map on which it was shown was the work of Guillaume Delisle, one of the first truly scientific cartographers, whose map, when compared with those of Champlain and Sanson, a few decades earlier, reveals the degree to which French knowledge of Michigan had been advanced by French exploration in the seventeenth century.

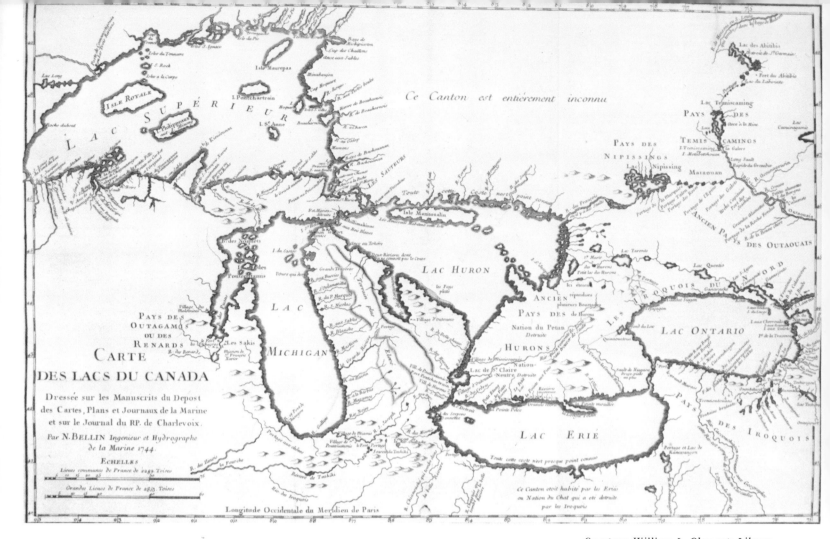

Courtesy: William L. Clements Library

Strangely enough, an increased familiarity with the area did not guarantee increased accuracy in the maps of Michigan. Witness this well-known map of 1744, produced by a distinguished French geographer, Jacques Nicolas Bellin. It shows large islands in Lake Superior which no one before or since has ever seen, geographical errors which Bellin added to such other misconceptions of earlier eighteenth-century map makers as the fictitious ridge (*Terrain plus Elevé*) running up the center of the lower peninsula, and the southeasterly slant of Lake Michigan. All this despite the existence of the French missionary, military, and fur-trading posts which Bellin shows at the Sault, at Mackinac, on the St. Joseph River, and at Detroit (*Fort Pontchartrain*), some of whose inhabitants would certainly have spotted a few of Bellin's mistakes and distortions.

The French settlements shown on Bellin's map have long since vanished. What physical remains survive are, for the most part, buried beneath the modern cities of Detroit, St. Ignace, Sault Ste. Marie, and Niles. Fortunately, however, the site on the south side of the Straits of Mackinac to which the French in 1715 removed the fort which previously had been established at St. Ignace remained undisturbed and undeveloped for nearly two centuries after it was finally abandoned. Thus, in 1959 and in the years following, archaeologists from Michigan State University, the University of Michigan, and other institutions have been able to uncover the foundations and other traces of the fort's buildings and its stockade.

36

Courtesy: Mackinac Island State Park Commission

In 1963, the site of the Jesuit church, which, in the early 1700's, had also been transferred from St. Ignace across the straits to what is now Mackinaw City, was excavated. Each shovelful of sand and dirt was sifted through screen frames mounted on roller skates. Like gold miners examining the final contents of their pans for precious metals, the archaeologists search through the objects remaining behind on the screens, hoping to find items that to them are equally priceless, artifacts dropped or thrown away by their owners during the sixty-five years Fort Michilimackinac was occupied in the eighteenth century.

Among the items found within the fort were many that related to the religious activities that had been an important part of the life of the inhabitants during the French period. These included a crucifix, a Jesuit medal, and, very close to the church site, part of a bell, which could very well have been the bell that was rung to announce a church service.

In 1964, the Mackinac Island State Park Commission, the agency in charge of this state historic site, reconstructed the old Jesuit church on the original footings uncovered by the archaeologists, and in a style which was as faithful to that of the original as it was possible to make it from a study of the evidence found in the earth, in the few relevant historical documents, and the surviving architectural examples from the same period in French Canada.

Courtesy: Mackinac Island State Park Commission

Courtesy:
Mackinac Island State Park Commission

Tens of thousands of artifacts have been uncovered in the excavation of Fort Michilimackinac. Much of it today appears to be junk or trash, which is precisely why it was tossed away two centuries ago. But a careful examination of these items reveals much about life in this frontier post, a life which, as the presence of such things as fine china indicates, was perhaps not as harsh as tradition tells us it was. (See also the two pictures at top of next page.)

38

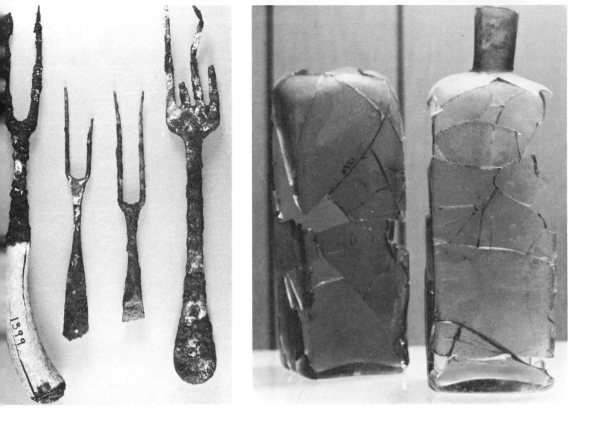

Gradually, Fort Michilimackinac is rising again from the sands along Lake Michigan, a lost page in the region's history that has been rediscovered.

Courtesy: Mackinac Island State Park Commission

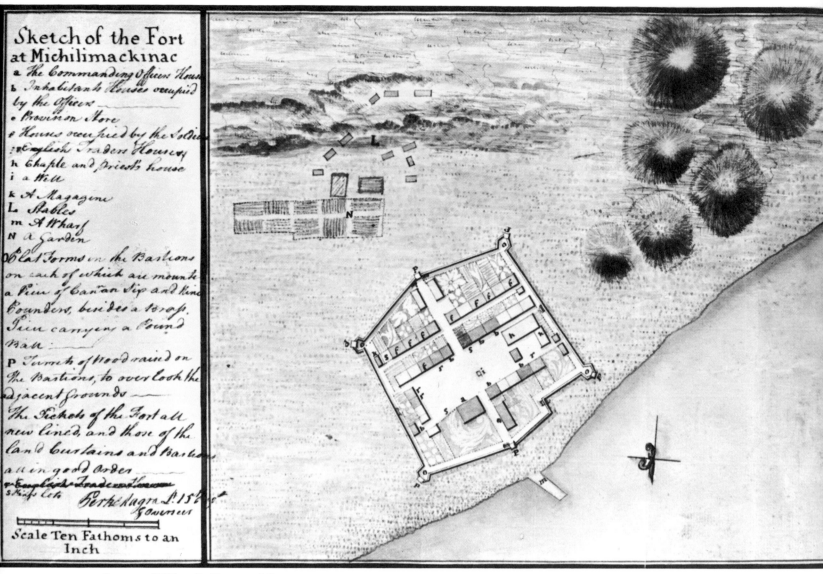

Compare the outlines of the twentieth-century reconstruction with this plan of the fort, drawn in 1766. (The long narrow building which appears in the center of the fort in the aerial photograph is a reconstruction of the soldiers' barracks, which was not built until some years after the 1766 plan was prepared.)

The British Period

The plan of Fort Michilimackinac (p. 40) was drafted by Lieutenant Perkins Magra of the British army in 1766. A new era had begun five years before when members of Great Britain's 60th or Royal American Regiment had occupied Detroit, Michilimackinac, and the other posts in Michigan after the final surrender of the French holdings in Canada to the British. The change was dramatically documented when archaeologists at Fort Michilimackinac discovered these buttons from the uniforms of some of these soldiers.

No buttons were likely to be absent for long from the uniform of Major Henry Gladwin, who took over command of a garrison of Royal Americans at Detroit in 1762. Gladwin, whose portrait was painted later in life by the English artist John Hall, was an above-average example of the hardheaded, stolid, no-nonsense British officer, without whose devoted service the British Empire could never have been built or maintained.

Courtesy: Detroit Institute of Arts

Gladwin's assignment at Detroit was a difficult one. The stockaded fort where he and his men were stationed was built by Cadillac in 1701. It was actually a tiny walled city, with narrow streets, packed with buildings, as shown on this map which was published in 1764 but was based on surveys made between 1749 and 1755, when Detroit was still under French rule. The French soldiers had now departed, but the French farmers who resided up and down the river, outside the fort, still remained. They and the Ottawas, Hurons, and Potawatomies who lived in villages nearby looked upon the English as unwelcome intruders.

Courtesy: William L. Clements Library

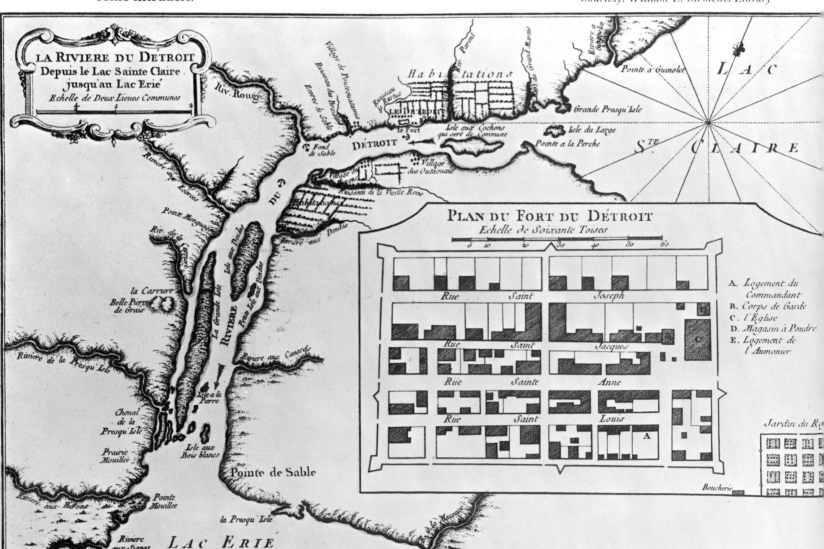

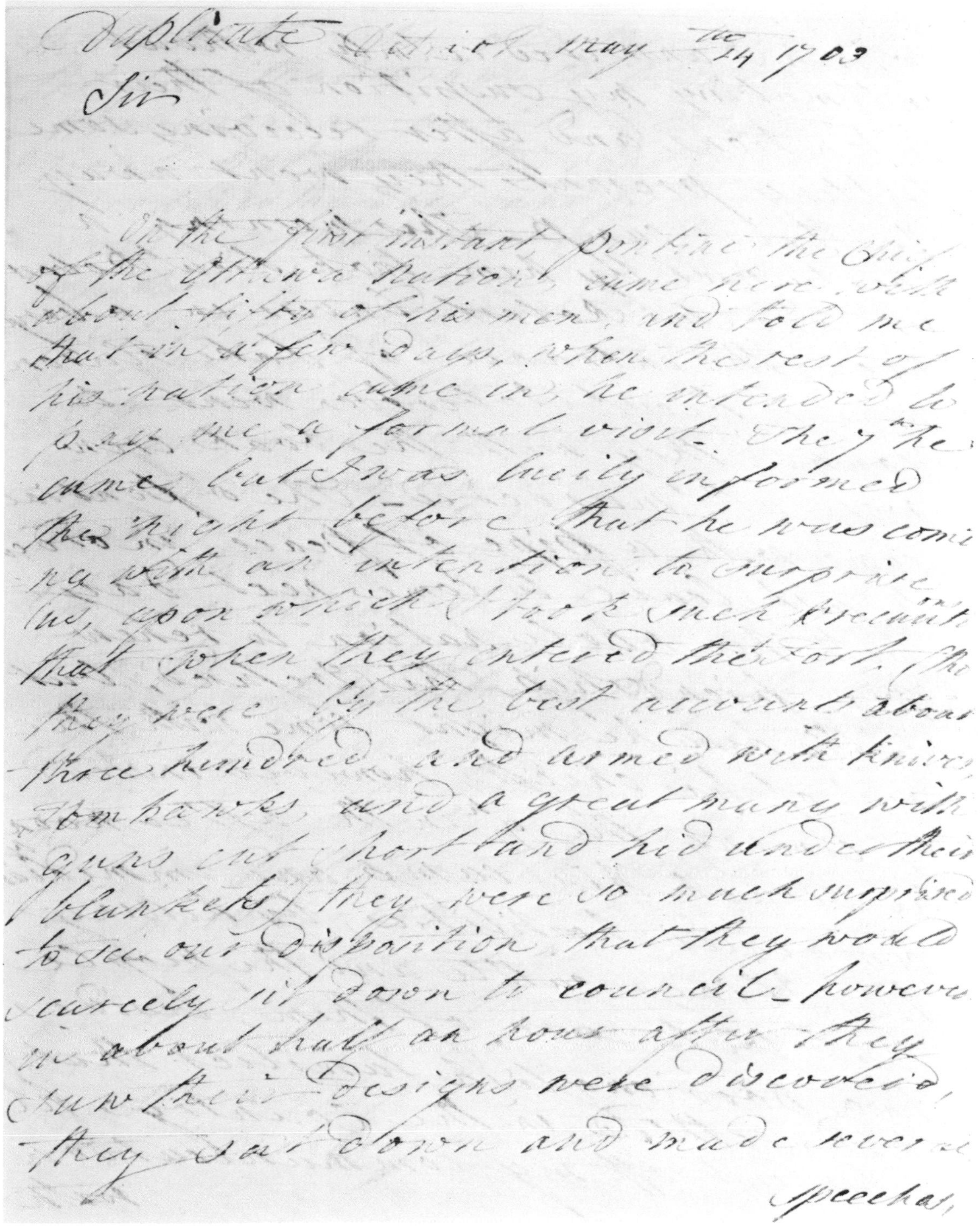

[Handwritten letter, reproduced in print below]

In 1763, the Indians in the Detroit area, led by a remarkable Ottawa chieftain, Pontiac, decided to capture the fort and expel the English. Today, in the sedate, sumptuously furnished William L. Clements Library at the University of Michigan, one can read Major Gladwin's report to his commander-in-chief, Sir Jeffery Amherst, in which he described how he foiled Pontiac's plot, forcing Pontiac to lay siege to the fort and thereby touching off the great Indian war that bears the Ottawa leader's name:

> On the first instant [May, 1763], Pontiac the Chief of the Ottawa nation, came here with about fifty of his men and told me that in a few days, when the rest of his nation came in, he intended to pay me a formal visit. The 7th he came but I was luc[k]ily informed the night before that he was coming with an intention to surprise us, upon which I took such precautions that when they entered the fort (tho they were by the best accounts about three hundred and armed with knives, tomhawks [sic], and a great many with guns cut short and hid under their blankets) they were so much surprised to see our disposition that they would scarcely sit down to council—however in about half an hour after they saw their designs were discover'd, they sat down and made several speeches, which I answered calmly without intimating my suspition [sic] of their intentions, and after receiving some trifling presents they went away to their camp—. This morning [May 7] a party sent by him [Pontiac] took Lieut. Robertson and Sir Robert Davers in a barge near

the entrance of Lake Huron, which Lieut. Robertson went to sound; they with the boat crew were all murdered. The 8th Pontiac came with a pipe of peace, in order to ask leave to come next day with his whole nation to renew his friendship. This I refused, but I told him he might come with the rest of his chiefs; however instead of coming the 9th in the afternoon he struck his camp and immediately commenced hostilities, by killing the Kings cattle and the people that took care of them, besides two poor english families that had settled in the country, he also cut off my communication with the inhabitants, and threatened them that the first that should bring me provisions or any thing else, he would put to death; they surrounded the fort and fired a vast number of shot at it and the vessels, which were anchored so as to flank the fort above and below. . . .

Gladwin goes on to relate the events of the following days, as Pontiac increased his pressure on the fort and Gladwin, in turn, refused the Indians' demand that he surrender. He concluded his report to Amherst by declaring, in the best traditions of the British army:

We are in high spirits and have provisions and ammunition enough to serve us till a relief arrives. I believe the enemy may amount to six or seven hundred. I have the honor to be Sir your most humble servant Henry Gladwin.

On July 31, a sortie against the Indians, led by Captain James Dalyell, ended in disaster for the English soldiers. In what is now Detroit's Elmwood Cemetery, along a stream which ever since has been called Bloody Run, Pontiac and his warriors ambushed Dalyell's men, killing Dalyell and many more of the soldiers, wounding and capturing still others, and forcing the survivors to fight their way back to the safety of the fort.

Courtesy: Ferris Lewis

Despite Pontiac's victory at Bloody Run, he was unable to maintain an effective siege of Fort Detroit since he could not prevent supplies and reinforcements from being brought in to Gladwin from the river. Finally, at the end of October, with winter approaching and his Indians anxious to return home, and with the receipt of news that all hope of French military aid must be abandoned, Pontiac, who could not write, dictated this note to Gladwin, whom he addressed as "My Brother":

> The word which my father [the French authorities] has sent me to make peace I have accepted. All my young men have buried their hatchets. I think you will forget the bad things which have taken place for some time past. Likewise I shall forget what you have done to me, in order to think nothing but good. . . .

Pontiac's siege of Detroit, the longest Indian military operation of this character in American history, had come to an end.

Courtesy: William L. Clements Library

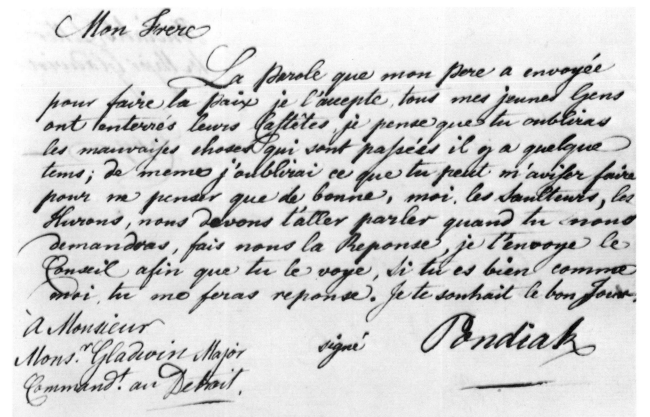

45

Pontiac's attack upon Detroit was followed in a few days by attacks by Indians elsewhere on every English outpost in the West. On June 2, 1763, outside the stockade at Fort Michilimackinac, a seemingly innocent game between the Chippewa and Sac Indians suddenly turned into a murderous assault on the unsuspecting English garrison, resulting in the capture of the fort by the Indians and in every Englishman at Michilimackinac either being killed or taken prisoner. Today, when the gate beneath this gun platform is opened, tourists, not hostile Indians, pour in, walking over the very ground on which took place what has gone down in history as the "Massacre of Fort Michilimackinac." White men wrote this history. To the Indians, it was a great victory that they had won at Fort Michilimackinac.

Among the Englishmen at Michilimackinac who were captured was the fur trader Alexander Henry, shown here in his prosperous later years in Montreal. The intervention of a friend whom Henry had made among the Chippewas saved him from death at the hands of the enraged savages. It was this ability of the English fur trader to establish amicable relationships with the Indians plus the need of the Indian for the trader and his trade goods that helped put an end to the Indian war of 1763.

46

CAPTAIN GRANT,

Informs the *Traders* at Michilimakinack, Detroit, *and* Niagara.
THAT he will transport their Merchandize in the Vessels on the Lake, at the following Rates:

New-York Currency.

From Ontario to Niagara, a three handed Boat, or 12 Barrels; the distance about 170 Miles, £ 6 - 0 - 0

From Fort William Augustus, per Barrel, to Niagara; the Distance about 300 Miles, 1 - 0 - 0

From Niagara to Detroit, a three handed Battoe Load, or 12 Barrels, exclusive of the Carrying-Place; the Distance about 300 Miles, 12 - 0 - 0

From Detroit to Michilimakinack, a three handed Battoe, or 12 Barrels; the Distance about 400 Miles, 12 - 0 - 0

All other Things will be transported in Proportion to the above, and nothing charged for any small Articles in a Battoe, over the 12 Barrels.

FREIGHT OF PACKS, &c.

From Michilimakinack to Detroit, per Pack, — — — — £ 0 - 4 - 0
From Detroit to Niagara, exclusive of the Carrying-Place, — — 0 - 4 - 0
From Niagara to Ontario, each Pack, — — — — — — 0 - 2 - 0
From Niagara to Fort William Augustus, per Pack, — — — — 0 - 4 - 0

The vessels (wind and weather permitting) will sail from Ontario the 10th of May, and 1st of September, and from Fort Erie, the 20th of May and 20th of September; as also at any other times when there is sufficient freight; and from Detroit to Michilimakinack, when most convenient for those who may have effects to send there. The vessels arriving from Ontario, will discharge at the Lower Landing, and at Little Niagara boats and men will be found to transport the goods and packs, to, and from, Fort Erie, gratis. The utmost care will be taken of every thing sent, and proper stores provided at Fort Erie. The masters of vessels will sign bills of lading for any merchandize that are shipped on the above conditions. As no charge will be taken at the Carrying-Place, at Niagara, every owner of goods, must provide a careful person to take charge of their effects at that place. By adopting this manner of conveyance to the several posts, the property of an Indian trader, and his credit (of course) with his merchant, will become infinitely less liable to hazard than in that of proceeding single and defenceless in small open boats, which subjects them to be seized by the Savages, who thereby become possessed of ammunition and cloathing, that may enable them to carry on a long series of hostilities against our posts and settlements; an event of the most mischievous tendency to the British government, destructive of human life, and which would produce a train of calamities horrible to be reflected on, yet ever to be apprehended from the uncertain duration of peace with our troublesome neighbours.

The English developed the fur trade in Michigan considerably beyond the level to which the French had brought it. For the first time since the ill-fated voyage of the *Griffin,* sailing vessels appeared on the upper Great Lakes, making it possible to bring trade goods to Detroit and Michilimackinac more efficiently, economically, and safely than by canoe or *batteau.* These advantages were pointed out in this advertisement in the Quebec *Gazette* for March 22, 1770, one of the earliest examples of the advertising man's art applied to Michigan.

Courtesy: Quebec Provincial Archives

Courtesy: Minnesota Historical Society

Despite the use of sailing vessels, the heavy work of the fur trade under the English continued to be handled by the French *voyageur.* It was these men, one of whom was portrayed by Mrs. Samuel B. Abbe in the mid-nineteenth century, whose arms and backs provided the muscle needed to propel the fur traders' *batteaux* over the hundreds of miles of lakes and rivers that had to be traveled to obtain the furs from the Indians. The *voyageur* also provided the brute strength required to portage boat and cargo around the numerous rapids and overland to the next waterway.

47

Courtesy: McCord Museum, McGill University

But the men who enjoyed the enormous profits of the fur trade were not the *voyageurs* or the Indians, or, for the most part, the traders who went out and obtained the pelts. It was the men at Michilimackinac and Detroit who hired the traders and *voyageurs,* and especially the men back in Montreal who provided the capital that profited from the trade. Such a man was James McGill, one of the Montreal entrepreneurs who was closely connected with the Michigan fur trade in the last four decades of the eighteenth century and whose name today is perpetuated in McGill University, Montreal, endowed with the fortune he made in the business.

Courtesy: William L. Clements Library

During these years of British rule, the land which would become Michigan continued to be governed by military men. As a group, these officers were less colorful than Cadillac, La Salle, and some of the others from the earlier French period. One redcoat who, although he may have lacked judgment, certainly did not lack color, was Major Robert Rogers, founder of Rogers' Rangers and the central figure in Kenneth Roberts' great novel, *Northwest Passage.* It was Rogers who had established British authority at Detroit in 1760 and had fought at Bloody Run during Pontiac's siege before he was named to head the garrison at Michilimackinac in 1766. Two years later he left the post under arrest, charged with "Designs of a Traiterous and Dangerous nature" against his king and his country. Although he was acquitted of the charge, Rogers' career was effectively ruined. This portrait, although published in 1776 during Rogers' lifetime, has been labeled fictitious, an attempt by the artist, Thomas Hunt, to cash in on the desire of the British public to secure copies of a likeness of the notorious officer.

A few years after the ignominious departure of Rogers from his Michilimackinac command, an officer of a very different, but likewise unusual, character took over at that post. Arent Schuyler de Peyster was a member of a distinguished New York colonial family, who, in later years, would retire to Scotland where he became a friend of the poet Robert Burns. This was a natural development, since De Peyster can be termed Michigan's first literary figure. He spent the long, boring hours at the Straits of Mackinac in composing poems. In 1779, about a year before this portrait was made, he was transferred to Detroit. He rose to the occasion with this lyric:

> *Now to Mitchilimackinack*
> *We soldiers bid adieu,*
> *And leave each squa a child on back,*
> *Nay some are left with two.*
> *When you return, my lads, take care*
> *Their boys don't take you by the hair,*
> *With a war-whoop that shall rend the air,*
> *And use their scalping knives.*

Courtesy: Burton Historical Collection

As Major de Peyster and his men were en route to Detroit in 1779, other British soldiers were locked in combat with the American colonists along the Atlantic seaboard. There was scant sympathy for the revolutionists among the English and French residents of Michigan, and yet, among the items uncovered in the archaeological excavation of Fort Michilimackinac is this political button honoring the English liberal and friend of the colonists, John Wilkes. Was its owner simply a collector of such trivia, or was he an admirer, if not an adherent, of the American cause, proclaiming his sentiments in a bastion of British military might?

Courtesy: Mackinac Island State Park Commission

Courtesy: Burton Historical Collection

Although far removed from the battlefields, Detroit and Michilimackinac played an important role in the war in the West, for it was at these posts that parties of Indians were organized to raid the American frontier. Henry Hamilton, who, in 1775, was named commander at Detroit and the first lieutenant-governor of the Detroit District in the enlarged province of Quebec, directed these campaigns. He was labeled "Hair Buyer" by the Americans for his action in paying the Indians for scalps. Historians have since proved that the Americans were being unjust to Hamilton, but whether deserved or not, Hamilton's nickname has been responsible for keeping his name alive in Michigan history when officers of equal or greater rank have long since been forgotten.

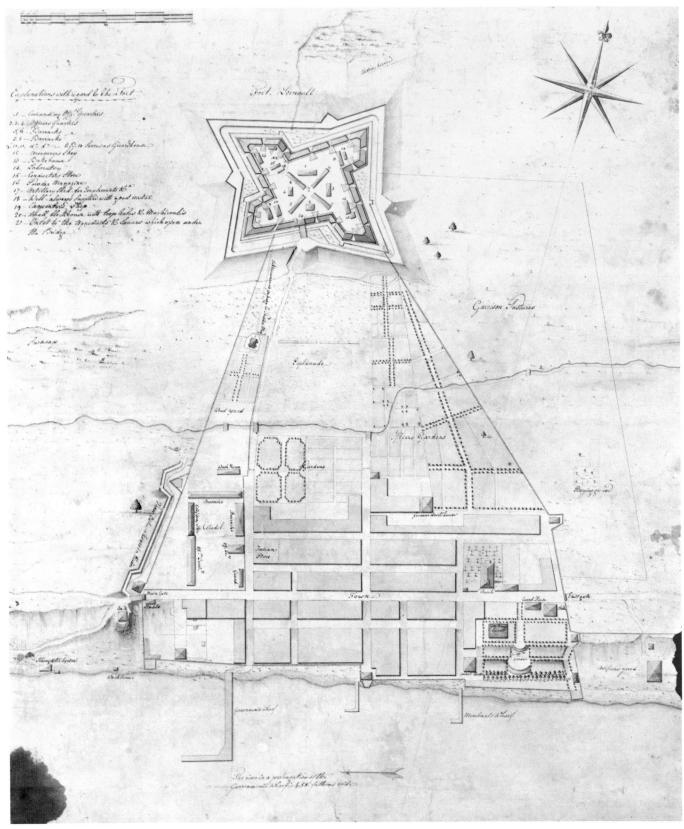

During the Revolution, the British, fearing American attacks in reprisal for the raids launched from Michigan, moved to strengthen their military positions. At Detroit, a new fort, named Fort Lernoult, was built in 1778-79, some distance inland from the old French fort site on the banks of the Detroit River. This map, drawn in 1799 by John J. Rivardi, shows how the new fort was connected with the town of Detroit to the south.

Courtesy: Detroit Bank and Trust Company

Detroit's central business district has been built on the ruins of eighteenth-century Detroit — a fact dramatically demonstrated in 1962 during the construction of a skyscraper addition to the Detroit Bank and Trust building at Fort and Shelby. The contractors suddenly struck something that was subsequently determined to be the remains of Fort Lernoult's southwest bastion. Work was halted on the twentieth-century building while archaeologists from Wayne State University, headed by Dr. Arnold Pilling, carefully uncovered the timbers of a structure that had stood on the same site two centuries earlier. A treasury of artifacts was rescued for later study after the construction crews had resumed their work on top of Fort Lernoult's reburied ruins.

Meanwhile, back in 1779, De Peyster had been replaced at Michilimackinac by Captain Patrick Sinclair, shown here in a silhouette made in his later years of retirement in his Scottish homeland. Sinclair, who in 1764 had brought the first sailing vessel up Lake Huron to Mackinac since the voyage of the *Griffin* eighty-five years earlier, had been named lieutenant-governor of the Michilimackinac District in 1775 but the war had delayed his arrival in northern Michigan until 1779.

Courtesy: Burton Historical Collection

Deciding that the post on the northern tip of the lower peninsula was too vulnerable to an attack by Americans or Indians, Sinclair, in the fall of 1779, laid out the plans for a new fort across the straits on Michilimackinac Island (as Mackinac Island was called until well into the nineteenth century). This is a late nineteenth-century reproduction of a sketch of the work on the new fort from British records. The reproduction was made before the modern era of photo-duplication techniques which have enabled an exact copy of manuscript drawings and plans to be made.

SKETCH OF THE FORT ON MICHILIMACKINAC ISLAND.
Temporary Lines of Pickets.

ADDITION TO BE MADE
PROVISION STORE RAISED
Double Lines filled in Platform high nearly.

OFFICERS BARRACKS WILL BE BEGUN IN JULY.

ROAD FROM THE LOWER GROUND

SOLDIERS BARRACKS WILL BE FINISHED IN JUNE IF CLASS ARRIVES.

Dotted line not filled in yet. Platform high out raised with logs.

GUARD HOUSE

WELL
Will be dug out 20 feet more in the course of the summer.

POWDER MAGASINE
Will be finished 24th June.

The Flank on this side of the Gate way was exten[ded] to overlook the ground which threatened the salient an[gle] of the other Half Bastion. This single line—to [the] steep bank will be raised in—the course of the summ[er.] The Half Curtain was reduced on this side the gate [by] the distance to which it was once extended would h[ave] exposed the Rampart to have been taken in reve[rse] from the ground without opposite side of the Fort.

Unlike Fort Lernoult, which was built at the same time but was later demolished in the 1820's, Sinclair's Fort Mackinac, as it would be called, survives today. In the Fort Mackinac which one now sees, however, as in this aerial photograph in which the fort appears in the left center as a pie-shaped cluster of buildings, scarcely any of the structures date from Sinclair's day.

Courtesy: Mackinac Island State Park Commission

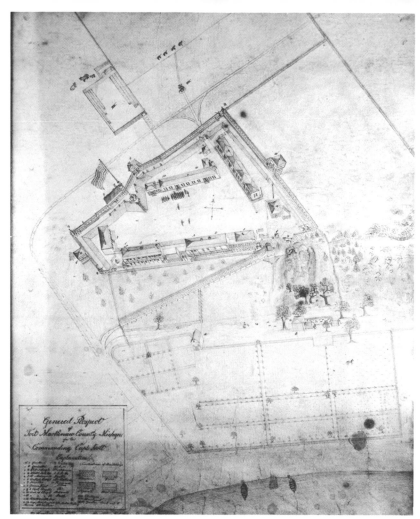

Not even this bird's-eye view, prepared by an American soldier in the early 1840's, contains much that the builders of the original fort would have recognized.

The impressive limestone escarpment, pierced by the South Sally Port, facing out over the harbor of Mackinac Island, probably dates from the early 1780's, although it has had to be repaired many times in the succeeding years.

Inside the fort, only the architecturally acclaimed Officers' Stone Quarters dates from Fort Mackinac's days as a British post, but even it was not completed by Sinclair or his successors. It remained for the Americans in the late 1790's to add the roof.

Courtesy: Michigan Tourist Council

Likewise, the fort's famed blockhouses, probably the most photographed man-made structures in Michigan, were apparently built by the Americans in the late 1790's and, despite what the guidebooks have been saying all these years, do not date from 1780.

Courtesy: Library of Congress

With the transfer of British troops to Fort Mackinac, the old fort on the mainland to the south was abandoned. Gradually this historic post disappeared before the ravages of time and shifting sands. By 1842, when this sketch was made, passengers on ships passing through the Straits of Mackinac could see no sign that the site had been inhabited only sixty years earlier.

Neither Fort Mackinac nor Fort Lernoult was attacked during the American Revolution, but in Niles a huge boulder and a historical marker locate the site of Fort St. Joseph which, on February 12, 1781, was briefly occupied by forces of Spain, which then controlled the area west of the Mississippi River and had entered the war as an ally of the Americans. It was an easy triumph for the Spaniards because the fort had not had a British garrison in eighteen years.

Today the Four Flags Motor Inn (formerly the Four Flags Hotel) in Niles helps to keep alive an aspect of that city's history in which it takes great pride—it is the only Michigan community over which the flags of four nations, France, Great Britain, Spain, and the United States, have flown.

In 1783 the Treaty of Paris ended the American Revolution. Great Britain recognized the independence of its rebellious colonies along the Atlantic and agreed upon the boundaries of the new United States of America. This map, published by John Wallis of London on April 3, 1783, less than three months after the treaty went into effect, was one of the first maps of the new country to be rushed into print. Although Wallis obviously was not well informed as to the location of the northwestern boundary, to the residents of Michigan the map made one thing clear: Michigan had become American.

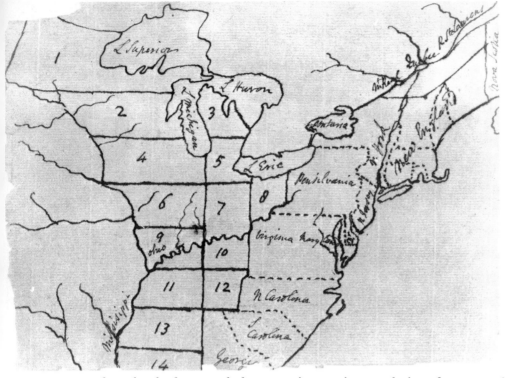

The United States government lost no time planning for the development of its western lands. In 1784, Congress passed an ordinance, prepared by Thomas Jefferson, in which the great Virginian proposed the creation of ten states in what is now the Middle West. Jefferson, with customary imagination, even named the states, and on this manuscript map showed their approximate boundaries. Most of what is now Michigan would have been included in Jefferson's states of Cherronesus (3) and Sylvania (1). Jefferson named one of his states Michigania, number 2 on his map, but it would have been confined primarily to the present state of Wisconsin. Jefferson's ordinance was never put into effect, but he had, nonetheless, set in motion a chain of events that eventually would result in the establishment, twenty years later, of a political division to which the name Michigan would be applied.

The Ordinance of 1784 was replaced in 1787 by what many historians regard as the most important act ever passed by any Congress, the Northwest Ordinance, establishing the Northwest Territory. This territory, which was delineated by Joseph Scott of Philadelphia in his *United States Gazetteer* of 1795, included the future states of Ohio, Indiana, Illinois, Wisconsin, a portion of Minnesota—and all of what would become the state of Michigan.

56

Getting title to Michigan's lands and waters was one thing, but getting actual possession was something else. The Americans had to deal with the British, who refused to leave until the Americans fulfilled certain conditions of the treaty of 1783. The Americans also had to deal with the Indians of the Great Lakes region, who did not recognize the right of any white man to give or take lands which the Indians regarded as their own. Only in 1795, after several years of difficult, costly fighting, did the United States Army get some of

these Indians to agree to relinquish their claims to most of Ohio and to narrow strips of land at Detroit and the Straits of Mackinac. An American soldier who was present at this historic event in Greenville, Ohio, is believed to be the artist who portrayed officers and chieftains negotiating the treaty.

General Anthony Wayne, the stern, tall officer in the painting, was the officer who organized and directed the defeat of the Indians, and who dispatched the American troops that finally occupied Michigan in 1796, the year in which this portrait was painted and the year in which he met his untimely death.

Anthony Wayne himself visited Detroit in the fall of 1796 to help set up American civil authority—and appropriately enough, the first county established was named in his honor. This is how Wayne would have seen Detroit as he looked up the Detroit River at the old fort on the river bank, standing about where Cobo Hall now stands. An unknown artist made this wash drawing in 1794, when the British flag still flew over the stockaded post and the royal naval vessels anchored in the river.

In 1804, a British army doctor, Edward Walsh, stood on the Canadian side of the Detroit River, in what is now Windsor, Ontario, and made this sketch of Detroit, over which the United States flag now waved.

Later in 1804, Walsh added a painting of the fur-trading posts at the rapids of the St. Mary's River, what is now Sault Ste. Marie, Michigan, and its sister community across the international boundary, Sault Ste. Marie, Ontario.

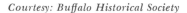

On the American side at Sault Ste. Marie, a Scotsman, John Johnston, maintained a trading post. He and his Chippewa wife, Susan or Ozha-Gus coday, had a remarkable progeny whose descendants today are found scattered through Michigan and elsewhere in the country and have included in their numbers some prominent individuals. Johnston, however, although he was now technically an American, remained loyal to the British, as did a great many more of the residents of Michigan who stayed on in the area after 1796. This would prove to be a serious problem for the American authorities, which was not resolved for many years.

South of Sault Ste. Marie, on St. Joseph Island at the head of Lake Huron, Dr. Walsh visited the fort and trading establishment which the British had built in 1796 when they finally had to evacuate the fort on Mackinac Island, some forty-five miles to the west.

Mackinac Island, shown here in an engraving published in 1813, continued under American control as an important fur-trading center. A small settlement hugged the shoreline of the harbor, while on the high ground overlooking the waterfront a small force of soldiers represented American authority in this most remote northern United States military outpost.

The year 1805 is one of the most important in Michigan's history, for it was at that time that Congress established a new territory in the northwest and called it Michigan. Now for the first time it was possible to refer to a political unit and a land area that bore this name. As is shown by Amos Bradley, Jr., of Philadelphia, in this map that is dated 1804 but apparently was actually printed in 1805 or later, the boundaries of Michigan Territory in 1805 were not the same as those of the present state. Only the eastern tip of the Upper Peninsula was part of the new territory.

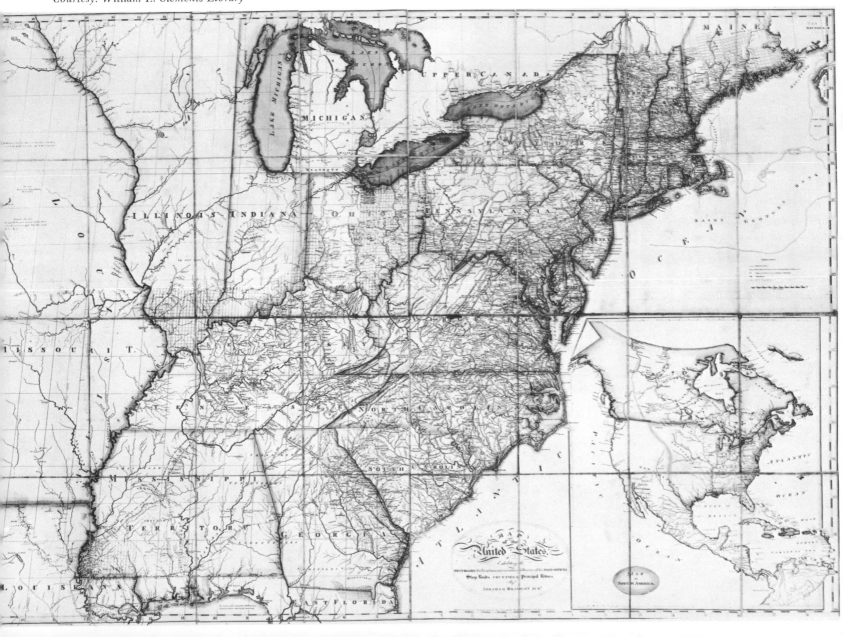

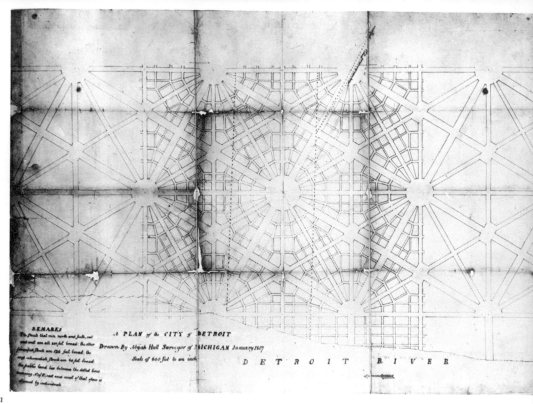

Left: William Hull, a 52-year-old New Englander and veteran of the Revolution, was selected by President Thomas Jefferson to be Michigan's first governor. This portrait was painted by Gilbert Stuart, probably in 1824, a short time before Hull's death. In the 1960's it was owned by Hull's great-great-granddaughter, Mrs. James E. R. Jones of Lakeville, Connecticut.

Right: When Governor Hull arrived in Michigan in the summer of 1805, he found that most of Detroit, the territorial capital, had been destroyed by a great fire on June 11. In the most forward-looking action of Hull's administration, a plan for rebuilding Detroit, drawn up by Judge Augustus B. Woodward, was adopted by the territorial government.

Below: Woodward's plan, an adaptation of the one prepared for Washington, D. C., by Major Pierre L'Enfant, was later abandoned by citizens who could see no need for two-hundred-foot wide avenues and numerous circular parks. Twentieth-century Detroit, however, as this 1930 aerial photograph reveals, still retained a few traces that Judge Woodward would have recognized. Had his plan been adhered to, Detroit might have been spared some of its monstrous traffic headaches of the past few decades.

Hull and Woodward represented the American wave of the future, but for some years the majority of the territory's white population would continue to be, as it had been since Champlain's day, French-speaking. Representing this element was a remarkable priest from France, Father Gabriel Richard, who came to Michigan in 1798, and although based at Detroit, was responsible for the Catholics throughout the entire upper Great Lakes region. He served the area in a variety of capacities until his death in 1832 from cholera, which he contracted while helping others during an epidemic that swept southeastern Michigan. This portrait was painted shortly after Richard's death by the artist James O. Lewis, and was based upon his examination of the dead man. Lewis was paid twelve dollars for what would become one of the most widely reproduced portraits ever made of a Michigan resident.

Courtesy: Burton Historical Collection

Father Richard was more than just another priest, faithfully serving the needs of his French Catholic parishioners. He was interested in many things that looked to the cultural and political development of Michigan. He imported a printing press, one of the first in Michigan, on which were produced some of the rarest, most sought-after Michigan imprints, including Michigan's first newspaper, the *Michigan Essay*. Michigan apparently was not ready for a newspaper, however, because there is no evidence that any other issues followed this initial issue of August 31, 1809. The Burton Historical Collection of the Detroit Public Library has one of the few known copies of this issue.

Courtesy: Detroit News

Governor Hull, although not an outstanding chief executive, did make at least one major contribution to the territory's subsequent development when in 1807 he negotiated a treaty with the Indians for the cession of their lands in southeastern Michigan. The northern boundary of the area ceded began near the town of Harbor Beach at a famous landmark in Lake Huron known then—and now—as White Rock.

Courtesy: Field Museum of Natural History

Opposition to the advance of American settlers into the West led some Indians to plan a united resistance to this movement. Some authorities believe that this portrait, whose origin is uncertain, is one of the leader of these Indians, Tecumseh, a Shawnee who lived in Indiana but whose influence with many Michigan Indians at this time was great. Ironically, a Michigan town in Lenawee County would be named in his honor by admiring white men of a later generation, the very people whose further intrusion into Indian country Tecumseh had fought against. Similarly, descendants of Pontiac's enemies would name a town, a lake, and an automobile after that earlier foe of the English-speaking white man.

The War of 1812

The feeling of the Western frontiersman that the British in Canada were inciting Tecumseh in his anti-American activities and that they were behind other Indian problems in the West was a primary cause of the War of 1812—a war which broke over Michigan in all its fury in the summer of 1812. On the night of July 16-17, a British force from St. Joseph Island quietly landed on the north end of Mackinac Island and by morning had occupied the high ground to the rear of Fort Mackinac, shown here in a late nineteenth-century photograph.

The American garrison of some sixty men had not yet learned that war had been declared. Faced by an overwhelmingly superior force, including hundreds of Indians who might massacre civilians on the island if a fight were made, the commander of the fort surrendered without a struggle and marched his men out of the fort through this North Sally Port.

Meanwhile, at Detroit, Governor William Hull had been given command of the American army in the northwest, with orders to invade Canada. He crossed the Detroit River and took up quarters in this brick house, then owned by François Baby, now a museum in Windsor maintained by the Hiram Walker Company.

By WILLIAM HULL, *Brigadier General and Commander of the North Western Army of the United States.*

A PROCLAMATION.

INHABITANTS OF CANADA! After thirty years of PEACE & profperity, the UNITED STATES have been driven to Arms. The injuries & aggreffions, the infults & indignities of Great Britain have *once more* left them no alternative but manly refiftance, or unconditional fubmiffion. The ARMY under my command, has invaded your country, & the Standard of the UNION now waves over the Territory of CANADA. To the peaceable unoffending inhabitant, it brings neither danger nor difficulty. I come to *find* enemies, not to *make* them. I come to *protect*, not to *injure* you.

Separated by an immenfe Ocean, & an extenfive Wildernefs from Great Britain, you have no participation in her Counfels, no intereft in her conduct. You have felt her Tyrany, you have feen her injuftice, but I do not afk *you* to avenge the one or to redrefs the other. The UNITED STATES are fufficiently powerful to afford you every fecurity, confiftent with their rights, & your expectations. I tender you the invaluable bleffings of Civil Political & Religious Liberty, & their neceffary refult individual and general profperity; That Liberty which gave decifion to our counfels and energy to our conduct, in our ftruggle for INDEPENDENCE, and which conducted us fafely and triumphantly, thro' the ftormy period of the Revolution. That Liberty which has raifed us to an elevated rank among the Nations of the world, and which has afforded us a greater meafure of PEACE and Security, of wealth and improvement, than ever fell to the lot of any people.

In the name of my *Country* and by the authority of my *Government*, I pomife you protection to your *perfons, property* and *rights*. Remain at your homes. Purfue your peaceful and cuftomary avocations. Raife not your hands againft your brethren. Many of your fathers fought for the freedom & INDEPENDENCE we now enjoy, Being children therefore of the fame family with us, and heirs to the fame heritage, the arrival of an Army of friends, muft be hailed by you with a cordial welcome. You will be emancipated from Tyrany and oppreffion, and reftored to the dignified ftation of freemen. Had I any doubt of eventual fuccefs, I might afk your affiftance, but I do not. I come prepared for every contingency. I have a force which will look down all oppofition, & that force is but the vanguard of a much greater. If contrary to your own intereft, and the juft expectation of my Country, you fhould take part in the approaching conteft, you will be confidered & treated as enemies, & the horrors & calamities of war will ftalk before you.

If the barbarous & favage policy of Great Britain be purfued, and the favages are let loofe to murder our Citizens, & butcher our women and children, this war, will be a war of extermination. The firft ftroke of the Tomahawk, the firft attempt with the fcalping knife, will be the fignal for one indifcriminate fcene of defolation. *No white man found fighting by the fide of an Indian, will be taken prifoner.* Inftant deftruction will be his lot. If the dictates of reafon, duty, juftice and humanity cannot prevent the employment of a force which refpects no rights, & knows no wrong, it will be prevented by a fevere and relentlefs fyftem of retaliation.

I doubt not your courage and firmnefs : I will not doubt your attachment to Liberty. If you tender your fervices voluntarily, they will be accepted readily.

The UNITED STATES offer you *Peace, Liberty* and *Security.* Your choice lies between thefe & WAR, *flavery,* and *deftruction.* Choofe then, but choofe wifely ; and may he who knows the juftice of our caufe, and who holds in his hand the fate of Nations, guide you to a refult the moft compatible with your rights and intereft, your Peace and profperity.

BY THE GENERAL

Capt: 13th. U. S. Regt: of Infantry and Aid de camp.

Hull issued a proclamation to the Canadian people, printing it on the press Father Richard had brought to Detroit. The bombastic tone of the message was in striking contrast to Hull's naturally cautious personality. Actually, he was fully aware of the weaknesses in his position which limited his ability to carry out his threats.

Downriver from Detroit, on the Canadian side, the British had military and naval forces at Fort Malden, which they had built in 1796 after they were forced to evacuate Detroit. The town of Amherstburg, the fort, and the navy yard are shown on the right and Bois Blanc Island (today's popular Bob-Lo summer amusement center) on the left in this painting made in 1813 by Catherine Reynolds, sister of the fort's commissary. One of the Indians in the lower right-hand corner is supposed to be Tecumseh, who was now openly supporting the British.

In August, Sir Isaac Brock, military commander of Upper Canada (present-day Ontario), arrived at Fort Malden with reinforcements. A career military man, General Brock not only had the edge on his opponent, Hull, in the matter of experience but also in the ability to make and to execute command decisions.

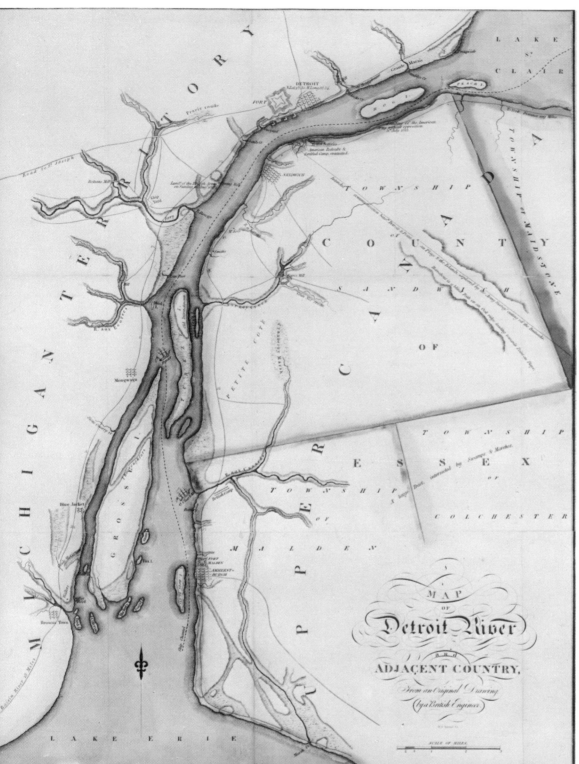

What happened on the Detroit River in July and August, 1812, is clearly shown on this map, published the following year and based on a drawing by a British engineer. From his positions on the Canadian side of the river, opposite Hog Island (today's Belle Isle), Hull had sent scouts probing as far south as the Canard River. But efforts to bring supplies overland up the American side of the river from the River Raisin were frustrated in battles between American troops and Indians led by Tecumseh and his British allies at Browns Town (in the modern community of Gibraltar) and in the area of the Indian village of Mongwaga (now the city of Trenton). This inability to bring supplies, plus British naval control of the Detroit River, and finally news of the fall of Mackinac Island and Brock's imminent arrival, caused Hull to abandon invasion plans and to pull back to the defenses of Detroit. The British and American artillery batteries on the opposite shores of the river engaged in a spirited duel on August 15. The following morning, Brock and his men crossed the river below Detroit, quickly advanced up the river road, and, at noon, Hull, fearful of what Britain's Indian partisans might do to the civilians living around Detroit, accepted Brock's demand that he surrender. Hull's career in Michigan thus came to an inglorious end. He departed as a prisoner of the British and he would later be made a scapegoat by the American government for the disasters it suffered early in the war.

Detroit—and Michigan—was again under British control, as this proclamation by Isaac Brock, coming from the same press that but a month before had printed Hull's proclamation to the Canadians, made perfectly clear.

Courtesy: Burton Historical Collection

More disasters lay ahead for the Americans. At the little settlement of Frenchtown, as Monroe was then called, near the mouth of the River Raisin, an American expedition which had come up from Ohio to protect the settlers was itself surprised and overwhelmed on January 22, 1813. The British marched their captives back to Fort Malden, but left behind a number of wounded Americans. Many of the latter were killed on January 23 by Indians who were enraged at the losses they had suffered in the fighting on the previous day. This graphic wartime print helped to make the cry, "Remember the River Raisin," an effective means of rallying Westerners throughout the remainder of the war.

Courtesy: William L. Clements Library

In the summer of 1813, the tide of the war turned in the Americans' favor. At Put-in-Bay, a few miles east of Michigan in Lake Erie, Captain Oliver Hazard Perry led a new American navy to victory over the British fleet in the decisive battle of the war and one of the most important in American history.

Perry sent this terse report of his victory to the American authorities. The phrase "We have met the enemy and they are ours" was enough to make the young New Englander one of the most frequently quoted American heroes.

The American victory on Lake Erie forced the British to abandon Detroit. American forces, commanded by General Duncan McArthur of Ohio, who had commanded a regiment that served with Hull in 1812, reoccupied Michigan's principal city on September 29, 1813. The authority of the American government had been restored, this time permanently, to southeastern Michigan.

The war in Michigan did not end with the reoccupation of Detroit, however. In the summer of 1814, troops commanded by young Lieutenant-Colonel George Croghan were sent north up Lake Huron to recapture Fort Mackinac.

Courtesy: Rutherford B. Hayes Library

Before attacking Mackinac Island, the Americans had several secondary objectives, including John Johnston's fur-trading post at Sault Ste. Marie, which was partially burned in retaliation for aid which Johnston had given the British. Johnston's home, which he built probably a year or so later, is preserved as a historic house museum in the Soo. Some of the construction details, such as the hand-cut laths, are exposed to view in the interior.

When the expedition reached Mackinac Island, the Americans found that it would be impossible to launch a frontal assault on Fort Mackinac. When Croghan sought to accomplish his goal by landing on the north side of the island, away from the fortifications on the south side, he ran into an ambush on Michael Dousman's farm where a strong British and Indian force drove the Americans back with considerable losses. Mackinac Island and all of northern Michigan only returned to American hands in 1815, after the treaty ending the war.

In the summer of 1815, the British garrison at Fort Mackinac packed its bags and moved to a new fort built a few miles to the northeast on Drummond Island, which the British believed to lie on the Canadian side of the international boundary. Here they could continue to exercise an influence over the Great Lakes Indians, some of whom are shown in the early 1820's rendezvousing on Drummond Island to receive gifts from the British. The buildings of the British fort are in the distance, behind the Indian encampment along the shore.

But in 1822, a British-American commission surveyed the international boundary through the lakes and decided that Drummond Island should be placed in American territory. Not until 1828, however, did the British finally leave the island. Today, stone chimneys are about all that survive of Fort Colyer, the last British-held military post on Michigan soil.

70

The Passing of the Old Michigan

In the fall of 1813, a young, vigorous Yankee arrived in Michigan to be the new governor of the territory. Lewis Cass, shown here in a rare youthful portrait of undetermined date by Abraham G. Tuthill, would be the dominant political force in Michigan for the next half-century. A New Hampshire native who had begun his political career in Ohio as a Jeffersonian Democrat, Cass had come to Detroit in 1812 as commander of one of Hull's regiments. His impatience with Hull's cautious conduct of the war had reached the point of outright mutiny. Now during the eighteen years that Cass would be governor of Michigan, this same quality would help him to become an energetic administrator who, more than anyone else, would be responsible for changing Michigan from a remote wilderness possession inhabited by a few Indians, fur traders, and government employees, to a booming area swarming with people who were hurrying to take up the rich lands in the southern part of the territory.

During the early part of this period, Governor Cass resided in this house. It reportedly dated from the early 1700's, having survived the fire of 1805. Scars of bullets which had struck the building during Pontiac's siege were still visible when Cass moved in. The house was torn down in 1882; thereby one of the last remaining ties was removed which linked Detroit, rapidly advancing into the modern world, with its historic French past.

This house, which Cass built in 1840, some years after he sold his first Detroit home, was a good example both of Cass's prosperity and of the progress Michigan had made since 1813. The house, which was located at Cass and Fort Streets in Detroit, was removed in 1876—a quick casualty of Detroit's accelerating growing pains.

At the same time that the new Michigan of the farmer and tradesman was emerging under the aegis of Governor Cass, the old Michigan of the fur trader, the Indian, and the soldier enjoyed one final fling. In the decade or so after the War of 1812, the American Fur Company, organized from New York by the German immigrant John Jacob Astor, enjoyed a complete monopoly of the fur trade in the United States.

Under Astor's American company, as earlier under the British and French trading companies, the backbone of the business was supplied by the French-Canadian *voyageurs* who formed the crews of canoes which took the trader and his goods to the distant Indian villages. This painting, *circa* 1870, was the work of Mrs. Frances Anne Hopkins, who depicted three traders' boats moving through a Lake Superior fog. Mrs. Hopkins knew her subject, since she had frequently accompanied her husband on trips that he had made as an agent for the Hudson's Bay Company.

Mackinac Island in these years was the hub of the fur trade for the Great Lakes and regions to the west. This painting by an unknown primitive artist of the period conveys some of the excitement that characterized life on Mackinac in the heyday of the fur trade.

Astor's trusted aide on Mackinac Island was Ramsay Crooks, who used up-to-date techniques to bring greater efficiency than ever before to the centuries-old fur-trading business, and rooted out competitors with a ruthlessness that any business tycoon of the late nineteenth century would have viewed with admiration.

During a few weeks each summer, hundreds of clerks labored in the buildings of the American Fur Company on Mackinac, keeping a record of millions of dollars' worth of furs which the traders had brought in. Two of these buildings have survived over the years. In the late nineteenth century they were joined together and put to a different use, as a popular resort hotel, the John Jacob Astor House. In the present century the buildings were restored to their original condition, with one of them, named the Stuart House, after Ramsay Crooks' long-time associate at Mackinac, Robert Stuart, being operated as a historic house museum. The buildings, probably the oldest surviving commercial structures in Michigan, are good examples of the classical style of architecture which was the fashion in the East in the early nineteenth century and which Americans brought with them when they emigrated to Michigan.

Down the street from the American Fur Company buildings was, and is, a modest house which is believed to be the oldest private residence on Mackinac Island, if not in Michigan. Its architectural style and mode of construction hark back to those that were popular in Michigan's pre-American period. Houses similar to it are still found in rural Quebec Province. The house was purchased in the 1820's by Edward Biddle, who was involved in the fur trade and in other island business and political activities for many years. The Biddle House ceased to be occupied in the 1930's, was boarded up, and its fate hung in the balance until it was restored in the late 1950's by interested architectural and construction groups.

In the 1820's and 1830's there were scattered through Michigan numerous trading posts that were subsidiaries of the operations at Mackinac. In the Grand River valley, Astor's agent during these years was Rix Robinson, a native of Massachusetts, who exemplified the high caliber of many of Astor's men. An educated man of great ability, Robinson was married twice, each time to an Indian woman, a fact which contributed to the great influence he had over the Indians around what is now Grand Rapids. Later in life, when he posed for this photograph, he became a potent political figure in western Michigan.

Courtesy: Jack T. Crosby, Jr.

On Grand Island, just off the
Upper Peninsula in Lake Superior,
these cabins stood until the
1960's, relics of a small trading
post built on the island in the
early nineteenth century. The
buildings were later converted to
use as summer cottages. Finally,
when this latter use had been
abandoned, some of the historic
cabins, with their squared-log
walls and stone fireplaces, were
removed to other locations off
the island or were threatened with
final destruction.

Courtesy: Jack T. Crosby, Jr.

Abraham W. Williams, a native of Burlington County, Vermont, operated the Grand Island post for many years. He lies buried on the island in an unkempt little graveyard, tucked away in a wilderness setting. This is appropriate, since he made his living from pelts of forest creatures. When he died, the forests remained, but the great fur trade had long since moved far to the west, ahead of the wave of settlers who swept into Michigan, disrupting the old patterns upon which the fur trade had been built.

Symbolic of the change that took place in Michigan in the 1820's and 1830's is the historic Mission Church on Mackinac Island, shown here in a photograph taken in the early twentieth century. Built in 1829-30, it was part of a Protestant Indian mission which also provided services for the increasingly large non-Catholic white population on the island. It is the oldest surviving church building in Michigan. As its Federal-style architecture and its austere interior suggest, its builders were Yankees from New England and New York. These were men who, like their Puritan forefathers, might be interested temporarily in trading and working with the Indians, but who ultimately looked to acquiring the land for themselves and to developing farms and settlements and all the other features of the culture and civilization in which they had been raised.

By 1842, the Indians of Michigan, through a series of treaties with the United States government, had ceded away their claims to all their lands with the exception of a few small areas reserved for their use. For a few years after signing these treaties, the Indians received annual payments from the government agents. A British visitor, Colonel Henry Ainslie, made this fine sketch of Mackinac Island, showing the Chippewa encampment at the time of the annual payment of 1842.

The government agents, of whom Henry Rowe Schoolcraft is Michigan's best known, worked with the dispossessed Indians and were charged with the supposedly desirable objective of aiding these native Americans in adapting to the ways of the white man.

Schoolcraft in the 1820's worked at Sault Ste. Marie, where the Indian Agency House, which dates from that decade, is still preserved.

At Mackinac, where Schoolcraft moved in the 1830's, a dormitory was built to provide a place where Indians having business on the island might stay, protected by the agent from the traders in the village, some of whom used liquor to take unfair advantage of the Indians. Few of the Chippewas and Ottawas who came to the island used the dormitory, and eventually it was used as a schoolhouse for ten times the length of time it was used as an Indian dormitory.

The full nature of the tragedy that had befallen the Indian now became increasingly clear. The independent native of the prehistoric era, living or dying by his own wits, the Indian of the fur-trading era, who, although he was more and more dependent on the white man, retained some measure of pride by the fact that he was the principal source of supply for an item highly valued by the white man—these were no more. In their place now were pitiful figures such as Chief Okemos, reputedly a leading aide of Tecumseh during the War of 1812, who in his last years in the 1850's was a familiar character in Lansing, where he and his tribesmen were reduced to cadging drinks from the white man.

Courtesy: Hartford Public Library

The policy of the federal government in the 1830's was to remove the Indians east of the Mississippi to new lands in the West, away from the flood of settlement that was sweeping over the regions of the Middle West and the Deep South. Some Potawatomi Indians in southwestern Michigan were removed to what later became Kansas, but Michigan's Indians as a whole escaped this fate and were allowed to remain in the state. They survived as best they could under difficult circumstances. Some achieved a certain kind of fame. Leopold Pokagon, whose portrait, painted in 1838, is owned by the Northern Indiana Historical Society, was the leader of a group of Catholic Potawatomi Indians living in Cass and Berrien Counties, who were exempted from the removal policy. Leopold's children, particularly Simon, added more luster to what was probably Michigan's best-known Indian family. . . .

. . . Chief Shoppenagon, shown posing with his wife and young daughter, was well known for many years to visitors in the Grayling area where he served in various capacities, and many a hunter and salesman has stayed in the hotel in Grayling that bears his name. . . .

. . . Indian dress continued to be worn by some Indians, such as the sad-eyed young girl, Full Moon, but many did so now because it was what the tourist and the photographer expected of them . . .

. . . More and more Indians adopted the white man's dress and ways, with more or less success as, for example, those in the Charlevoix area who, in the mid-nineteenth century, built a little log Methodist church at Greensky Hill, where they and their descendants have worshipped ever since. . . .

. . . But for many others, the problems of adjustment, compounded by the white man's neglect and prejudice, led only to the poverty which was the lot of the Indian family standing outside its cloth-covered dwelling on the shores of Lake Superior, opposite Grand Island, in 1870, . . .

... or the Indian fish dressers standing outside their log hut at Whitefish Point, late in the century.

Until the end of the nineteenth century, vestiges of the frontier military fort continued to be found in Michigan, as they had since the 1600's. General Hugh Brady, who built a fort at Sault Ste. Marie that bore his name, and who served in Michigan well into his seventies, was in the tradition of Cadillac and Gladwin—guarding the frontier from the Indian.

As late as the 1840's, a traditional stockaded wooden fort was built at the tip of the Keweenaw Peninsula. A sketch of the fort, called Fort Wilkins, appeared in 1846 in a unique handwritten camp journal, *The Agate*. . . .

Courtesy: Michigan Tourist Council

. . . Supposedly the fort was built to protect the copper miners who were swarming into the area from the Indians, but many have speculated that the garrison actually was intended to protect the Copper Country's hapless natives from the miners. At any event, the need for troops to be stationed at the fort, which is now a state park, was short-lived.

In the late nineteenth century, soldiers continued to drill, . . .

Courtesy: Mackinac Island State Park Commission

... perform guard duty, and go through the rest of the military routine at Fort Mackinac, but with the passing of the fur trade and the Indian danger the post had long since become an anachronism. The last garrison was evacuated in 1895, and the fort was turned over to Michigan as part of the first state park.

Courtesy: Mackinac Island State Park Commission

In the 1830's the Detroit Arsenal was built, oddly enough, not in Detroit, but ten miles to the west in what is now Dearborn. It was an arms depot designed to supply the military posts throughout the Old Northwest. With the passing of the frontier and the closing down of many of these posts, the need for the arsenal decreased, until finally it was abandoned in 1877. Today, the one-time headquarters of the arsenal's commandant serves as the headquarters of the Dearborn Historical Museum.   *Courtesy: Dearborn Historical Commission*

In the late 1840's, Fort Wayne was built at Detroit. Some of its buildings, such as the massive barracks, contrasted sharply with the smaller and simpler structures of Michigan's earlier forts. The reason is easily determined. Fort Wayne was not intended to be a frontier post but a military base in the settled part of the country, where the troops were trained in peacetime and in times of war were assembled and transported to the areas of military action.

The Coming of the Pioneers

Late in 1836, tragedy struck the family of J. and A. Darling, who lived in western Wayne County. Louesa, a daughter not yet two years old, died on December 1. Six and a half years later, Louesa's brother Charles, aged seven years and six months, also died. None of the Darling family became famous. Rather, history files the family away, along with tens of thousands of others, under the heading "Pioneers." Louesa and Charles Darling are buried in a tiny, rural cemetery on a bank overlooking US-12, which in pioneer days was the Chicago Road, one of the main routes west out of Detroit. A stone, now much weathered, gives probably as much information about these children as we will ever have. Similar graveyards, often neglected and overgrown, are scattered by the hundreds throughout Michigan, with grave markers whose inscriptions may now be illegible, if the markers themselves are not broken or fallen over. But the real monuments to the Darlings and their fellow pioneers are the farmlands which they cleared and the villages and towns and cities they founded.

In the late 1800's, some pioneers set down their reminiscences as they looked back over their lives and recognized how they and their contemporaries had, in a few years, altered the entire appearance of southern Michigan. Among the best-known memoirs are those of William Nowlin, which he recorded in *The Bark Covered House,* published, as were so many of these historical works, in the year of the nation's centennial, 1876. Illustrations, drawn, presumably, under the watchful eye of the author, depict the stormy passage of the Nowlin family in 1834 from New York in the steamboat *Michigan;* . . .

. . . the tavern whose proprietor was hired by the Nowlins to move them from Detroit over the Chicago Road to the land John Nowlin had purchased in Dearborn; . . .

. . . the bark-covered log cabin which was the Nowlin's first home; . . .

. . . the larger house which they built in 1836; . . .

. . . the rapid development of the area, symbolized by the coming of the railroad to Dearborn in 1837; . . .

. . . and finally the well-cleared, fenced acres of the Nowlin farm, with its barns and its three-story brick house, built in 1854, "not as palatial as some might admire, but a good substantial house." The series of illustrations effectively summarize the problems and triumphs of the successful pioneers of the middle decades of nineteenth-century Michigan.

Before the Nowlins or anyone else could legally settle in Michigan, the land, after it had been relinquished by the Indians, had to be surveyed by federal surveyors. This tremendous task of literally walking over the entire surface of Michigan and marking township and section corners at half-mile intervals began in earnest in 1815 and was substantially completed by 1850. Lucius Lyon, one of the most prominent of those who carried out this project, started as a young surveyor in Michigan in the 1820's, gaining a knowledge which he used to good advantage subsequently in a variety of real estate promotions, including the town of Lyons and a large section of what would become Grand Rapids. Lyon also served as one of Michigan's first two United States senators before returning to his earlier profession as surveyor general for Ohio, Indiana, and Michigan.

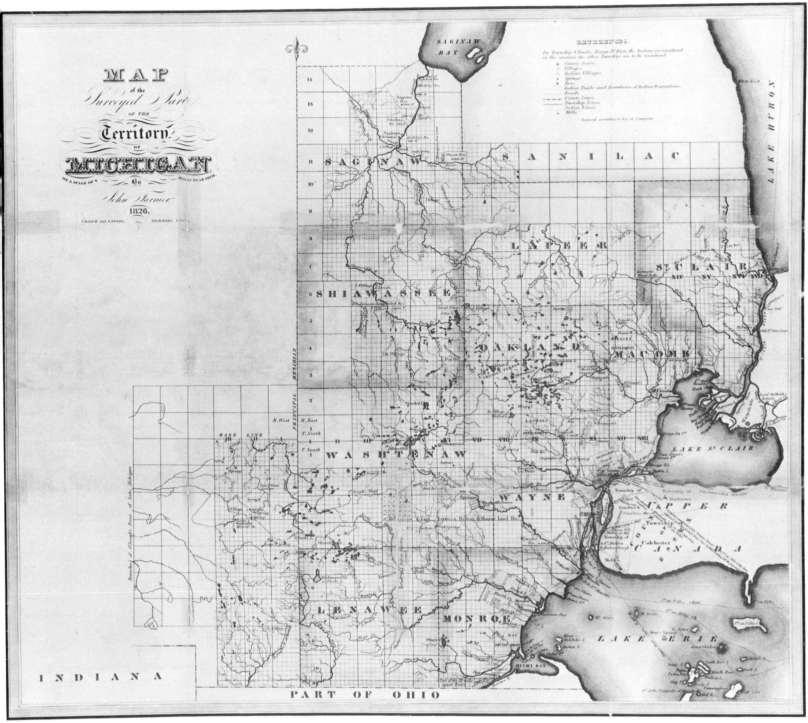

By the mid-1820's, the surveyors had carried out their task across the southeastern part of the lower peninsula, as shown on this 1826 map, which was one of the first maps produced by John Farmer, the founder of Michigan's most famous map-making firm which continued in business into the twentieth century. The difference between the American system of surveying the land into neat square sections measured off from the Principal Meridian running north and south, and the east-west Base Line (the origin of today's Meridian Road in Ingham County and Base Line Road along the Wayne County-Oakland County boundary), and the earlier French system, under which lots were laid out at ninety-degree angles to the rivers, is graphically illustrated by examining the pattern along the Detroit River and the River Raisin which had been settled in the eighteenth century.

Courtesy: University of Michigan General Library

By about 1847, the federal survey of Michigan was well on its way to completion, as indicated on this map, which shows that by this time the job was completed in southern Michigan, the field work was virtually completed in the rest of the lower peninsula, while in the Upper Peninsula a good start had been made on laying out the townships. William A. Burt, who probably did more of the land survey than any other single individual, includes a note on this map that the dotted lines running from the Saginaw valley up to Grand Traverse Bay and the Straits of Mackinac indicated the best routes for roads into these areas which were still almost totally unsettled.

Surveyed land could be purchased from United States land offices, the first of which was opened in Detroit in 1818, a second a few years later in Monroe, and a third in 1831, at White Pigeon, the first land office in western Michigan. This office was moved to Kalamazoo in 1834, but the building in which it was housed while in White Pigeon is believed to be a dilapidated structure now occupied by a restaurant. The land office buildings at Detroit and Monroe are not known to have survived.

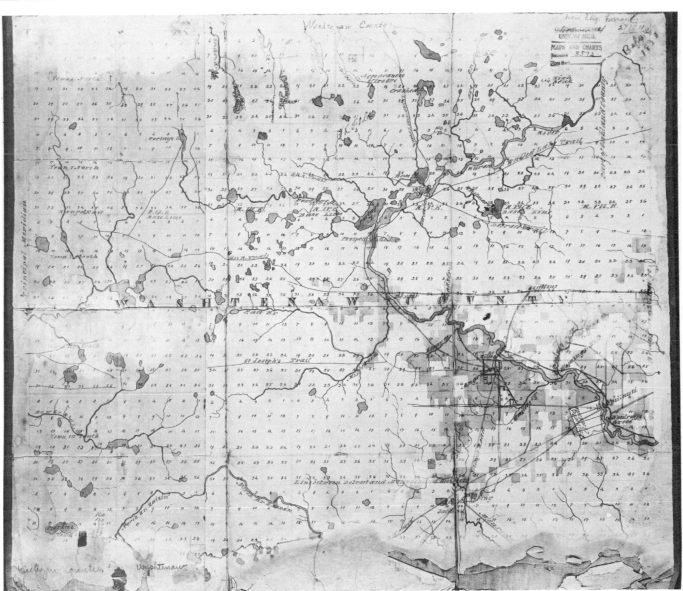

Courtesy: University of Michigan General Library

At the land office, the seeker after public land, whether a prospective settler or a speculator, could quickly learn if the section he was interested in was still available. On this Washtenaw County map from the late 1820's, those lands around Ypsilanti and "Anarbour" which had been taken up were shaded in a solid color by a land office employee. The non-shaded areas were still for sale at the low, low price of $1.25 an acre. Later, after the passage of the Homestead Act in 1862, over three million acres of land were obtained in Michigan by homesteaders who paid nothing except a small registration fee, if they had resided on the land for five years.

called *Lac des Illinois*; is fifteen miles long, of an oval figure, and subject to a flux and reflux.

SURFACE, SOIL, TIMBER.

There are no mountains in this territory; the interior is table land, having a western and northern inclination, interspersed with small lakes and marshes, from which issue the head branches of the rivers. Prairies exist, from the banks of the St. Josephs to lake St. Clair; some are of an excellent soil; others, sandy, wet and sterile. There are, nevertheless, extensive forests, of lofty timber, consisting of oak, sugar maple, beach, ash, poplar, white and yellow pine, cucumber, buckeye, basswood, hickory, cedar, plum, crab apple, cherry, black and honey locust. The last flourishes as far north as the margin of lake Huron—yet east of the Allegany mountains, it is never found north of the Delaware. The bottoms, and high prairies are equal to those of Indiana. A considerable part of the coast of lake Michigan consists of a range of sand-hills, thrown up by the surf and "eddying winds." The timbered uplands are well adapted to the production of most kinds of grain; and appear to bear a long series of crops, as is the case with the ridge in the rear of Detroit.

EXTENT OF CEDED LANDS.

At a treaty held at Detroit in November, 1807, between Gen. Hull and the chiefs of the Pottawattamie, Ottawa, Wyandot, and Chippawa tribes, all the lands within the following limits, except the reservations hereafter described, were ceded to the United States, viz: "Beginning at the mouth of the Miami river of the lakes, and running thence up the middle thereof, to the mouth of the great Au Glaize river ; thence running due north until it intersects a parallel of latitude, to be drawn from the outlet of lake Huron, which forms the

Courtesy: Michigan Historical Collections

Land sales in Michigan proceeded at a very slow pace for a number of years. The great Michigan land boom, one of the most spectacular in American history, did not come until the mid-1830's, nearly two decades after land in Michigan first went on the market. Despite a legend that has persisted for many years, this delay was not the result of unfavorable publicity. Actually, reports of Michigan soil were overwhelmingly favorable, as, for example, these comments from Samuel R. Brown's *The Western Gazetteer; or Emigrant's Directory,* published at Auburn, New York, in 1817.

On August 27, 1818, the *Walk-in-the-Water* completed its first trip from Buffalo to Detroit. By 1819, it was bringing passengers and freight to and from Mackinac Island and other points up the Great Lakes beyond Detroit.

92

Courtesy: Clarke Historical Library

Courtesy: William L. Clements Library

Michigan, in the early years of the nineteenth century, was a remote area. Americans were slow to come to the territory because it was accessible by land or water only after a long and expensive journey. One step toward removing this major impediment to large-scale settlement is illustrated in this 1820 painting of Detroit by George Washington Whistler, gifted father of an even more gifted artist son. Dominating the scene is the *Walk-in-the-Water,* the first steamboat on the Great Lakes above Niagara Falls.

MANIFEST of the whole Cargo on board of the Steam-Boat WALK-IN-THE-WATER— whereof JOB FISH is at present Master ; burthen 338 and 60-95ths Tons, bound from the Port of *Mackinac* to the Port of *Black Rock June 21th* 1819

Marks and Numbers.	No. of Entries.	Packages and Contents.	Shippers.	Residence.	Consignees.	Residence.
J F W	1	Box	Capt Knapp	Mackinac	John H White	Erie
D Deacon	1	Mocock Sugar	D Deacon	on Board	D Deacon	on Board
I H Carr	1	Do Do	I H Carr	do	I H Carr	do
I B Stuart	45	Barrels Fish	I B Stuart	do	I B Stuart	do
D G Jones	18	Hams	D G Jones	do	D G Jones	do
do	1	Pack Furs	do	do	do	do
do	1	Keg	do	do	do	do
do	1	Box Dry Goods	do	do	do	do
do	1	Barrel Do	do	do	do	do
do	4	Boxes Nails	do	do	do	do
L H	4	Barrels Fish	L Hodge	do	do	do
Cheesborough	1	Barrel Fish	Cheesborough	do	do	do
D D	1	Barrel Fish	D Deacon	do	do	do

40 ARTICLES OF ENTRY.

DISTRICT OF BUFFALO CREEK, } ss.
PORT OF BUFFALO CREEK,

JOB FISH, Master of the Steam-Boat WALK-IN-THE-WATER, having, as the law directs, made oath to the above Manifest consisting of Forty articles Black Rock Articles of Entry; and delivered a duplicate thereof, permission is hereby granted to the said Master to proceed to the Port of Black Rock in the State of New York, Given under my hand and seal of office, at the Custom-House of the Port of Buffalo Creek, de Mackinac this 21 June 1819, and of the Independence of the United States the forty third year,

COLLECTOR.

FACSIMILE REPRINT from the original in the Sault Ste. Marie Collection in the Clarke Historical Library of Central Michigan University.

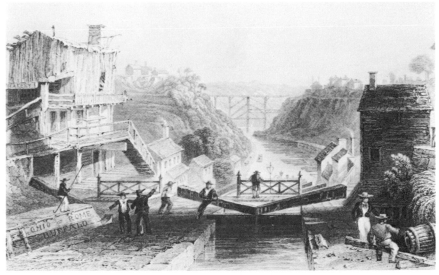

In 1825, the Erie Canal opened, an event that was equally as important to the development of such western areas as Michigan as it was to the economy of New York. The famous canal provided an all-water route connecting New York City and other Eastern markets with Michigan, cutting many days and dollars off the time and the expense that had previously been involved in transporting passengers and goods between these points.

Later, in its financially disastrous internal improvements program of the late 1830's, Michigan would attempt to build its own canal system across the lower peninsula. Traces of the never-finished Clinton-Kalamazoo Canal which was to have linked Mount Clemens, at the mouth of the Clinton River, with what is now Saugatuck, at the mouth of the Kalamazoo, may still be seen in Macomb and Oakland Counties. This ruined aqueduct near Utica was to have carried canal traffic over the Clinton River.

At Detroit, as traffic from the East now rapidly increased, facilities were built to take care of the travelers. Woodworth's Steamboat Hotel, opened in 1819, was, until the 1840's, the most famous establishment of its kind in the city; and its proprietor, Uncle Ben Woodworth, was one of Detroit's best-known personalities. The hotel was located on the corner of Woodbridge and Randolph Streets in downtown Detroit.

When settlers began arriving at Detroit, roads were needed over which they could move into the interior of the lower peninsula. The most famous of these was the Chicago Road, which was surveyed in the late 1820's with funds appropriated by Congress. This is a part of a map published in 1825 which showed the surveyed route, with some of the notations made by the surveyors regarding the terrain and other topographical features. Like so many of Michigan's major roads, the Chicago Road's route followed very closely an old Indian trail. The pioneers, however, did not necessarily follow the route as it was surveyed. Since the road was little more than a track worn by the vehicles that passed over it, the drivers of these vehicles did not hesitate to abandon the surveyed route when an easier and shorter path could be found.

Courtesy: Transportation Library

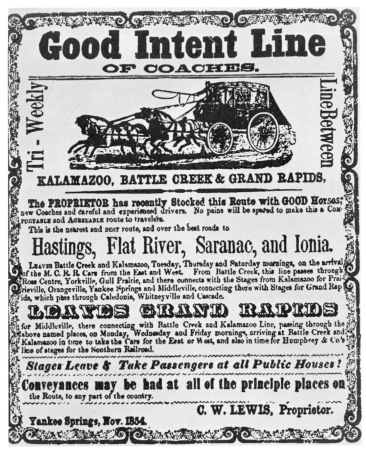

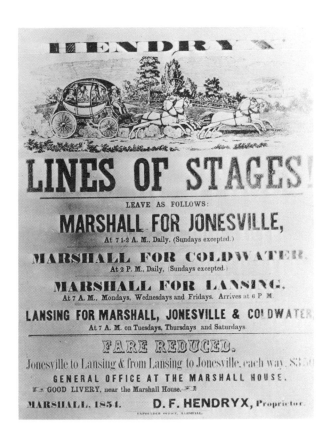

By the 1830's there was regular stagecoach service between Detroit and Chicago over the Chicago Road, and before long, similar service was provided throughout southern Michigan. One of the stages of the Good Intent Line is shown in Plainwell in 1865.

Courtesy: Grand Rapids Public Library

One of the best-known stagecoach stops along the Chicago Road was this inn at Clinton, built in 1830, which, by the 1920's, had fallen into ruinous condition. At that time, Henry Ford acquired the building and had it removed to the outdoor museum he was developing at Dearborn. Since that time, the Clinton Inn, restored to all of its nineteenth-century majesty, has provided food and relaxation to far more people visiting Ford's Greenfield Village than it ever did during its stagecoach era. The inn is also a fine example of Greek Revival architecture in a commercial structure.

Courtesy: Henry Ford Museum

Farther west along the Chicago Road, at Cambridge Junction (the intersection of US-12 and M-50), the old Walker Tavern, built originally in 1832, is another stagecoach stop which has survived and now, after many years of operation as a private historical museum along the lines indicated in this picture, has been purchased by the state to form the nucleus of a historical park.

Another onetime stage stop, the Botsford Inn, located in Farmington on the old Grand River Trail, continues to serve travelers of the modern era as both a restaurant and a hotel. Additions made in the 1950's and 1960's since this photograph was taken have greatly enlarged the original facility, part of which dates from the 1830's.

Courtesy: J. W. Anhut

Not all stagecoach inns were sumptuous affairs, however, as witness this modest establishment, the Robinson Tavern on the Hastings-Battle Creek stage road. Although this tavern was probably more typical of the inns of the day than were the Clinton or Botsford inns, there has been little effort to preserve examples of this type. Here, as elsewhere, the historical preservation movement has always been primarily interested in preserving the superb structures rather than the commonplace.

WINTER ARRANGEMENT
FOR 1866-7.

WHILE THE SLEIGHING IS GOOD
—A—
LINE OF STAGES
WILL RUN FROM
Traverse City to Muskegon
—IN—
3 DAYS.

Leaving TRAVERSE CITY every Monday, Wednesday and Friday, at 7 o'clock A. M.
Returning Leave MUSKEGON every Tuesday, Thursday and Saturday, at 7 o'clock A. M., stopping both ways, for the night, at Manistee and Pentwater,
And, to take on and leave off passengers or freight, at White Lake, Pere Marquette, Lincoln, Freesoil, Norwalk, Pleasanton, Benzonia, Homestead, Sherman's or any other point on the route.
☞ Express goods carried with safety and responsibility.
Accommodations as GOOD, Fare as LOW, and QUICKER TIME than by any other line.
STEWARD & BAILY,
RODY & COLLINS,
PITTENGER & CO.

The stagecoach era continued in parts of Michigan until the end of the nineteenth century with special arrangements sometimes made to take advantage of winter road conditions.

In the 1830's the railroad arrived, the final addition to Michigan's nineteenth-century transportation system. Hoping to emulate the success of short-line railroads that developed in the East in the 1820's and early 1830's, many Michigan railroad companies were chartered, although few ever laid a track. The earliest such company to be chartered in Michigan, indeed the first railroad company chartered in the Old Northwest, was the Pontiac and Detroit, whose charter was dated July 31, 1830. The company failed to get anywhere and, in 1834, an entirely new corporation, the Detroit and Pontiac Railroad Company, was organized. Eventually, in 1843, service was actually provided between these two cities. At the Detroit end, travelers could get a room at Hiram R. Andrews' Rail-road Hotel. . . .

Courtesy: Transportation Library

The advertisement (left column):

DIRECTORY.   151

1846.} [train illustration] {1846.

RAIL-ROAD HOTEL,

BY

HIRAM R. ANDREWS,

Opposite the Central & Northern railroad depots,

DETROIT, MICHIGAN,

THIS House has been greatly enlarged and fitted up in a style equal to any Public House in Detroit for comfort and convenience. Its location is one of the most healthy and pleasant in the city,

BEING ON THE PUBLIC SQUARE,

and in the immediate vicinity of the Central and Pontiac Railroad Depots, Auditor General's office, and at the junction of all the leading turnpike roads from Detroit.

GENERAL STAGE OFFICE AT THE HOTEL.

☞ The Proprietor assures the Public that no pains will be spared to furnish his Table with as good as the market affords, and his guests with every attention requisite for their comfort.

TRAVELERS

Wishing to take the Cars or Boats will be FURNISHED MEALS AT TWENTY-FIVE CENTS, And Carriage and Baggage Wagon in readiness at all times to convey them to the Cars or Boats, *gratis.*

BOARD BY THE DAY 75 CENTS.

Courtesy: Michigan Historical Collections

. . . A full-page ad in the 1846 Detroit city directory trumpeted some of the services which this hotel offered, including meals "furnished . . . at twenty-five cents" (note the inverted "N's" in the original line!) .

Michigan's first operating railroad, however, and the first railroad in the West was not the Detroit and Pontiac but the Erie and Kalamazoo, which began running horse-drawn trains between Toledo and Adrian in 1836 and in 1837 started steam operations with a Baldwin locomotive. Just what Michigan's first train looked like is a matter of conjecture. This sketch appeared a half-century after the event, showing the train rolling through the countryside, the pioneers, who were still busily clearing their land, waving at this welcome link with the outside world.

Courtesy: Michigan Historical Collections

A banknote issued by the Erie and Kalamazoo itself is decorated with a picture of a very different-appearing train. It was perhaps not intended to be an exact representation of the Michigan company's rolling stock.

99

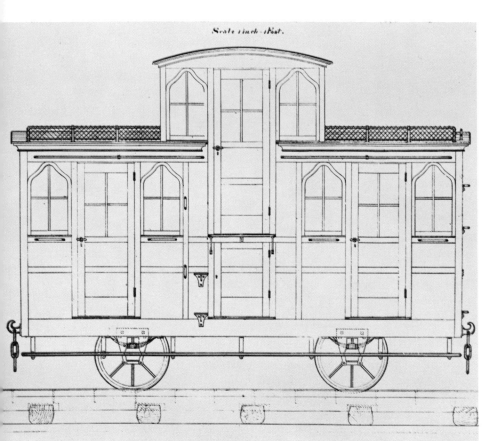

Scale 1 inch 1 Foot.

At any event, this plan for the first Erie and Kalamazoo passenger car does not resemble the cars shown in the two sketches of the railroad's first train.

In the late 1830's railroad lines began to reach across the lower peninsula. By 1838, the Michigan Central offered service from Detroit to Dearborn, and before the year was out its tracks had reached Ypsilanti.

By the 1840's more and more communities in southern Michigan were being served by one or more lines. Much of the early impetus came from the state government which began building both the Michigan Central and the Michigan Southern, but in a few years was forced by financial necessity to sell the railroads to private companies, which by the 1850's completed the laying of rails across the state and on to Chicago.

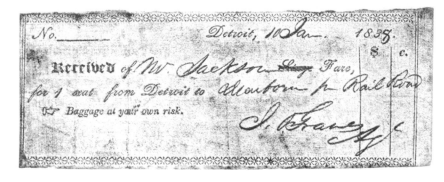

MICHIGAN CENTRAL RAIL-ROAD LINE.

ROUGH IN 34 HOURS IN OPPOSITION TO A VOYAGE FROM 4 1-2 TO 9 DAYS LONG.

OR DETROIT, CHICAGO,

AND OTHER PORTS ON LAKE MICHIGAN.

bin Fare through, (*Meals and Berths on Lakes Erie and Michigan included,*) $

THROUGH TO DETROIT WITHOUT LANDING !

ROUGH TO CHICAGO IN 34 HOURS—TO MILWAUKEE IN 44 HOURS,
AND TO ST. LOUIS IN 3 1-2 DAYS.

THE NEW AND SPLENDID STEAMER

ATLANTIC,

CAPT. S. CLEMENT,

ves the Michigan Central Railroad Wharf, EVERY MONDAY and THURSDAY EVENING, at NINE
LOCK, P. M., in connection with the MICHIGAN CENTRAL RAILROAD, through without landing,
ing at Detroit in time for the Evening Train going West.

m Buffalo to Detroit in 17 Hours. From Detroit to New Buffalo in 11 Hours.
m New Buffalo to Chicago in 4 Hours. From Chicago to St. Louis in 48 Hours.

Passengers arriving by the Eastern Cars wishing to take this Boat will please have their Baggage
d under the MICHIGAN CENTRAL RAILROAD SIGN, in the Depot. A Baggaman will be in
dance to convey Baggage to the Boat.

or Passage or Freight, apply on board, or at the Office, at the Michigan Central
Railroad Wharf, Buffalo.

Press of Jerome & Brother, Daily American Office, Rochester.

The completion of the Michigan Central between Detroit and Chicago led the railroad company to offer this combination steamboat-train trip linking the East and the West. By taking a steamboat from Buffalo to Detroit, the traveler could then board the Michigan Central, whose depot was located on the Detroit River shore, and proceed to Chicago, thereby cutting several days off the time it took to go from Buffalo to Chicago by boat alone.

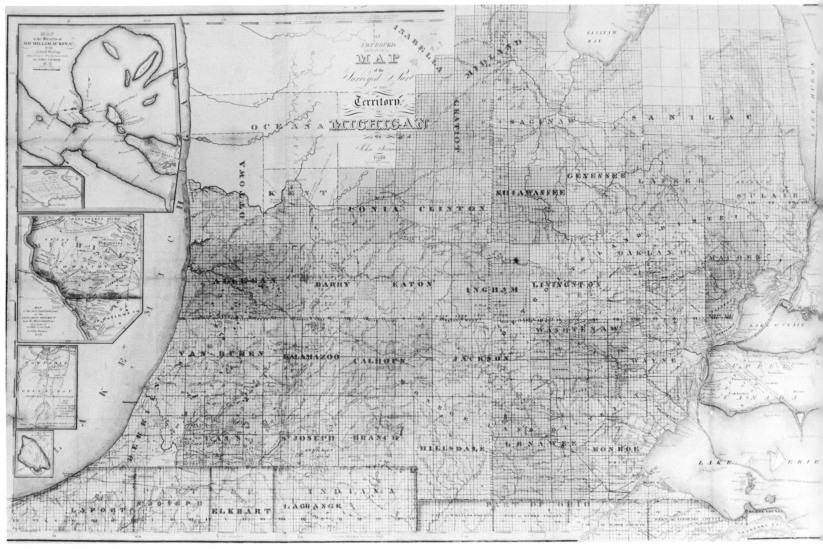

In a matter of but two or three decades, the once remote wilderness had become an easily accessible area to which settlers eagerly flocked. By 1836, John Farmer showed the surveyed parts of Michigan and settlement as stretching clear across the southern third of the lower peninsula from Lake Erie and Lake Huron on the east to Lake Michigan on the west. The advances made since Farmer's first map of 1826 are also shown by the host of new counties that had been created, many of which were named for such prominent officials of the period as Andrew Jackson, Lewis Cass, Martin Van Buren, and John C. Calhoun.

By this time, the population of Michigan Territory was at least one hundred thousand, in contrast with a figure of less than five thousand a quarter of a century earlier. This was far in excess of the population of sixty thousand free inhabitants which had been set by the Northwest Ordinance as the number a territory must contain in order to become a state. Stevens T. Mason, who, as a nineteen-year-old youth, had been named secretary of the territory in 1831, was acting governor much of the time after Cass left in 1831 to become secretary of war. Mason asked Congress to authorize the territory to draw up a state constitution and elect a state government.

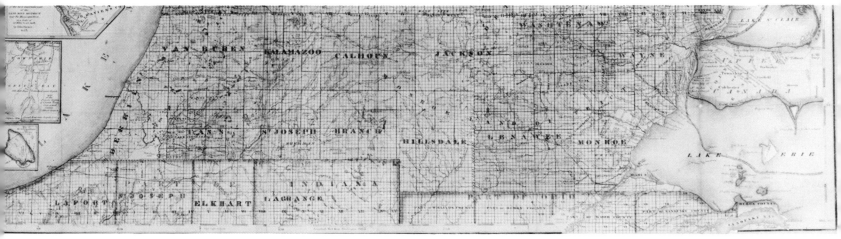

Congress refused Mason's request because of a boundary dispute between Ohio and Michigan. Congress in 1787 had declared that the line separating the northern and southern states that would be carved out of the Northwest Territory was to be an east-west line running through the southernmost point of Lake Michigan. This line, as the maps of the period, such as Farmer's map of 1836, clearly showed, intersected Lake Erie some distance south of Miami (Maumee) Bay, placing this area, where the important industrial and port city of Toledo would develop and also a rich band of farm land, in Michigan Territory. Ohio, however, insisted that the Northwest Ordinance line of 1787 had been laid down at a time when no one had realized how far south Lake Michigan extended, and that the direction of the line should be altered in order to give Ohio control of Maumee Bay. Its case was strengthened by the fact that Indiana, as well as Illinois, had successfully pushed their boundaries northward beyond the limits imposed by Congress in 1787. Nevertheless, Michigan insisted that the Toledo strip was rightfully part of its domain. This was the origin of the so-called Toledo War between Michigan and Ohio.

Denied authorization from Congress to proceed with the steps necessary for statehood, acting Governor Mason went ahead on his own. A constitutional convention convened in 1835 and drew up Michigan's first state constitution, a brief document that established a strong central government with few restrictions to hamper the actions of the elected officials, such as would characterize all of Michigan's later constitutions.

103

A state seal was adopted by the convention. It was designed by Lewis Cass, who had also designed the seal used by the territorial government since 1814. Its motto, *Tandem fit surculus arbor* ("The shoot at length becomes a tree"), had probably expressed the ultimate desire of Cass to see Michigan grow to statehood. Now, as that goal was being attained, he paraphrased a motto that appears on the tomb of Sir Christopher Wren to point out the unique aspect of the new state: "If you seek a pleasant peninsula, look around you." The word *Tuebor* ("I will defend") was probably intended to indicate Michigan's determination not to give up its claim to the Toledo strip. In the center of the seal, a man is shown holding a gun, standing on a point of land jutting out into the water. The two seals are shown here in their exact original size. The state seal as Cass designed it in 1835 has remained the seal of the state to the present day, although the delineation of the various figures on it has varied considerably over the years, so that today the animals, the eagle, and even the man, bear little resemblance to those shown on the original seal. The great seal can be used on documents or for other purposes only with the permission of the secretary of state. Such permission is not required to use the state coat of arms, which is that material within the outer circles of the seal.

Although Michigan voters late in 1835 approved the state constitution and elected Stevens T. Mason as the first state governor, Congress still would not approve the action and admit Michigan to the union until in 1836 a convention meeting at Ann Arbor in the Washtenaw County Courthouse agreed to surrender the Toledo strip in return for the western two-thirds of the Upper Peninsula. The courthouse in which this historic decision was made was torn down later in the nineteenth century and was replaced by a new building on the same site. The same process was repeated in the middle twentieth century to provide for the present Washtenaw County Courthouse, which will be lucky to survive into the next century.

Courtesy: Michigan Historical Collections

104

Twenty fourth

CONGRESS OF THE UNITED STATES;

At the *second* Session,

Begun and held at the City of Washington, on Monday, the *fifth* day of December, one thousand eight hundred and *thirty six*.

AN ACT

to admit the State of Michigan into the Union, upon an equal footing with the original States.

Whereas, in pursuance of the act of Congress of June the fifteenth, eighteen hundred and thirty-six, entitled "An act to establish the northern boundary of the State of Ohio, and to provide for the admission of the State of Michigan into the Union upon the conditions therein expressed," a convention of delegates, elected by the people of the said State of Michigan, for the sole purpose of giving their assent to the boundaries of the said State of Michigan as described, declared, and established, in and by the said act, did, on the fifteenth of December, eighteen hundred and thirty-six, assent to the provisions of said act, therefore: Be it enacted by the Senate and House of Representatives of the United States of America in Congress assembled, That the State of Michigan shall be one, and is hereby declared to be one, of the United States of America, and admitted into the Union on an equal footing with the original States, in all respects whatever. Section 2. And be it further enacted, That the Secretary of the Treasury, in carrying into effect the thirteenth and fourteenth sections of the act of the twenty third of June, eighteen hundred and thirty-six, entitled "An act to regulate the deposites of the public money," shall consider the State of Michigan as being one of the United States.

James K. Polk Speaker of the House of Representatives.

M Van Buren } Vice President of the United States, and President of the Senate.

Approved this 26th January 1837 —
Andrew Jackson

Courtesy: Library of Congress

President Andrew Jackson on January 25, 1837, signed the act of Congress which conferred statehood on Michigan. After more than two centuries of colonial status under French, British, and American rule, Michigan had become a self-governing state with a voice in the affairs of the federal union equal to that of the twenty-five other established states.

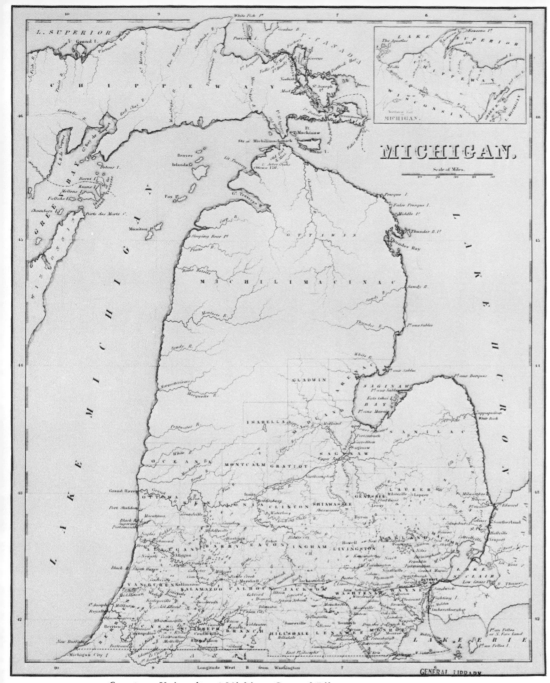

MICHIGAN.

Scale of Miles.

Courtesy: University of Michigan General Library

In a short time, maps of the new state of Michigan began to appear, such as this one, published in 1838 by T. G. Bradford. Much information was yet needed before the geographical knowledge of Michigan would reach the level it has since attained, but the geographical unit that was called Michigan in 1837 is the same one that exists under this name today. Because of the peculiar shape of the state, which makes it difficult to show the entire area on a normal atlas page, Bradford showed the western half of the Upper Peninsula, in much reduced scale, in an inset, a practice that map makers have commonly used, to the disgust of many residents of those western portions. (Bradford was a little premature in showing the extent of railroad operations in southern Michigan in 1838 and also in showing a canal running from Saginaw to Ionia, which was planned but never completed.)

The famous "war" between Michigan and Ohio fortunately never amounted to much and never reached the stage of real combat and bloodshed. Not until 1915 was the land boundary agreed upon in 1836 officially surveyed. At that time, Governor Woodbridge N. Ferris of Michigan (left) and Governor Frank B. Willis of Ohio shook hands across the state line. The "war," however, is not quite over even yet because the location of the water boundary in Lake Erie is still a matter of dispute between the Wolverine State and the Buckeye State.

Pioneer Architecture

Statehood and self-government were but two of the goals which American pioneers were determined to achieve. The ambitions of the Michigan pioneers are perhaps best exemplified in the buildings which they erected soon after their arrival. Not content with practical, utilitarian structures, they ultimately insisted on importing the best styles they had known in the Eastern states from which they had emigrated. It was appropriate, therefore, that Adrian in 1870 erected as a monument to its Civil War dead a marble Greek Ionic column which had been part of Philadelphia's Bank of Pennsylvania building. Today, this column, the only known fragment from the building with which the architect, Benjamin H. Latrobe, in 1798 had inaugurated the Greek Revival style of architecture in America, stands as a fitting memorial to the pioneers whose building activities adhered to a style which the architectural historian Rexford Newcomb declares "was more exclusively classic than that of any other state of the Old Northwest."

This was Grand Rapids in 1831. In the foreground is the camp of Chief Noonday, a leader of the Ottawa Indians, who still lived in villages along the Grand River and hunted over the surrounding lands, as they and their ancestors had done for centuries. In the background are buildings associated with a Baptist mission, established in 1823, and the fur-trading post of Louis Campau, which he had been operating since 1826.

Courtesy: Michigan Historical Collections

Within a few months after the Rev. J. Booth portrayed Grand Rapids as it looked in 1831, Louis Campau, Lucius Lyon, and others who now bought land here began to promote the development of a city and by the time Michigan became a state in 1837, Grand Rapids was a booming community which, its boosters (many of them from western New York) declared, would be the "Rochester of the West." Had photography been sufficiently advanced by this time, the scene in Grand Rapids would probably have been quite similar to this one, taken in May, 1886, in the new Upper Peninsula town of Ironwood, looking west down Aurora Street. The process of pushing back

the frontier was one that did not end in Michigan until the twentieth century, and, in fact, still continues, to some extent, with each new suburban development.

In an amazingly short time, considering the transportation facilities and the construction materials and equipment that were then available, the new towns in Michigan advanced beyond the raw frontier stage. Men of means in these communities were soon moving their families into homes such as this one, built by the Grand Rapids merchant Abraham Pike, in 1844 or 1845, when that city was scarcely a decade removed from being simply an Indian trading and mission settlement.

Courtesy: Allen Stross

Although the Pike House, now the home of the Grand Rapids Art Gallery, is in itself an example of how rapidly southern Michigan was transformed from a wilderness into an area of thriving settlements, the great Doric columns that support the central pedimented portico illustrate this movement in an even more startling fashion. They were originally part of a $200,000 hotel built in the 1830's by the promoters of Port Sheldon, a town located on Lake Michigan, some twenty-five miles west of Grand Rapids. Port Sheldon failed to fulfill the dreams of its developers and the town soon disappeared. But the four columns from the hotel, which Abraham Pike bought for the house he was building, epitomize the high ambitions of the Michigan pioneer.

The traditional pioneer dwelling, as every school child knows, was a log cabin, but contrary to what many believe, the Michigan log cabin was not necessarily the typical cabin with walls of round, untrimmed, bark-covered logs. Rather, these cabins, since fur-trading days, were more likely to be constructed of squared logs, as in this abandoned building, located between Lansing and Williamston.

Courtesy: Michigan Historical Collections

Courtesy:
Michigan Historical Collections

Here was a larger log farm house, again of squared-log construction, which was found in the Houghton Lake area.

This family in the Traverse City area had either begun with, or advanced to, this larger, unpainted frame house, with such luxuries as a stoop outside the entrance for rocking chairs, flower pots, and, hanging from the eaves, a bird cage.

Courtesy: Clarke Historical Library

The examples of nineteenth-century houses which are carefully preserved and pointed out to visitors who want to see old buildings, however, are not the average residential buildings of the period, few of which have survived, but the exceptional and very fine architectural examples, especially the Greek Revival house. The best known, certainly the most frequently mentioned and pictured, is the Harold Brooks House, on the corner of North Kalamazoo Avenue and Prospect Street in Marshall. With its great two-story portico of five fluted Ionic columns, its carved ornamental window in the pediment above the columns, . . .

. . . its entrance through a one-story Ionic porch on one side, its interior decoration (we overlook the jarring note of the mid-1930's furnishings), this brick house is a magnificent structure, built by Jabez S. Fitch around 1840, scarcely a decade after Marshall was founded.

113

Courtesy: Historic American Buildings Survey

The Brooks House is by no means unique. Numerous other superb examples of Greek Revival architecture abound in southern Michigan, including such other examples of the two-story, temple-style mansion as the Wilson-Wahr House at 126 North Division Street, Ann Arbor, built in 1843. Its location on a smaller corner lot does not set off the house to such an advantage as do the more extensive grounds of the Harold Brooks House, but the Wilson-Wahr House is considered by Rexford Newcomb to be "one of the finest Greek Revival houses in America." Great full-length windows beneath the portico look out from the parlor.

Courtesy: Historic American Buildings Survey

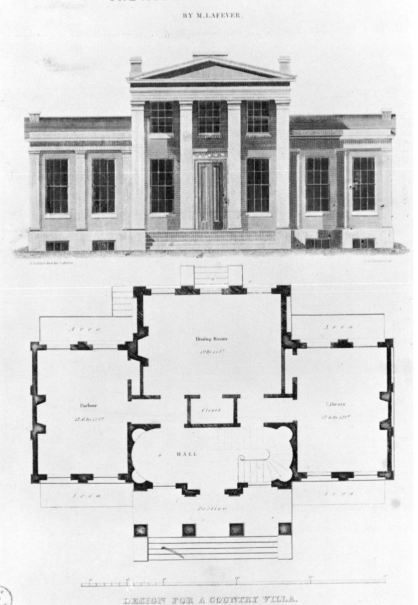

There were innumerable variations of the Greek Revival style. Somewhat similar to the Pike House in Grand Rapids is the Sidney T. Smith House on Michigan Road, just west of Maute Road, in the vicinity of Grass Lake. The house, built in 1840, has a two-story central section, flanked by one-story wings, all fronted by square-columned porticoes. It appears that Smith, like modern home builders who pore over books of model homes to get ideas, patterned his house after a model for a country villa in Minard Lafever's *Modern Builder's Guide,* first published in 1833.

Courtesy: University of Michigan Architectural Library

115

Not all Greek Revival houses present a massive appearance. An early and unusual type is the Elijah Anderson House, West Chicago Boulevard at North Union Street, Tecumseh, built in 1832. Some of its features, such as the dormer, were added at a later date and serve to detract from the original classic design.

Courtesy: Historic American Buildings Survey

Courtesy: Historic American Buildings Survey

A house does not have to have an imposing, multi-columned portico to qualify as a Greek Revival building, as witness the Sibley House at 976 East Jefferson Avenue, Detroit, which was built by the political leader Solomon Sibley in the 1840's. It is now the rectory of Christ (Episcopal) Church.

Although the Greek Revival style was the dominant one for many years in the homes built by successful Michiganians, other types were not unknown. Traits of the earlier Federal style were evident in the John Palmer House in Detroit, which was built in 1829 and torn down four decades later.

116

Courtesy: Allen Stross

Somewhat later came such modifications of the Greek Revival style as the bracketed Italianate style, exemplified by the Chauncey M. Brewer mansion at 410 North Eagle Street, Marshall, which was completed in 1859.

Courtesy: Grand Rapids Public Library

Then there were the unusual types, such as the octagon houses, whose supposed virtues were advocated by the eccentric phrenologist Orson A. Fowler. He found a number of converts to his ideas in mid-nineteenth-century Michigan, from which period dates the Ira Jones cobblestone octagon house at 706 Butterworth Street, Grand Rapids.

The one-story brick octagon house at 1520 Long Road, Kalamazoo, now owned by Mrs. J. Stanley Gilmore, shows the eight-sided form of the main mass of the building carried through in the cupola which lights the central interior.

Courtesy: Kalamazoo Gazette

Courtesy: Allen Stross

In a class by itself is the Honolulu House, located at 107 North Kalamazoo Avenue, in that city of well-preserved old houses, Marshall. Abner Pratt built this house in 1860, supposedly using as his model a house which he had occupied while serving as United States consul to Hawaii. Both in its exterior appearance and in its ornate interior decoration, the Honolulu House, now maintained as a historic house museum, has been hailed by the architectural historian Harley J. McKee as "a unique and highly interesting piece of architecture and decoration."

Courtesy: Michigan Historical Collections

Michigan is fortunate to have so many well-preserved residential houses from this great architectural era. Many more, like this neglected, rundown country home in Livingston County, have disappeared or are gradually falling into a state virtually beyond repair.

Politics and Government

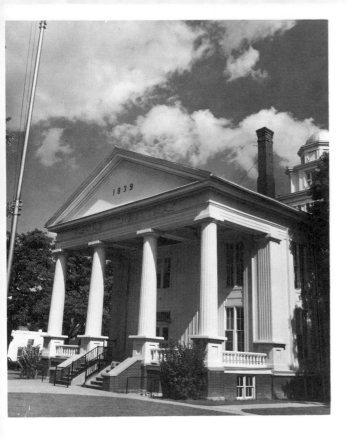

As the date inscribed on the pediment indicates, the Lapeer County Courthouse in Lapeer was erected in the midst of the period when classic models were the fashion among Michigan's builders and architects. The degree of attrition that has taken place among Michigan's public buildings dating from the pioneer period, however, has been far higher than that which has occurred among the private residences built at that time. For many years the Lapeer County Courthouse has held the distinction of being Michigan's oldest courthouse, but it has been in constant danger from those who have wanted to replace it with a larger, more efficient, modern structure.

It must be admitted, however, that the pioneers were often much more conservative in providing adequate housing for their government offices than they were for themselves. The first Ingham County Courthouse in Mason was built in 1843 at a cost which the county supervisors directed must not exceed $800. Within a few years the need for larger quarters for the county officials led to the construction of a new courthouse, this time at an expense of $12,229.19. Completed in 1858, the new building, designed by Matthew Elder of Lansing, was a more imposing structure, but it barely survived into the twentieth century before it, too, was replaced.

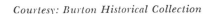

Courtesy: Burton Historical Collection

So far as the government of Michigan was concerned, the story was somewhat reversed. In the 1820's, the territorial government moved into what was for the time an impressive and commodious brick capitol, after having met in various temporary quarters since the establishment of the territory in 1805. The new capitol, which later, until it burned in 1893, was used by Detroit as a school building, cost $21,000 and was one of the earliest Greek Revival buildings in Michigan, with a fine Ionic portico and a tower which rose to a height of 140 feet.

In 1847, ten years after Michigan officially became a state, the state constitution required that a decision be made as to where the capital of Michigan should be permanently located. Communities throughout southern Michigan contested with Detroit, which had been the temporary capital, for the honor, with the Legislature finally choosing a wilderness site in central Michigan which would later be named Lansing. Here, by the next session of the Legislature in January, 1848, a plain, quietly modest frame capitol was built at an original cost that was considerably less than the cost of the first Michigan capitol building in the 1820's. Economy-minded legislators knew at the time that the new capitol would be totally inadequate for the needs of the state in a few years, but not enough of them were willing to risk their careers by supporting the appropriations that would have been required to build a structure of more realistic dimensions.

The only state building in Lansing from this early period that still survives is this house, which the Legislature, with a wisdom it has not shown since, had built in 1850 as the official residence for the governor. The state's chief executives, however, refused to use the house, declaring that it did not meet the requirements necessary for such an important office. For a time, other state officials lived in the house, which stood at the corner of Allegan and Capitol in downtown Lansing. Later, in the twentieth century, after the house had been sold to a private individual, it was moved far out to what were then the outskirts of town at 2003 West Main, where the house is still used as a private residence.

Towering over Michigan's political and governmental affairs throughout these years, as few men since have done, was Lewis Cass, still a very active figure when he sat before the camera in the 1850's. Cass did not need to caution the photographer, as he had some earlier portrait painters, not to hide any warts or wrinkles. The daguerreotype taken that day was brutally frank in the image it left of an old statesman, now in his seventies, tired and disillusioned from the strains and conflicts and frustrations of half a century of unending political life. He had been governor of Michigan Territory, secretary of war in Andrew Jackson's cabinet, minister to France, and United States senator from Michigan. Ahead of him lay one of his most important jobs, that of secretary of state under President James Buchanan, but he knew that his ultimate dream, that of becoming President of the United States, was now a thing of the past, something that he could now no longer hope to achieve.

From an earlier period in his life is this rather ridiculous portrait of Cass in which he is shown with a Roman toga thrown over his nineteenth-century dress. Such a pose, which reflected the same obsession with classical models that spawned the Greek Revival fad, had been popular in paintings and statues of the founding fathers of the republic, in whose footsteps Cass, like any other ambitious politician of his day, sought to follow.

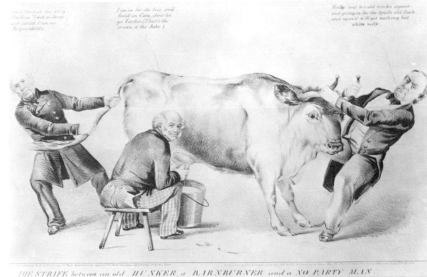

THE PRESIDENTIAL FISHING PARTY OF 1848.

THE STRIFE between an old HUNKER a BARNBURNER and a NO PARTY MAN.

Cass came very close to becoming President in 1848 when he was nominated for the office by the Democratic Party, the only resident of Michigan to be so honored by a major party. (Thomas E. Dewey, who was born in Owosso, had long since become a New York resident when he was the two-time Republican presidential candidate a century later.) As these cartoons suggest, however, in the labored style typical of the era, Cass had to contend not only with the other major party candidate, the military hero Zachary Taylor, but also with a formidable nominee of the Free-Soil Party, former President Martin Van Buren. Van Buren's opposition to slavery won him enough votes among antislavery Democrats in New York to prevent Cass, whose stand on slavery did not please the ardent foes of that institution, from winning that state's electoral votes. This in turn was enough to give Taylor the majority he needed to win and therefore deny Cass the office for which he had been preparing throughout his adult years.

Lewis Cass was one reason why the Democrats were the dominant party in Michigan from the time that elections were first held in the territory in the 1820's until the decade of the fifties. In the first election after Michigan became a state in 1837, the hero of Michigan's struggle to achieve statehood, Stevens T. Mason, was returned to the governor's office by an overwhelming Democratic majority. The painter T. H. O. P. Burnham depicted the scene in Detroit on election day in a somewhat Hogarthian manner. Mason is shown left center in a tall black hat, with a cigar in his mouth, caught in the act, some think, of buying votes. Nearby, two drunks seem to be standing in line for their payment, while over on the right a heated discussion on the merits of the candidates is underway and a Mason supporter seated on horseback holds aloft a Democratic banner. In the background, a procession of Whig Party people, one carrying a banner that states, "Provisions for the poor if the Whigs carry the day," advances from the left toward city hall, into which a ballot box is being carried.

Courtesy: Burton Historical Collection

Two of the figures in Burnham's painting hold copies of Detroit newspapers, which is certainly no accident in this political panorama. In that period, newspapers were identified far more definitely than in modern times with a particular political party or faction. Many papers survived as long as they did simply because they were a necessary organ. The Detroit *Gazette*, the second newspaper to be published in Michigan and the first to continue to appear over an extended period of time, was, from its founding in 1817 until its demise in 1830, a Democratic paper.

Courtesy: Burton Historical Collection

The need for a Democratic Party paper to take the place of the Detroit *Gazette* led to the appearance on May 5, 1831, of the first issue of the Detroit *Democratic Free Press and Michigan Intelligencer,* which continues today as the Detroit *Free Press,* Michigan's oldest newspaper. The *Free Press,* which remained a staunch supporter of the Democrats until the end of the nineteenth century, in the fall of 1835 became the first Michigan paper to be issued on a daily basis.

Kalamazoo Gazette.

BY H. GILBERT, PUBLISHER OF THE LAWS OF THE UNITED STATES AND OF THE STATE OF MICHIGAN.

VOLUME III]   KALAMAZOO, JANUARY 23, 1837.   [NUMBER 142.

The second oldest paper in Michigan published under the same name down to the present is the Kalamazoo *Gazette,* which originated in 1833 as the *Michigan Statesman and St. Joseph Chronicle* and was published in White Pigeon. Shortly after the United States land office at White Pigeon was moved to Kalamazoo, the newspaper was moved to that city also. Beginning on January 23, 1837, the paper began to appear under the title of Kalamazoo *Gazette.*

126

GREAT WHIG MEETING.

WHIGS to the RALLY.

A MASS MEETING

Of the Whigs of Washtenaw county will be held at the court house in Ann Arbor on Saturday, the 26th inst. at one o'clock, P. M. By invitation of the county convention held yesterday, William Woodbridge and others are expected to address the meeting. Freemen of old Washtenaw, let us have a glorious rally. Let us gather from all quarters of the compass, and teach the office-holding tories by our numbers that we can triumphantly put them down at the ballot boxes. To the rally, then, farmers, by thousands!

H. CHUBB,
J. T. ALLEN,
N. C. WELLS,
M. EACKER,
WM. R. PERRY,
October 22d, 1839. County committee.

Courtesy: Michigan Historical Collections

The good times that contributed to the success of Governor Mason and the Democrats were soon forgotten in the late 1830's, when a severe depression hit the nation. The new state government found itself in serious financial troubles which were blamed on the Democratic administration. The Whig Party took advantage of the opportunity in 1839 to throw out "the office-holding tories," as the Democrats were described in this campaign poster.

Scoring its only statewide victory in its history, the Whig Party of Michigan elected William Woodbridge governor. Woodbridge, shown here in a portrait made a few years later, had held numerous public offices since coming to Michigan in 1815 as secretary of the territory. He was an honest, conservative, and unimaginative man who would resign as governor early in 1841 to serve a term as United States senator.

Stevens T. Mason's career, which had begun so brilliantly, ended tragically in 1843 when he died at the age of thirty-one in New York City. He had gone to New York shortly after completing his second term as governor, his reputation and popularity in Michigan greatly diminished by the difficulties which, in modern terminology, had given the young state a poor image. Early in the twentieth century, Mason's remains were brought to Michigan and buried on the old capitol grounds in Detroit and a statue erected to honor belatedly the man who had successfully led Michigan into the union.

127

In 1841, the Democrats turned to an outstate man, John S. Barry, to return to power. Barry made frugality in government his watchword and thereby succeeded in becoming Michigan's only three-term governor in the nineteenth century. His home in Constantine, built about 1840, is still preserved.

Courtesy: Michigan Historical Collections

Courtesy:
University Archives, Western Michigan University

Robert McClelland (left) of Monroe and Detroit, who served as governor, represented Michigan in Congress, and was secretary of the interior under President Franklin Pierce; Alpheus Felch (center) of Ann Arbor, who, at one time or another in a long career, held the offices of governor, United States senator, and state Supreme Court justice, along with miscellaneous other positions; and Charles Stuart (right) of Kalamazoo, who was one of the leading Democratic United States senators in the 1850's—these were some of the most important Michigan Democrats in this era of Democratic ascendancy. The list of offices they held is more impressive than the list of their accomplishments in office, which perhaps explains why their names are now generally forgotten.

128

By the 1850's the question of slavery forced all others to the background, bringing about a fundamental realignment of Michigan's political factions. Opponents of slavery had been active in Michigan for many years, with women emerging for the first time in Michigan as major leaders in such a movement. Elizabeth Margaret Chandler, whose talents as a poet are symbolized in this portrait by the pen she holds in her hand, was already, when she came to Lenawee County in 1830 from the East, one of the better-known figures in the antislavery movement, although she was only twenty-three years old. Like so many of her fellow Quakers in the Lenawee County area and elsewhere, she opposed slavery on moral grounds. In 1832, Miss Chandler took the initiative in the organization of the Michigan Antislavery Society. Elizabeth Chandler died in 1834, but the antislavery work she had begun was carried on by others.

Courtesy: Michigan Historical Collections

Through the efforts of Miss Chandler, another Lenawee County Quaker, Laura Smith Haviland, became interested in the fight against slavery. Mrs. Haviland spent most of her remaining years before, during, and after the Civil War working to free the Negro and at the Raisin Institute, which she and her husband founded, to provide the training and other assistance that the Negro would need when he gained his freedom.

Courtesy: Burton Historical Collection

Sojourner Truth, a Negro who had been born a slave in New York early in the nineteenth century and who was subsequently freed, came to Michigan in the 1850's and made her home in Battle Creek. Long active in the abolitionist movement as an untrained but effective speaker and singer at meetings, she continued her work from Battle Creek until her death in 1883, leaving behind a record in which fact had become so mixed with legend that biographers have unraveled her life's story only with great difficulty.

Michigan residents sheltered fugitive slaves who escaped from the South and fled to the North. In later years, an amazingly large number of people would claim to have been engaged in this illegal activity, the penalties for which, if caught and convicted, became especially severe in the 1850's. There is scarcely a town in southern Michigan which does not have one or more buildings which the local residents will swear was a "station" on the Underground Railroad. This house in Union City is apparently one whose claim is more authentic than that of some others.

This marker in Marshall locates the site of the cabin which an escaped slave from Kentucky, Adam Crosswhite, and his family, occupied in 1847 when several Kentuckians, including Crosswhite's owner, arrived to take the family back South. The citizens of Marshall forcibly prevented the Kentuckians from carrying out their mission, although the Southerners had the law on their side. The Crosswhites were spirited away to final safety in Canada, and the Crosswhite Case became one of the legal battles over the return of fugitive slaves that served to divide the North and the South.

STOCKHOLDERS
OF THE UNDERGROUND
R. R. COMPANY
Hold on to Your Stock!!

The market has an upward tendency. By the express train which ar-rived this morning at 3 o'clock, fifteen thousand dollars worth of human merchandise, consisting of twenty-nine able bodied men and women, fresh and sound, from the Carolina and Kentucky plantations, have arrived safe at the depot on the other side, where all our sympathising coloniza-tion friends may have an opportunity of expressing their sympathy by bringing forward donations of ploughs, &c., farming utensils, pick axes and hoes, and not old clothes; as these emigrants all can till the soil. N. B.—Stockholders don't forget the meeting to-day at 2 o'clock at the ferry on the Canada side. All persons desiring to take stock in this prosperous company, be sure to be on hand.   By Order of the
Detroit, April 19, 1853.   **BOARD OF DIRECTORS.**

Detroit was the last stop on the road to freedom for the fugitive. This was a handbill distributed in Detroit in 1853, openly proclaiming the successful passage of twenty-nine slaves across to the Canadian side of the Detroit River and calling for donations to help the escapees establish themselves as farmers.

130

Slavery as a political issue had been agitated in the 1840's by the ex-Alabama slaveholder James G. Birney, who settled in Bay City in 1841, the year after he ran for President on the Liberty Party ticket. Birney ran for governor in 1843, and for President again in 1844, and although the votes he received were relatively few, he paved the way for the subsequent Free-Soil Party, which torpedoed the presidential ambitions of Lewis Cass, and finally the Republican Party, on whose ticket Birney's son James would be elected lieutenant governor in 1860.

In 1854, a new party sprang up throughout the North as a result of the Kansas-Nebraska Act, which opened to the slaveholder territories in the West which the farmers of Michigan and other states in the Old Northwest had looked upon as future homesites for themselves and their sons. At Jackson, Michigan, on July 6, a convention of men opposed to the act met "Under the Oaks" because no hall was large enough to accommodate all of the delegates. Here the term "Republican" was first applied to the nascent party. This is the origin of Jackson's claim to being the birthplace of the Republican Party, a claim that received considerable support in 1910 when President William Howard Taft took part in a parade, his car preceded by the famous Jackson Zouave Drill Team, as part of a great civic celebration that was climaxed by the dedication of a bronze plaque at Second and West Franklin Streets which proclaims that "here . . . was born the Republican Party."

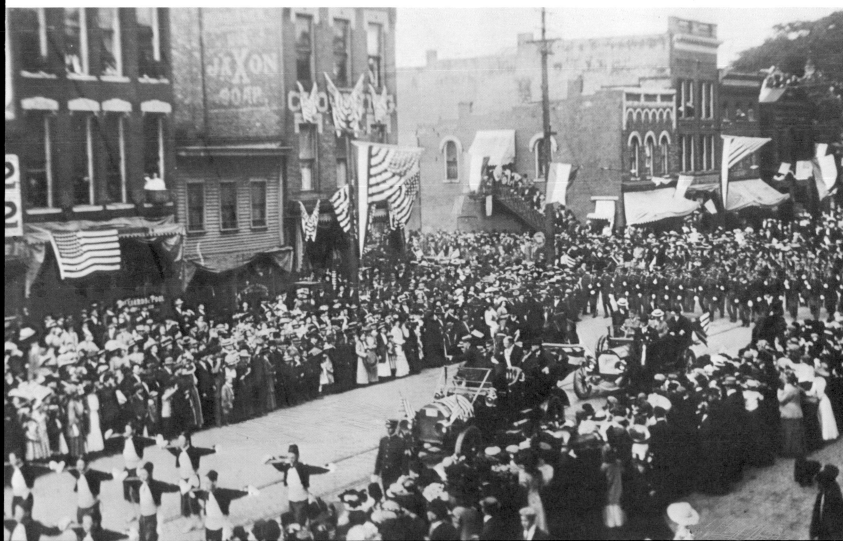

MASS MEETING!
AT MASON, SEPT. 9th, 1854.

To the People of Ingham County, without distinction of Party:

In view of the recent action of Congress in regard to the organization of Nebraska and Kansas Territories, and the evident designs of the Slave power to attempt still further aggressions upon Freedom, we invite all our Fellow Citizens, without reference to former political associations, who think that the time has arrived for a Union at the North, to protect Liberty from being overthrown and down-trodden, to assemble in

Mass Convention,

On Saturday, the 9th day of September next, at 10 o'clock A. M., at the Court House, in the Village of Mason, for the purpose of putting in nomination suitable persons to fill the County offices, Representative to the State Legislature, delegates to the Congressional and Senatorial Conventions, and to transact such other business as may be deemed expedient.

D. G. McClure, J. W. Holmes, W. Jones, Geo. W. Dart, R. Foster, W. Foster, C. O. Stiles, G. A. Brown, J. W. Soule, A. W. Williams, H A. Rueght, D. M. Bagley, M. K. North, H. Bisby, J. O. Smith, C. Thomas, H. H. North, Roswell Everitt, O. D. Skinner, Joshua North, H. Lester, F. R. West, J. Paul, M. T Hicks, R Stephens, W M Stephens, H. D. Granger, J. D. Reeves, A. P. Hicks, A. H. Roble, S. S. Green, C. E. Royce, David Hale, R. Howell, K. Johnson, J. N. Bush, H. Baker, H. L. Baker, J P. Powell, O. D. Parker, E. C. Barker, S. Lovell, J. H. Lobdell, J. W. Demerest, W. S. Calkins, James I. Mead, J. Robson, L. D. Quackinbush, E. N. Grilley, S. A. Tooker, A. Nois, S. Harrington, A. Cline, S Sanderson, S Dunn, J W Phelps, John Dunsbach, Jr, Sanford Marsh, Geo Smith, Levi Buck, Geo Chappell, E L Holmes, Thos Treat, C White, H Bristol, W H Child, H Converse, S B Wilcox, S Cromeen, S B Wessels, N Parks, J W Ball, Wm Tanner, D J Cobb, E F Thompson, N Brace, A Olds, Wm Baldwin, L Merrill, L H Spancer, W F Lindsey, E V Van Epps, E W Cooledge, W B Holdren, T Lester, R W Burdick J T Irish, S Roth, J E North, J North, S Barton, S R Greene, Wm Lee, W H Packney, H B Shank, O B Webster, S D Newles, E P Newles, J H Rowley, A B Bagley, N C Branch, U M Chappell, C C Durling, John G Durling, W B Everitt.

August 30th, 1854.

Similar meetings, on a smaller scale, were held throughout Michigan in 1854, drawing antislavery Democrats, Whigs, and Free-Soilers together into a new party.

The Michigan Republicans nominated as their gubernatorial candidate Kinsley Bingham of Livingston County, a former Democratic congressman whose antislavery views now brought him into the new party, which he led to victory in 1854, defeating his old Democratic colleague John S. Barry.

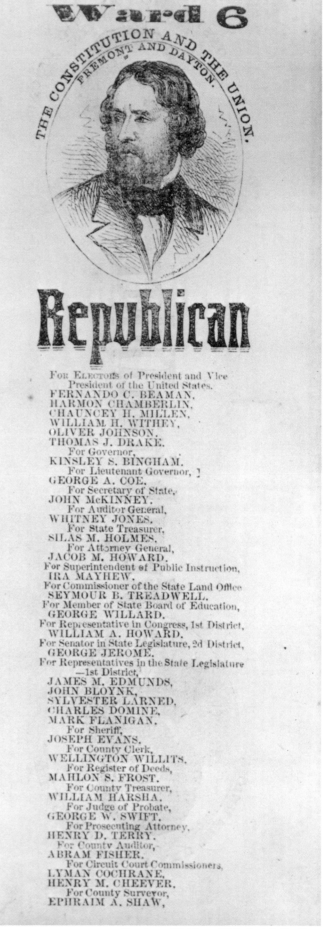

Ward 6
THE CONSTITUTION AND THE UNION.
FREMONT AND DAYTON.

Republican

For Electors of President and Vice President of the United States.
FERNANDO C. BEAMAN,
HARMON CHAMBERLIN,
CHAUNCEY H. MILLEN,
WILLIAM H. WITHEY,
OLIVER JOHNSON,
THOMAS J. DRAKE.
   For Governor,
KINSLEY S. BINGHAM.
   For Lieutenant Governor, }
GEORGE A. COE.
   For Secretary of State,
JOHN McKINNEY.
   For Auditor General,
WHITNEY JONES.
   For State Treasurer,
SILAS M. HOLMES,
   For Attorney General,
JACOB M. HOWARD.
For Superintendent of Public Instruction,
IRA MAYHEW.
For Commissioner of the State Land Office
SEYMOUR B. TREADWELL.
For Member of State Board of Education,
GEORGE WILLARD.
For Representative in Congress, 1st District,
WILLIAM A. HOWARD.
For Senator in State Legislature, 2d District,
GEORGE JEROME.
For Representatives in the State Legislature
   —1st District,
JAMES M. EDMUNDS,
JOHN BLOYNK,
SYLVESTER LARNED,
CHARLES DOMINE,
MARK FLANIGAN.
   For Sheriff,
JOSEPH EVANS.
   For County Clerk,
WELLINGTON WILLITS.
   For Register of Deeds,
MAHLON S. FROST.
   For County Treasurer,
WILLIAM HARSHA.
   For Judge of Probate,
GEORGE W. SWIFT.
   For Prosecuting Attorney,
HENRY D. TERRY.
   For County Auditor,
ABRAM FISHER.
   For Circuit Court Commissioners,
LYMAN COCHRANE,
HENRY M. CHEEVER.
   For County Surveyor,
EPHRAIM A. SHAW,

Courtesy: Michigan Historical Collections

Two years later, in 1856, Bingham ran for re-election on a ticket headed by John C. Fremont, the first Republican presidential candidate.

On August 26, 1856, a Republican campaign rally was held in Kalamazoo's Bronson Park, shown here in a nineteenth-century photograph. One of the orators on this occasion who spoke from the old Indian mound on which the girl in the photograph stands, was Abraham Lincoln of Illinois. He disappointed his more radical listeners by his position on the slavery question, which they felt was too mild. This may have been one of the reasons why Lincoln never spoke in Michigan again.

Courtesy: Kalamazoo Public Museum

Courtesy: National Archives

There was nothing mild about the antislavery views of Zachariah Chandler, a Detroit merchant who had been the unsuccessful Whig candidate for governor in 1852 and then two years later had been one of the leaders of the group that organized the Republican Party. In 1857, Chandler succeeded Lewis Cass in the United States Senate. Like Cass, Chandler had been born in New Hampshire, and like Cass, who had dominated his party in Michigan for decades, Chandler would dominate Michigan Republican politics until his death in 1879. As this Mathew Brady photograph suggests, Chandler was a grim, fire-eating partisan, who would lead the Radicals in Congress in violent opposition to many of Lincoln's policies during the Civil War and to those of Andrew Johnson in the post-war years.

As the fifties drew to a close, events moved toward the final break between the North and the South. In March, 1859, John Brown, an activist *par excellence* among abolitionists, arrived in Detroit with a dozen slaves he had helped escape from Missouri. In this house on Congress Street, long since torn down, Brown met with the Negro leader, Frederick Douglass, and several members of Detroit's Negro community, including the owner of the house, William Webb. The group certainly discussed the question of slavery, although there is little solid evidence to substantiate the tradition that Brown at this time outlined his plans to attack Harper's Ferry later that year.

133

POLITICAL DEMONSTRATIONS OF THE PRESIDENTIAL CAMPAIGN   TREMENDOUS GATHERING OF REPUBLICANS IN DETROIT ON SEPTEMBER 4, 1860.   PROCESSION OF THE WIDE AWAKES   FROM A SKETCH BY MR. LUM, OF DETROIT.   (See page 310.)

Courtesy: Burton Historical Collection

In the fateful year of 1860, the rising tide of support in the North for the Republican Party, as evidenced by this parade of "Wide-Awakes" in Detroit on September 4, resulted in the election of the Republican presidential candidate, Abraham Lincoln.

In Michigan, Austin Blair, a Jackson attorney, a strong antislavery man, and a veteran of many political campaigns since coming to Michigan from New York in 1841, was elected governor on the Republican ticket. The office was then only a part-time job, with an annual salary of $1,000. The duties were so light, however, that the governor had ample opportunity to carry on his private business at home, without even bothering to reside in the state capital except during the brief legislative session, normally held every two years. But for Blair the governorship would be no sinecure. Barely three months after he took office, he would suddenly be faced with responsibilities and duties beyond anything his predecessors had encountered. Blair handled them well and was ever after affectionately known as Michigan's "War Governor." But while he was earning this title he had to forget about his law practice and, honest man that he was, he left office virtually impoverished.

134

The Civil War

In 1861, screaming headlines of the type familiar to modern newspaper readers were as yet undreamed of, but the firing on Fort Sumter and the subsequent surrender of that federal post in South Carolina was an event of such obvious importance that no reader of the Marshall *Statesman* or any other Michigan paper of that day needed any assistance to realize the momentous nature of these events. War had broken out—a civil war that would disrupt the union of which Michigan had been a voting member for less than twenty-five years.

FROM WASHINGTON.

THE ATTACK ON SUMTER!

THE SURRENDER!

THE BOMBARDMENT AND DEFENSE!

Effect of the News in Washington

ABSURD AND CONTRADICTORY RUMORS!

PRESIDENT LINCOLN'S PROCLAMATION!

CALLS FOR THE STATE MILITIA!

Action of the States!

The Prevailing Excitement—Thrilling War News—Preparations for War!

MARSHALL STATESMAN.

Wednesday, April 17, 1861.

THE CRISIS IN DETROIT.

MAY APPOINTMENT.

Throughout Michigan, public meetings were held to voice the concern of the citizens and to express their united support of the federal government's initial steps to combat the rebellion of the Southern states. At this April 20th meeting on Detroit's Griswold Street, public officials of the federal, state, county, and city governments renewed their oaths of allegiance, as a great crowd, some of them standing on roofs and ledges, looked on. In the background is the old capitol building. The Detroit photographer J. Jex Bardwell recorded this and other wartime events in Detroit, providing the first extended photographic record of any phase of Michigan's history.

By the end of April, the first Michigan troops were assembling, in response to President Lincoln's call upon the states to supply the federal government with the forces needed to put down the revolt. In contrast with the wars of the twentieth century when the task of filling the manpower needs of the nation's armed services has been directed primarily from Washington, in the nineteenth century it was the states who were given the major responsibility for raising troops for the army. During the Civil War, Michigan would furnish nearly sixty military units of infantry,

cavalry, artillery, and miscellaneous other types, each of which was designated throughout the war as a Michigan outfit, although serving in the Union army. Lincoln first called for men for terms of only three months. The First Michigan Infantry Regiment, composed of previously organized state militia companies, assembled to meet this call and went through a brief training program on the rolling terrain of Fort Wayne, Detroit.

On May 11, a ceremony was held in Campus Martius (one of the areas on Judge Woodward's city plan from which several streets radiate like spokes from the hub of a wheel) at which the First Michigan received its regimental colors. Hiram Andrews' Rail-road Hotel provided a good vantage point from which to view the proceedings. Two days later, the regiment shipped out for Washington and war service.

137

Scarcely a week after it arrived in Washington, the First Michigan Infantry, which was the first regiment from the Western states to come to the defense of the nation's capital, was leading an advance across the Potomac to capture Alexandria, Virginia. When Michigan subscribers to *Harper's Weekly* opened their June 15 issue, they found this sketch depicting Confederate cavalrymen surrendering to the regiment.

COMPANY OF SECESSION CAVALRY SURRENDERING TO COLONEL WILCOX, OF THE FIRST MICHIGAN REGIMENT, IN FRONT OF THE SLAVE-PEN AT ALEXANDRIA, VIRGINIA.—[DRAWN BY OUR SPECIAL ARTIST.]

Courtesy: Burton Historical Collection

Courtesy: Burton Historical Collection

The members of the First Michigan Infantry were not gone from Michigan very long. Their three-month term of enlistment having expired, they arrived back in Detroit on August 2 on board a flag-decorated train of the Detroit and Milwaukee Railroad, the successor to the old Detroit and Pontiac. The crowd that turned out to greet the soldiers was so excited that many of the spectators are only blurs on the photograph which Jex Bardwell took with the slow-speed equipment of the day. (The black line down the middle of the picture is the result of a break in the glass negative.) At the station, Lewis Cass, now nearly eighty years old, made a welcoming address to Michigan's first Civil War veterans. They had acquitted themselves well in the Union army's disastrous defeat at Bull Run, and although many of the officers joined other Michigan regiments, most of the enlisted men decided to quit while they were ahead and returned to civilian life.

138

Below:

Meanwhile, other military units were being formed. The Second Michigan Infantry was mustered into federal service at Fort Wayne on May 25, 1861, as Michigan's first regiment to enlist for the three-year term which now became standard. Its commander was Colonel Israel B. Richardson of Pontiac, a West Point graduate, a man itching to lead his troops into battle, as this superb Brady portrait reveals. He got his wish. At Antietam in 1862, Richardson, now a division commander, rallied his men with the cry, "Boys! Raise the colors and follow me!" As he advanced, hatless, his sword drawn, Richardson was mortally wounded, but his example inspired his soldiers to drive back the Confederates.

Courtesy: Library of Congress

Also at Fort Wayne in May, 1861, was a group of Coldwater men who were training as an artillery unit, known as Loomis' Battery, after their commander, Cyrus Loomis. As Battery A of the Michigan Light Artillery Regiment, it would become one of the state's most famous military units, serving with distinction until war's end, more than four years later.

One of the ten-pounder Parrott guns which the Loomis Battery received when it went south in 1861 is displayed in a park in Coldwater at the junction of US-27 and US-12. The gun was captured by the Confederates in 1863 at the battle of Chickamauga, where the battery suffered its heaviest losses of the war. Later, other Union forces recaptured the gun and returned it to its surviving gunners.

THIRD REGIMENT MICHIGAN VOLUNTEERS MARCHING DOWN JEFFERSON AVENUE, DETROIT, MICHIGAN. Sketched by J. B. Nankert See page 139

Companies and regiments were formed at various points in the state. The Third Michigan Infantry, organized at Grand Rapids, was sketched by an artist for the New York *Illustrated News* as it marched down Jefferson Avenue, Detroit, en route to Virginia. The havelocks that make the men look like something out of a foreign legion movie were one of the exotic uniform styles affected at the outset of the war and soon discarded in favor of more practical battle garb.

Courtesy: University Archives, Western Michigan University

In the early days of the war military companies were formed in local communities faster than there were places for them in the regiments the state was organizing. Rather than wait until additional Michigan regiments were created, a number of these companies offered their services to and were accepted by regiments of other states. Such a company was the Lafayette Light Guard of Paw Paw, shown here on the day that it left home to serve as Company C of the Seventieth New York Infantry Regiment.

Probably the most unusual regiment organized in Michigan was the Lancer Regiment, a mounted unit organized by Colonel Arthur Rankin, a veteran of the British army. An artist for *Harper's Weekly* made this sketch late in 1861, showing some of the men with their lances, which were made in Michigan from Michigan white ash. The lances were to be the regiment's principal, if not sole, weapon in battle. However, because Rankin and his men would not comply with army regulations regarding arms and equipment, the regiment was not accepted by the army and had to be disbanded.

Courtesy: Burton Historical Collection

COLONEL RANKIN'S LANCER REGIMENT, NOW AT DETROIT, MICHIGAN.—Sketched by B. R. Erman.—[See Page 811.]

140

Courtesy: Michigan Historical Collections

Although the Lancer Regiment never got into action, eleven regular cavalry regiments were mustered in from Michigan, as, for example, the Fifth Michigan Cavalry. This colorful broadside is typical of those published during the war as souvenirs for soldiers and their families. One wonders, however, how many copies were sold to the twenty-one members of Company H who deserted, particularly to William H. Watson, who appears on the scroll of honor as a two-time deserter. Not every Civil War soldier was a hero.

It was as commander of the Michigan Cavalry Brigade, composed of the First, Fifth, Sixth, and Seventh Michigan Cavalry Regiments, that George Armstrong Custer first won fame as a twenty-three-year-old brigadier general. Custer was born in Ohio, but his family had subsequently moved to Monroe County, Michigan. Custer spent considerable time there and during the war married the daughter of a leading citizen of Monroe. In this Brady photograph, the rakish tilt of the hat, the folded arms, and the facial expression give an inkling of the personality traits which would make Custer one of America's most controversial military figures.

After leaving Michigan, the regiments were sent either to the eastern or western theaters of operation where they spent long months in camp. This was undoubtedly an idealized sketch of the camp of the Sixteenth Michigan Infantry during the winter of 1862-63, after a full year of campaigning in Virginia during the war's second year.

More realistic were the many photographs of Michigan men in camp that were taken by Mathew Brady or his assistants or by some other army photographers. Here a group of men from the Twenty-first Michigan Infantry pose with their Enfield rifles in front of some rather permanent-appearing quarters in their camp in the West where this regiment spent its time during the war.

Courtesy: National Archives

The Fourth Michigan Infantry seems to have been a favorite of the cameramen, judging by the number of photographs of members of this unit that are found in the Brady Collection at the National Archives. With his sword, his Colt revolver tucked in his belt, his mustache, and his erect figure, Lieutenant Henry G. Hill of Company D of the Fourth made a fine picture of a Union officer.

At the other extreme from the trim, assured image of Henry Hill is this splendid photograph of Private Emory Eugene Kingin, who enlisted in the Twenty-first Michigan Infantry early in 1864 at the age of seventeen. The strictly non-regulation checked shirt, the bowie knife, and the nonchalant pose all may have been efforts to cloak the true feelings of a frightened youth.

Courtesy: National Archives

The Negro boy, clad in a Union uniform, seated on the ground with these men of the Fourth Michigan, was a familiar sight in the regimental camps in the South as slaves from nearby plantations entered the Union lines. These Michigan men had apparently solved the problem of what to do with this particular boy—a problem which, multiplied by many thousands, was a source of bitter debate among army commanders and government leaders. As the war progressed, however, more and more people in the North began to ask: Weren't young boys like this what the war was all about?

As is the case in every war, there were long hours in which there was nothing to do. Members of Company M of the Fourth Michigan here seem to be demonstrating, somewhat stiffly, to be sure, how they filled these empty hours by smoking, drinking, and card-playing.

The ultimate objective of Michigan's soldiers was to fight and defeat the Confederate armies. These men are identified as members of the Twenty-first Michigan Infantry who had been wounded in battle. Brady identifies the battle as Fair Oaks, which occurred in Virginia on May 31 to June 1, 1862. If this is correct, then Brady's identification of the regiment is in error since the Twenty-first had not been organized by that date, and when it was, it saw action not in Virginia but in the western campaigns.

For these men of the Twenty-fourth Michigan Infantry, the war ended with the battle of Gettysburg. The thirteen or so men who can be counted in this memorable photograph by the great Timothy O' Sullivan were but a small fraction of the total number of casualties that decimated the ranks of the Twenty-fourth and gave it the dubious honor of having suffered heavier losses in this turning point of the war than those of any other Union regiment at Gettysburg.

During the Civil War, more than ninety thousand Michigan men entered the army. The great majority of them volunteered for service, attracted by recruiting posters such as these three from the collection of Norm Flayderman of New Milford, Connecticut. After the initial wave of enthusiasm of the first weeks of the war had passed, however, a variety of inducements, financial and otherwise, had to be resorted to by the organizers of the state's later military units, such as the Seventeenth Michigan Infantry, which needed three months to fill its ranks in 1862.

Form 31.

CERTIFICATE OF NON-LIABILITY TO BE GIVEN BY THE BOARD OF
ENROLLMENT.

We, the subscribers, composing the Board of Enrollment of the *Fifth*
District of the State of *Michigan*, provided for in section 8, Act of
Congress "for enrolling and calling out the national forces," approved March 3, 1863,
hereby certify that *Cyrus S. Farrar* of *Armada*
Macomb county, State of *Michigan*, having given
satisfactory evidence that he is not properly subject to do military duty, as required by said
act, by reason of *Substitute Furnished* *not liable to Draft* is exempt from all liability to military
duty for the term of *for which said Substitute is not liable to Draft*
not exceeding the term for which said Substitute was Accepted

Wm McConnell
Provost Marshal, and President of Board of Enrollment.

Henry Miller
Member of Board of Enrollment.

S. Paddack
Surgeon of Board of Enrollment.

Dated at *Pontiac*
this *20* day of *Aug* 186*4*

Note.—This certificate is to be given in all cases where it is applicable, according to the 2d, 3d, 13th, and 17th sections
of the act of Congress referred to above.

Courtesy: Michigan Historical Collections

As the war dragged on and the casualty totals swelled (one of every six Michigan soldiers would die as a result of war service), it became ever harder to find volunteers. If all else failed, men might be drafted. But the Civil War draft was a far cry from the military conscription of the twentieth century. The draft was used only if a state failed to fill its assigned quota of troops with volunteers. However, even if a man were drafted, he could be exempted not only for the usual medical or family reasons but also by furnishing a substitute to go in his place, as Cyrus S. Farrar of Armada is hereby certified as having done in 1864, or by paying a commutation fee of $300.

SAGINAW COUNTY, MICH.
SAGINAW CITY—FIRST WARD.

FOR THE UNION

LINCOLN & JOHNSON

NO COMPROMISE WITH TREASON!
" Rally 'round the Flag, boys, rally once again."
For Electors of President and Vice President of the
United States,
ROBERT R. BEECHER,   CHRISTIAN EBERBACH.
THOMAS D. GILBERT.   PERRY HANNAH.
FREDERICK WALDORF,   OMAR D. CONGER,
MARSH GIDDINGS,   GEORGE W. PACK.
For Governor—HENRY H. CRAPO.
For Lieutenant Governor—EBENEZER O. GROSVENOR.
For Secretary of State—JAMES B. PORTER.
For Auditor General—EMIL ANNEKE.
For State Treasurer—JOHN OWEN.
For Attorney General—ALBERT WILLIAMS.
For Commissioner of Land Office—CYRUS HEWITT.
For Superintendent of Public Instruction,
ORAMEL HOSFORD.
For Member of State Board of Education,
WITTER J. BAXTER.
For Associate Justice of the Supreme Court—(to fill vacancy,)
THOMAS M. COOLEY.
For Representative in Congress—Sixth District,
JOHN F. DRIGGS.
For Senator in State Legislature—Twenty-Seventh District,
DAVID H. JEROME.
For Representative in State Legislature—First District,
WILLIAM H. TAYLOR.
For Sheriff—AUGUSTUS LULL.
For Judge of Probate—OTTO ROESER.
For County Clerk—WILLIAM MOLL.
For Register of Deeds—THOMAS W. HASTINGS.
For County Treasurer—EMIL MOORES.
For Prosecuting Attorney—CHAUNCEY W. WISNER·
For County Surveyor—IRA W. LA MUNYON.
For Circuit Court Commissioner—DANIEL W. PERKINS·
For Coroners—ISRAEL N. SMITH. SETH WILLEY.

STATE OF MICHIGAN
County of Oakland,
TOWN OF HIGHLAND

McCLELLAN TICKET.
For Electors of President and Vice President
SAMUEL T. DOUGLASS,
RIX ROBINSON,
HENRY HART,
ROYAL T. TWOMBLY,
D. DARWIN HUGHES,
JOHN LEWIS,
MICHAEL E. CROFOOT,
RICHARD EDWARDS.
For Governor,
WILLIAM M. FENTON.
For Lieutenant Governor,
MARTIN S. BRACKETT.
For Secretary of State,
GEORGE B. TURNER.
For Auditor General,
CHARLES W. BUTLER.
For State Treasurer,
GEORGE C. MUNRO.
For Superintendent of Public Instruction,
JOHN D. PIERCE.
For Commissioner of State Land Office,
GEORGE M. RICH.
For Attorney General,
LEVI BISHOP.
For Member of State Board of Education,
OLIVER C. COMSTOCK.
For Associate Justice of Supreme Court (to fill vacancy),
ALPHEUS FELCH.
For Representative in Congress, Fifth District,
AUGUSTUS C. BALDWIN.
For Senator in State Legislature, Sixth District,
JAMES M. HOYT.
For Representative in State Legislature, Third District,
JOHN HADLEY.
For Sheriff,
SAMUEL E. BEACH.
For County Clerk,
JAMES D. BATEMAN.
For Register of Deeds,
JOHN V. LAMBERTSON.
For County Treasurer,
CHARLES C. WALDO.
For Judge of Probate,
FRANCIS DARROW.
For Prosecuting Attorney,
MICHAEL E. CROFOOT.
For County Surveyor,
ELIAS C. MARTIN.
For Circuit Court Commissioners,
JAMES A. JACOKES,
JOSEPH R. BOWMAN.
For Coroners,
ORRIN E. BELL.

Courtesy: Michigan Historical Collections

(For description, see caption at the top of next page.)

Courtesy: National Archives

This was Camp Blair in Jackson, where, beginning in March, 1864, those men who were drafted were inducted into service. The first reception center for draftees had been in Grand Rapids. At the close of the war, Camp Blair would become one of the two principal centers in Michigan where soldiers were paid off and returned to civilian life.

(See the two illustrations at the right-hand top of preceding page.)

In 1864, Michigan's vote helped re-elect Abraham Lincoln to a second term as President, although war weariness gave the Republicans some anxious moments during the campaign. Austin Blair retired after two terms as governor and was succeeded by a Flint lumberman, Henry H. Crapo. On the losing Democratic ticket were such formidable names out of the past as Alpheus Felch, Rix Robinson, and John D. Pierce, Michigan's first superintendent of public instruction under Governor Mason, three decades before. As respected as these men were, they were not able to reverse the trend which would make Michigan a safe Republican state almost continuously for the following seventy years.

In the spring of 1865, the great national testing came to an end. At the beginning of April, after a bitter nine-month siege by Union forces, General Robert E. Lee was forced to abandon the Confederate capital of Richmond, Virginia, with its neighboring stronghold, Petersburg. On April 3, a Michigan brigade, consisting of the Second and Twentieth Michigan Infantry and the First Michigan Sharpshooters Regiments, were the first federal troops to enter Petersburg. Here, an artist for *Harper's Weekly* shows the Second Michigan hoisting its colors over the customs house.

Courtesy: Michigan Historical Collections

Within less than a week after Michigan's soldiers occupied Petersburg, General Lee and his men surrendered at Appomattox Courthouse, and Michigan residents across the state assembled to celebrate the happy news.

SURRENDER OF GEN. LEE!

"The Year of Jubilee has come! Let all the People Rejoice!"

200 GUNS WILL BE FIRED

On the Campus Martius,

AT 3 O'CLOCK TO-DAY, APRIL 10,

To Celebrate the Victories of our Armies.

Every Man, Woman and Child is hereby ordered to be on hand prepared to Sing and Rejoice. The crowd are expected to join in singing Patriotic Songs.

ALL PLACES OF BUSINESS MUST BE CLOSED AT 2 O'CLOCK.

Hurrah for Grant and his noble Army.

By Order of the People.

147

Within a week, however, the same Detroiters who had met to commemorate Lee's surrender were back in Campus Martius for a solemn observance of the death of President Lincoln from an assassin's bullet.

At Irwinsville, Georgia, on May 10, 1865, the fleeing Confederate president, Jefferson Davis, was captured by the Fourth Michigan Cavalry Regiment. This satirical contemporary sketch accepts the first report by Union officers that Davis was dressed in women's clothes when he was taken. Later, this was denied, and the subject is still a controversial one.

"Don't provoke the President, or he may hurt some of you!"

THE CAPTURE OF JEFF DAVIS.

His last official act "The adoption of a new rebel uniform".
He attempts to "Clear his Skirts", but finds it "All up in Dixie".

Courtesy: Michigan Historical Collections

The year 1865 marked the end of the Civil War. The news of the year was summarized in poetic form in this sheet which the Kalamazoo *Gazette*'s carrier boys distributed to their patrons on January 1, 1866. The "Carrier Boy's Address," issued annually on New Year's day, was a charming custom common to most newspapers in Michigan in the nineteenth century.

Courtesy: Burton Historical Collection

Courtesy: Michigan Historical Collections

On July 4, 1866, with the last Michigan regiments now mustered out of service, Michigan's veterans assembled in Detroit for a great parade that preceded a ceremony in Campus Martius in which each of the state's military units returned to the governor the colors which they had carried into battle. These flags are today preserved in cases in the rotunda of the state capitol in Lansing, and are in many ways the most touching mementos of the sacrifices the young state made in the Civil War.

In the years following the war, determined efforts were made to see that Michigan did not forget the war. The custom of setting aside May 30 each year as a national holiday on which the graves of soldiers would be decorated was begun in 1868. (The observance in 1869 was held on May 29 because the 30th fell on a Sunday.)

At the foot of Emerald Street in Houghton, this statue since 1912 has served as a reminder of the members of Company I (the Houghton Company) of the Twenty-third Michigan Infantry and of the other men, numbering five hundred in all, from this Upper Peninsula mining county who marched away to war in the 1860's.

Courtesy: Adrian Daily Telegram

Throughout Michigan, monuments began to be erected to the state's Civil War soldiers. The first of these was this simple sandstone shaft, costing $1,500, which was placed in the cemetery at Tipton in Lenawee County and was dedicated on July 4, 1866. (The monument was blown over in the Palm Sunday tornado of 1965 but has since been restored.)

Courtesy: Houghton Daily Mining Gazette

This dramatic monument, the work of the distinguished American sculptor Lorado Taft, stands in a small park at First Street and West Michigan and Wildwood Avenues, Jackson. It was donated by one of Jackson's best-known soldiers, William H. Withington, who served with the original First Michigan Infantry at the start of the war, was captured at Bull Run, and returned to Michigan to become colonel of the Seventeenth Michigan Infantry. Unforeseen production problems delayed the actual erection and dedication of the monument until July 14, 1904, despite the date inscribed on the base. By this time, General Withington had died.

Austin Blair, Michigan governor during all but the last few months of the Civil War, died in 1894. The last thirty years of his life had not been especially happy ones for him. He had been denied by the party he had helped to found the office he most desired to hold, the office of United States senator, and for a time in the 1870's he went over to the Democratic Party. His finances continued in such bad condition that in 1892 friends took up a collection of some four thousand dollars which they presented to him at Christmastime as "a little aid, not as charity, but as a token of affection." In 1898 this statue of Blair was erected on state capitol grounds in Lansing, at a cost to the state of $7,200. In the years since its unveiling, the statue, the work of Edward Clark Potter, the same sculptor who also completed the famous equestrian statue of General Custer in Monroe, has acquired the patina and discoloration associated with bronze and has become one of Lansing's most celebrated landmarks.

Michigan, *the* Farm State

During the Civil War, Congress passed the Homestead Act, offering up to 160 acres of public land free to American citizens or aliens who had declared their intention to become citizens, if they lived on the land for five years and began to farm it. The northern two-thirds of Michigan was still largely unsettled at this time, and it was therefore, for a number of years, one of the principal areas in the country to which settlers came to obtain this free land. This photograph, taken at the end of the century, shows what is described as a "typical home" of one of these Michigan homesteaders.

Courtesy: Library of Congress

Agriculture in the nineteenth century was the bulwark of the state's economy. This father and his son, unsmiling in the midst of a hard life but proud of their achievements, were representative of the majority of Michigan residents who made their living from the soil.

Courtesy: Al Barnes

Courtesy: Grand Rapids Public Museum

For those who established this farm near Lowell, and for most Michigan farmers, except those fortunate enough to buy land on one of southern Michigan's scattered and small prairies, clearing the land of its timber cover was a back-breaking task.

154

Courtesy: Michigan Historical Collections

Stump pullers, such as the Little Giant Rock and
Stump Extractor and the home-made but effective model
which these Michigan farmers used, were a welcome aid.

Once they were pulled, the stumps were burned. Sometimes pioneers in southern Michigan, weary of the task of cutting down trees, saved themselves the trouble by simply burning the trees down, destroying hardwood that was potentially of enormous value to the lumberman, but to farmers was only an obstacle which had to be removed if the land was to be plowed and planted.

A scene such as this, photographed near Otsego Lake in 1939, was a strange one in the mechanized twentieth century, but in the nineteenth century the ox-drawn plow was a familiar sight in Michigan, along with the more familiar horse-drawn plow.

155

Courtesy: Michigan State Highway Department

On this pioneer farm near Greenville, in west-central Michigan, a successful grain crop was being harvested laboriously by hand in a field that was still not completely cleared of stumps.

Michigan by the mid-nineteenth century was one of the leading agricultural states in the nation, and wheat and other grains were the main cash crops. This was the scene in Eaton Rapids in the 1870's as the farmers of the area assembled for the wheat market auction.

As the century wore on, however, the diversity that would come to characterize Michigan agriculture was beginning to appear. Farmers in central Michigan, many of them drawing on their New England background, supplemented their regular farm income by tapping the maple trees on their wood lots to obtain sap for maple sugar and maple syrup.

Northern Michigan would become famous for its potatoes.

Beginning in the 1890's, sugar beets would become a major crop of the Saginaw Valley and the Thumb, where this photograph was taken in 1939. This region, too, would become the nation's great bean-producing area.

Michigan's most famous specialized agricultural area, however, became a narrow band of land along the Lake Michigan shore of the lower peninsula. Here, due to the moderating effects of the lake's waters and the prevailing westerly winds, warmer year-round temperatures and a longer growing season from that found a few miles farther inland enabled the farmers living here to concentrate on the growing of fruit. Here, in Michigan's Fruit Belt, springtime became one of the most beautiful in America as the great orchards burst into bloom.

These were strawberry pickers near Frankfort, in the northern half of the Fruit Belt.

157

Courtesy: Al Barnes

This elderly, bearded farmer was supervising the packing of apples, grown on a farm at Old Mission, in the Traverse Bay area.

Courtesy: Al Barnes

The Traverse Bay region, however, became most famous for its cherries, such as these people on the Brinkman farm at Old Mission were picking.

In Berrien County in southwestern Michigan, the Fruit Belt reaches its greatest distance inland, some thirty miles, making this county consistently among the most prosperous agricultural counties in the country. At Benton Harbor a great fruit market developed, shown here in the twentieth century, where the products of the area's fruit farms could be sold.

From St. Joseph and Benton Harbor, at the mouth of the St. Joseph River, fruit was shipped across Lake Michigan to Chicago, the same route that later became popular for lake cruises.

Around 1880, histories of most of the counties of southern Michigan were published, which was part of a nation-wide program promoted by several publishing firms who cashed in on the historical interest that was generated in 1876 by the celebration of the centennial of the Declaration of Independence. More than any other group of citizens in the state, Michigan's farmers yielded to the temptation to pay to have their portraits and sketches of their farms appear in these volumes. The farm scenes are invariably as flattering and as idealized as the portraits, on the other hand, are unflattering and starkly realistic in the view they give of their subjects. This was the relatively modest farm of Rodolphus Tryon in Alaiedon Township of Ingham County, together with the portraits of Tryon and his wife, Lavina, which were included in the expensive two-page spread which Tryon paid for in the *History of Ingham and Eaton Counties,* published in Philadelphia in 1880. Tryon, the accompanying biographical sketch declared, had gone heavily in debt when he first moved to Ingham County in 1844, but by this time he had "a well-won competency." The sketch, which was approved, if not written, by Tryon, described the farmer as a man "possessed of many of the virtues and but few of the failings of mankind." His wife was "a lady of more than an ordinary amount of resolution and stamina."

In contrast with the Tryon farm is this view of the farm of George B. Vanatta in the neighboring Ingham County township of Meridian Township. Although their portraits made them look older, the Vanattas were only in their mid-forties and, what was somewhat uncommon at that time, both were natives of Michigan, having been born in Washtenaw County. Vanatta was described as "raising all kinds of farm productions," but, as the sketch makes clear, he was proudest of his livestock, "of which he is an extensive breeder." Some of Vanatta's eight children can be seen in front of the farmhouse, which fortunately was quite large.

159

Levi Arnold of Gun Plain Township in Allegan County was obviously very proud of his Poland China hogs, for in the two-page sketch of his farm which he paid to have printed in the *History of Allegan and Barry Counties,* published in Philadelphia in 1880, he had the artist devote the foreground to portrayals of his prize pigs: Dauntless, Oxford Belle, Lady Broadham (at two years), King of Riversides, Black Nell (weight: 625 pounds), Pride of Michigan, Lady of Oxford, and Victor. An inset provided a close-up of Arnold's piggery and office.

In this view of the S. S. Fairbank's farm near Litchfield, in the *History of Hillsdale County* published at Philadelphia in 1879, the emphasis is on the crops that were grown on the farm.

This was the farm of William Curtis and Sons near Wheatland, also in Hillsdale County. The large house, the many fine farm buildings, the well-landscaped grounds, the cattle in the foreground, and the inset sketch of the tenant's house all denote a prosperous agricultural enterprise.

160

"Gothic Ridge" was the name which Albert D. Healy gave to his farm at Casco in Allegan County. The house was, in fact, a good example of Gothic-style architecture that was fashionable in the third quarter of the nineteenth century. The farm itself, with Lake Michigan but a short distance away, was given over entirely to fruit growing, with seventeen acres covered with peach trees, 880 plum trees, and six acres of miscellaneous other fruits.

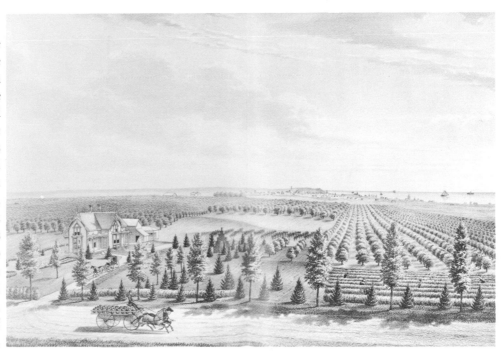

The Hustons established this farm in Galien Township in Berrien County in 1858, two years after they were married. By the time this view appeared in the *History of Berrien and Van Buren Counties*, published at Philadelphia in 1880, farm machinery was assuming an increasingly greater role in farm operations.

This photograph taken on a farm at Mulliken in Eaton County shows a steam threshing machine in operation which is not unlike the one depicted on the Huston farm. At least twenty-two men can be counted who are taking part in the threshing activities.

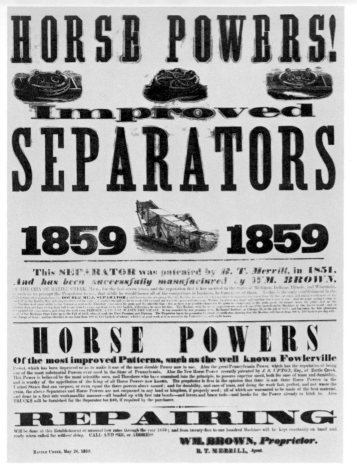

Courtesy: Michigan Historical Collections

This monstrous contraption, drawn by sixteen horses, was a harvester-combine patented by Hiram Moore of Climax in 1836. In this faded photograph, believed to date from the late 1840's, Moore, in the tall black hat, sits on top of his machine, which was capable of harvesting twenty to thirty acres a day. Lucius Lyon was Moore's financial backer, but defects in the machine, which caused it to break down frequently, and costly lawsuits between Moore and Cyrus H. McCormick over patent rights finally forced Moore to abandon plans to manufacture the harvester.

Much of the early manufacturing that developed in Michigan was in response to the need for farm machinery. Here William M. Brown of Battle Creek advertizes the separator he manufactured, which, he boasted, would "thresh from 300 to 700 bushels per day without change of team; and has threshed in one hour from 100 to 125 bushels of wheat; which is as good work as is on record in the United States, with eight horses."

Courtesy: Library of Congress

Despite Hiram Moore's failures, by the end of the nineteenth century machines had taken over much of the work which the early Michigan farmers had done by hand. Here one of them drives a machine that was cutting and binding the corn in his field much faster and more efficiently than it had taken several men to do the same tasks by hand a few years before.

The changing times were spelled out on Charlie Goodwin's Implement Shop in Colon in the 1880's, a place where farmers of the area could buy McCormick or Champion harvesters, South Bend or Oliver plows, and other equipment. Such shops were now found in every country village.

The mechanization of farm operations marked the passing of the pioneer farming era. With it also gradually disappeared such fine old customs as the barn raising, when relatives and neighbors would gather to build a new barn. . . .

163

. . . More than 125 men, women, and children can be counted in this group picture. Both pictures date from around the turn of the twentieth century when the practice was still observed in some areas.

Courtesy: Michigan Department of Conservation

Rising farm costs resulting from the use of machines and other factors drove many small farmers out of business and caused scenes such as these to become common, especially in northern Michigan, where poor soil conditions and a short growing season crushed the hopes of thousands of young farm couples who settled in that region in the latter years of the nineteenth century and the early years of the twentieth.

Courtesy: Michigan Historical Collections

164

The Age of the Lumberman

The old man lit up his pipe and recalled the days of his youth when he participated in the final stages of one of the major events in American history: the logging of the immense forests of central and northern Michigan. It had been a rough, rigorous life, but in the tradition of the pioneer period, he and his fellow woodsmen had wrested from the wilderness the raw materials with which the cities and towns and the farmhouses and barns of the Middle West were built.

Lumbering had been carried on in Michigan long before the period of peak activity in the late nineteenth century when it was the foremost lumber-producing state in the country. Small operations, centering around mills such as Adams' Mill, near Plymouth, shown in this painting dated January 18, 1856, supplied the local market in the rapidly developing settlements of southern Michigan.

The Landlooker.

The lumber industry, as such, however, did not develop until markets opened up outside the local area and outside the state. To take advantage of such markets required large-scale operations, beginning with the land-lookers who sought out the good stands of timber. This sketch of one of these skilled woodsmen accompanied an article in *Scribner's Magazine* in 1893, which was written by the great Saginaw lumberman Arthur Hill, who began his career in the industry in this capacity.

The Bay City lumberman W. D. Young and an employee were dwarfed by some of the pines in one of Young's tracts. Big as they were, however, vast quantities of trees even larger awaited the logger's axe, just as Young himself was but one among many in the Saginaw Valley who made fortunes, large and small, while turning that area into the most important center of the Michigan lumber industry.

When the land had been purchased, a logging camp was set up and a camp meant men—men who loved the outdoors and did not object to working from dawn to dusk, six days a week for at least half the year, including the winter months. Such were these men at Reed and Redy's Camp on the Tittabawassee River in the winter of 1890-91 . . .

. . . or these men in a small crew in western Michigan in 1906. Some were only boys while others were much older in appearance than they were in years as hard labor and a hard climate took their toll.

The Kitchen.

Head cook.   Chore-boy.   Cook's "devils."

A good cook was essential to a lumber camp. In a series of illustrations he did in 1893 for *Scribner's Magazine*, Dan Beard made this sketch of the kitchen in a Michigan lumber camp, with the head cook, the chore boy, and the cook's "devils."

Courtesy: Grand Rapids Public Museum

The tables in the mess hall are set, ready for the men to sit down for their meal.

And here was the dinner hour in a Michigan lumber camp, "drawn from life" by Dan Beard.

The bunk house was home for the Michigan woodsmen from fall through to the following spring. This was the scene inside one such bunkhouse, on a Sunday, the only day off the men got, as sketched by Dan Beard during his tour of several Michigan camps.

168

Also essential to a successful lumber camp were strong, healthy horses and skilled teamsters who could move the logs out of the woods where they were cut. Some of the teams in the Rust Brothers Camp II in the Saginaw Valley area are shown here in front of the camp's barn.

Courtesy: Michigan Historical Collections

In the woods, choppers and sawyers felled the great giants of the forest, some of which rose to a height of as much as 170 feet and might be three centuries old. A photographer from Chapman Bros. studio in Stanton, in February, 1888, snapped sawyers of the Cutler & Savidge Lumber Company in Montcalm County cutting a felled tree up into lengths to be hauled away by the team which is standing in the background.

Finally, the logs were piled on sleds and hauled out of the woods over the iced roads. There was always a natural interest among the men as to what was the heaviest and tallest load they could haul. A large crowd gathered in the spring of 1892 to inspect this great load, estimated to weigh a hundred thousand pounds, which a team of four horses was bringing to the mill of the Wisconsin Land and Lumber Company in Hermansville.

Courtesy: Manistee County Historical Museum

The famous "big wheels," developed and manufactured by Silas C. Overpack of Manistee in the early 1870's, provided a method of hauling small quantities of logs out of the woods at any time of the year, thereby freeing the logger, to a degree, from the necessity of confining his operations to the months when frozen roads permitted the use of horse-drawn sleighs. . . .

169

... The wheels are shown being used in Oceana County.

Far more important than the "big wheels," however, in opening the way to year-round logging was the logging railroad, first successfully developed by a Michigan lumberman, Winfield Scott Gerrish, in 1877. Scenes such as this one in January, 1882, became a common and welcome sight to the lumberman. Logs are being hauled by horses and oxen out of the forest to this logging train which will then move the load six miles to the Cummer Lumber Company mill in Cadillac. The train is drawn by a tiny Shay Geared Locomotive, which was invented by Ephraim Shay, who came to Michigan after the Civil War and entered the lumber business. His locomotive, which he developed when he encountered difficulty in moving logs to his mill at Cadillac, was manufactured at the Lima Locomotive Works in Lima, Ohio, and was one of the most popular engines used by the logging railroads.

Here in Cadillac in 1882 a narrow-gauge logging train has just brought in a load of 393 logs.

170

Even after the coming of the railroads, however, the numerous rivers that flow out of the interior of Michigan's peninsulas into the Great Lakes provided the easiest and least expensive means of transporting the logs to Saginaw, Muskegon, and the other great mill and shipping centers. The logs were hauled from the woods to the river bank where they were stacked, awaiting the river drive. These logs at the Clam River banking grounds were the result of fifteen days of hauling over the D. A. Blodgett Logging Railroad in 1884.

With the spring thaw and the breaking up of the ice, the logs were dumped into the river, down a runway, or sometimes down a chute, such as this one on the Big Manistee River in the 1890's, and the river drive, the most exciting aspect of the entire lumber industry, was ready to begin.

It was an awesome sight—the logs filling the length and breadth of the river, with more still to be dumped in from the banks—and this photograph was taken on the Muskegon River in the 1890's, several years after the peak years of production along this river in the 1880's.

To keep the drive going smoothly required a crew of men trained in the dangerous tasks of spotting trouble spots and moving across the floating logs to prevent or break up log jams. This was part of the crew on the main drive down the Muskegon River in 1886 as the drive passed Evart. In the rear are the floating quarters that were used to house and feed the men.

Courtesy: Grand Rapids Public Museum

This picture shows the wanigan or floating cook shack, the cook, his helpers, and some of the river men on the Muskegon River log drive.

Courtesy: Besser Company

Left: The drive ended at the mouth of the river, as here at Alpena, where the logs entered a great "boom" from which they were sorted into pens according to the log marks of the various companies which were stamped in the end of each of their logs. These log marks had to be registered in the county seats of the counties where the companies operated. *Below*: Some of the log marks of companies in the Saginaw Valley lumber area are shown.

Once the logs were sorted, they were fastened together into rafts and hauled to the mills to be cut into timber. These logs at Saginaw, probably in the 1870's, have been pegged and roped together by employees of the Tittabawassee Boom Company, the largest of the companies which handled both the river drives and the tasks of sorting and rafting at the end of the drive.

Martha A. Hay — Palmerton Wooden-Ware Co. — E.O. & S.L. Eastman Co.

W. R. Burt — Charles Lee — Rust Bros. Co.

Wells, Stone & Co. — Gebhart & Estabrook — Arthur Barnard

Gebhart & Estabrook — Charles Merrill & Co. — Mumford & Avery

Bliss & Van Auken — Sewell Avery — Whittier & Co.

Merrill & Ring — W. B. Mershon & Co. — Brand & Hardin

Courtesy: Saginaw Museum

Here was one of the sawmills of the
fabled Louis Sands at Manistee. The
mill is on Manistee Lake at the mouth
of the Manistee River. In the foreground is the Manistee log boom
from which logs are taken to the mill
to be made into lumber of varying kinds
and dimensions which could then be
loaded on board vessels for shipment
out of Manistee.

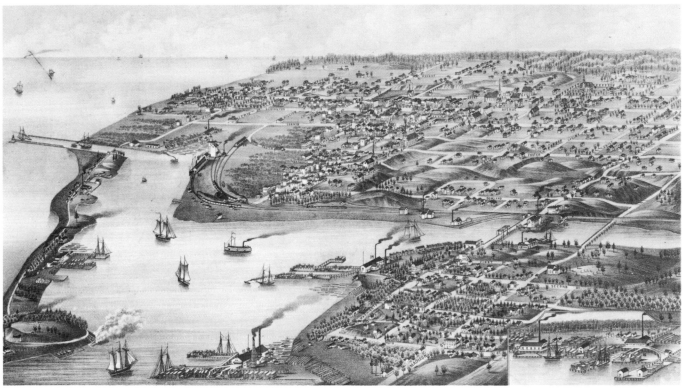

Ludington, shown here in 1880 near the peak of the lumbering era in the lower peninsula, was typical of numerous ports along Lake Michigan whose situation could scarcely have been better for the
lumberman. The logs that had floated down the Pere Marquette River arrived at the mouth of the
river which widens into a lake as a result of the natural dam formed by sand bars. Around this lake were
located a number of sawmills and shingle factories. The finished lumber was then loaded on boats at
the docks of these mills, from which point the boats then passed through the channel leading out into
Lake Michigan. (The degree to which the lumber industry attracted foreign immigrants to Michigan
is suggested by the fact that three of the nine churches located on this bird's-eye view were either Ger-
man- or Scandinavian-speaking.)

In the mill towns, the company store sold
a variety of staples, including good old
Log Cabin Maple Syrup, and provided a
place where the workers could gather
around the stove and talk or simply re-
lax, as these men were doing in this unidentified Michigan company store.

173

Courtesy: Michigan Historical Collections

The boardinghouse was one of the most important institutions in every lumber town. This was Boarding House No. 1 in the Upper Peninsula lumber center of Hermansville in 1891. The place was operated by Mrs. McMonigle and her daughter Rose. They appear at the left. The man wearing an apron was Mr. Fisher, the cook. At the right rear is the home of G. W. Earle, head of the lumber company.

Courtesy: Michigan Historical Collections

The lavish Victorian mansions of the great lumber barons were the most obvious evidences of the enormous profits that many men made in the lumber industry. The home of James Shearer of Bay City, shown here in 1875, was more tasteful than some others because Shearer, in addition to being the successful operator of a sawmill in Bay City, was also an architect.

A half-century later, in 1959, this was the view at exactly the same site, a dirt road following the same curve as the long-since-vanished logging railroad had once followed. The great forest is now only decaying stumps and scrubby second growth.

Courtesy: Michigan Department of Conservation

Courtesy: Michigan Department of Conservation

The story of Michigan's great lumbering days began in the forests, at a scene such as this one in the lower peninsula, in 1905.

174

Courtesy: Michigan Department of Conservation

Between 1901 and 1912, one of the last big virgin pine tracts remaining in the lower peninsula was cut down in operations around Deward, now a ghost lumber town northeast of Grayling, marked by acres of decaying stumps.

The forest fires threatened everything in their path. The great fire of 1871 cut a path of destruction across the central lower peninsula, leaving behind it communities such as Holland, which, as this proclamation of the mayor of the neighboring city of Grand Haven states, was virtually wiped out. By coincidence, this fire occurred at the same time as the great Chicago fire.

Courtesy: Michigan Historical Collections

Courtesy: Al Barnes

Close behind the loggers came the scourge of fire which swept through the cutover lands, feeding on the cuttings left behind by the lumberman. In the hot summer months, these cuttings became tinder-dry. Any spark might ignite them, destroying in the process thousands of acres of land. This was the scene in the area of the Upper Manistee River after a fire in July, 1894.

The most terrible of Michigan's forest fires was one that roared through the Thumb area in September, 1881, destroying not only much of the remaining timber but vast amounts of farm property as well and killing at least 125 people who were unable to escape ahead of the fast-moving flames. A state marker in a roadside park on highway M-25, near Bay Port, stands amidst some of the forest growth that has come back since 1881.

Courtesy: Bay City Times

PROCLAMATION!

Our sister City of Holland is nearly destroyed by fire. More than two thousand people are left homeless and exposed to to the pittiless storm. Food and Clothing is the immediate want.

I, HENRY GRIFFIN, Mayor of the City of Grand Haven, do hereby call upon all good citizens to contribute to the relief of these sufferers.

For this purpose I have caused Subscription Papers to be opened at my office.

Any provisions, cooked or otherwise, and clothing, will be of comfort, and such donations taken to the Office of E. P. FERRY, will be there received and record kept of Donors.

HENRY GRIFFIN, Mayor.
Grand Haven. Oct. 10th, 1871.

GREAT FIRE OF 1881
Small fires were burning in the forests of the Thumb, tinder-dry after a long, hot summer, when a gale swept in from the southwest on Sept. 5, 1881. Fanned into an inferno, the fires raged for three days. A million acres were devastated in Sanilac and Huron counties alone. At least 125 persons died, and thousands more were left destitute. The new American Red Cross won support for its prompt aid to the fire victims. This was the first disaster relief furnished by this great organization.

175

MICHIGAN'S
TERRIBLE CALAMITY.

DANSVILLE SOCIETY OF THE

RED CROSS.

A CRY FOR HELP!

The Dansville Society of the Red Cross, whose duty it is to accumulate funds and material, to provide nurses and assistants if may be, and hold these for use or service in case of war, or other national calamity—has heard the cry for help from Michigan. Senator O. D. Conger wrote on the 9th of September that he had just returned from the burnt region. Bodies of more than 200 persons had already been buried, and more than 1500 families had been burned out of everything. That was in only twenty townships in two counties. He invoked the aid of all our people. The character and extent of the calamity cannot be described in words. The manifold horrors of the fire were multiplied by fearful tornadoes, which cut off retreat in every direction. In some places whole families have been found reduced to an undistinguishable heap of wasted and blackened blocks of flesh, where they fell together overwhelmed by the rushing flames. For the dead, alas! there is nothing but burial. For the thousands who survive, without shelter, without clothing, without food, whose every vestige of a once happy home has been swept away, haply much, everything, can be done. The Society of the Red Cross of Dansville proposes to exercise its functions in this emergency, and to see to it that sympathy, money, clothing, bedding, everything which those entirely destitute can need, shall find its way promptly to them. But the society is in its infancy here. It has in fact barely completed its organization. It has not in possession for immediate use the funds and stores which will in future be accumulated for such emergencies. It calls therefore upon the generous people of Dansville and vicinity to make at once such contributions, money or clothing, as their liberal hearts and the terrible exigency must prompt them to make. Our citizens will be called upon for cash subscriptions, or such subscriptions may be left with James Faulkner, Jr., Treasurer of the Society, at the First National Bank of Dansville. Contributions of Clothing and Bedding may be left at 154 Main street, Maxwell Block, Sewing Machine Agency of Mrs. John Sheppard.

☞A special agent of the Society will be dispatched with the money and goods to see to their proper distribution. Please act promptly.

EXECUTIVE COMMITTEE RED CROSS.

Dansville, Sept. 13, 1881.

DANSVILLE ADVERTISER STEAM PRINT.

Courtesy: Library of Congress

Courtesy: Michigan Department of Conservation

Finally, around the turn of the century, the initial steps were taken to conserve what remained of Michigan's once mighty forests. The state and federal forest services began to take action to guard against fires, and at Higgins Lake the state forest nursery began the first planting of seedlings which now have developed into impressive pine plantations.

This fire of 1881 in Michigan resulted in the first disaster relief by the newly formed American Red Cross. The relief program was directed by the founder of the Red Cross, Clara Barton, from her headquarters in Dansville, New York. (Estimates of the death toll in this tragedy vary considerably, but the figure of "more than 200" in this handbill is too high.)

Monuments often fail to accomplish the purpose for which they were erected, but few who view the Lumbermen's Memorial, placed in a wilderness setting sixteen miles northwest of Tawas City, with the Au Sable River, the scene of so many log drives, just down the hill to the rear of the memorial, can fail to come away without a sense of the tremendous accomplishment of Michigan's lumbermen. Despite their wasteful methods and their lack of regard for the needs of future generations, the results of which can still not be clearly measured, these men, through the more than one hundred sixty billion board feet of pine that they produced, did indeed, as the inscription declares, make "possible the development of the prairie states."

Courtesy: Michigan Tourist Council

The most famous rock in Michigan history is the Ontonagon boulder, which weighs some six thousand pounds, is fifty inches long, forty-one inches wide, and eighteen inches thick. This is no ordinary boulder, however, as evidenced by the fact that it has been owned and displayed by the Smithsonian Institution in Washington for more than a century. The Ontonagon boulder, which was originally found on the upper reaches of the Ontonagon River in the western part of the Upper Peninsula, contains a huge mass of pure copper, and it was for many years the most visible evidence of the great mineral wealth to be found in this section of Michigan.

Courtesy: Smithsonian Institution

Although upper Michigan's deposits of copper had been known to some of the area's early prehistoric Indians who made artifacts from the outcroppings of the metal in its pure state which they found, the white men who came to the area made almost no attempt for over two centuries to exploit this wealth. In 1841, however, the first detailed scientific report on the extent of these deposits was made by Michigan's first state geologist, Douglass Houghton. The information was contained in Houghton's report on the work of the state geological survey, and despite Houghton's warnings that the mining of this copper would require the expenditure of large amounts of time and money, hundreds of men soon descended upon the Upper Peninsula after a cursory reading of the report, expecting to get rich quickly. The brilliant Houghton, who had already made his mark not only as a geologist but as a chemist and doctor and as a politician (mayor of Detroit), continued the work of the geological survey until his life was cut short at the age of thirty-six when he drowned in 1845 off the shores of the Keweenaw Peninsula, an area that was already becoming known more familiarly as the "Copper Country."

LAKE SUPERIOR NEWS

AND

MINERS' JOURNAL.

VOLUME 1.]   COPPER HARBOR, LAKE SUPERIOR, MICHIGAN, JULY 11, 1846.   [NUMBER 1.

Courtesy: Sylvester Lucas

By the time of Houghton's death, the Keweenaw Peninsula was in the midst of the first really important mining boom in American history. In an area which as recently as 1842 had been owned by the Indians, towns suddenly appeared, with the early activity concentrated at the northern tip of the peninsula around Copper Harbor, where, in 1846, northern Michigan's first newspaper appeared, its name and the stories it contained obviously reflecting the interests of the area.

The expenses involved in establishing a successful copper mine were soon enough to discourage the adventurers and to bankrupt the many companies that were formed in the 1840's. This sketch in the 1850's of the Cliff Mine near Eagle River, the most profitable of the early Michigan copper mines, gives some idea of the increasingly complex nature of the mining operations.

In later years, as the copper deposits at or near the surface were exhausted, underground mining had to be resorted to. Here in 1892 in a candle-lit underground level of a Michigan copper mine, three miners go about their business, one grimly holding a drill which the other two, hopefully, will hit with their sledgehammers, thereby loosening chunks of copper ore.

At the surface of the copper mines, a structure was erected over the mine shaft to house the equipment that was needed to transport the men down into the mine and to hoist the ore to the ground level. The most picturesque of these shaft houses was that of the Quincy Mine at Hancock, which was, because of its numerous gables and the interesting lighting effects they created, a favorite of photographers and artists until the building burned in 1956.

180

To free the copper from the other material found in the ore, the ores had to be crushed and the pure copper removed in a series of operations in stamping and concentrating mills.

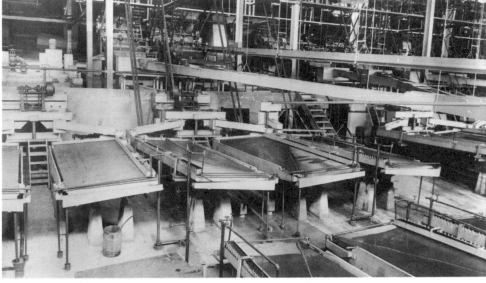

Finally, pure copper, concentrated into ingots, was stacked on the dock at Houghton, awaiting shipment.

In the heart of the Copper Country, which stretches from the tip of the Keweenaw Peninsula on the north to the Ontonagon region in the south and west, is Houghton, shown here in 1881, with its twin city of Hancock, a small portion of which shows at the bottom of this view. Located on the waterway which was cut across the peninsula, following the natural water-route system of Portage Lake, Houghton and Hancock became not only major copper-mining centers but also the most important shipping point for much of the copper produced in the entire area.

The great Calumet and Hecla mining operations around Calumet, which began to develop after the Civil War, soon came to dwarf the production of other copper mines and have continued to the present day.

181

Until the late 1880's, Michigan was the leading copper producer in the country. After that, although its production continued to rise for several decades, it lost its national leadership to Western copper-mining states, and ultimately the high cost of mining in Michigan's Copper Country forced most mines out of business, leaving the area dotted with ghost towns, such as Central Mine, located on US-41 in Keweenaw County, where mining ended in the 1890's and the descendants of the Cornish mining families who lived here return each summer for a reunion amidst the crumbling mine buildings and the empty frame houses, once so full of activity and life.

Courtesy: Michigan Department of Conservation

Courtesy: Marquette County Historical Society

Courtesy: Ray A. Brotherton

On September 19, 1844, a surveying team headed by the great William A. Burt, was conducting a combined land and geological survey in the Upper Peninsula on the site of the present city of Negaunee. When the surveyor's compass needle began to fluctuate wildly, Burt called out to his men, "Boys, look around and see what you can find!" In a short time, the cause of the needle's action was found with the discovery of numerous specimens of iron ore. Burt's party had stumbled on the first of the major deposits of iron ore in the Lake Superior region.

The following year, 1845, a group of men from Jackson who had come to the Upper Peninsula in search of copper were led instead by an Indian, Marji-Gesick, to a mountain of iron ore in the area that Burt's party had surveyed. Local tradition in Negaunee declared that the first ore was found amidst the roots of this fallen tree stump.

182

In the next thirty years, the western part of the Upper Peninsula was combed by parties of men, such as this one employed by the St. Mary's Canal Mineral Land Company in 1863, searching for more mineral wealth. Eventually, three great areas of iron ore deposits, known as ranges, were discovered, including the original Marquette Iron Range, which had been discovered by Burt and his men, the Menominee Iron Range, and the Gogebic Iron Range.

Among the most famous of these prospectors was Richard Langford, who came to upper Michigan in the early 1850's. In 1872 or 1873 he claimed to have discovered an ore body which, a few years later, would be exploited by the Colby Mine, the first mine on the Gogebic Iron Range at the extreme western end of Michigan's Upper Peninsula. Langford never received the one-quarter interest in this highly profitable mine that he said he had been promised, and he lived out his life as a hermit, dying blind and penniless at the Ontonagon County infirmary in 1909.

This was Peck's Camp, established in 1883 in what would become the mining town of Ironwood. The men in the camp were there to explore for ore, and their efforts ended in the opening of the **Pabst** Mine, one of the most successful in the history of the Gogebic Range.

183

The early iron mines, beginning with the Jackson Mine at Negaunee, the Lake Superior region's first iron mine and for three-quarters of a century one of its most productive and profitable operations, were open-pit mines. This was the No. 1 pit of the Jackson Mine in 1860. The equipment, by later standards, was primitive.

Courtesy: Michigan Department of Conservation

But the bulk of the Upper Peninsula iron ore was found deep in the ground. Here at the Jackson Mine in 1865, horizontal-tunneling operations had begun to reach ore deposits which no longer could be reached conveniently by open-pit methods.

Courtesy: Michigan Historical Collections

At the Aurora Mine in Ironwood in 1886 vertical shafts were beginning to be sunk in order to reach the levels of ore that were located many feet below the surface.

184

This was the famous "C" Shaft of the Norrie Mine at Ironwood in 1899. The mining was now entirely underground, where the ore was loaded into skips which were lifted to the surface by great hoists and then run out along the trestle and dumped, to await subsequent reloading on railroad cars.

To keep the underground mines from filling up with water, like a gigantic well, pumps had to be installed. This is the huge Cornish Pump from the old Chapin Mine at Iron Mountain which was capable of pumping out of the mine three thousand gallons of water per minute.

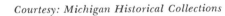

Mining in the early days was a slow, laborious process, depending on the strength and skill of the individual miners, such as these three workers at the Jackson Mine in June, 1863, pipes clenched between their teeth, who were engaged in the grim business of hand drilling.

A new element of danger was added when underground mining began. These miners working in an Ishpeming mine, depended for light on a candle attached to their hat. If it went out, they might plunge to their death in the darkened underground labyrinth. The miners also faced the constant prospect of being buried alive in a cave-in if the wooden timbers that supported the level in which they were working collapsed; or they might drown if the pump failed and the shaft suddenly filled with water.

185

Courtesy: Michigan Department of Conservation

Iron ore is a bulky product to ship, and thus companies at first made an effort to reduce the ore to pig iron or other forms of iron at furnaces near the mines, using the abundant forests of the area as a source of fuel. One of the most extensive of such operations was at Fayette on the southern shore of the Upper Peninsula, where the Jackson Iron Company built a blast furnace in 1867. It was operated for nearly three decades before being abandoned, a fate all of these forges and furnaces of northern Michigan eventually suffered. The ruins of Fayette today are preserved as a state park.

Most of Michigan's iron ore was shipped out by boat, via the Great Lakes to the iron and steel centers of the East. This was the dock of the Jackson Mine in 1854 at Marquette, a new community on Lake Superior that developed as a shipping port for the Marquette Iron Range.

Courtesy: Ray A. Brotherton

186

MARQUETTE.L.S.,MICH.
1881.

This was Marquette in 1881, by which time the number of mines on the Marquette Iron Range and the total production of ore had vastly increased since the pre-Civil War beginnings. Railroads from the mines to the west brought the iron ore to the docks where it could then be loaded on boats for final shipment to the mills.

This was an early ore train, carrying ore in May, 1865, from the Jackson Mine to the new ore port of Escanaba on Lake Michigan, . . .

... which in a few years developed as a worthy rival of Marquette and later would become the chief outlet for the ores from the mines of the Menominee Iron Range, some thirty to forty miles to the west.

Courtesy: Rev. Edward J. Dowling, S. J.

The first small shipments of ore were made in existing vessels, but in 1869, the *R. J. Hackett,* a 211-foot wooden vessel, was built at Cleveland exclusively for the bulk iron ore trade. It became the prototype of the great ore boats that would become the most easily recognized symbol of the Great Lakes shipping industry.

188

Before the Upper Peninsula's mineral resources could be fully developed and the Great Lakes waterway system completely utilized, the bottleneck of the rapids in the St. Mary's River, where the waters from Lake Superior descend to the lower level of the waters of Lake Huron, had to be broken. Portaging had been the solution since the days of the fur trade, and in 1845 the steamer *Independence* was portaged around the rapids to become the first steamer on Lake Superior. (Certified here in 1849 as "sound and in all respects sea-worthy," the *Independence* blew up in 1853.)

190

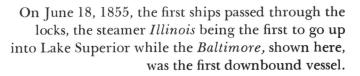

In this 1850 sketch of Water Street in Sault Ste. Marie, the artist Wheaton Metcalf shows how tracks had been laid to make it easier to haul goods around the rapids so that they might be reloaded on ships below—at best, however, a costly method of handling such heavy products as copper and iron.

Then, in the 1850's, the final solution came with the building of the canal around the rapids and the locks needed to raise or lower vessels passing between Lake Superior and Lake Huron, thereby eliminating the need for passengers and cargoes to change vessels. This was the scene as the workers cut through rock to construct the locks.

Many men were involved in the Soo Canal project but Charles T. Harvey, shown here in a portrait made some years later, claimed and probably deserves much of the credit for being one of the prime movers, if not the principal one.

On June 18, 1855, the first ships passed through the locks, the steamer *Illinois* being the first to go up into Lake Superior while the *Baltimore,* shown here, was the first downbound vessel.

191

In two decades the total freight tonnage passing through the original locks increased from not quite 15,000 tons in 1855 to more than 1,500,000 tons in 1875. In 1876 the army engineers began constructing the Weitzel Lock, the first of several new locks that had to be built in the years ahead as the canal traffic became the heaviest on any canal in the world. In 1881 control of the locks passed from the state of Michigan to the federal government, since it was felt that Michigan should not have to bear the entire expense of maintaining a facility that benefited the entire nation.

Year-round use of the Great Lakes has always been prevented by the ice which clogs the narrow waterways connecting the lakes, as well as the harbors, and in some cases freezes over the entire lake. Here a small fleet of ships is frozen in for the winter at the Soo in December, 1926, awaiting the spring thaw.

It now became possible to board a steamer in Lake Erie and stay on the same vessel all the way to the western end of Lake Superior, as described here by one of the first steamship lines offering such service.

THE ICE-CRUSHING STEAMER "ST. IGNACE."—Drawn by E. J. Meeker.—[See Page 186.]

To keep service operating throughout the winter between St. Ignace and Mackinaw City, the Duluth, South Shore, and Atlantic Railroad developed "an ice-defying ferry boat," as *Harper's Weekly* called it in the story that accompanied this picture layout in 1892. "Yankee ingenuity has circumvented nature in a clever way," the magazine declared, by constructing a vessel that was "like a ram or a steam-hammer, or both combined." In its initial voyage in 1888, the *St. Ignace*, piloted by Captain Lewis R. Boynton, carried a load of eight locomotives across the straits through three feet of ice. The degree to which the eastern end of the Upper Peninsula had been isolated from the world during the long winter months was now substantially reduced.

Courtesy: Clarke Historical Library

For many years, however, communications across the frozen waterway that separates Michigan's two peninsulas were maintained by sleds and sleighs pulled by horses or, in this case, by teams of dogs. In the background are the docks used by the ferries that began carrying passengers and railroad cars over the straits in the 1880's.

Courtesy: Michigan Historical Collections

Courtesy: Library of Congress

Another hazard to shipping was the lake storm, such as this one off Sleeping Bear Dune in 1839, depicted in Francis, Comte de Castlenau's *Vues et Souvenirs de l'Amérique du Nord,* published in Paris in 1842.

An artist of the period depicted the sinking of the steam barge *H. C. Akely* in a storm off Saugatuck in November, 1883, traditionally one of the worst months for lake storms. The captain of the *Akely* and five of her crewmen drowned, one of hundreds of such tragedies that have occurred on the Great Lakes since the loss of the *Griffin* in 1679.

Courtesy: Clarke Historical Library

As early as 1825 a lighthouse was built by the federal government at Port Huron, and other beacons to aid the navigators of shipping passing through Michigan waters were soon provided at harbor entrances and in dangerous waters. This was a typical Michigan lighthouse of the period, tended by a keeper who, in the automated world of the future, would become as obsolete as the sailing vessel passing by out in the lake.

194

Courtesy: Detroit Institute of Arts

The Great Lakes were the highways on which a great shipping industry developed in the nineteenth century. Detroit was the chief port of entry into the hinterlands of southern Michigan, a fact dramatically demonstrated in this painting by William J. Bennett in 1837 showing the busy Detroit River and the city of Detroit in the background. The Detroit area was also a center for shipbuilding. The 473-ton, 156-foot steamship *Michigan,* second from the left, was launched at Detroit in 1833 and was the largest steamer on the Great Lakes until it was surpassed in 1838 by the *Illinois,* another Detroit-built ship.

By the time this Detroit waterfront scene was photographed in the last quarter of the nineteenth century, sailing vessels and the early side-wheeling steamships had largely given way to more advanced steam vessels that were capable of carrying much larger quantities of freight and numbers of passengers to and from Detroit's docks.

In nineteenth-century Michigan, however, the waters of the Great Lakes were not only means of transporting goods and people. They were also a source of income for the thriving fishing industry. The fishermen's nets drying on the dock at Whitefish Point in Lake Superior was a common scene along Michigan's more than three thousand miles of Great Lakes shoreline.

Courtesy: National Archives

Courtesy: Burton Historical Collection

This was the commercial fishing fleet at the mouth of the Au Sable River. The waters of Lake Huron outside this harbor were as important to these fishermen and their families as were the waters of the Atlantic to a New England fishing village.

An adventurous photographer went out in a fishing canoe in the rapids of the St. Mary's River and photographed these raging waters where fishing was done with dip-nets and the boats were carried along at a rate of a mile in three minutes.

Courtesy: National Archives

In the winter time on Saginaw Bay, and elsewhere, fishermen went out and obtained great quantities of fresh fish through the ice and brought their catch back on sleds.

Courtesy: Clarke Historical Library

The same scene was enacted daily during the fishing season at many other points, such as here at Port Huron in the 1890's, as enormous amounts of whitefish, lake trout, and other fish were shipped fresh or salted to cities throughout the Middle West.

Here at Whitefish Point fish caught in Lake Superior are being brought off the fishing tug and loaded onto cars.

Courtesy: National Archives

Courtesy: National Archives

Courtesy: Michigan Department of Conservation

The fishing industry would continue on well into the twentieth century, but it became less and less important and scenes such as this one of an abandoned boat and fish house became all too common—outward signs of changes that were taking place in Michigan.

Michigan in the latter part of the nineteenth century was changing rapidly. It was growing up. In Lansing, in the 1870's, a new state capitol building, costing over a million dollars, was erected. When it was completed, its dome towered over the modest frame capitol building which a much younger state had built thirty years before and which would soon disappear in a fire in 1882.

Although not as elaborate as some state capitols that were constructed in this period, Michigan's was impressive enough when it opened in 1879 to be the subject of a picture study in *Harper's Weekly*, with line drawings of, among others, the Senate Chamber and the Governor's Room.

Building construction reflected the expansion of the state governmental services in other areas also. At Jackson, in the 1880's, an impressive new state prison was constructed to replace the earlier structures that had been built since Jackson in 1837 was selected as the site of the new state's first prison. By the fourth decade of the twentieth century, however, these new facilities were long since outmoded, and they were abandoned for a huge new structure at a different site. The grim ruins of the old prison remain, resembling some kind of medieval fortress.

Courtesy: Michigan National Guard

At Kalamazoo, where the state's first "asylum for the insane" had been located by legislative act in 1848, this handsome building was erected between 1854 and 1859, according to plans prepared by the Philadelphia architect Samuel Sloan, and Dr. Thomas Kirkbride, of the same city, who collaborated in establishing a new standard for mental hospitals of this period. By the 1960's, Sloan and Kirkbride's work was judged to have outlived its usefulness, and although it was acclaimed by architectural historians such as Harlcy McKec as "a remarkably advanced building for the 1850's," it was written off by the state as expendable and was scheduled for demolition.

Courtesy: Allen Stross

Courtesy: Allen Stross

On the county level, the late nineteenth century was an era in which many of the courthouses that still survive and are in use in Michigan were built. A splendid example of the rather eclectic style employed is the Eaton County Courthouse in Charlotte. Built in 1883, it is a red brick building with white trim, topped by a dome on which stands a statue of justice. Eaton County has maintained the building in excellent condition, and when the need for more office space arose the county did a rather remarkable thing: it built new facilities while retaining the old.

203

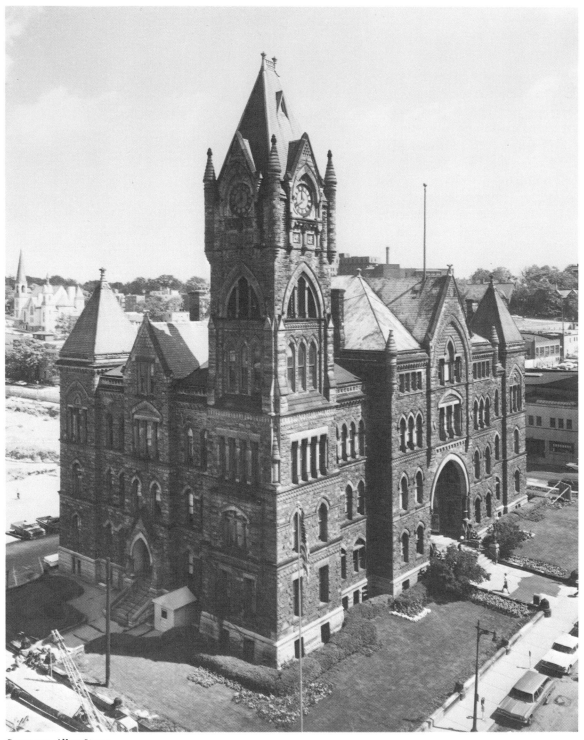

Erected in 1888 and demolished in 1967 during America's latest urban renewal craze, the Grand Rapids City Hall was designed by Elijah E. Myers, the architect who had earlier designed the state capitol. It was another excellent example of the attention that was given to details, both large and small, in the public buildings of that day which gave to them a distinctive character, details that many people of a later, faster-moving generation would regard as fussy an unnecessary.

Education

Courtesy: Michigan Historical Collections

This was the town of Hillsdale in the 1870's. The houses, some modest, some more pretentious, the fenced yards with the woodshed and privy in the back, the dirt streets—these are what one would expect in a small farming community. But what of the large building in the background? Although it looked out of place, it really was not, because it was part of Hillsdale College, one of many private and public institutions of higher learning founded earlier in the century which now made rapid strides forward that were indicative of the high degree of concern for education that Michiganians shared with the rest of their countrymen.

Michigan, together with the other states of the Middle West, had a heritage of public support for education that went back to the provisions of the Land Ordinance of 1785 and the Northwest Ordinance of 1787. A special, quite unique feature of Michigan's educational development, however, occurred in 1817, only a dozen years after the territory had been established and in a period when the few settled areas were just recovering from the ravages of the War of 1812. The territorial government, under the leadership of Judge Augustus B. Woodward, attempted to set up a complete system of schools from the elementary through the university level, plus libraries, museums, and assorted other institutions— all under centralized control. The entire system was called the University of Michigania or the Catholepistemiad, a name dreamed up by Woodward, who also believed that all disciplines and sciences could be grouped into thirteen categories which he here names and describes. A professor was to be appointed to teach each of these categories in the territory's university.

206   *Courtesy: Michigan Historical Collections*

In the fall of 1817, a two-story brick building was erected on the west side of Bates Street, near Congress, in Detroit. The instruction that was given in this building over the years never advanced beyond the primary and secondary school level to that of a university. Later, the building, the only one erected for the original University of Michigan in Detroit, was used by Detroit for public school classes until 1858 when it was razed.

In 1827, the territory moved from centralized direction of education to complete decentralization, turning over to the townships the power to establish school districts. The first such local district was created in rural Monroe County where the Bridge School District operated from the 1820's to 1955 when it was consolidated into a large school system. The two-room brick school building, five miles east of Dundee, where classes were held from the 1860's, is now owned and preserved by the Monroe County Historical Society.

Through the efforts of the Rev. John D. Pierce (right) and Isaac Crary (left), over-all supervision of Michigan's schools was provided for in the state constitution of 1835 with the establishment of the office of superintendent of public instruction. Pierce was appointed to this office by Governor Mason in 1836.

Courtesy: Michigan Historical Collections

Although free public education was the goal of many educational leaders, it was not until 1842 that tuition-free schooling was provided for the first time in Michigan in this Detroit school, located above a grocery store on Woodbridge Street near Shelby.

In most school districts, until well into the second half of the nineteenth century, tuition was charged. The schedule of fees, according to the course of study the pupil desired to pursue, was set forth by the trustees of the Pontiac Union School in 1851.

CONTRACT BETWEEN DISTRICT BOARD AND TEACHER.

See Sections 39, 43, 60 and 85, School Law of 1864.

It is Hereby Contracted and Agreed, Between

Alfred Gifford of District N° _16_ in the Township of _Flint_, County of _Genesee_, and State of Michigan, and _Hattie E. Southard_, a legally qualified Teacher in said Township, that the said _Hattie E. Southard_ shall teach the Primary School of said District for the term of _sixteen_ weeks, commencing on the _eighteenth_ day of _November_, A. D. 18 _67_, and the said _Hattie E. Southard_ agrees faithfully to keep the List and Record required by law, (Section 43,) and to observe and enforce the Rules and Regulations established by the District Board.

The said _Alfred Gifford_, in behalf of said District, agrees to keep the School House in good repair, and to provide the necessary Fuel, and to pay said _Hattie E. Southard_ for the said services as Teacher, to be faithfully and truly rendered and performed, the sum of _Eighty eight_ —— $\frac{}{100}$ Dollars, the same being the amount of wages above agreed upon to be paid on or before the _first_ day of _June_ 18 _68_.

PROVIDED, That in case said _____ shall be dismissed from School, by the District Board, for gross immorality or violation of this Contract, or shall have _____ Certificate annulled by the School Inspectors, _____ shall not be entitled to any compensation from and after such annulment or dismissal.

In Witness Whereof, We have hereunto subscribed our names this _eighteenth_ day of _November_, A. D. 18 _67_.

Alfred Gifford Director.

H. E. Southard Teacher.

Approved by

_____ Moderator.

Corydon Crane Assessor.

In this contract with School District 16 of Flint Township in 1867, Hattie Southard agreed to teach the students of the primary school for the sixteen-week winter term at a salary of eighty-eight dollars. She agreed to enforce all rules and regulations established by the board. In turn, Alfred Gifford, school board director, agreed to keep the schoolhouse in repair and provide the fuel to heat it.

Courtesy: Allen Stross

In the towns, the first crude school facilities were replaced by larger, more elaborate buildings as the need increased. The architectural style of the Capitol Hill School in Marshall, built in 1860 at 602 Washington Street, reflected the Gothic architectural influence of the period. The building is still used by the Marshall school system, although for storage purposes, not classroom instruction.

The Union School in Niles was typical of the larger, two- or three-story school buildings that were erected in the last half of the century as the city schools expanded to include high school as well as the primary grades.

For the students of Room 3 of the Grandville Avenue School in Grand Rapids, with tiny American flags clutched in their hands, and for their teacher, too, having the class picture taken on the school steps was apparently a solemn occasion. For some of the children, a photographer seems to have been a person who was regarded with suspicion.

Courtesy: Michigan Historical Collections

Courtesy: Michigan Historical Collections

But in the last half of the nineteenth century and on into the twentieth, the tiny one-room country schoolhouse remained the most common school building in Michigan.

The University of Michigania which was to have been established in Detroit under the act of 1817 died before it really got started. In 1837, the state legislature provided for a new University of Michigan and located it in Ann Arbor on forty acres of land which the Ann Arbor Land Company had donated free of charge. The company capitalized on the fact that the state university would be established in the town as a means of promoting the sale of a thousand village lots.

Courtesy: Michigan Historical Collections

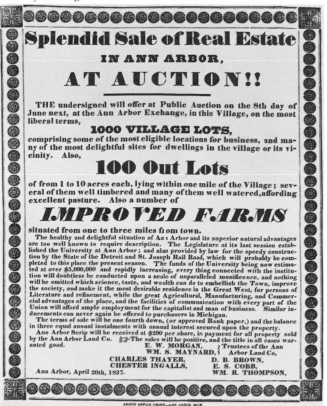

Courtesy: Grand Rapids Public Library

This was the interior of the Collins School, a one-room school located three miles east of Reeds Lake. For most of these children, the instruction they received would very likely be all the formal education they would get. Only a few would go on to high school in a neighboring school district and even fewer would go on to college.

The University of Michigan in Ann Arbor developed slowly in its early years. In the 1850's, however, under the leadership of its first president, Henry Philip Tappan, the university began to break out of the traditional classical curriculum and to offer programs in the sciences as well. For example, Tappan decided that the university should have an observatory for classes in astronomy. He raised money in Detroit for such a building, which was opened in 1854, the first observatory in the West and today one of the last structures surviving from this period in the university's history.

Courtesy: Michigan Historical Collections

211

From 1871 to 1909, James B. Angell was president of the university. These were the golden years when the school achieved recognition as one of the truly great universities in the nation.

Courtesy: Michigan Historical Collections

The State Street side of the original campus of the University of Michigan in the 1870's looked like this. Many of the trees have grown up with the school and still remain, but the buildings have disappeared.

These are members of the distinguished faculty that had been assembled by the 1870's. President Angell is seated third from the right.

Courtesy: Michigan Historical Collections

This is a group of the university's students during the same era—sober, well dressed, prepared to face the world.

Medical students tackle some cadavers in their anatomy class in the 1880's. The development of the medical school in the 1840's was one of the clearest indications that the University of Michigan intended to be a full-fledged university.

Important as its academic programs were, another aspect of the university would receive disproportionate attention in the years ahead—years that followed the appearance of the first intercollegiate football team in 1879—the future Champions of the West.

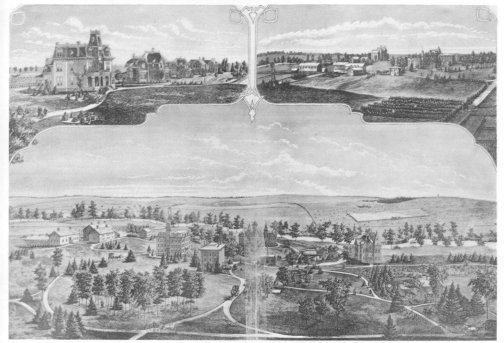

Meanwhile, east of Lansing, another state school was becoming well established. After a shaky start following its founding in 1855, Michigan Agricultural College, as this bird's-eye view in the 1879 Ingham County history indicates, had an extensive campus, with the school's farmlands to the rear providing room for the enormous expansion that would be needed in the following century as the school's enrollment went from a modest 264 in 1880 to more than forty thousand by the end of the 1960's.

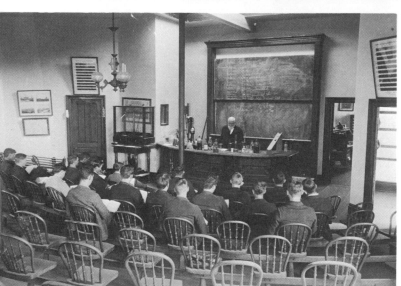

Professor Robert C. Kedzie, shown here in 1892 lecturing to his chemistry class, was one of the most influential Michigan State faculty members in persuading farmers to adopt more scientific agricultural methods and in other ways to improve their economic position. Kedzie and his colleagues thereby built up a backlog of good-will in the rural areas that would prove of inestimable value in securing the school the increased appropriations it would need as it advanced toward ultimate university status.

At Ypsilanti, Michigan Normal School was established by the legislature in 1849 to fill the need for more teachers. The school's library, shown here in 1894, would need to move into larger quarters twice within the next seventy years as the school's curriculum expanded and its student body greatly increased.

In addition to Michigan's burgeoning system of state-supported colleges and universities, there were scattered through the southern part of the state numerous private, denominational colleges, some of which would die, but most of which survived their initial growing pains. The oldest such college, the Baptist-supported Kalamazoo College, which opened its doors in 1836, began to earn an enviable reputation for excellence under the leadership of its principal, James A. B. Stone, and his wife, the talented educator Lucinda Hinsdale Stone, who headed the college's female department.

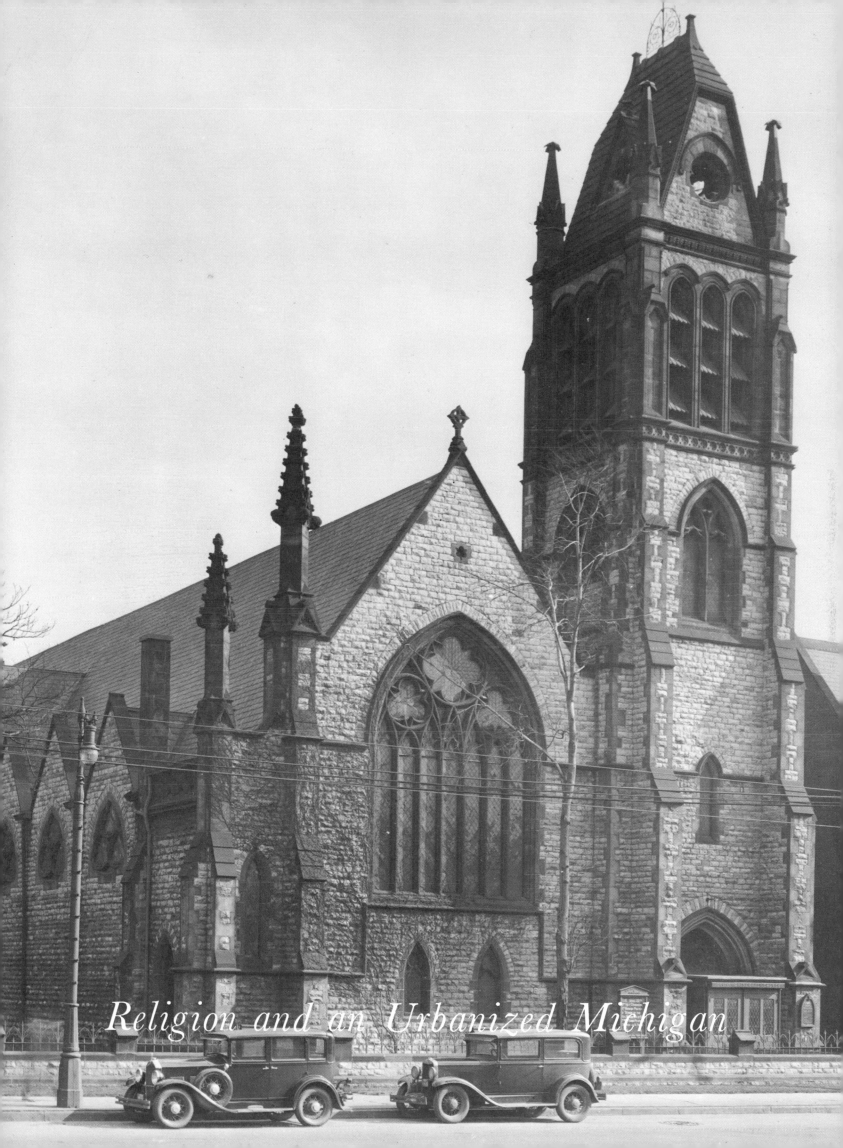

Religion and an Urbanized Michigan

Courtesy: Netherlands Museum

This was the campus of Hope College in Holland, Michigan, in 1876. Like almost all the state's private colleges, it was church-affiliated, but its particular affiliation demonstrates the greater diversity in the peoples and their churches that came to comprise the state's population as the nineteenth century wore along.

Hope College was founded by Dutch settlers who had come over from the Netherlands in the late 1840's, under the leadership of the revered church leader Albertus C. Van Raalte.

Van Raalte established a colony at the mouth of the Black River, near Lake Michigan, which was called Holland. It is shown here in a bird's-eye view dated 1875, only four years after the community was almost totally destroyed by fire. Holland and its neighboring Dutch settlements in west Michigan added to the state not only a new nationality group but also a new religious denomination, the Reformed Church.

Germans, virtually unknown in Michigan previously, began immigrating to the state in large numbers in the first half of the nineteenth century. Many settled in the cities where they added an important new dimension to the life of these communities. Typical of this influence was Harmonie Hall, which was built at Lafayette and Beaubien Streets in Detroit in 1874-75, to house the city's oldest musical organization which had been founded by German immigrants in 1849.

Other German immigrants came to Michigan to farm and settled in or near rural communities which almost invariably were oriented around a religious denomination. Most were either Catholic or Lutheran settlements, but in the case of the most unusual of all, the short-lived communitarian settlement of Ora et Labora in the Thumb, shown here in a painting of around 1860, the founders were German Methodists.

217

Courtesy: Rt. Rev. Msgr. J. Maksymowski

The imposing lines of St. Adalbert's Church, with its archangels blowing golden trumpets, are seen by the modern traveler driving through Grand Rapids on the I-196 expressway. The church typifies the increasingly cosmopolitan nature of Michigan's population in the latter years of the 1800's, for it was built by Polish immigrants who came at this time and became second only to the Dutch in the foreign-born population of Grand Rapids.

The devotion of many of Michigan's European immigrants to the Catholic faith served to strengthen the denomination which had been the only one in Michigan in the seventeenth and eighteenth centuries. In northern Michigan, Father (later Bishop) Frederic Baraga, himself an immigrant from eastern Europe, labored diligently in the middle decades of the nineteenth century among the Indians and the white settlers.

But the astonishing growth that took place in Michigan in a few decades is clearly shown in the character of the church buildings erected during these years. The new St. Ann's Church built between 1818 and 1820 was in itself a considerable advance over the first sanctuaries in which Detroit's original Catholic parish had met in the eighteenth century.

Courtesy: Bishop Baraga Association

Baraga built many churches, among which the Holy Redeemer Church in Eagle Harbor still stands and is still open for services in the summer months.

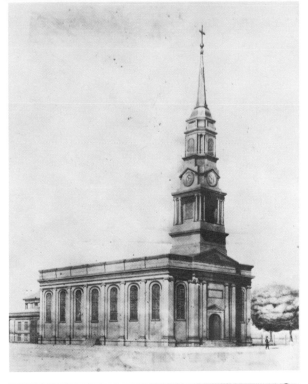

Courtesy: Historic American Buildings Survey

In the 1840's, Sts. Peter and Paul Cathedral was built at East Jefferson Avenue and St. Antoine's Street in Detroit. The tall spire called for on the original plan was not erected, but in other details the brick church, with its elaborate entrance, was a considerably more imposing edifice than the simple chapels in which Fathers Allouez, Marquette, and the other Catholic pioneers had introduced Christianity to Michigan only a century and a half earlier.

With the influx of Americans into Michigan in the nineteenth century, the Protestant denominations quickly passed the Catholic Church in members and in church buildings. In rural communities of southern Michigan these settlers sought to create the life they had known in the communities from which they had come. In Vermontville's Congregational Church (*above and left*), built in 1843, one could easily imagine that he was in a New England church, rather than in one located in central Michigan.

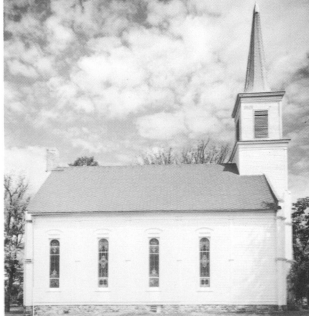

Courtesy: Allen Stross

The tiny rural sanctuary of the Sashabaw Presbyterian Church in Independence Township, Oakland County, was originally built in 1840 through the joint efforts of the Congregational and Presbyterian denominations, which pooled their resources in the initial missionary work in frontier settlements of the West. Ultimately, the members of these new churches, once they had gotten on their feet, decided with which denomination they wished to affiliate.

The Fort Street Presbyterian Church at Fort and Third Streets, Detroit, built in 1855, is impressive evidence of the degree to which this denomination was established in Michigan by that date—as well as being an example of the English influence on church architecture of this period. Although it was damaged severely by fire in 1876 and 1914, its appearance today is approximately what it was a century ago.

Similarly, the modest Greek Revival lines of the Dixboro Methodist Episcopal Church, built in 1858, and shown here in an old photograph but still standing today, . . .

. . . were a far cry from those of the First Methodist Episcopal Church of Kalamazoo, erected a few years later.

Courtesy: Michigan Historical Collections

Courtesy: Historical American Buildings Survey

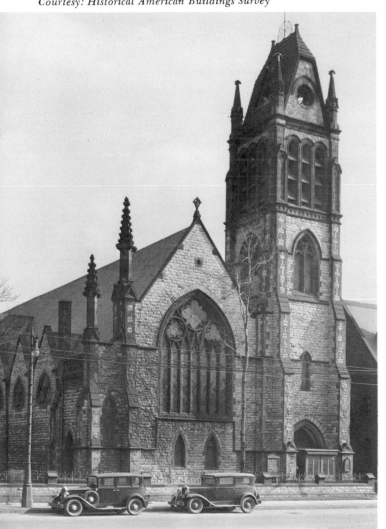

Nevertheless, while a Christ Episcopal Church, at 960 East Jefferson Avenue, Detroit, built in 1861-63, was needed by the large parishes of the cities, tiny church buildings, some of them, such as St. Katherine's Episcopal Chapel near Williamston, built in 1888, of equally distinguished architectural design, were still very much needed in the rural areas.

Courtesy: Allen Stross

221

Some of the most unique personalities in Michigan history represented the smaller denominations. Mrs. Caroline Bartlett Crane, who would become a leading urban reformer of the Progressive era, came to Michigan originally in the 1880's to serve as the minister of Kalamazoo's Unitarian Church.

Courtesy: Detroit News

Courtesy: Stanley L. Johnston

Courtesy: Henry Ford Museum

In mid-century, James J. Strang sought to establish his claim as the chosen successor to Joseph Smith as head of the Mormon Church. Strang founded a Mormon colony on Beaver Island which was achieving considerable success until Strang's assassination in 1856 resulted in the dispersal of his followers. It was Strang's espousal of the doctrine of polygamy and his assumption of the title of king, however, which won him his greatest notoriety with the public, inspiring the unknown artist of the 1850's who painted this highly imaginary scene showing King Strang and his wives indulging in the luxuries of life on Beaver Island.

Then there was Dr. John Harvey Kellogg, a lay member of the Seventh-day Adventist Church, who, as a young boy, had come with his parents to Battle Creek in the 1850's. Within a few years, the Adventists established their headquarters in Battle Creek. Young Kellogg went away to medical school and when he returned to Battle Creek in 1875 he took over the management of the Health Reform Institute which his denomination had established in 1866.

Courtesy: Burton Historical Collection

Dr. Kellogg renamed the institute the Battle Creek Sanitarium about the time this photograph was taken in the late 1870's. Here at the "San," which he headed for sixty-seven years, Dr. Kellogg became one of America's best-known medical figures. But it is not for this that he is remembered, important as his medical work was. The name Kellogg became world famous because of the special foods the doctor developed for his patients to make the dietary practices of the Adventist faith as palatable as possible. Dr. Kellogg's investigations proved to be the seed from which sprang a new industry which in turn would help to transform Battle Creek in the years ahead into a manufacturing city.

Courtesy: Michigan Historical Collections

Growth—this was the word of the day in the towns and cities of Michigan in the latter years of the nineteenth century. Under the influence of the industrial revolution that was changing the economy of the entire country, some Michigan communities advanced, while others remained stationary. Tecumseh and Battle Creek in mid-century were approximately of equal population. By the 1880's, Battle Creek's population had increased threefold or more, while Tecumseh's had remained about the same. The contrast between the two communities was strikingly revealed in their railroad stations. The Lake Shore Railroad Station in Tecumseh in 1885 was entirely adequate to handle the freight and passenger business of this community which served as a center for a rich farming area. In Battle Creek, on the other hand, a large new depot was built in 1887-88 to handle the increased business of the Michigan Central in that growing city.

The contrast between the street scene in Battle Creek in 1860 and that in Jackson only four decades later told a story of improved street paving, larger buildings and many more of them, new transportation facilities—all indicative again of a rapid growth in these urban areas.

Courtesy: Detroit News

Woodward Avenue, Detroit, in the 1890's presented a view that would have been startling enough to Judge Woodward, who had been dead for only seventy years, not to mention La Salle or Cadillac, whose statues looked down from the city hall which had been built in 1870-71. It was no accident that two of the statues on the city hall tower were supposed to represent commerce and industry since these were the forces that were pulling people to Detroit and expanding it from a city with a population of 20,000 in 1850 to a metropolis with one of a quarter of a million by the end of the century. The Majestic Building across the street from the city hall, an early approach to the skyscraper, provided office space for a few of the city's business activities. The tenants entered the building through revolving doors, the first used in Detroit, and they came to work on streetcars. Only one thing is missing—the automobile. Horse-drawn vehicles are still much in evidence, keeping the white-clad street cleaners busily occupied. Within a decade this would change. The automobile would be seen on every street and Detroit, as the center of the most important new industry of modern times, would be leading Michigan into the industrialized and urbanized world of the twentieth century.

226

The Indian community of Middle Village, near **Petoskey** . . .

. . . the mining and fishing town of Eagle Harbor in the Copper Country, . . .

... the farming community of Manchester, ...

... the little boy and his father riding in an ox cart—these were the symbols of an earlier day in Michigan's history, a day that was drawing to a close in the last years of the nineteenth century. The day of the fur trader, the pioneer farmer, the lumberman, the miner, and the fisherman was ended. The day of the factory worker, the white-collar employee, and the scientist was dawning.

Courtesy: Mrs. Otto Lee

228

INDEX

ACKNOWLEDGMENTS

In selecting illustrative material for this volume, I began with the pictorial collections of the Michigan Historical Commission Archives in Lansing. Although some of the items in these collections were acquired in the earlier years of the Commission's history since its establishment in 1913, it is only in the past decade and a half that a systematic effort has been made to build up these holdings. Under the direction of the present archivist, Dennis Bodem, and his predecessors during this period, Bruce Harding and Philip Mason, and especially through the continuing work during these years of Miss Geneva Kebler and Mrs. Elizabeth Rademacher of the Archives staff, a most extensive file of pictures and maps has been brought together. These have been organized in a logical fashion, greatly facilitating their use.

All illustrations in this book that are not accompanied by a credit line have, in general, been taken from the pictorial collections of the Archives. Many more of the illustrations were also in the Archives but they are credited to the sources from which the Archives originally obtained the picture. Since I also went to many of these same sources and obtained additional pictures which I have credited to these sources, it would be too confusing and not too rewarding to try to provide a complete list of all illustrations, no matter how credited, that have been reproduced from copies I found in the Archives. Suffice it to say that anyone interested in pictures relating to all aspects of Michigan history would be well advised to begin his search at the Michigan Historical Commission.

Important as the collections of the Archives were in my research, more than half of the illustrations in this book have been collected from other sources. It is a pleasure to express my gratitude to the following persons who, either as individuals or as employees of the organization, institution, or business that precedes their name, assisted me in assembling materials and information for this pictorial history.

American Antiquarian Society, Worcester, Massachusetts: Marcus A. McCorison.

Bacon Memorial Public Library, Wyandotte, Michigan: Mrs. Joseph C. DeWindt.

Bartlett, Herbert, Ann Arbor, Michigan, for advice on early maps.

Bay City *Times*: R. Neil Smith.

Burton Historical Collection, Detroit Public Library: James M. Babcock.

Chamber of Commerce of Greater Niles, Niles, Michigan: Justin F. McCarty, Jr.

Chicago Historical Society, Chicago, Illinois: Clement M. Silvestro.

Clarke Historical Library, Central Michigan University, Mount Pleasant, Michigan: John Cumming and Alexander Vittands.

College Sainte-Marie, Montreal, Canada: Paul Desjardins, S.J.

Cunningham, Wilbur M., Benton Harbor, Michigan, who supplied the illustration on page 30 which is credited to its original owner, Cecelia B. Buechner.

Davis, George, Grand Rapids, Michigan.

Dearborn Historical Museum, Dearborn, Michigan: Winfield H. Arneson.

Detroit Bank and Trust Company: Darwin D. Martin, Jr.

Detroit *News*: Ruth Braun and Ray O. Williams.

Field Museum of Natural History, Chicago, Illinois: E. Leland Webber.

Flayderman, N., & Company, New Milford, Connecticut: John Bachner.

Foehl, Harold M., Red Keg Press, Bay City, Michigan, who supplied the illustration used on pages 165 and 167 which is credited to its original owner, Mrs. Clover Gougeon.

Grand Rapids *Press*: David B. Osborne.

Grand Rapids Public Museum: W. D. Frankforter.

Hartford Public Library, Hartford, Michigan: Mrs. J. A. Dohrow.

Haynes, Virgil D., Harbor Springs, Michigan.

Henry Ford Museum, Dearborn, Michigan: John Still.

Kalamazoo *Gazette*: Jean Brink and Robert Maxwell.

Kalamazoo Public Museum: Alexis Praus.

Klima, Joseph, Jr., Detroit, Michigan, who is responsible for most of the photographic reproductions of materials from the Burton Historical Collection which are used in this book.

Lang, Henry C., Fayette, Michigan.

Lemmer, Victor F., Ironwood, Michigan, who, in addition to supplying the illustrations credited to him, also supplied the illustration on page 185 which is credited to the original owner, the Carnegie Library of Ironwood.

Lewis, Ferris E., Henry Ford Community College, Dearborn, Michigan.

Loughin, Mrs. Esther, Michigan State University, East Lansing, Michigan.

Mackinac Island State Park Commission, Lansing, Michigan: Eugene T. Petersen.

Maksymowski, Rt. Rev. Msgr., St. Adalbert's Church, Grand Rapids, Michigan.

Marquette University, Milwaukee, Wisconsin: Raphael N. Hamilton, S. J.

Mason, Philip P., Wayne State University, Detroit, Michigan, who supplied the two illustrations on page 58 which are credited to the original owner, the Buffalo Historical Society.

McCord Museum, McGill University, Montreal, Canada: Mrs. I. M. B. Dobell.

Michigan Department of Conservation, Lansing, Michigan: Russell McKee and Helen Wallin.

Michigan Department of State, Lansing, Michigan: James McClure.

Michigan Historical Collections, University of Michigan, Ann Arbor, Michigan: Robert M. Warner and the members of his staff, particularly Miss Ida Brown and Mrs. Janice Earle.

Michigan Historical Commission, Lansing, Michigan: in addition to those members of the Archives staff listed at the beginning of this section, the following past and present members of the Commission staff contributed in various ways to the success of the project: the former executive secretary, Lewis Beeson, and the present administrative head, Harry Kelsey, and also Donald Chaput, Jack T. Crosby, Jr., John B. Fortier, and Solan Weeks.

Michigan State Highway Department, Lansing, Michigan: Ed Boucher.

Michigan Tourist Council, Lansing, Michigan: William McGraw and John Maters.

Minnesota Historical Society, St. Paul, Minnesota: Eugene D. Becker and Russell Fridley, who, in addition to the illustrations credited to that organization, also supplied the illustration used as background for pages 2 and 3, and on pages 71 and 73, which is credited to the original owner, the Glenbow Foundation of Calgary, Canada.

Monroe County Historical Society, Monroe, Michigan: Mrs. Vincent Barker.

Netherlands Museum, Holland, Michigan: George Cook.

Pilling, Arnold R., Wayne State University, Detroit, Michigan.

Public Archives of Canada, Ottawa, Canada: W. I. Smith.

Quebec Provincial Archives, Quebec, Canada: Bernard Weilbrenner and Antonio Drolet.

Soini, Paul D., Bad Axe, Michigan, who supplied the illustrations on pages 62 and 175 which are credited to the original sources, the Detroit *News* and the Bay City *Times,* respectively.

State Historical Society of Wisconsin, Madison, Wisconsin: Raymond S. Sivesind and Paul Vanderbilt.

Steiner, Fred, Detroit Edison Company, Detroit, Michigan, who supplied, from the files of Detroit Edison, copies of five photographs on pages 143 and 144 which are credited to the original owner, the National Archives.

Stross, Allen, Detroit, Michigan.

Thorpe, Daniel, Wayne, Michigan.

Transportation Library, University of Michigan, Ann Arbor, Michigan: Robert T. Freese and Miss Sharon Hafeman.

University of Michigan General Library, Ann Arbor, Michigan: Mrs. Mary K. De Vries.

University of Michigan Museum of Anthropology, Ann Arbor, Michigan: James E. Fitting.

University of Michigan Photographic Services, Ann Arbor, Michigan: Fred Anderegg and Audie Herndon, who were always patient and prompt in handling the orders for photographic reproductions of so many of the items used in this book.

Wells, Joe E., Michigan Department of Agriculture, Lansing, Michigan.

Western Michigan University, Kalamazoo, Michigan: Willis F. Dunbar and Wayne C. Mann.

William L. Clements Library, University of Michigan, Ann Arbor, Michigan: Howard H. Peckham and Nathan Shipton.

PICTORIAL HISTORY
OF MICHIGAN

PICTORIAL HISTORY OF MICHIGAN:

The Later Years

To my wife and my grandson —
my sources of inspiration in good times and bad

CONTENTS

FOREWORD

When the project to publish a *Pictorial History of Michigan* was undertaken by the Michigan Historical Commission, only one volume was planned. Then, through the efforts of Dr. Philip Mason and, later, of Dr. George May, so many wonderful pictures were discovered that it was determined to expand the work to two volumes. This, the second of the two volumes, is largely devoted to a portrayal of life in Michigan in the twentieth century. Dr. May, formerly on the staff of the Michigan Historical Commission and now a professor of history at Eastern Michigan University, fortunately was willing to carry the project to completion. His wide knowledge of Michigan history and his discerning judgment are reflected in every page of these volumes.

The publication of this work was made possible through the John M. Munson Michigan History Fund, held by the Ann Arbor Trust Company and administered by the Michigan Historical Commission. Proceeds from this fund have been utilized by the Commission to publish F. Clever Bald's *Michigan in Four Centuries*, more than half a dozen pamphlets dealing with various phases of Michigan history, a like number of film strips, and several other publications. In 1969 publication of the four-volume "History of Education in Michigan" series was completed. The first volume, *The Michigan Record in Higher Education*, appeared in 1963. The second, third, and fourth volumes deal with elementary and secondary education. Through prudent management, a sizable balance remains in the John M. Munson Michigan History Fund, which enables the Commission to continue its program of publishing materials related to the history of Michigan and the history of education in the state.

Much has been accomplished in recent years, both by the Commission and by other agencies and individuals, to supplement the printed word in the presentation of Michigan history. The Consumers Power Company has produced a series of three excellent films depicting Michigan's development. These are available from the company for showing without cost. The Michigan Bell Telephone Company commissioned artist Robert Thom to execute a series of authentic paintings portraying different episodes in Michigan's past. These have been shown in many Michigan cities. Through the John M. Munson Michigan History Fund, reproductions of these paintings, suitable for framing, are available from the Michigan Historical Commission.

It is the hope of the Michigan Historical Commission that the two volumes of the *Pictorial History of Michigan* will find their way to the bookshelves of thousands of Michigan homes. Those who acquire them will find them exciting and fascinating, but they also have a lasting value. Children and grandchildren of the original purchasers will take them from the shelves in evenings or rainy days in the years ahead and will glean from their pages a better understanding of the growth of their state. What they will see in these pages may make them proud of their heritage and perhaps will inspire in them a determination to do their part in preserving the best of our heritage and enhancing it for future generations.

WILLIS DUNBAR, President 1968-69
Michigan Historical Commission

INTRODUCTION

The last years of the 1800's and the early years of the 1900's in Michigan marked not only the passing of the old century and the dawn of the new. They also served to divide the Michigan of an earlier era from the Michigan that recent generations have come to know. That earlier Michigan, which was very much a reality in the 1880's, had been one of the younger states in the Union. It was a land of opportunity, rich in resources, many still untapped. It was, because of its natural wealth, primarily a state of farming, lumbering, and mining activities.

Then in a few short years all this changed. The lumbermen, mindless of the needs of the future, stripped the state of most of its great virgin forests by the end of the nineteenth century and moved on to forest areas further west. During the same years, an awakening knowledge of the undeveloped farmlands of the Great Plains and new sources of iron ore in northern Minnesota and copper in Montana, Arizona, and other western states tended to make the agricultural and mineral resources of Michigan pale by comparison. By the turn of the century, Michigan was no longer the number-one source of copper and iron ore in the country, while the state's farmers were turning from their earlier concentration on wheat production to a variety of specialized products that would not compete with those of the big farm states of the West. Agriculture, mining, and lumbering would continue to be important sources of wealth for Michigan in the years ahead, but they alone would no longer be sufficient to provide for the needs of a growing state.

Michigan by the end of the nineteenth century, then, had long since ceased to be an area on the outskirts of settlement. The frontier had moved far to the west, leaving Michigan deep within the well-developed, heavily populated regions of the eastern United States. But at the same time this change spelled the decline of one type of

economy it ushered in a new one to take up the slack. As the center of the nation's population moved steadily westward, the nation's industrial facilities, which had been concentrated in the northeast, had to keep pace in order to produce a ready source of the manufactured goods this population needed. Thus it was that southern Michigan in the last half of the nineteenth century became an increasingly important manufacturing center, turning out stoves, railroad cars, carriages, furniture, drugs, shoes, and a host of other products for the populous states of the Middle West. Some of these plants were located in Michigan because of the availability of the materials required in the product's manufacture. Many others, however, developed simply because the market was there or, if it was not, it could be created.

Michigan's emergence in the twentieth century as a great industrial state was already foreshadowed by the work of these pioneering manufacturers of the nineteenth century. But it was not until the Detroit area, partly by accident, partly by dint of the hard work of a few individuals, became the center of the automobile industry that the twentieth century image of the Wolverine State was fixed. By 1910 the turning point had been reached. After this date the census began to show that a majority of the state's residents no longer lived in rural surroundings but in urban areas.

The trend toward increased urbanization continued almost without a break during the succeeding decades, paralleling the rise in industrial production. The percentage of people living in the rural areas and in the northern, largely nonindustrial, regions of the state became ever smaller, while the highly industrialized counties of southeastern Michigan became home for the overwhelming majority of the population — a population whose racial and national origins were now far more diversified as a result of the attraction of factory jobs that once again made Michigan the land of opportunity for those who sought it. It is with these later years of Michigan's history and the social and political changes that resulted from the changes in the state's economy that this second volume of the *Pictorial History of Michigan* is concerned.

In dealing with the earlier years of Michigan's history one faces a problem in finding enough contemporary illustrative material to depict that history adequately. This problem does not exist when the pictorial historian moves into the later years. The camera had then become a common household possession, and the historian is therefore threatened with a flood of photographs, by both amateur and professional cameramen, on most subjects in which he is interested.

I have made a determined effort, however, to go beyond the photographs in order, through a liberal selection of advertisements (how better can one show the rise of business and commercial enterprises than through these announcements of the wares they had to sell), front pages of newspapers, and other types of illustrative items, to add some of the same variety that maps, portraits, documents, and similar materials provided in the first volume. Likewise, I have continued to pay considerable attention, as I did in *The Early Years,* to the surviving buildings and other structures of the different eras in the belief that this will prove useful to those readers who wish to turn from these pages to an examination of the physical, three-dimensional objects that remain from those bygone times and thereby gain some insight into the aspirations and accomplishments of those who built and used them.

Again, as in the case of the first volume, it is a pleasure to acknowledge my debt to the people without whose help and cooperation this book could never have appeared. At the conclusion of this volume I attempt to list each individual and organization that has aided me in obtaining material. But at this point I would like to express my special appreciation to the Michigan Historical Commission and its staff for the assistance it continued to give on this volume as on the first, and for its sponsorship of this project through the fund it administers and which, appropriately enough, was established by the late president of the university where I now teach. My thanks also go to William B. Eerdmans, Jr., who once again took the initiative in launching this book to complete the pictorial history his firm had begun with the publication of the first volume in 1967. All teachers and students of Michigan's history owe a debt of gratitude to the Wm. B. Eerdmans Publishing Company for the increasing attention it has paid to the history of the state and region in which it is located and the growing list of books that have resulted from this interest. A word of special thanks goes again to the Eerdmans book designer, Cornelius ("Casey") Lambregtse, who once again has succeeded in putting all my material into a most beautiful and worthy companion to Volume I.

Above all, words cannot express my appreciation to my wife who, during the most hectic year of our life together, nevertheless found time to type the manuscript for this book and to spur me on to complete this project that began some four years ago when I first started to assemble the materials for what ultimately turned out to be a two-volume pictorial history of Michigan. If the response to this volume is half as good as that accorded the first, the time will have been well spent.

GEORGE S. MAY

Ypsilanti, Michigan

12

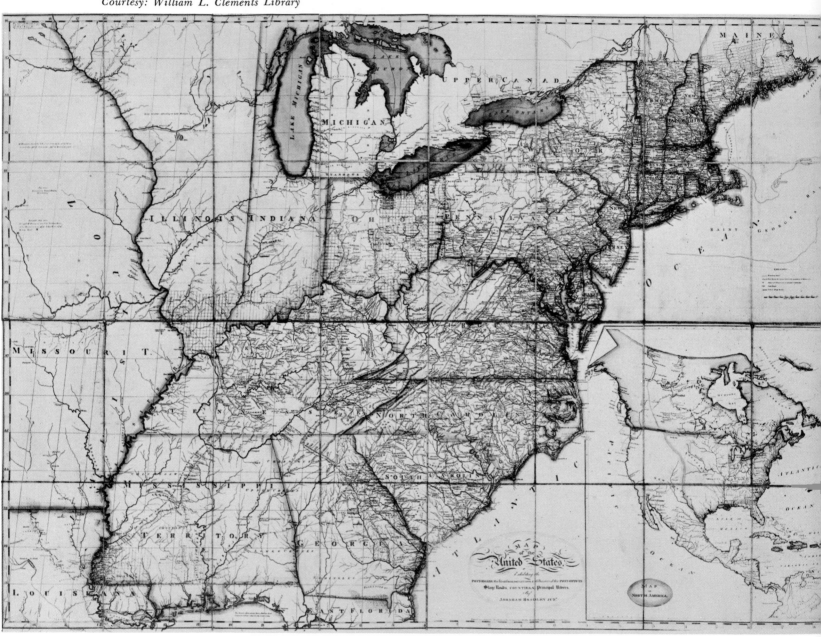

As the nineteenth century drew to a close, Michigan was a far different place than it had been at the start of the century when Abraham Bradley published one of the earliest maps showing the new Territory of Michigan, created in 1805. Then Michigan had been one of the most remote and least developed sections within the United States. Compared with areas to the east and south, where the profusion of lines and lettering evidenced the degree of development that had taken place, Michigan was virtually a blank spot on the map.

Courtesy: Michigan Historical Collections

By 1897, when this official map was published by the Commissioner of Railroads, Michigan was a state with a population of 2,400,000. An average of 400,000 new inhabitants had been absorbed during each of the past five decades. Settlers had fanned out from southern Michigan across the two great peninsulas, establishing new towns and counties as they went. This process seemed to have been completed by the 1890's. The last of Michigan's eighty-three counties, Dickinson, had been organized in 1891. No more would be created, but in the twentieth century, great changes in the distribution of population would result in the rise of many new towns and cities in the southern part of the lower peninsula and the decline and, in some instances, the disappearance of many of the settlements in the northern reaches of the state that are shown on this map.

Courtesy: Detroit News

More than one of every ten Michiganians in the 1890's lived in Detroit, which by 1900 would be the thirteenth largest city in the United States. Open-air streetcars, horse-drawn vehicles, bicycle riders, and pedestrians moving at what appears to have been a leisurely pace — this was the scene in downtown Detroit's Cadillac Square in 1902. The smoke that fills the sky beyond the domed county building was a clear indication of Detroit's importance as a manufacturing center even in this pre-automobile era.

Grand Rapids was a distant second among Michigan cities in 1900, with a population of 87,000 — 200,000 less than Detroit's. Behind Grand Rapids came a whole host of cities with populations ranging from a few thousand up to forty thousand. Lansing, the state capital, stood near the midpoint in this group. Here at the corner of Washington and Michigan Avenues, looking north, a great many of the commercial buildings that stood when this photograph was taken in the early 1900's continued in use as late as the 1960's. But the automobile turning the corner onto East Michigan was a harbinger of coming events that would dramatically alter the character of the city and many other southern Michigan communities in the next few years.

Courtesy: Michigan Historical Commission

At a time when such present-day products of the urban population explosion as Dearborn, Warren, Livonia, and Wyoming did not exist or had populations of only a few hundred, the still potent attraction of mining and lumbering enabled such northern Michigan cities as Negaunee, where the saloon was the first place to be shoveled out after a storm in March, 1899, and Cheboygan, in spite of its Siberialike appearance, to rank well up on the list of Michigan's larger cities.

But in the 1890's the majority of Michigan's residents were not city dwellers. At the end of the century, sixty-one percent of the people in the state lived on farms or in small towns with populations under 2,500.

Such a town was Constantine, whose 1,226 citizens made their living from their dealings with the farmers of the surrounding area of St. Joseph County.

The most familiar sight in Michigan was a quiet country dirt road running past the fields of the rich agricultural region of southern Michigan, such as these along the Holland to Grand Rapids road in Ottawa County. It was a scene that would undergo great change as the twentieth century progressed and a different image arose in the public's mind of the Wolverine State.

Courtesy: Michigan Historical Commission

In American history the last decade of the nineteenth century is known as the Gay Nineties. In a broader sense, these years marked the culmination of the Victorian era. Life in Michigan reflected the styles, the fashions, the customs, and the pastimes associated with those years. Throughout Michigan, particularly in the smaller towns, there are still many surviving examples of the great homes that come to mind when the term Victorian is mentioned. Such a one is this mansion in St. Clair, built in 1880 by William Hopkins.

Courtesy: Michigan Historical Commission

The interiors of these homes were as charmingly busy and cluttered in appearance as were the exteriors. This was the parlor of the home of Oliver Lyman Spaulding, a prominent Republican political figure from St. Johns. The picture was taken in 1889 and shows part of the dining room through the open door on the left.

Courtesy: Michigan Historical Collections

In the library of Donald M. Dickinson of Trenton, the high-ceilinged rooms, typical of the period, were used effectively to display pictures and other memorabilia collected by Dickinson during his distinguished career as a Democratic Party leader and Postmaster General in the cabinet of President Grover Cleveland, whose portrait can be spotted high on the wall at the right.

Courtesy: Michigan Historical Commission

One might have difficulty in moving swiftly through the living room in the Bay City home of lumberman James Shearer, but one could hardly have become bored for lack of things to look at along the way.

Courtesy: Michigan Historical Collections

Courtesy: Michigan Historical Commission

In such a living room — or was it the parlor? — two young women in St. Johns visited over a cup of tea in February, 1898. Their floor-length apparel, the profusion of pillows, rugs, and draperies, and the rather unappealing grouping of wall decorations — these, too, were a part of the Victorian way of life.

19

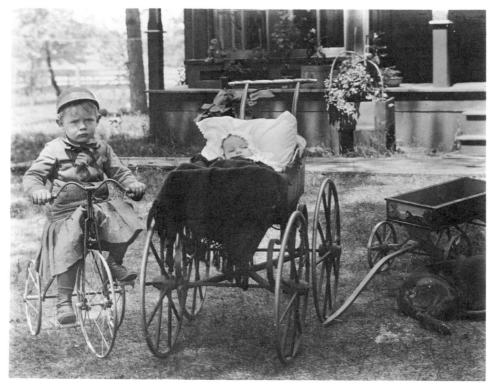

While the women gossiped indoors, the children amused themselves in a variety of ways, with a variety of playthings. The proud parents dressed them in their best clothes for these photographs, reproduced from the superb collection of glass negatives owned by Al Barnes, Traverse City newsman and historian.

"Laugh With Us To-Night," the banner reads, as a comic band gives a crowd in Cheboygan a sample of the fun that lies in store for those who plan to attend the evening's festivities. The Gay Nineties may not always have been gay, but in the period leisure activities were amazingly varied.

The cultural life of nearly every town was enriched by the services of an organization such as the Tipton Cornet Band, which posed in its colorful uniforms and gave ample proof that the musicians in a cornet band did not all play the cornet.

These are the members of the Coldwater Singing Society, a rather forbidding-looking group of men and women who performed for and, hopefully, entertained the citizens of their community around the turn of the century.

These young girls, grimly clutching their tambourines and cymbals — or are they pan lids? —, were part of a St. Johns organization in the 1890's which apparently gave evidence to an awakening interest in the dance as a form of expression.

On a different level, the annual May Festival, instituted at the University of Michigan in 1894, brought musical performers of the highest order to Ann Arbor. The audiences gathered in the auditorium of University Hall, long since demolished by the wrecker's hammer, to listen to the long-forgotten Boston Festival Orchestra.

No Michigan town felt itself worthy of the name unless it had at least one theater, which, in keeping with the extravagances of the day, was called an opera house. This is the interior of Steinberg's Opera House in Traverse City, where live dramatic and musical entertainments were presented at frequent intervals for many years.

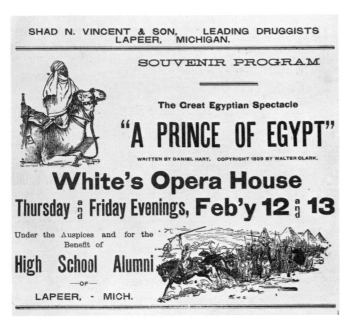

The majority of the performances in these local opera houses were of theatrical productions no more memorable than this one that played in Lapeer for the benefit of the high-school alumni. But the offerings on the whole were probably as distinguished as those presented by the new entertainment media of the twentieth century.

In one six-day period in 1904, the theatergoer from the Detroit area could see the great Maude Adams in James Barrie's sentimental comedy, "The Little Minister," and the almost equally renowned Richard Golden starring in one of the potboilers of the period. The Detroit Opera House, and some of the larger opera houses elsewhere in the state, offered a variety of entertainment to satisfy even the most discriminating person. If one did not care for what was playing at the moment, he had only to wait a day or two until the show changed.

The Detroit Opera House, shown here on the cover of one of its weekly program descriptions as it looked after the reconstruction that followed a fire in 1898, brought to that city a continuous series of performances of the most popular plays and musical shows, starring the great theatrical names of the day.

In 1896, the management of the Detroit Opera House installed Michigan's first motion-picture projector, to provide still more variety to its programs. Eventually, however, nearly all of the opera houses in the state, including the famous Kerredge Theatre in Hancock, became movie houses, and live entertainment became more and more of a rarity.

In the latter years of the nineteenth century, spectator sports began to become increasingly popular. In 1881, the Detroit Wolverines baseball team was admitted to the National League. The wealthy Detroit pharmaceutical manufacturer, Frederick Stearns, gained control of the team in 1885 and for $7,000 bought several of the greatest hitters of that era, including the immortal Dan Brouthers, second from the left in the top row. Two years later, in 1887, Detroit's awesome lineup of sluggers carried the team to the league championship and to victory over the St. Louis Browns in the World Series that fall. W. H. Watkins (in the business suit) was Detroit's manager, but Captain Ned Hanlon, seated with arms folded to the right of Watkins, and Catcher Charley Bennett, at the far left in the top row, were the real leaders of the team.

But the crowds that came to see the Wolverines play in Recreation Park at Brush and Brady Streets in Detroit were disappointing, even on July 4, 1887, and at the end of the 1888 season the Detroit franchise was sold and transferred elsewhere.

By the early years of the twentieth century, however, not only Detroit residents, but sports fans across the state were coming in great numbers to see Detroit's Tigers play the other teams in the new American League. Opening day became one of the major events of the year, although, as this view of a portion of the crowd at the 1912 opener indicates, interest in the sport was still confined to men only.

24

Nevertheless, even women and others who cared little about baseball could hardly be unaware of the stars of the sport, particularly Detroit's great Ty Cobb, shown here in 1909 sliding into third and driving his spikes into Philadelphia's "Home Run" Baker. With the exception of Henry Ford, one would be hard put to think of another individual connected with Michigan during the first three decades of the present century who was better known across the state and nation than Detroit's perennial batting champion.

Courtesy: Detroit News

Courtesy: Michigan Historical Collections

Although football had been played at the University of Michigan and other state schools in the later decades of the nineteenth century, it was not until young Fielding H. "Hurry-Up" Yost arrived in 1901, a football tucked under his arm, to coach the Michigan Wolverines that the university's national reputation in the sport was established.

On January 2, 1902, Yost's first Michigan squad, the famous "point-a-minute" team led by two-time All-American Halfback Willie Heston and Fullback Neil Snow, demolished Stanford, 49 to 0, in the first Rose Bowl game. The chagrined California sponsors did not schedule another football contest as part of the annual Tournament of Roses until 1916.

Weeks, Shorts, Snow, Heston, Herrnstein

TACKLE-BACK-RIGHT PLAY.

Courtesy: Michigan Historical Collections

25

Harper's Weekly, *March 12, 1892*

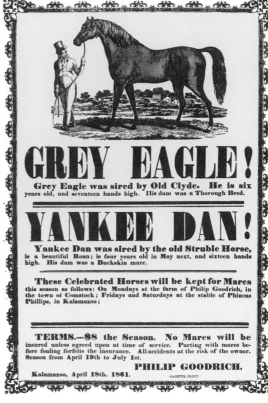

Courtesy: Michigan Historical Collections

A new sport that won adherents in northern Michigan gained prominence in 1888 when the first ski-jumping tournament ever held in Michigan was staged at Ishpeming. The jumps were short by later standards, but the tournament helped establish Ishpeming as the historic center of the sport in the United States and the future site of the National Ski Hall of Fame. Speaking of the sport of skiing in general, a correspondent for *Harper's Weekly* declared in the story that accompanied this picture that the beginner "will find the pastime exhilarating and fascinating, but decidedly dangerous."

One reason given for the failure of Detroit fans to support their championship baseball team of the 1880's was that they preferred the sport of horse racing — a sport that had a much longer history in Michigan. Kalamazoo was a major center for both the racing of horses and the breeding of these thoroughbreds.

In the 1870's East Saginaw had a trotting course that was considered one of the best in the land. Here on July 18, 1874, a large and excited crowd watched as Goldsmith Maid (left), the premier trotter of the day, defeated Judge Fullerton (right) in a special race in which Goldsmith Maid's average time for the three heats established a new record for the mile run.

Courtesy: Smithsonian Institution

Horse racing was a major attraction at the annual agricultural fairs. Here the artist, Frederick E. Cohen, depicts the secretary of the nation's first state fair, held at Detroit in 1849, announcing the premium awards for the exhibits that were presumably the reason for staging such an event. Through the window in the rear, however, can be seen the entertainment features of the fair, which soon overshadowed its more serious aspects.

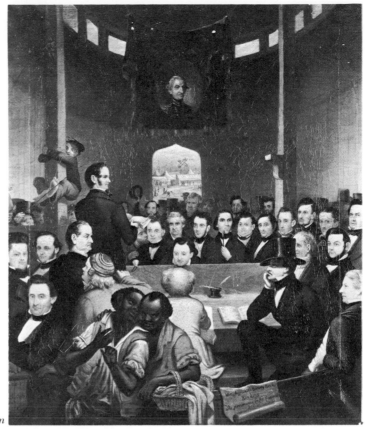

Courtesy: Burton Historical Collection

County fairs, such as that held at the Hillsdale County Fairgrounds, provided welcome relaxation each summer for the large majority of area people who could not attend the state fair.

History of Hillsdale County (1879)

Summer was also circus time, offering young and old an assortment of wonders, such as these on a midway of a circus that appeared in Detroit in 1898.

Courtesy: Burton Historical Collection

27

But while one had to pay to see Wallack, the lion tamer, perform his daring deeds, the circus parade that heralded the arrival of these attractions was free, and these boys had the thrill of seeing elephants walking, not on the sawdust under the big top, but on the brick pavement at the corner of Gratiot and Broadway in Detroit.

If this photograph of the parade of Forpaugh's Circus through downtown Kalamazoo in 1887 is fuzzy, so is the memory of more and more of the residents of Michigan who witnessed such an event, which was so typical of the life of that earlier age that it was out of place in the twentieth century and, before long, was not seen again.

Parades were a welcome feature also of the festivities on holidays and other special occasions. This fancifully decorated team of horses and the float which they pulled added color to Gladstone's Fourth of July parade in 1898, while the Pabst beer which was advertised and displayed denoted another aspect of the day's celebration of the nation's independence by this Upper Peninsula town.

HEAR YE! HEAR YE!

1776! Yᴱ Grande Centeniale 1876!

—AN EXACT COPIE OF—

Yᵉ Grande Philadelphia Exhibition!

——WILL BE GIVEN IN——

Yᴱ CITY OF FLINT,
——AT——

Yᴱ TOWNE HALL

Which is yᵉ same wherein yᵉ curious machines for squirting water upon yᵉ fires, are kept, upon

Yᵉ Night of Friday, yᵉ 9th day of June, Anno Domini, 1876.

Information of Yᵉ Goings on:

Yᵉ evening's diversion will comprise many strange and curious things not before seen in this towne. If so be yᵗ any person be kept at home from yᵉ Citye of Philadelphia by reason of corn planting, or peradventure by reason of not having sufficient of yᵉ world's filthy lucre, or any other cause, let him not grieve, for here he may see yᵉ same showe on a smaller scale for a smaller sum of money.

He Shall See:

1st. Yᵉ Gallerie of Art, containing pictures and graven images, unlike anything in yᵉ Heavens above or yᵉ earth beneath.

2d. Yᵉ exhibition of yᵉ products of all nations, under yᵉ direction of natives of far countries, wherein may be seen things rare and quaint, and many things yᵗ will fill ye observer with wonder and amaze.

3d. Yᵉ Womens' Pavilion, wherein many of yᵉ comliest maydens in yᵉ towne will gladden yᵉ eyes of yᵉ younge menne.

P. S. Parson Cordley, who knows how it is himself, will not object to yᵉ sparking on yᵉ part of yᵉ younge menne and maydens, provided it be done in a sober-minded, seemly way. Undue levity will be reproved by yᵉ Deacons and tithing menne.

4th. There will be quilted a fair, greate quilte, by some of the good wives, which will be made of yᵉ flags of alle nations, and will be sold to any one who may wish to keep it till the next Centenniale.

N. B. So be it that no one may hunger or thirst, there will be great store of food prepared of rare kinds, and some simple posset made of lemons and sugar, which shall not flye to yᵉ head; also, good sweet cream, frozen by yᵉ new fangled process. Yᵉ children can buy candy and oranges, and eat yᵉ same, if so be their parents will let them.

Ye younge menne may buy nosegays to give to their sweethearts.

Yᵉ moon shall shine all over yᵉ towne, for this occasion, at the time of going home—so no one need bring their lanthorn.

Yᵉ show will begin at dusk, after ye milking is alle done. Yᵗ will cost each one ten cents to get into yᵉ exhibition, and peradventure much more to get out.

Yᵉ moneys taken from yᵉ publick is to be devoted by yᵉ good wives and maydens to yᵉ purchase of a musickal organ for yᵉ Congregational Meeting House.

Printed at yᵉ Office of yᵉ Flint Globe Newspaper.

Courtesy: Michigan Historical Collections

The centennial of the signing of the Declaration of Independence was the occasion for extraordinary celebrations not only in Philadelphia but also in communities across the country, such as Flint, where the announcement of the events that would take place on June 9, 1876, was written in a tongue-in-cheek manner. But it was all for a good cause: "yᵉ purchase of a musickal organ for yᵉ Congregational Meeting House."

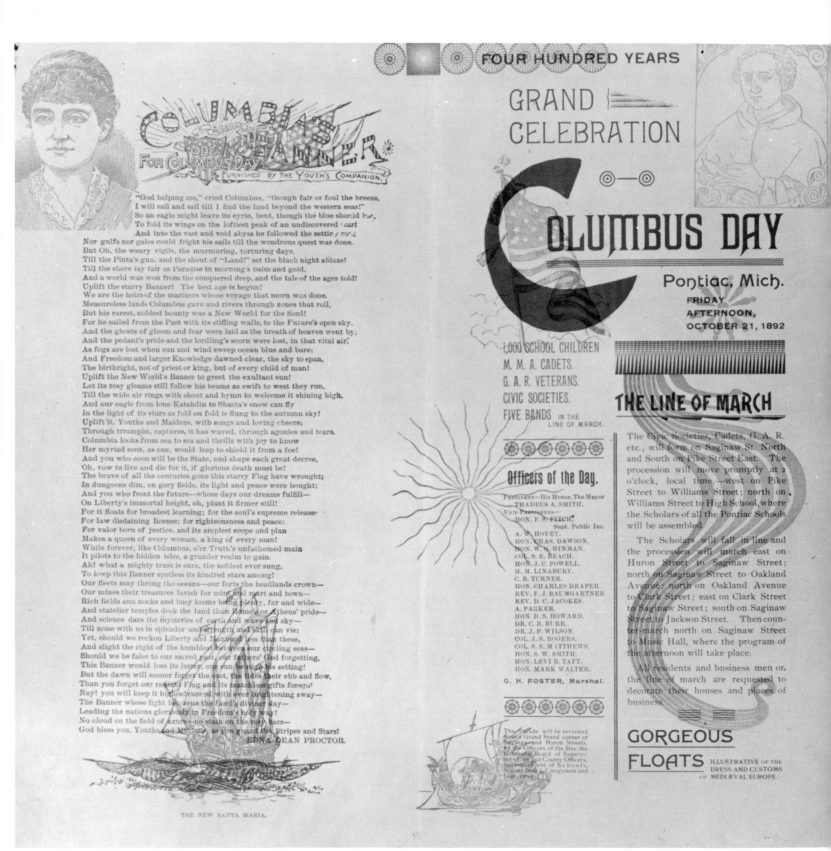

Courtesy: Michigan Historical Collections

Although the floats
may have been "gorgeous," the program
for Pontiac's observance
of the four-hundredth anniversary

EXERCISES

BY SCHOOLS

PROGRAM

1. Reading of President's Proclamation,
   By the Master of Ceremonies.
2. Raising of the Flag,
   By the Veterans.
3. Salute to the Flag and Song, "America,"
   By the Pupils.
4. Acknowledgment of God,
   Prayer.
5. Song of Columbus Day,

Air—"Lyons."

Columbia, my land! all hail the glad day
When first to thy strand Hope pointed the way;
Hail him who thro' darkness first followed the flame
That led where the Mayflower of Liberty came.

Dear Country, the star of the valiant and free!
Thy exiles afar are dreaming of thee,
No fields of the Earth so enchantingly shine,
No air breathes such incense, such music as thine.

Humanity's home! thy sheltering breast
Gives welcome and room to strangers oppress'd,
Pale children of Hunger and Hatred and Wrong
Find life in thy freedom and joy in thy song.

The fairest estate the lowly may hold,
Thy poor may grow great, thy feeble grow bold,
For worth is the watchword to noble degree,
And manhood is mighty where manhood is free.

O union of States and union of souls!
Thy promise awaits, thy future unfolds,
And earth from her twilight is hailing the sun
That rises where rulers and people are one.

THERON BROWN.

6. Address, "The Meaning of Four Centuries."
7. The Ode, "Columbia's Banner."
   A Reading of the Poem written for the occasion by Edna Dean Proctor
   [The poem appears on last page of this Program.]

THE PRESIDENT'S PROCLAMATION.

Now, therefore, I, Benjamin Harrison, president of the United States of America, in pursuance of the aforesaid joint resolution, do hereby appoint Friday, Oct. 21, 1892, the 400th anniversary of the discovery of America by Columbus, as a general holiday for the people the United States. On that day let the people, so far as possible cease from toil and devote themselves to such exercises as may best express honor to the discoverer and their appreciation of the great achievements of the completed centuries of American life.

In testimony whereof I have hereunto set my hand and caused the seal of the United States to be affixed.

Done at the city of Washington, this 21st day of July, in the year of our Lord one thousand eight hundred and ninety-two, and of the Independence of the United States the one hundred and seventeenth.

(signature)

EXERCISES

BY CITIZENS

PROGRAM

1. Music, By the Band.
2. Prayer, Rev. C. C. Miller.
3. Chorus, By Pupils of "A" Grammar School.
4. Reading of President's Proclamation, Mary Phelps.
5. Music, By The Schools—Mrs. Owen, Director.
6. Columbus Day Address, Parker Lyon.
7. Columbus Day Ode, Minnie Smith.
8. Music, By the Band.
9. Address—"The Historical Event," James H. Lynch.
10. Music, By the Schools—Mrs. Owen, Director.
11. Address.—"The American Public Schools,"
    Rev. W. S. Jerome.
12. Music, By the Band.
13. Tableau, "America," By Wm. Anderson.
14. Tableau,
15. Music,—"America," Audience and Schools.
Benediction, Rev. T. C. Pillsbury.

ARRANGEMENTS COMMITTEE

- COSTUMES
- FURNISHED BY
- A. BRUESSER & CO.,
- DETROIT.

47 MACOMB STREET.

DR. M. W. GRAY, Chairman.
HON. J. E. SAWYER, Secretary.
CHAS. A. NISBETT,
Representing the G. A. R.
O. L. BACKENSTOSE,
Representing the School Board.
REV. W. S. JEROME,
SUPT. FERRIS S. FITCH.
SUPT. F. E. CONVERSE.
J. S. STOCKWELL and
I. B. MERRITT,
Representing the Citizens.

Courtesy: Michigan Historical Collections

of the discovery
of America by Columbus indicates there
was to be little levity
in this "Grand Celebration."

Courtesy: Michigan Historical Commission

No special occasion was needed for those who wanted to pack a picnic lunch and enjoy an outing on a pleasant Michigan summer day, as these women may have been intending to do after they left the photographer's studio.

These young people were finding a variety of ways to amuse themselves while camping at Acme, on the shores of Grand Traverse Bay in the summer of 1894.

Courtesy: Michigan Historical Commission

These men, with their nineteenth-century version of a camping trailer, were enjoying a hunting and fishing vacation at Portage Lake, while another party of campers in northern Michigan secured photographic proof of the success of their hunting expedition.

These women were enjoying Michigan's most publicized recreation asset — the waters of the four Great Lakes that wash its two peninsulas and its innumerable inland lakes.

The attraction of Michigan's lakes was emphasized in a brochure issued by the Jackson, Lansing, and Saginaw Railroad Company in 1875, which sought to sell land which it owned by featuring this picture of sportsmen fishing the waters of Higgins Lake and shooting the waterfowl that frequented the area.

Rowing was popular, both as a pleasant form of relaxation, as in the case of this woman and four companions on the Detroit River in the 1890's, or as a competitive sport in which crews from clubs in various Michigan communities challenged crews from other parts of the country and Canada.

Excursion boats on the Grand River near Grand Ledge provided a welcome Sunday outing for residents of the area in a period when leisure time was a much more precious commodity to men who worked a ten-hour day, six days a week.

Grand Rapids & Indiana Railroad.

 1880 1881

Mackinac, Grand Rapids and Cincinnati

SHORT LINE.

THROUGH EXPRESS TRAINS DAILY BETWEEN

Cincinnati, Traverse City and Petoskey,

——LUXURIOUS——

COMBINATION SLEEPING AND CHAIR CARS AT LOW RATES
ATTENTIVE PORTERS IN CHARGE.

Steamer Connection During the Summer Season for

Mackinac, Marquette and other Points in the Lake Superior Iron Country.

THROUGH TICKETS and Baggage Checks to Prominent

SOUTHERN and EASTERN POINTS

——DIRECT CONNECTION AT——

FORT WAYNE with through Trains of the Great Pittsburgh, Fort
Wayne and Pennsylvania Railroads to PITTSBURGH, HAR-
RISBURG, WILLIAMSPORT, BALTIMORE, PHILA-
DELPHIA and NEW YORK.

The All Rail Line to the Great Methodist Park and Camp Ground at Petoskey

Summer Excursion Round Trip Tickets

*To MACKINAC, CHEBOYGAN, PETOSKEY, TRAVERSE CITY and POINTS in the
LAKE SUPERIOR IRON COUNTRY.*

FISHERMEN, SPORTSMEN, TOURISTS, see Summer Excursion Books of the
G. R. & I. R. R. for full information as to the unrivaled fishing and shooting facilities of Northern
Michigan. Enquire at Ticket Offices, or of

A. B. LEET, Gen'l Pass. Agent, GRAND RAPIDS, MICH.

Grand Rapids City Directory, 1880-81

John Bailey, Mackinac, Former Michilimackinac

In the latter part of the nineteenth century, northern Michigan was promoted as a prime vacation spot, not only for residents of the state, but also for tourists from outside Michigan who took advantage of the rail service to that area that now was offered. None of the railroad companies was more active in seeking such business than the Grand Rapids and Indiana, which was often referred to as the "Fishing Line."

For those who wanted to reach their northern Michigan resort by a more leisurely mode of travel, the Detroit and Cleveland Navigation Company and other Great Lakes steamship companies offered frequent service during the summer months.

Courtesy: Michigan Historical Commission

Of all northern Michigan resort areas, none was more popular than Mackinac Island, and with the construction in 1887 of the Grand Hotel by a group of railroad and steamship interests, the island had accommodations second to none among summer hotels in the Great Lakes region.

Courtesy: Michigan Historical Commission

This colorfully costumed group, part of the Trades Carnival held in Grand Ledge in 1891, illustrates another aspect of the life of the times — the different kinds of business activities that served the needs of the growing towns and cities in Michigan and the residents of the surrounding rural areas.

The most popular store was no doubt the grocery store, which, like today's supermarkets, might sell many items besides groceries. These Marshall grocers advertised gloves and mittens in bolder type than any of their "choice family groceries."

Marshall City Directory, 1885-86

Donavan's Store in Petoskey, shown here around 1880, had a friendly atmosphere, with its round stove in the rear, its bushel baskets of vegetables out in the center of the store, and its glass cases containing cigars on one side, candy on the other. This was no modern serve-yourself store. Frank Donavan stood behind the huge coffee mill, ready to grind your coffee for you or to get whatever canned goods you wanted from the shelves that lined the walls.

Courtesy: Michigan Historical Commission

There was nothing fancy about Henry Kebler's shoe store in North Lansing (the older section of the state capital), and the customer might have to sit on the padded bench in the foreground, but Henry did not have to move very far to find the style and size of shoe that was desired.

The larger and more elaborate department store was beginning to appear, however. Steketee's Wholesale Store moved into this new building on Fountain Street in Grand Rapids in 1885. The building is still being used today by the greatly expanded firm that operates under the famous Steketee name.

Courtesy: Michigan Historical Commission

Courtesy: Michigan Historical Commission

This was the horse-and-buggy era when shoppers or diners in Detroit parked their horse-drawn rigs at the curb, while they went into the drugstore or the restaurant.

Courtesy: Michigan Historical Commission

Courtesy: Michigan Historical Commission

Mr. and Mrs. Alison L. Bryant of Mayville posed in their fringe-covered carriage on a country knoll, but ownership of one or more horses and buggies was commonplace among city residents as well as rural families.

This was a time when a Detroit company described itself in national advertisements as the "largest manufacturers of fine Harness in America."

For those who did not own a carriage or needed something special, the local livery stable stood ready to rent a variety of kinds of conveyances for both happy and sad occasions.

Wright's Directory of Ironwood, *1893-94*

It was also a time when the J. Allen Gray Company at Cass and Adams Avenues, and several other companies with like products, attracted considerable attention to Detroit as a center for the manufacturing of vehicles of the horse-drawn variety.

Courtesy: Burton Historical Collection

But the times were changing. New services introduced in the late nineteenth century were adding to the comforts of life. Rural free delivery, first offered in Michigan in 1896 to the rural inhabitants around Climax, reduced the isolation of those who lived in the country. The rural mail carrier, in his horse-drawn wagon, shown here on his way out of Battle Creek to cover his rural route, soon appeared throughout the state.

Courtesy: Michigan Historical Commission

Courtesy: Michigan Bell Telephone Company

The telephone was introduced on an experimental basis in Detroit, Grand Rapids, Houghton, and several other communities in 1877, just a year after the new device had been displayed at the Centennial Exposition in Philadelphia. In September, 1878, the state's first telephone directory appeared, listing the 124 customers in Detroit who had subscribed to the services of Michigan's first commercial company offering the "speaking telephone." By the time this unique float appeared in a Battle Creek parade in 1899, this new means of communication was an indispensable part of the lives of an ever-growing circle of Michigan residents. (The Michigan Telephone Company was a predecessor of the Michigan Bell Telephone Company.)

39

The water tower in Ypsilanti, a fantastic structure that must rank as one of Michigan's most unique and familiar landmarks, was completed in 1890, signaling the establishment of a city water system and the introduction of indoor plumbing to those residents of that city who wanted it. (In the foreground is a bust of Demetrius Ypsilanti, hero of the Greek War of Independence, after whom this Michigan city was named.) Such conveniences now became the norm for city residents, helping to set them apart from the state's less fortunate rural families.

The poles might be somewhat bowed, but the men on them and their equipment, and the name painted on the wagon, clearly indicate the dawn of the age of electricity. By the 1890's, firms such as Detroit's Edison Illuminating Company were stringing their lines above Michigan's streets and providing power not only to businesses but to more and more private residences as well.

By the end of the nineteenth century Michigan was spanned by a network of over eight thousand miles of railroad lines, linking all sections of the state. Thirty railroad companies operated in the state, bearing such romantic names as the Duluth, South Shore, & Atlantic, one of whose trains is seen here pulling into a station in the Copper Country.

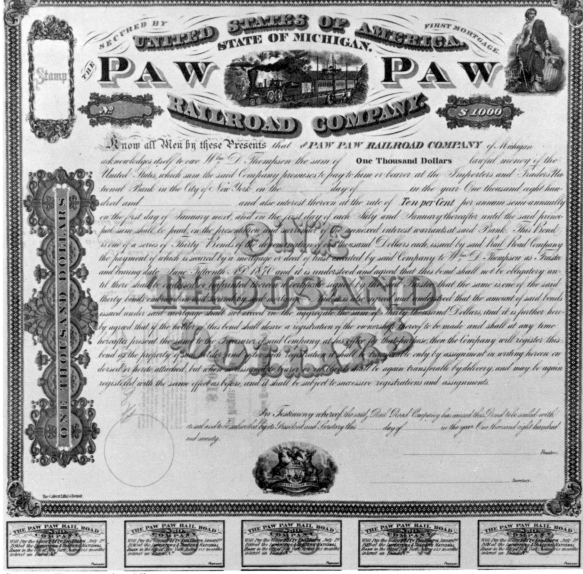

Courtesy: Transportation Library

Other companies had come and gone by this time, leaving little behind but beautifully engraved bond or stock certificates.

Courtesy: Transportation Library

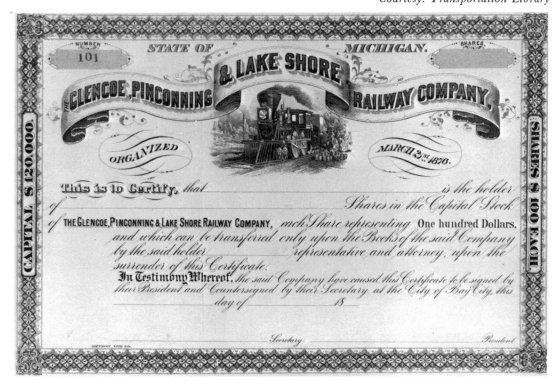

To residents of such tiny communities as Bruce Crossing in the western part of the Upper Peninsula, the railroad was the most tangible tie with the rest of the world. On the wooden platform at the station a number of people, young and old, always gathered as the train's arrival neared. Some carried coats and bags as they prepared to take a trip. Others were there just because they liked to watch trains.

Courtesy: Michigan Historical Commission

Courtesy: Michigan Historical Collections

Courtesy:
Michigan Historical Collections

In the nineties, the interurban, an outgrowth of the street railway lines that had appeared in Detroit and Grand Rapids in the 1860's, began to connect neighboring communities, offering frequent and cheap service for these short trips. The first of these ran between Ann Arbor and Ypsilanti, beginning in 1891 with a steam-powered train and then in 1896 converting to electric cars. These lines, which soon crisscrossed over much of southern Michigan, accustomed people to the idea of commuting to a job in one town while continuing to reside in another. The development of other modes of transportation in the twentieth century would accomplish the same purpose and with less inconvenience for the individual, resulting in the early demise of the interurban.

For a time in the last years of the century, it appeared that the new mode of transportation of the future would be the bicycle, although some may have doubted if the high-wheel ordinary would be the style that would prevail.

As the popularity of the bicycle caught on, riding enthusiasts formed clubs, as did these men in Calumet in 1886.

To the passengers in these carriages on East Michigan Avenue in Lansing, it must have seemed as though cyclists were taking over the world. The occasion was no doubt a special one which had attracted this many riders. In any event, the bicycle craze died out in a very short time, leaving the horse-and-buggy still the king.

43

Courtesy: Michigan Historical Commission

But people, not bicycles, interurbans, telephones, and wagons, are the important ingredients of history. This grandmother and her daughter and granddaughter in the kitchen of their home in the tiny rural community of Maple Rapids — how were their lives being affected by the innovations of the nineties, and what would happen to them as a result of the far greater changes that lay in the future? These were the important questions as Michigan passed into the twentieth century.

Politics and the Spanish-American War

Grand Review
~ DAY! ~

The REPUBLICANS of LIVINGSTON COUNTY will for[m]
their last

GRAND PROCESSION!

of this Campaign, on the STREETS OF HOWELL, on

SATURDAY, OCTOBER 30th, 188[0]

and then leave the Verdict with the People.

THIS MAMMOTH
MASS MEETING

will be the **GRANDEST POLITICAL DEMONSTRATION** eve[r]
witnessed in Livingston County, and "don,t you forget it,"

SIX BRASS BANDS

The *ASSEMBLED THOUSANDS* will be addressed by the most talent[ed]
men of the land. Behold the Eminent Orators that are to appear
and address you:

GEN. JASPER A. PACKAR[D]

of INDIANA; fresh from the field of battle, and inspired with
Republican Victory, he will tell the people why

☞ 20,000 DEMOCRATS ☜

in Indiana joined the Republicans of that State, and said that a graspi[ng]
"Solid South" shall now be confronted by an unbroken Loyal North.

GEN. O. L. SPAULDING

the popular Nominee for Congress in this District, will be present
and address the people.

COL. O. T. BEARD

the Eloquent Orator of Detroit, is also among the Distinguished
Speakers of the day.

HON. W. M. KILPATRICK

Nominee for State Senator, and one of the best speakers and finest
men in Michigan, will be heard from by his constituency.

HON. JAS. A. PARKINSON

of JACKSON, one of the most Original Speakers on the Michigan
stump, will be here.

Other Prominent Men from abroad will grace the occasion with their presenc[e]

The Speaking will continue through the Afternoon and Evening, an[d]
Booming of Cannon, Music by Cornet and Marshal Bands, display of F[ire]
Works, etc. etc. ☞ The different Towns of the County are expected to [be]
present, with several decorated 4-horse teams, accompanied with Banner[s]
Flags, etc.

SHERIFF BEURMANN,
Chief Marshal of the Da[y]

☞ Turn out, and give Your Country one full day. A "Solid South["]
must be confronted by the Loyal North.

The Republican Party in Michigan was stronger in the dying years of the nineteenth century than it had been for a quarter of a century. After the halcyon days of the Civil War and the reconstruction when its principal candidates had rolled up impressive majorities, the GOP frequently had to appeal to old wartime emotions, as was the case in this Republican rally held at Howell in 1880. Fifteen years after the war had ended, speakers designated by their wartime military rank, although they had long since resumed their civilian careers, spoke of the "Loyal North" standing firm against "a grasping 'Solid South.'"

The Republican tactic of "waving the bloody shirt" failed to work only in 1882, when the Democrats combined with the Greenback Party to elect the luxuriantly bearded Josiah W. Begole of Flint to the governorship, and in 1890, when a split in Republican ranks enabled the Democratic gubernatorial candidate Edwin B. Winans, a Livingston County farmer, to be elected. Winans was the only Democrat to serve as Michigan's chief executive between 1854 and 1913.

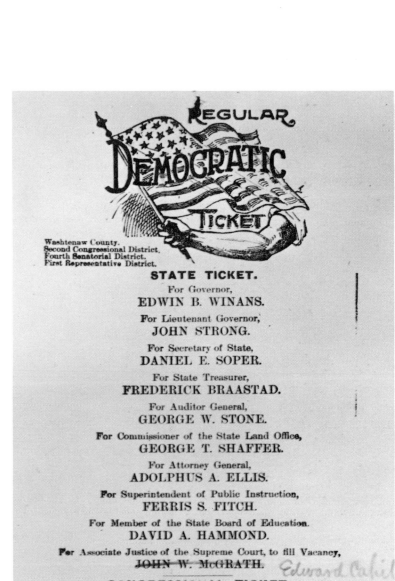

REGULAR

DEMOCRATIC TICKET

Washtenaw County.
Second Congressional District.
Fourth Senatorial District.
First Representative District.

STATE TICKET.

For Governor,
EDWIN B. WINANS.

For Lieutenant Governor,
JOHN STRONG.

For Secretary of State,
DANIEL E. SOPER.

For State Treasurer,
FREDERICK BRAASTAD.

For Auditor General,
GEORGE W. STONE.

For Commissioner of the State Land Office,
GEORGE T. SHAFFER.

For Attorney General,
ADOLPHUS A. ELLIS.

For Superintendent of Public Instruction,
FERRIS S. FITCH.

For Member of the State Board of Education.
DAVID A. HAMMOND.

For Associate Justice of the Supreme Court, to fill Vacancy,
~~JOHN W. McGRATH.~~ *Edward Cahil*

CONGRESSIONAL TICKET.

For Representative in Congress, Second District.
JAMES S. GORMAN.

LEGISLATIVE TICKET.

For Senator in State Legislature, Fourth District.
AUGUSTUS C. McCORMICK.

For Representative in State Legislature, First District,
JOHN V. N. GREGORY.

COUNTY TICKET.

For Sheriff,
CHARLES DWYER.

For County Clerk,
~~ARTHUR BROWN.~~ *Wm. G. Dieterle*

For County Treasurer,
GUSTAVE BREHM.

For Register of Deeds.
MICHAEL SEERY.

For Prosecuting Attorney,
~~MICHAEL J. LEHMAN.~~ *A. F. Freeman*

For Circuit Court Commissioners,
PATRICK McKERNAN.
FRANK JOSLYN.

For Surveyor,
CHARLES S. WOODWARD.

For Coroners,
MARTIN CLARK.
EDWARD BATWELL.

Printed by Authority: Gilbert R. Osmun, Secretary of State.

The boss of the Michigan Republicans was James McMillan, a wealthy Detroit businessman, under whose direction the leadership of the party came to resemble an exclusive millionaires club. Elected United States senator in 1889 by the Republican-dominated state legislature, McMillan was able to retain a firm hand on the controls of his machine from Washington and effectively block any actions that would endanger his economic interests.

Courtesy: Detroit News

Courtesy: Michigan Historical Commission

The most serious challenge to McMillan's control came from Hazen S. Pingree, a highly successful Detroit shoe manufacturer, who in the 1890's gave Michigan a preview of the maverick political reformer who would become more common a few years later during the Progressive Period. As mayor of Detroit from 1889 to 1897, Pingree vigorously battled the corrupt influences that permeated many city departments, fought the utility and streetcar companies in an effort to get them to lower their rates, and, during the depression of 1893 and 1894, sought to relieve the suffering of the unemployed by turning over to them vacant land in the city on which they could plant gardens. Pingree's potato patches, which he is shown inspecting, helped to win him enormous popularity with the voters, while his other actions won him the enmity of those with a vested interest in the status quo.

In 1896, the Democratic Party, hoping to capitalize on the discontent that had arisen in some quarters as a result of the depression, nominated a vigorous young candidate for President, William Jennings Bryan, who, as the spokesman for the Silver Democrats, advocated certain inflationary fiscal policies as a means of restoring prosperity. Supporters of Bryan in Michigan made a brave showing. The faithful gathered at rallies, such as this one at Jail Hill in Traverse City, with banners that proclaimed: "Bryan is the poor man's friend."

Courtesy: Michigan Historical Commission

Courtesy: Burton Historical Collection

Not all Michigan Democrats, however, supported Bryan, since a significant minority was opposed to the policies he advocated. In its July 12 issue, the Detroit *Free Press*, which had been the leading spokesman for the Democrats in Michigan since the paper's founding in 1831, issued this "Declaration of Independence." The editor stated: "For ourselves we have no hesitation in declaring that The Free Press will stand by its convictions, and will not indorse the Chicago platform or candidates." The earlier close ties between Detroit's famous morning paper and the Democratic Party were only occasionally reestablished thereafter.

The more numerous Republicans overcame the oratorical eloquence of William Jennings Bryan. Here at Leslie, members of the First Voters Republican Club wait at the railroad station for the arrival of ex-governor Russell Alger and other Republican leaders who would address a rally in that Ingham County town on behalf of the Republican presidential candidate, William McKinley, and the party's candidate for governor, Hazen Pingree. Arthur J. Tuttle, on the right in the front, wearing his father's silk wedding hat, would later serve as federal judge for the Eastern District of Michigan.

In Coldwater, a McKinley rally included an elaborate arch over the main street, replete with party slogans and a large bandstand on top.

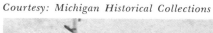

Courtesy: Michigan Historical Collections

Such efforts were probably not necessary to assure the party of the victory which was gleefully reported by such staunch Republican papers as the Adrian *Times and Expositor* of November 4, 1896. Pingree was elected governor by a majority substantially greater than that given to McKinley.

Pingree's shoe company, which was reportedly the largest firm of its type west of the Appalachians, soon capitalized on the chief's political triumph by adopting the title of his new office as the trade name for one of its shoes for men.

Scribner's Magazine, *Vol. 26 (1899)*

Courtesy: Michigan Historical Collections

During Governor Pingree's second year in office, the United States was involved in its "splendid little war" with Spain, which arose over Spanish administration of its colony in Cuba. In response to President McKinley's call for 125,000 volunteers, Pingree on April 24, 1898, ordered up the Michigan National Guard. Two days later, a great mass of humanity assembled in Campau Square in Grand Rapids to bid farewell as the Grand Rapids Battalion marched off to war.

At Island Lake, just east of Brighton, Michigan's Spanish-American War infantry regiments assembled to train, under the watchful eye of Governor Pingree. Among the members of Pingree's staff who posed with him for their picture was a future two-term governor, Fred W. Green, seated second from the left. The numbering of Michigan's regiments started at thirty-one, taking up where the state's Civil War infantry regimental numbers ended. Only the Thirty-third and Thirty-fourth Regiments saw action in Cuba before the brief war ended. *(See also the two top pictures on page 53.)*

Courtesy: Detroit News

Courtesy: Clarke Historical Library

Courtesy: Clarke Historical Library

Meanwhile, another Michigan Civil War veteran, former Governor Russell A. Alger, was serving as secretary of war in McKinley's cabinet. An artist sketched Alger, on the left, conferring with two men who were offering their services to the government. Alger would later be blamed, unjustly it now seems, for some incredible blunders by the army in supplying the men in the Caribbean with winter uniforms and rotten beef. The wealthy Detroiter's political influence in Michigan was not seriously harmed, for in 1902 he was elected to the United States Senate.

Commanding the American invasion of Cuba was Major General William Rufus Shafter of Galesburg, who had won a Congressional Medal of Honor for service as a Michigan officer in the Civil War and then had continued on in the regular army after the war. Now an obese sixty-three years old, Shafter, shown here directing the embarkation of troops to Cuba from Tampa, Florida, performed creditably but without the recognition given to other, younger and more glamorous, officers.

Harper's Weekly, July 2, 1898

Harper's Weekly, May 28, 1898

Pingree's career, meanwhile, which included a second term as governor in the two years following the war, was cut short by death when he was on a tour abroad in 1901. Citizens of Michigan raised $25,000 for a bronze statue which was erected in Grand Circus Park in downtown Detroit in 1903 to honor the memory of a political figure who, even when sitting down, towers above the run-of-the-mill, colorless figures who too often have held Michigan's top elective office.

Sixty years after the Spanish-American War, on May 15, 1958, a few surviving Michigan veterans returned to Island Lake, now a popular state park, for the dedication of a state historical marker honoring them and their departed comrades. Raised in Michigan in the nineteenth century, these men had lived through over half the twentieth century and had witnessed changes they could hardly have dreamed of in their wildest youthful imaginings. To the young people of the Brighton High School Band who performed at the dedication, these changes aroused no wonder at all. They had never known a world that was any different.

54

Michigan Becomes Industrialized

Frank J. Hecker was among the men from Michigan who served in the Spanish-American War. The fact that he was appointed chief of the army's division of transportation indicates that he was a man of some stature in civilian life.

The Detroit home to which he returned at war's end left no doubt of that. Hecker's mansion at 5510 Woodward Avenue, today occupied by the Smiley Brothers Music Company, had been built in the early 1890's. The architects were influenced by the French Renaissance style, and the château they designed was replete with towers and carved ornamentation on the limestone exterior...

...and lavish details throughout the interior—as shown in these contemporary photographs taken apparently soon after the residence was completed. The structure was a magnificent testimonial to the money that was being made by the state's industrialists in the last years of the nineteenth century—years in which the numbers of such men were rapidly becoming legion. By 1900, one out of every four gainfully employed individuals in the state held factory or manufacturing jobs, compared with less than one in a hundred in 1850. The railroad car company Hecker headed employed thousands of men and was but one of many major manufacturing establishments located in Michigan at the dawn of the twentieth century.

57

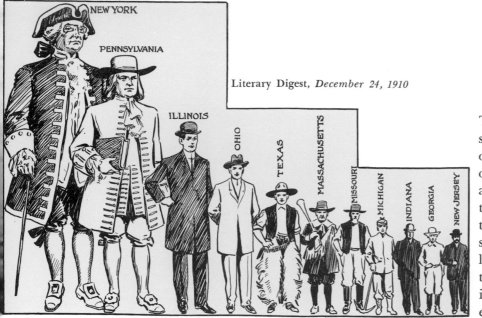

Literary Digest, *December 24, 1910*

The nation's older image of Michigan as a source of raw materials, not as a processor of them into manufactured items, lingered on well into the present century. In this attempt in 1910 to illustrate pictorially the relative size of the states according to the census of that year, it is notable that the symbol chosen to represent the eighth largest state was a miner, despite the fact that such workers were now far surpassed in numbers and in their impact on Michigan's economy by the state's factory employees.

Courtesy: Michigan Historical Commission

Much of Michigan's industrial development was a logical outgrowth of the exploitation of the state's rich natural resources. The older, extractive, type of economy, in fact, continued to play a major part in the state's economy along with the newer processing activities. Farming in the twentieth century was far different from what it had been in the pioneer period only a few decades earlier. Although horse-drawn and gasoline-powered farm vehicles existed side by side for some years, the introduction of the truck and other motorized equipment ultimately made the horse as a work animal a thing of the past on the farm.

Courtesy: Michigan Historical Commission

Farm machinery, such as this hay baler, contributed to the rising costs of farm operations while they reduced the need for the large force of farm workers that previously had been needed to perform the tasks now efficiently handled by machines. The trend in the twentieth century was toward fewer and larger farms, as the small farmer found it ever more difficult to break even.

Grain elevators, such as those of the Saginaw Grain Company, stored the agricultural products for which Michigan had once been chiefly noted and which in the twentieth century still were a bulwark of the state's agricultural prosperity.

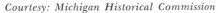

The greater diversity that has come to characterize Michigan farm products is typified by this poultry farm near Alma and a dairy herd on a Shiawassee County farm. The market for dairy and poultry products developed hand in hand with the increased urbanization of southern Michigan, for as cities grew in size, it soon was no longer possible for families to own a cow and a few chickens, as many residents of towns and villages in an earlier age had been able to do.

59

Courtesy: Michigan Historical Commission

Courtesy: Burton Historical Collection

Some of Michigan's most famous business firms at the turn of the century were agriculturally oriented. Dexter M. Ferry of Detroit had made a fortune from the firm he had helped to found in 1856. After 1867 this firm bore his name and by the 1870's it was reportedly the largest seed house in the world.

In addition to hundreds of workers whom Ferry employed in his huge Detroit warehouse, many more laborers, both men and women, worked as field hands on the seed farm the company established in 1891. This photograph, dating from that period, is not an illustration of peasants in eastern Europe from a school geography book, but was taken on the Ferry Seed Company's farm outside Detroit where pedigreed seed stocks were developed.

Courtesy: Michigan Historical Commission

Harper's Weekly, *March 2, 1901*

Always Fresh.
Always the Best.

FERRY'S SEEDS

are sold everywhere.
1901 Seed Annual free.
D. M. FERRY & CO., DETROIT, MICH.

It was almost true that Ferry's seeds were "sold everywhere." The company was so well known to farmers and city gardeners alike that often in its advertisements in national publications the company felt it necessary to mention little else but the name.

The Gale Manufacturing Company of Albion was one of Michigan's busiest farm equipment manufacturers. Starting with a few plows made by George Gale and his son in Hillsdale County in the 1840's, the company, after moving to Albion, had outstripped its facilities by 1887 and was shopping about for a new location for a larger factory. The city of Albion quickly voted to bond itself for $30,000 to keep the company from leaving the city. A tract of land for the firm was obtained on which the expanded plant was constructed. The largest building in the complex was a thousand feet long.

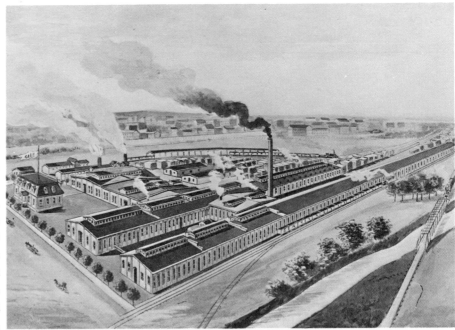

Courtesy: Eastern Michigan University Library

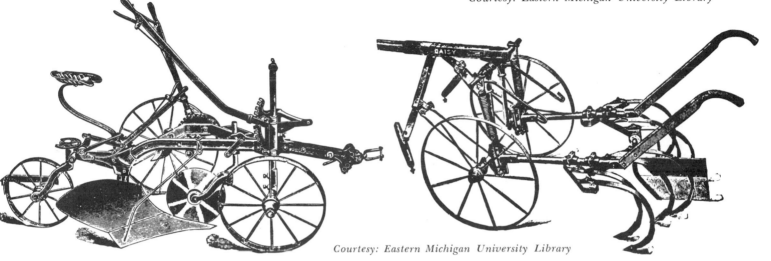

Courtesy: Eastern Michigan University Library

In the mid-1890's, three hundred thousand Gale implements, such as the Little Injun three-wheel sulky plow and the Daisy walking cultivator, were shipped out over the Michigan Central and the Lake Shore and Michigan Southern Railroads, both of which had spurs running past the Albion plant. Sales were reported not only throughout the United States but in many foreign countries as well.

Courtesy: Michigan Historical Commission

This apple-drying operation at Yankee Springs in Barry County was a modest forerunner in 1890 of the food-processing industry that developed in Michigan to can, and later to freeze, the bulk of Michigan's fruit and vegetable crops that were not sold fresh to the consumer while these crops were in season.

61

Factories sprang up in Bay City, Saginaw, Alma, and other central Michigan communities in the late 1890's and early 1900's to process the sugar beets that many farmers in the area were encouraged to grow during these years. This was the Owosso Sugar Company's plant in Lansing in 1912, sugar beets piled high along the railroad siding, ready to be transformed into sugar. Although this plant is now only a memory in the state capital, the sugar packaged in Michigan in the twentieth century has placed the state consistently up among the top half-dozen states in the nation from which this product is obtained.

Courtesy: Michigan Historical Commission

Courtesy: Eastern Michigan University Library

In 1902 the National Grange recognized Michigan's important agricultural standing by holding the annual convention of that farmers' organization in Lansing. The souvenir booklet printed up for the delegates included this advertisement that makes the extravagant claim that a Battle Creek factory manufacturing threshers was the "most interesting place in Michigan." Other developments that were underway at that time, however, would soon give Battle Creek a far more interesting and unique ranking among factory towns anywhere in the world, let alone in Michigan.

At the beginning of the twentieth century, Battle Creek, population nineteen thousand, was already known to many people far removed from Calhoun County or southern Michigan as the site of a nationally advertised health sanitarium maintained by the Seventh-day Adventist denomination.

62

Dr. Kellogg developed a variety of new foods that would make the menu at the sanitarium as interesting as possible for those who came there. Among these was a substitute for coffee that became so popular that many patients wanted to continue to use it after they had returned home. As a result, a separate health food company was formed for the purpose of marketing, on a very modest scale, Caramel-Cereal and some of Dr. Kellogg's other products.

As the ads suggested, an important feature of the treatment at the Battle Creek San was the proper diet, which, in accordance with the beliefs of the Seventh-day Adventists, meant no meat and no stimulating drinks of any kind. Regulating the diet of the patients was part of the responsibility of Dr. John Harvey Kellogg, who had headed the institution since the late 1870's.

In 1896, a former patient at the sanitarium, Charles W. Post, began to advertise a product that he called Postum, a coffee substitute that was remarkably like Kellogg's Caramel-Cereal. Unlike Kellogg, however, Post launched a vigorous national advertising campaign, promoting the health-giving benefits of Postum at the same time that he attacked the evils of coffee.

Caramel= Cereal

A Morning, Noon, and Evening Drink.

A Delicious and Wholesome Substitute for Coffee.

CARAMEL-CEREAL has been used by the Greatest Sanitarium in the World for more than twenty years.

Send two two-cent stamps for sample package if your grocer does not keep it.

MANUFACTURED BY

The Battle Creek Sanitarium Health Food Company,

BATTLE CREEK, MICHIGAN.

CARAMEL CEREAL

Although Post reportedly started his company with only $69, Postum caught on and from his profits Post was soon expanding and buying more equipment, such as these cooling pans that were used in the preparation of his imitation of Kellogg's imitation of coffee.

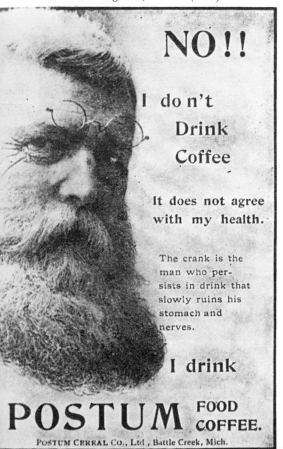

NO!!

I don't Drink Coffee

It does not agree with my health.

The crank is the man who persists in drink that slowly ruins his stomach and nerves.

I drink **POSTUM** FOOD COFFEE.

POSTUM CEREAL CO., Ltd., Battle Creek, Mich.

63

In 1898, Post also came out with Grape-Nuts, a prepared breakfast food involving various baking processes. It, too, was strangely reminiscent of a granulated cereal that Kellogg had been serving his patients for nearly two decades. Kellogg, in turn, seems to have followed closely the work of Dr. James C. Jackson of New York, who had developed a similar granulated cereal for his patients as early as the 1860's. Post, however, was the first to realize the potential market for these products and to take advantage of that realization.

Courtesy: Michigan Historical Commission

By the turn of the century, Post was netting a million dollars a year. This was a part of the office staff he employed in 1906 to take care of the ever mounting volume of orders. The sight of working women, whether on the Ferry Seed Farm or in the offices of the Post Cereal Company, became a familiar one as industrialization advanced in Michigan and the opportunities and need for women to seek jobs outside the home increased.

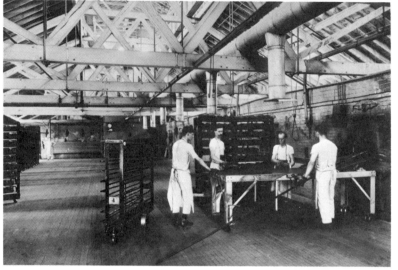

Courtesy: Michigan Historical Commission

The irony of Charles W. Post's life, however, was that although he advertised his products as health foods, his own health was not good. This was one reason why he spent less and less time in Battle Creek and more and more time at the home he built in the warmer climate of California. Finally, in 1914, despondent over his continued ill-health, he committed suicide. The company he founded was subsequently merged with several others to form the General Foods Corporation.

Courtesy: Michigan Historical Collections

Post's own office was a resplendent, albeit somewhat dark, affair. This photograph was taken around 1906. Scarcely more than a decade earlier Post was virtually penniless, and his wife had had to sell suspenders door to door in Battle Creek to pay for the care he was receiving in the sanitarium.

Courtesy: Michigan Historical Commission

Harper's Weekly,
June 21, 1902

Courtesy:
Chicago Tribune

The fortune that Post uncovered in breakfast foods touched off a fantastic boom in Battle Creek in the early years of the twentieth century, with forty-two separate companies springing up between 1902 and 1904, offering various imitations of products developed by Dr. Kellogg or Post. The Chicago *Tribune's* great cartoonist, John T. McCutcheon, commented wryly on the frenzied efforts of each of the competing firms to grab a share of the market. Several of the would-be millionaires, hoping to steal some secrets, are shown peeking through the windows, the transom, and the keyholes of the building in which Dr. Kellogg carried on his experiments.

One of these new companies that achieved some success, although it did not last, was the Malta-Vita Pure Food Company, which was the first to awaken a large number of Americans to the flaked cold cereal. Malta-Vita wheat flakes were a copy of a product developed by Dr. Kellogg and his younger brother, W. K. Kellogg, in 1894, to which the Malta-Vita company had added some malt as flavoring.

Courtesy: Kellogg Company

W. K. (he was christened Willie Keith, but later shortened his first name to the more adult-sounding Will) Kellogg had managed the separate food company his brother had organized. In 1906, frustrated by his desire to promote large-scale sales of these products while his brother was primarily interested in research, W. K. Kellogg broke away from the doctor's control and established the Battle Creek Toasted Corn Flakes Company, the origin of today's Kellogg Company, in these rented quarters.

65

TOASTED CORN FLAKES

Literary Digest, *October 1, 1910*

The Morning Chorus: Post Toasties – "The Memory Linger" 'Most as much fun as a Christmas tree!

Harper's Weekly, *April 13, 1912*

Kellogg launched an advertising campaign, virtually unprecedented in its day, to interest the public in corn flakes, a product he had had a hand in developing and which he believed had the greatest potential appeal of any of those the Kelloggs had worked on. Kellogg sold corn flakes not as a health food but simply as a wholesome product that tasted good. The "sweetheart of the corn" became a symbol of this wholesomeness and was featured in Kellogg ads for many years. In addition, in an effort to protect his corn flakes from the products of his imitators, W. K. Kellogg began printing his signature on every package of the breakfast food.

Imitations did appear, however, and Kellogg's principal rival, Post, was soon out with the most successful of these, Post Toasties. Post also took a leaf from Kellogg by adopting the same kind of homey, "cute" advertising for its corn flakes.

Kellogg's original rented factory burned down on July 4, 1907, but sales of his corn flakes were so good that he did not hesitate to proceed at once to acquire land at a new location between the Grand Trunk and Michigan Central railroad tracks, where, on the side of his first building, Kellogg emblazoned the name of his home town, a name that ever since has figured prominently in the Kellogg Company's advertisements. *Courtesy: Kellogg Company*

In the new plant Kellogg installed the latest machinery, which was operated, in many cases, by women dressed in smock-type uniforms and caps that served the purpose for which they were designed — to cover the head.

Kellogg himself took a direct interest in all aspects of the business. Here he is testing equipment in a new power plant.

Here Kellogg sits in a rocking chair beside an economy-size box of corn flakes at his company's first board of directors' meeting. The gentleman with the cane, also seated in a rocking chair, is Dr. John Harvey Kellogg, who had been made one of the principal stockholders in the company as part of the deal to obtain his permission to make corn flakes, using his processes. Subsequently the doctor sold nearly all his stock to his brother, and the two men became involved in a series of bitter legal battles over the rights to the commercial use of the Kellogg name, battles in which W. K. on the whole was the victor. After that they scarcely spoke to each other the rest of their long lives.

Courtesy: Kellogg Company

The Kellogg Company, despite its late start, soon vaulted ahead of Post and all other breakfast food companies. As it continued to expand its facilities to those of the present day shown here, it, together with Post and several other companies, maintained Battle Creek's position as the cereal capital of the world.

Lumbering, Michigan's most spectacular industry in the last three decades of the nineteenth century, continued to make a significant, although greatly reduced, contribution to the state's economy in the twentieth century. The devastated, burned-over lands of northern Michigan were restored.

Courtesy: Michigan Historical Commission

Reforestation projects, such as this one in the Au Sable State Forest, near Higgins Lake, which began in the early part of this century, have restored beauty and value to many thousands of acres of scarred and worthless land.

Courtesy: Michigan Historical Commission

Courtesy: Michigan Historical Commission

Courtesy: Michigan Historical Commission

With the use of newer techniques and equipment to fight forest fires, the young second growth has had a chance to develop and once again to cover northern Michigan with great forests.

The wasteful lumbering practices of the nineteenth century have been replaced in more recent decades by a more careful management of the timber resources and, as in the case of agriculture, the use of labor-saving, time-cutting mechanized means of carrying on logging operations that had required much larger crews of men, not to mention work animals, in earlier years.

Courtesy: Michigan Historical Commission

Courtesy: Michigan Historical Commission

Many industries in Michigan arose wholly or in part because of the proximity of timber resources. Long after the giant, centuries-old, virgin white pines had fallen before the loggers' axes and saws, the young growth that was left provided pulpwood for the paper mills and the paper-products industry. The woodyard at the Filer City plant of the Packaging Corporation of America in the 1960's attested to the fact that lumbering still provided income to many in the Manistee area many decades after the boom years of the nineteenth century.

Courtesy: Michigan Historical Commission

Courtesy: Michigan Historical Commission

The stacks of pulpwood at Munising began to appear in 1904 with the opening of that city's paper mill, part of an industry that would provide one of the few bright spots in the otherwise gloomy view that characterized the economic prospects of a vast section of the Upper Peninsula between the Soo on the east and the mining towns on the west.

Courtesy: Kalamazoo Public Library

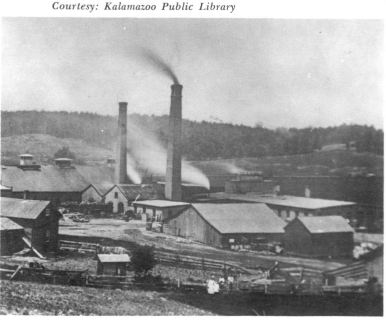

The leading center of the paper industry in Michigan was Kalamazoo, where the Kalamazoo Paper Company, shown here around the time of its founding in 1867, was the nucleus around which numerous other mills arose in the Kalamazoo area in later years.

70

Unlike some of Michigan's other industrial activities, the paper industry did not make the communities where it was located or the state as a whole nationally or

internationally renowned because of the public's familiarity with its advertisements and products. The only ad in the mass-circulation publications that was remotely related to Michigan's importance as a source of paper at the beginning of this century was an occasional notice promoting the sale of Golf Playing Cards, printed in Kalamazoo, hopefully on locally made pasteboards.

Harper's Weekly, *March 9, 1901*

One Michigan lumber firm that advertised on a modest scale was Mershon and Morley of Saginaw, one of several companies in that area that helped develop the concept of prefabricated buildings that could be shipped anywhere, assembled quickly, and used for a variety of purposes, even, this ad points out, as "automobile houses."

A major industry that arose because of the availability of wood was shipbuilding, one in which Michigan led all other states in the 1890's. The largest number of ships was launched from the shipyards of Wayne County, such as the Orleans Street dry dock of the Detroit Shipbuilding Company, while the Bay City shipyards led in the tonnage of ships they produced.

Courtesy: Michigan Historical Commission

71

World's Work, *Vol. 1 (1900-01)*

At the turn of the century, an occasional
full-page advertisement for the Michigan
Yacht and Power Company — although it
scarcely suggested the over-all importance
of Michigan's shipbuilding industry — did
provide a portent of the bright future ahead
for the pleasure-craft industry. Although
this company offered yachts and launches
built of steel or wood, the failure of the
Michigan shipbuilders as a whole to switch
over to metal construction cost them dearly
in the early years of the twentieth century,
as shipping firms turned to shipyards in Ohio
and other states to obtain the larger,
sturdier vessels needed to handle the growing
volume of freight carried on the Great Lakes.

Review of Reviews, *Vol. 22 (1900)*

Another company that did not hesitate to place
large ads in national magazines, in fact one
of the few Michigan companies to advertise
extensively and regularly at the beginning of
the century, was Berry Brothers, the leader of
Detroit's important paint and varnish industry.
Its finishes were widely used by many
manufacturers of wood products, including the
shipbuilders and the furniture manufacturers.

Review of Reviews, *Vol. 24 (1901)*

"Furniture made Grand Rapids famous," was
the proud claim of that city's furniture
manufacturers' trade organization in 1901 —
and indeed it had. Since the 1870's, Grand
Rapids had meant furniture to people in all
parts of the United States and in the many
other parts of the world where the handiwork
of thousands of Grand Rapids furniture
craftsmen was marketed. This kind of
identification, a foreshadowing of the
subsequent identification of Battle Creek
with breakfast foods and Detroit with
automobiles, would effectively create the
twentieth-century image of Michigan, the
manufacturing state.

Actually, Grand Rapids was not the only Michigan city in which furniture was manufactured. The hardwood forests of the southern part of the state made this section a logical one in which to produce furniture, which, until the twentieth century, was made almost entirely of wood. There were many Michigan communities where furniture factories developed. At Grand Ledge, up the Grand River from Grand Rapids, the Grand Ledge Chair Factory, founded in 1884, soon established an enviable reputation for the high quality of its specialty.

Why Grand Rapids became the great furniture center that it did is something of a mystery. Michigan's largest river, the Grand, not only furnished water power to the factories but also brought logs to the very doors of such famous furniture manufacturers as Berkey and Gay (on the opposite side of the river in this picture, just beyond the covered bridge). But other Michigan communities enjoyed equal, if not greater, advantages. In terms of adequate railroad connections to the great markets of the country, Grand Rapids was for a number of years at a decided disadvantage compared to cities further south that were located on the main east-west lines.

Grand Rapids achieved its position largely as a result of the efforts of individuals. William Haldane, shown here in a photograph taken years later, arrived in the young frontier community in the 1830's and set up shop as the first cabinetmaker in Grand Rapids. One of his hand-crafted chairs is exhibited today in the city's public museum. Other skilled craftsmen followed Haldane to Grand Rapids, together with able, imaginative business organizers whose success persuaded other men to establish similar businesses in the city, where a large force of trained workmen was now available.

History of Kent County, Michigan *(1881)*

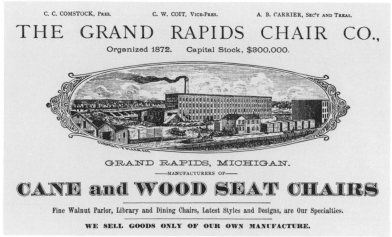

Grand Rapids City Directory, *1880-81*

After a few years, Comstock sold out his interest in his company, but in 1872 he helped found the Grand Rapids Chair Company, which, as this advertisement indicates, manufactured only certain types of chairs. Beginning in 1882, however, the company branched out into bedroom and dining-room furniture and became one of the largest furniture companies in Grand Rapids.

Among the early leaders of the Grand Rapids furniture industry was Charles C. Comstock, who had been a lumberman in New Hampshire and continued in the lumber business when he came to Grand Rapids in 1852. In 1857 he bought a furniture company, and after some initial failures he launched in 1862 the city's first wholesale furniture company. He was a pioneer in seeking markets outside Grand Rapids and Michigan, opening branch outlets in some of the major cities of the Middle West.

Country Life in America, *February, 1906*

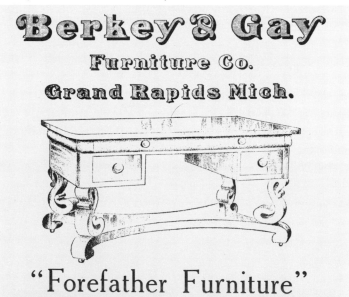

In the years after the Civil War, Julius Berkey is credited with steering the Grand Rapids industry into the emphasis on high quality that has characterized it ever since. Berkey's own company, Berkey and Gay, became a symbol of furniture of the very best quality. It further expanded the market for the city's furniture by opening a branch in New York City.

Berkey and Gay furniture is displayed in the company's showroom for dealers and buyers to examine.

In 1878 a semiannual furniture market was inaugurated in Grand Rapids where buyers could come to see the latest work of the city's companies exhibited. Within a few years manufacturers from other areas began to exhibit their products, providing additional recognition of the leading position Grand Rapids had assumed in the furniture industry. This was one of the displays prepared for the one hundredth market in 1928. Only in the last few years has the market been abandoned in favor of newer methods of acquainting buyers with company products.

Most Grand Rapids furniture manufacturers advertised infrequently in national publications, if at all. The Fred Macey Company, which specialized in office and library furniture, was an exception. The $35.00 price tag on this "luxurious Turkish Rocker," with its "machine-buffed Genuine Leather" upholstering, is in itself an interesting commentary on the value a dollar could command in 1900 and on how times have changed.

Scribner's Magazine, *Vol. 27 (1900)*

Courtesy: Michigan Historical Commission

Courtesy: Michigan Historical Commission

In the twentieth century, the emphasis among Grand Rapids furniture makers continued to be on quality, as other areas, such as North Carolina, moved to the forefront in the large-scale production of cheaper furniture. Firms such as the John Widdicomb Company now took pains to point out the fine materials and the hand labor that went into its products. Although Grand Rapids no longer held the position it once did in terms of its total share of furniture production, the reputation it had gained from the high standards of its manufacturers was unchallenged.

Leonard Cleanable Porcelain Lined Refrigerators

Excel all others.
The porcelain lining is real porcelain fused on sheet steel and indestructible. The doors are air-tight.

This Means Your Ice Bill is Cut in Half.

The shelves slide in metal bars and are adjustable to any height (see cut). There are nine walls to preserve the ice——(see cut below.)

The price is ⅓ less than tile lining and the refrigerator better. Write for free sample of porcelain lining and catalog showing 50 other styles.

This style, 35x22x16
Polished Oak Case
Quarter Sawed Panels
$27.50

For sale by all the best dealers or will ship direct from factory. Freight prepaid as far as the Mississippi and Ohio Rivers. Beware of imitations made with white paint; the lead is poisonous and not durable, *you can scratch it with a pin.*

GRAND RAPIDS REFRIGERATOR CO.
8 Ottawa Street, GRAND RAPIDS, MICH.

The LEONARD LOOK that makes it AIR TIGHT

Sliding Adjustable Shelves

The Nine Walls of Leonard Cleanable Refrigerator

Cosmopolitan Magazine, *Vol. 40 (1905-06)*

The Bissell Sweeper

The handy, useful, every-day labor-saving convenience of the home.

It is not enough to take up carpets once a year, or to clean them with compressed air process, for after this comes the daily necessity for a good carpet sweeper. Dust accumulates fast, and unless you have a good carpet sweeper always at your command, your house is bound to get very dirty.

The corn broom simply scatters the fine grit and dust, whereas the Bissell sweeper gathers it completely, depositing it in the pan receptacles.

Then consider how it lessens the labor of sweeping 95 per cent., raises no dust; making sweeping a positive pleasure instead of a drudgery.

It's a great economy, too, as a Bissell will last longer than fifty corn brooms.

For sale by all the best trade.
Price $2.50 to $5.50.

Buy now, send us the purchase slip, and receive a neat, useful present *free.*

Bissell Carpet Sweeper Co.
Grand Rapids, Mich.
Dept. 64.
(Largest Sweeper Makers in the World.)

Cosmopolitan Magazine, *Vol. 41 (1906)*

The economic well-being of Michigan's second largest city was not solely dependent on the furniture industry. Magazine ads at the beginning of this century gave some evidence of that fact, although some of the city's other industrial activities were closely related to household furnishings. The emergence of Grand Rapids as a major center for the production of refrigerators was a logical move to expect of men trained in such work as building cabinets, while the housewife with a home full of elegant Grand Rapids-made furniture could just as logically be expected to turn to a carpet sweeper, not a corn broom, to keep that home clean.

Harper's Weekly, *January 4, 1890*

Michigan's position as a mineral-producing state was firmly established by the time these sketches of iron-mining operations in the Upper Peninsula appeared in *Harper's Weekly* in 1890. Although Michigan was no longer the leading source of copper in the nation, the expanding output of its three iron ranges continued to make it the number-one iron ore state until 1900. The complexity of these mining operations was suggested by the artist Charles Graham who depicted a miner (1) with his candle in his hat to light his work underground and a woodsman (2), whose services were essential in providing the timbers needed as framing and supports for the underground levels (6). By the end of the century, fewer and fewer Michigan miners who picked up their pay (3) were engaged in open-pit operations (5). Most of them did their work deep beneath the surface, going down inclined shafts (7) or the vertical shafts that became more common.

In 1900, ores from Minnesota's Mesabi Iron Range pushed that state into the leadership. Michigan, however, remained a strong second as the methods of extracting its underground ores were constantly improved. Cages lowered the miners several thousand feet beneath the surface to the sources of the ore. Battery-operated lights had replaced the candles, and many other features had been developed to add to the safety of the miners' work.

Once they had been lowered to the required depth, the miners proceeded from the shaft into the main-level drift, a man-made cave cut through the rock to the area of ore deposits. The well-lit tunnel, the tracks, and the pipes that carried fresh air and water, were indicative of the increasingly sophisticated methods of mining that were developed in the twentieth century.

To remove the ore, the miner placed dynamite in a drill hole, and the ore was blasted loose. The chunks of ore were then pushed down into the main level below, where cars would haul the material to the shaft where it could be lifted to the surface. As the mining companies became more safety conscious, shatterproof glasses were made required equipment to protect the eyes of the miners, while steel sets provided greater protection from falling debris underground than the timbers that had been the only framing material in the earlier years.

At the surface, the ore was reloaded into specially built railroad cars to be taken to the lake port serving that iron range: Marquette for the Marquette Iron Range, Escanaba for the Menominee Iron Range, or Ashland, Wisconsin, for the Gogebic Iron Range. At the railroad crossings in these mining areas, the slow-moving, incredibly long ore trains constantly halted pedestrian and vehicle traffic during the shipping season, but to the waiting residents of the ranges the trains were a welcome sight, a visible index of the health of the mining industry.

The ore cars were run out onto the ore dock, in this instance the Lake Superior and Ishpeming Railroad dock at Marquette, and the ore dumped into pockets from which chutes ran it into the holds of ore boats that tied up at the dock.

The great ore boats that were loaded at the Lake Superior ports proceeded with their cargoes to Sault Ste. Marie and entered the locks. The water level was lowered to that of Lake Huron, and the boats then sailed on their way. As the twentieth century wore on, an ever greater proportion of the ore passing through the locks came from the open-pit mines of Minnesota. The costs of Michigan's underground operations increased, bringing closer the day when it would no longer be profitable for these mines to compete with the Minnesota mines.

Iron ore and copper were not the only valuable resources that lay beneath Michigan's two peninsulas. Around the time of the Civil War, the enormous reserves of salt found in great pools of brine deep underground or in solid form began to be commercially exploited. Wells, such as this one at the R. G. Peters plant in Manistee, raised the brine to the surface where the water was evaporated off and the salt pulled away in barrels.

By the 1880's, Michigan was the leading source of salt in the country, accounting for about half of the nation's total production. This salt was obtained by various evaporation processes, but in 1910, mining of the rock salt deposits beneath the city of Detroit was inaugurated and has continued since that time in a manner similar to the methods used in mining other minerals. In a vast network of tunnels under Michigan's largest city, electrically powered dump trucks carry twenty-ton loads of sterling rock salt to the primary crusher thousands of yards away.

Here at the Diamond Crystal Salt Company plant in St. Clair the same formation of crystallized salt that is mined at Detroit is tapped by forcing water into the salt to form brine, which is then pumped out and evaporated.

Northern Michigan contains major deposits of limestone, which began to be developed around the turn of the century. The most spectacular of these quarrying operations was initiated near Rogers City. The limestone was hauled in cars from the quarry to port facilities nearby where the Great Lakes waterway system was conveniently available to provide an inexpensive means of shipping this bulky product to the steel mills where it was needed.

This mid-twentieth-century view of the operations of the Michigan Limestone Division of the United States Steel Corporation at Calcite Harbor, Rogers City, when compared with the earlier views, a half-century before, demonstrates again the rapid advances in technology that have characterized the economic activities of this period.

Gypsum deposits are found in several places in Michigan, but probably the most famous of the operations that developed is at Alabaster, where the quarrying and crushing of gypsum began in the 1860's. The product is conveyed to ships out in Lake Huron by this unusual method that never fails to arouse the curiosity of tourists driving along the lake-shore highway south of Tawas City.

At the tip of the Thumb, across Saginaw Bay from Alabaster, another town arose whose name even more clearly identified the product for which it was famous. These two scenes show some of the activity at the Wallace Quarry in Grindstone City in 1884 that helped to make that city known far beyond the bounds of the United States as the source of some of the finest grindstones in the world.

The development of carborundum around the time of World War I killed off the demand for grindstones. Today the abandoned grindstones that lie along the beaches are added attractions for the tourists and vacationers who come to Grindstone City in the summer and provide enough income to keep the little community from becoming a ghost town.

By the end of the nineteenth century, the manner in which Michigan's minerals were used was revealing the same shift from purely extractive activities to those of a processing type that characterized the state's economic development in general during these years. At Alpena in the early years of this century, the abundant resources of limestone found in that area of northern Michigan were quarried and then heated and processed to form portland cement. The Huron Portland Cement Company's plant at Alpena, the world's largest, was a welcome addition to that city's economy in the years following the lumber boom of the nineteenth century.

Less fortunate was the community of Marlborough in southern Lake County, which sprang up after 1901 when the Great Northern Portland Cement Company was incorporated to manufacture cement from the marl found in this area. The process soon proved too costly to be practical, and the plant was shut down in 1908. Efforts to keep the community alive through the development of other activities proved unsuccessful. A half-century later, the imposing ruins of the million-dollar plant and a few old-timers who had stuck it out were about all there was to the town of Marlborough.

Courtesy: Michigan Historical Commission

Some of the same brine pools that gave birth to Michigan's salt industry also were a source of bromine. At this rented brine well in Midland, Herbert Dow in 1891 developed his successful method of producing bromine commercially through the process of electrolysis.

Courtesy: Michigan Historical Commission

From that humble beginning, Dow ultimately went on to create the huge Dow Chemical Company. Some of the Midland units are shown in the 1950's, turning out innumerable chemical products, many of them still based on Michigan bromine.

Courtesy: Michigan Historical Commission

At the same time that Herbert Dow was using the brine at Midland as the springboard to the development of a chemical industry in that city, J. B. Ford was establishing an experimental plant in Wyandotte for the purpose of converting the salt deposits in the Detroit area into soda ash. He was successful, and the great Wyandotte Chemicals Corporation was the result. In the process, the fortune of Detroit's "other Ford family" was made.

84

Courtesy: Michigan Historical Commission

Silas Farmer, History of Detroit

Silas Farmer, History of Detroit Harper's Monthly, *Vol. 101 (1900)*

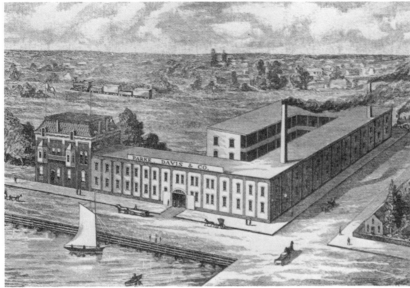

Closely related to Michigan's important chemical industry was its pharmaceutical industry, which developed somewhat earlier. Hervey C. Parke, a Detroit businessman who knew nothing about the making of drugs, invested his money in a small Detroit pharmaceutical laboratory in 1866. Reorganized as Parke, Davis and Company in 1871, the company's rapid growth into one of the largest pharmaceutical houses in the world is suggested by the contrast between the original plant of 1866 and the one built in the 1870's on the Detroit River at the foot of McDougall Avenue.

Michigan's importance in the chemical and pharmaceutical industries at the end of the nineteenth century was not reflected in the advertisements that appeared in national magazines, unless this one for Wright's Dentomyrh Tooth Paste is counted. Charles Wright had founded a company in Detroit in 1880 to manufacture pharmaceuticals, but after 1890 he had turned to the proprietary drug field, manufacturing a variety of headache remedies, syrups for rheumatism, and soap for teeth. Wright, therefore, really represented the patent medicine industry, which was also prominent in Michigan in that day.

Nothing Too Good for Uncle Sam.

DENTOMYRH is purchased by the U. S. Gov. The soldier is taught, and *you should know,* that good Teeth, a clean Mouth, firm Gums, a sweet Breath, are necessary for good health, and good health is necessary to be **A Victor in the Battle of Life.**

WRIGHT'S

Dentomyrh

For the Teeth, Mouth, Gums and Breath.

A delicious, creamy **TOOTH PASTE** in collapsible tubes, made after same formula as Wright's renowned Tooth Soap, Powder or Wash.

Is purifying and healing. It whitens and preserves the teeth. Prevents decay. Hardens the gums. Removes offensive breath. Is convenient to use. Endorsed by eminent medical and dental scientists.

Once tried, always used.

At all druggists, **25c.**, or from

Charles Wright Chemical Co.

Dept. N.,

DETROIT, MICH.

Booklet, "*A Tooth Treat,*" testimonials and sample, FREE.

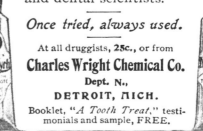

Scifert's Improved Oil of Gladness ("Sure and Speedy"), and Steketee's Worm Destroyer, which not only would destroy Pin Worms but was "highly recommended" as a cure for epileptic fits, were typical of the products of innumerable patent medicine companies scattered over Michigan. They required few resources to bottle their magical potions, and few were in a position to advertise and market their products except in the immediate area where they were situated.

Chapin & Page's Tecumseh Directory *(1869)*

Grand Rapids City Directory *(1880-81)*

The presence of iron ore in the Upper Peninsula led in 1853 to the establishment by Eber Brock Ward of the Eureka Iron Company on land down-river from Detroit. Ward, who was probably the first Michiganian to become a millionaire, had already made a fortune as a shipbuilder and shipowner. Not content to stay in that field, he had begun acquiring large tracts of timber in Michigan and had also invested in the new iron-mining activities in the northern part of the state.

The Eureka Iron Company soon developed into one of Ward's most successful endeavors. The city of Wyandotte sprang up around the plant, to which Ward's ships brought ore from the Marquette Iron Range. The ore was smelted into iron, for which some of Ward's timber holdings were used as the source of charcoal. In 1864, Ward pioneered in the production of Bessemer steel in America.

Courtesy: Bacon Memorial Public Library, Wyandotte

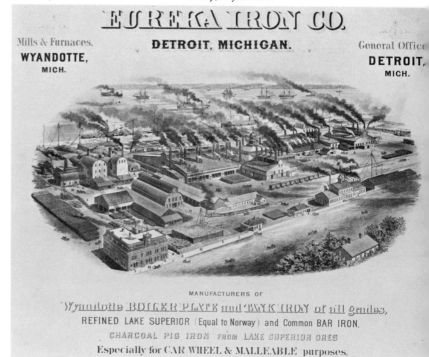

EUREKA IRON CO.

DETROIT, MICHIGAN.

Mills & Furnaces, WYANDOTTE, MICH.   General Office DETROIT, MICH.

MANUFACTURERS OF

Wyandotte BOILER PLATE and TANK IRON of all grades,
REFINED LAKE SUPERIOR (Equal to Norway) and Common BAR IRON.
CHARCOAL PIG IRON FROM LAKE SUPERIOR ORES
Especially for CAR WHEEL & MALLEABLE purposes.

Courtesy: Michigan Historical Commission

Ward's death in 1875 was a severe blow to the further development of the Eureka Company. Then, on June 1, 1888, a boiler explosion, which shattered windows within a one-mile radius in Wyandotte and killed nine people, contributed to the eventual demise of one of Michigan's most important and promising early industrial developments. In any event, charcoal was an inadequate source of fuel to enable Michigan companies to compete with the iron and steel companies in the East with their abundant resources of coal.

Courtesy: Michigan Historical Commission

A major user of iron and steel in the Detroit area was the railroad-car industry, which, by the 1890's, employed nine thousand workmen and turned out a hundred freight cars a day. Senator James McMillan made his fortune initially as a founder in 1864 of the Michigan Car Company, whose operations, as shown here in a bird's-eye view, forecast the mass-production techniques for which the name Detroit would become synonymous. Freight cars produced in the company's plant moved steadily along a track through the woodworking department, the setting-up shop, the blacksmith shop, and the paint shop, with the cars emerging painted, lettered, numbered, and ready to roll.

Courtesy: Transportation Library

87

An 1895 blurb for the Sheffield Car Company, manufacturers of a variety of light handcars for railroad repair work and also for use in mining, lumbering, and plantation operations, claimed that it had "done more to make Three Rivers known to the outside world than any one thing."

W. J. WILLITS.

One of the important industries in Michigan, and indeed of the United States, is the Sheffield Car Company, manufacturers of light cars of every description for railroad repair work, also for plantation, contractors, mining and lumbering operations of all kinds. This is the largest concern in the world making a specialty of cars of this class. Their reputation is such that "Sheffield" is almost a household word among the railroad men of the United States, and they are recognized all over the world as experts in the manufacture of cars of

special design for special work, and their advice is sought after by the miner and the planter, the lumberman and the contractor.

This company was established in 1879 and incorporated in 1883, with a paid up capital of $200,000. The president is W. J. Willits; secretary and treasurer, E. B. Linsley; who are the active managers of the business. Richard H. Webb is vice president. The output is $500,000 a year, which goes all over the world; in fact, there is scarcely a time that they have not several orders on their books from foreign countries and to meet these requirements they publish a finely illustrated catalogue in several languages.

To the uninformed it might seem that there was no great demand for these cars, but when one considers

the immense number of hand cars alone used in the repair of track, they can readily realize the importance of this industry. Their regular catalogue of 100 pages, which, by the way, is one of the finest ever issued in Michigan, gives thirty different kinds of cars, most of which are made in several different styles; for instance, there are hand cars for section work, bridge work, inspection work, weed cutting, plantation work and mining tunnels; then there are special cars for logging, mining, plantation, track laying, transfers and also velocipede cars. They

E. B. LINSLEY.

Courtesy: Eastern Michigan University Library

Courtesy: Eastern Michigan University Library

Three Rivers' fame from its manufactured products did not, however, equal that which came to another southwestern Michigan town, Dowagiac, as a result of the location there of the Round Oak Stove Works.

Established in 1871 by Philo D. Beckwith, the company's stove was reportedly the leading heating stove in the country by the time of Beckwith's death in 1889. The company continued in the hands of Beckwith's estate, adding a Round Oak Furnace to the line of stoves. Three hundred fifty men were employed in the various buildings that occupied the fifteen-acre factory site. Forty tons of pig iron alone were used each day to make the cast portions of the stoves.

Courtesy: Western Michigan University Archives

Estate of P. D. Beckwith

FRED E. LEE, Manager,
DOWAGIAC, MICH.

Manufacturers of

Round Oak Stoves, Ranges and Furnaces.

The Famous Air Tight Round Oak Furnace.

Literary Digest, *August 23, 1913*

The stove industry was not confined to Dowagiac but was widespread across southern Michigan. The Kalamazoo Stove Company would shortly capitalize on its geographical location through its memorable slogan: "A Kalamazoo Direct to You (and Gas Stoves Too)." Note the introduction of the easy-payment plan in this ad in 1913 — the only method by which Michigan's high-priced consumer products of the twentieth century could be marketed on a sufficiently large scale.

Courtesy: Burton Historical Collection

But it was Detroit that was the leading producer of stoves, not only in Michigan but in the entire world. The individual most responsible for this development was Jeremiah Dwyer, shown in a caricature drawn early in the present century. Dwyer had learned the stove business in New York State, the early center of the industry. Then, in 1861, Dwyer established his first stove company in Detroit.

Courtesy: Eastern Michigan University Library

PLANT OF THE DETROIT STOVE WORKS, JEFFERSON AVENUE.

By the 1890's, in addition to numerous smaller firms, the Detroit stove industry was dominated by three giants, in the establishment of which Dwyer, his brother, or his associates had had a hand. These were the Detroit Stove Works, the oldest of the three, the Peninsular Stove Company, . . .

89

... and the Michigan Stove Company, which claimed in its ads to be the largest manufacturer of stoves and ranges in the world and that its Garland stoves were the "World's Best." In 1892 it employed twelve hundred men, had a payroll of nearly $600,000, and produced 75,699 stoves. By 1900, however, the days of the wood stove were numbered, and the Detroit Stove Works was ready for the change with its Detroit Jewel Gas Range. One of its advantages: "no soot, no smoke, no ashes."

Long after Detroit had become far better known for other manufactured products, its onetime renown for stoves had been recalled by the "Big Stove," a huge iron replica originally built as an exhibit at the Chicago's World Fair of 1893. Subsequently, as shown here, it was displayed on the grounds of the merged Detroit and Michigan stove companies at Jefferson Avenue and the Belle Isle Bridge. When the stove works went out of business several years ago, the giant model was moved to the Woodward Avenue entrance to the State Fairgrounds in Detroit where it still can be seen.

Courtesy: Burton Historical Collection

Although the presence of iron ore, timber resources, and agricultural products might explain much of the industrial development in Michigan by the turn of the century, there were numerous instances of industries that defied such explanations. In those less complicated days when the ownership of guns was not the controversial subject that it became in the late 1960's, generations of boys pored over ads for Daisy Air Rifles and hoped they would find one under the Christmas tree. In the process they also learned that there was a town located somewhere in Michigan by the name of Plymouth where "that safest of all guns for a boy" was manufactured.

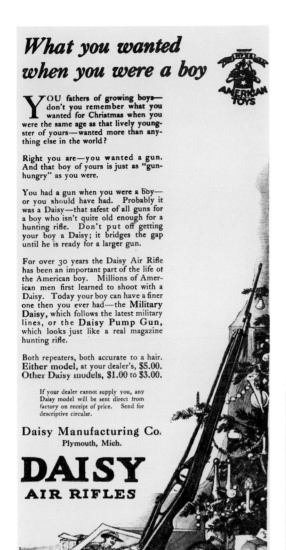

Literary Digest, December 13, 1919

After 1904, advertisements for the Burroughs Adding Machine carried a Detroit address where earlier these devices, resulting from a patent obtained by William Seward Burroughs in 1888, had been produced in St. Louis, Missouri. The relocation in Detroit of the company, including some 253 workers and their families, was an example of how the growing importance of Michigan as a center of industrial activity helped to attract additional manufacturing companies to the state when reasons of larger facilities or other considerations made a move necessary.

Literary Digest, September 10, 1910

If the furniture industry made Grand Rapids famous, the town of Belding in neighboring Ionia County owed its very existence to the silk industry, which was established at that site in the 1860's. Dormitories were built near the silk mills to house the women who constituted the bulk of the laboring force, an example of how, in this region where the New England influence was so strong, Belding's silk industry was modeled after the textile industry in such cities as Lowell, Massachusetts. By the middle of the twentieth century the silk industry had pulled out of Belding, although some of the buildings still survive and spools of the popular Belding Thread still suggest to later generations the economic origins of the small Michigan town.

Courtesy: Michigan Historical Commission

On the whole, the textile or clothing industries were never of major significance in Michigan. But in a day when ads from Michigan companies were relatively uncommon in national publications, these advertisements for Michigan-made socks and underwear appeared in two of the more widely read magazines.

Cosmopolitan, Vol. 29 (1900)

Harper's Weekly, June 8, 1901

In a state that produced very little tobacco (although this has long been a major crop in parts of southern Ontario a hundred or so miles to the east), the importance of the manufacturing of various tobacco products in Michigan in the nineteenth century is rather curious. As a matter of fact, in Detroit, where John Bagley, governor of Michigan in the 1870's, made a fortune from the sale of his Mayflower chewing tobacco, the value of the cigars and chewing tobacco that were produced in 1880 exceeded that of any other industry in the city, and as late as 1909 tobacco products ranked fourth among Detroit industries. Other Michigan towns also had their local cigar makers.

Courtesy: Ann Arbor **News**

Times changed, however, and in Ann Arbor, where there had once been a dozen cigar factories, each employing from five to twenty men, there was by 1948 only one cigar maker left, John E. Kranich, who, at age seventy-eight, symbolized a departed era in Michigan's economic growth. Young men no longer thought of rolling cigars, or making stoves, or mining iron as a career, as they had in Kranich's youth. The big money for men with similar occupational interests was now to be made in an industry that had not even existed when Kranich was deciding upon his lifetime occupation.

*Michigan Puts
the World on Wheels*

Going Like The Wind

yet gliding along so smoothly that only the rapidly moving panorama, the exhilarating breeze and the surprised faces of those you pass, tell you how fast when riding in

The Winton

No shock or bump, no vibration or jar. The greatest luxury of automobile travel. The new 1903 model Winton has a 20 horsepower, double cylinder motor which can make you shoot over the roads or will let you "just crawl along," according to the pressure put upon the spring governor button, which is conveniently placed beneath the right foot. It is so simple to operate, yet as sensitive and effective as the throttle control of a railroad locomotive.

The Winton double cylinder motor, of the opposed type, has behind it an unparalleled success, demonstrating beyond cavil the correctness of the principles on which it was designed. The 1902 car, with its 15 horsepower motor, is the foundation of our present model, which has fulfilled our most sanguine expectations. The intensely gratifying results shown by this new model give added strength to our position as leaders in the world's automobile-building industry.

Price of the 20 horse-power, 1903 Winton Touring Car, including detachable tonneau, two full brass side lamps, tools, etc., $2500. Visit any of our branch or agency depots and the many features of Winton excellence will be fully demonstrated.

Branches and Agencies:

New York, The Winton Motor Carriage Co., 150-152 E. 58th St., Percy Owen, Manager
Chicago, The Winton Motor Carriage Co., 1400 Michigan Ave., Chas. H. Tucker, Mgr.
Boston, The Winton Motor Carriage Co., 41 Stanhope St., Harry Fosdick, Manager
Philadelphia, The Winton Motor Carriage Co., 246-248 No. Broad St., A. E. Maltby, Mgr.
Baltimore, Md., Cook & Owesney
Buffalo, N. Y., W. C. Jaynes Automobile Co., 873-875 Main St.
Binghamton, N. Y., R. W. Whipple & Co.
Cincinnati, O., The Hanauer Automobile Co., 24 E. Sixth St.
Columbus, O., Avery & Davis, 1197 Franklin Ave.
Dayton, O., Kiser & Company
Denver, Colo., Colorado Automobile Co., 521 Sixteenth St.
Derby, Conn., N. L. Biever
Detroit, Mich., W. E. Metzger, Jefferson Ave.
Grand Rapids, Mich., Adams & Hart, 12 W. Bridge St.
Indianapolis, Ind., Fisher Automobile Co., Cyclorama Place
Keene, N. H., Wilkins Toy Co.

Los Angeles, Cal., The Locomobile Co. of the Pacific.
Louisville, Ky., Sutcliffe & Co.
Milwaukee, Wis., Bates-Odenbrett Automobile Co.
Minneapolis, Minn., A. C. Bennett, 112 South Sixth St.
New Haven, Conn., H. C. Holcomb, 105 Goffe St.
Omaha, Neb., H. E. Fredrickson.
Pittsburg, Pa., Seely Mfg. Co., East End.
Providence, R. I., H. G. Martin & Co., 196-200 W. Exchange St.
Rochester, N. Y., Rochester Automobile Co., J. J. Mandery, Manager
San Francisco, The Locomobile Co. of the Pacific, Market St.
St. Louis, Halsey Automobile Co., 2250 Olive St.
Syracuse, N. Y., Syracuse Automobile Co.
Toledo, O., Toledo Motor Carriage Co., Charles M. Hall, Manager.
Toronto, Canada, Canada Cycle & Motor Co.
Troy, N. Y., Jas. Lucey, 359 Fulton St.
Washington, D. C., Cook & Owesney.

The Winton Motor Carriage Co., Berea Road, Cleveland, U. S. A.

Cleveland Sales Depot (Downtown) Euclid Ave. and Huron St., Chas. B. Shanks, Mgr.

The January 17, 1903, issue of *Collier's* was devoted to the subject of automobiles, one of the first times that a mass-circulation magazine devoted so much attention to what was still a novel contraption, with only 23,000 registered motor vehicles in the entire country. Thirteen makes of cars were advertised in the issue, including the Winton, manufactured in Cleveland,...

The HAYNES-APPERSON

is unique. It is its own type. It has proved the best for American Roads—better than Foreign types—better than the so-called "American type" of motor car. It is the oldest make in America—one of the oldest in the world—the most thoroughly developed.

We are about to issue (in addition to our regular catalogue) an interesting booklet that tells *why* it is the best. Shall we put you down for one? You will greatly oblige us by naming this publication when you write. Catalogue FREE, too. ∴ ∴ ∴

RUNABOUT	PHAETON	SURREY
$1200	$1500	$1800

Tonneau — ready for spring — particulars later.

HAYNES-APPERSON CO., Kokomo, Ind., U.S.A.

A primitive method of locomotion used in Ecuador, South America.

Simplicity
Durability
Reliability

are the three cardinal virtues in motor-carriage construction. You will find them in their highest development and efficiency in the

Rambler
Touring Car

Built for practical, every-day service, on all kinds of roads, in all kinds of weather, the Rambler has proved its genuine merit under all conditions.

Its many points of superiority are stated in detail in our

Complete Illustrated Catalogue

mailed free on request. The best grade of materials, backed by the highest class of skilled labor, make the Rambler a guarantee of quality.

MODEL E (like cut) $750.00
Thomas B. Jeffery & Co.
Kenosha, Wis.

...the Haynes-Apperson from Kokomo, Indiana, the Stevens-Duryea of Chicopee Falls, Massachusetts, and Kenosha's Rambler....

97

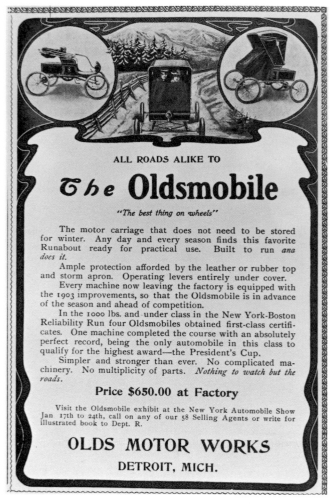

ALL ROADS ALIKE TO

C h e **Oldsmobile**

"The best thing on wheels"

The motor carriage that does not need to be stored for winter. Any day and every season finds this favorite Runabout ready for practical use. Built to run *and does it.*

Ample protection afforded by the leather or rubber top and storm apron. Operating levers entirely under cover.

Every machine now leaving the factory is equipped with the 1903 improvements, so that the Oldsmobile is in advance of the season and ahead of competition.

In the 1000 lbs. and under class in the New York-Boston Reliability Run four Oldsmobiles obtained first-class certificates. One machine completed the course with an absolutely perfect record, being the only automobile in this class to qualify for the highest award—the President's Cup.

Simpler and stronger than ever. No complicated machinery. No multiplicity of parts. *Nothing to watch but the roads.*

Price $650.00 at Factory

Visit the Oldsmobile exhibit at the New York Automobile Show Jan 17th to 24th, call on any of our 58 Selling Agents or write for illustrated book to Dept. R.

OLDS MOTOR WORKS
DETROIT, MICH.

...The only advertisement for a Michigan-made motor vehicle was one for the Oldsmobile. But it was a winner — the first popular, inexpensive car, whose sales of 4,000 in 1903 (up from 2,500 in 1902 and 425 in 1901) far exceeded the production figures of the Winton (700), the Pierce-Arrow (297), and all other cars of that day. Oldsmobile's success was a major contributing factor in the subsequent rise of Michigan to world leadership in the auto industry.

The automobile industry in 1903 was less than a decade old. It had emerged in the late 1890's after many years of experimentation, first in Europe, then in the United States, with various types of mechanically driven vehicles. It was not surprising that a number of young men in Michigan with the necessary mechanical abilities were devoting their spare time to such experiments in these years. On March 6, 1896, several years after others outside Michigan had achieved similar success, Charles B. King, a college-trained, twenty-seven-year-old engineer, drove the first gasoline-powered horseless carriage on the streets of Detroit. In this photograph, taken a short time after this historic event, King is on the right, gripping the tiller with which he steered the thirteen-hundred-pound vehicle, while his assistant, Oliver Barthel, is on the left.

Courtesy: Burton Historical Collection

Barthel would later be an assistant to a friend of King, Henry Ford, who in 1896 was the chief engineer of the Edison Illuminating Company of Detroit. In June, Ford drove out of the shed behind his Bagley Avenue home in the tiny, five-hundred-pound vehicle that he had been putting together during the past two years. Ford posed for this picture in October, 1896, by which time he had enclosed the engine, which is at the rear, beneath the buggy seat. In the Henry Ford Museum at Dearborn this first Ford car may be seen today, restored to its original condition, with the engine uncovered.

Courtesy: Michigan Historical Commission

Courtesy: Michigan Historical Commission

Of more immediate importance than either King's or Ford's car, however, was a third gasoline-powered vehicle that appeared in Michigan in the summer of 1896, one driven on the streets of Lansing by Ransom E. Olds. This historic vehicle eventually wound up in the Smithsonian Institution in Washington, D.C.

Courtesy: Automotive History Collection

Until he was supplanted by Henry Ford, Olds would be Michigan's best known auto maker. The successful industrialist, who is depicted in this portrait made in the early twentieth century, had not achieved his position overnight, however, but only after a decade and a half of effort.

A GASOLINE STEAM CARRIAGE.

The steam carriage recently invented by Ransom E. Olds, of the Olds & Son's engine works, Lansing, Mich., proves to be such a practical success that we give herewith an engraving of its appearance, as photographed. The frame is made of steel arched over the forward wheels, and is low enough at the rear end to form a platform on which the engines and boiler rest fifteen inches from the ground, so that the engines are low enough to make connections on main axle in front, on which the cranks are placed at each end at right angles, there being an engine on each side with a 3×8 inch cylinder.

The boiler is upright and placed between the two cylinders on the rear platform, both engines being connected so as to work as one engine. Just behind the seat are the water and gasoline tanks. The water tank is sufficient for a ten or fifteen mile run, while the gasoline tank is sufficient for a forty mile trip. Over the entire vehicle extends a canopy top, so that the general appearance of the rig is like an ordinary surrey. The fire regulation is automatic, so that more or less gasoline is admitted to the burners as is required by the grade of the road, and when the vehicle is stopped it also closes off the gasoline so that the steam will not rise above its given point. The steering lever is adjusted so that any one can operate the steering, while the throttle and reverse lever are by the operator's seat.

It carries two passengers besides the operator and it is the intention to couple on another vehicle behind if wishing to carry more passengers. The steam from the engines is entirely done away with by an ingenious contrivance of the inventor, and there is no smoke. The engines couple on direct, so that there is no gearing whatever, and the rig runs as quietly as an ordinary carriage. The boiler and engines at the rear end are inclosed by curtains which shut out all view of the machinery, so there is nothing about it to scare horses and they do not seem to mind it any more than an ordinary carriage. Its usual speed on good roads is fifteen miles per hour, and it will ascend any ordinary grade.

The vehicle as a whole includes many new merits. Mr. Olds states that its great advantages are that it never kicks or bites, never tires out on long runs, and during hot weather he can ride fast enough to make a breeze without sweating the horse. It does not require care in the stable, and only eats while it is on the road, which is no more than at the rate of 1 cent per mile. Weight 1,200 pounds.

Scientific American, *May 21, 1892*

Olds, who was first an employee and later the owner of a Lansing engine-manufacturing and -repairing company founded by his father, had developed a steam-powered experimental vehicle as early as 1887. In 1892 he put together a more sophisticated vehicle, also powered by a steam engine, which was sufficiently advanced for its day to be written up in the May 21, 1892, issue of *Scientific American* — almost certainly the first national notice given to a mechanically driven vehicle made in Michigan. Impressed by the article, perhaps especially by the "many new merits" cited in the last paragraph, and by the accompanying picture, a company in London, England, bought this car. When it was shipped abroad in 1893, the Olds steam vehicle became the first American-made car to be sold for export and very possibly the first sold to anyone.

A GASOLINE STEAM CARRIAGE.

100

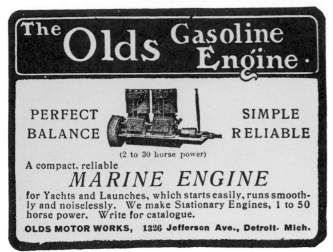
Harper's Monthly, *Vol. 101 (1900)*

Olds' experimentation did not lead immediately to commercial production of cars for the market, even after he had turned to the internal-combustion gasoline engine to power his third car in 1896. The Olds Motor Vehicle Company, organized in 1897, manufactured only a handful of vehicles, and in 1899 was reorganized as the Olds Motor Works, with its operations moved from Lansing to Detroit at the insistence of the principal investor, a wealthy Detroiter, Samuel L. Smith, who became president of the company, with Olds holding the position of vice-president. The company concentrated on the manufacture and sale of gasoline engines while Olds continued his efforts to develop a car that would be commercially successful.

Review of Reviews, *Vol. 23 (1901)*

In 1900, Olds finally settled on a tiny motorized buggy with a curved dash. The car was tested in October, 1900, and ads for it began appearing early in 1901 in national magazines that had previously carried advertisements for automobiles manufactured in Connecticut, Ohio, and other states, but not from Michigan.

Courtesy: Automotive History Collection

Sales of the curved-dash Oldsmobile were stimulated in November, 1901, when the durability of the vehicle had been demonstrated by a young Olds employee, Roy D. Chapin, who drove one of the cars from Detroit to the Waldorf-Astoria Hotel in New York for the annual auto show. This was a daring feat in a day when paved roads were virtually unheard of. It took Chapin seven and a half days to make the trip of 820 miles, and he drove up to the hotel so dirty and mud-splattered that he was at first denied entrance to the hotel where Olds was anxiously awaiting his arrival. The publicity given to Chapin's odyssey led to sales of 750 Oldsmobiles in 1902 in New York City alone, close to double the entire production of the car in 1901. The price tag of $695 for the little runabout brought an automobile, which had previously been little more than an expensive toy of the wealthy, within the reach of the less affluent masses.

The cars that came from the Detroit plant of the Olds Motor Works were the first to awaken in the public's mind an association of the automobile with that city. In addition, these same cars served to spawn other automobile manufacturing operations in Detroit because of the interest in motor vehicles that was generated among the local companies that made parts for the Olds. One of these suppliers was the Leland and Faulconer Company, which made engines for the curved-dash Olds. Robert Faulconer, seated at his desk on the left in the company's stark main office, put up nearly all the capital when the firm was organized in 1890, but he was completely overshadowed by his partner, seated at the right, Henry M. Leland, a mechanical genius who, despite the fact that he was nearly sixty years old, was soon to strike out on an entirely new career as an auto manufacturer.

Another supplier of engines and also transmissions for the Olds was a machine shop recently formed by John Dodge, left, and his brother Horace, the original Dodge boys. Horace Dodge had received some of his early training as a machinist from Henry Leland when he was an employee of Leland and Faulconer. Now the two brothers, like Leland, were encouraged by the success of the Oldsmobile to expand their activities in the auto industry, activities that would ultimately net their widows about $155,000,000 when they sold Dodge Brothers, Incorporated, in 1928.

Lansing business leaders now realized the economic loss to the city resulting from the transfer of the Olds operations to Detroit. They induced Olds to return to the state capital by offering the company the land it needed to build a larger plant to handle its rapidly expanding business. These Oldsmobiles were lined up beside the new Olds Lansing factory that was completed by the end of 1901.

102

In 1903, this parade of Oldsmobiles through Lansing's business district helped to emphasize the fact that the city was now not only the center of the state's government but also the headquarters of what was by far the nation's largest manufacturer of automobiles, although cars also continued to be produced at the Olds plant in Detroit for a few months.

Like so many of the pioneers in the auto industry, Ransom E. Olds did not stay with the company that bore his name. The majority stockholders forced him out in 1904 in a dispute over the kind of car the company should manufacture. But Olds bounced back later the same year to participate in the formation of a new Lansing firm, the Reo Motor Car Company. Olds observed that he had given his name to his first car, but only his initials were needed to identify his new venture. Within two years, the production figures of the Reo factory, located just south of the Grand Trunk Railroad station in Lansing, had made Olds again one of the leaders in the industry.

While Ransom E. Olds was making his name famous, Henry Ford was still unknown outside of his native Wayne County, where he was born in 1863 in a farmhouse near the tiny rural community of Dearborn. The building has now been removed to Greenfield Village in Dearborn, where it is maintained as a historic house museum.

Ford was endowed with a natural curiosity concerning machines and an ability to make them operate. With these talents he had become chief engineer of Detroit's electric light company by the 1890's and was living a comfortable life. Here in 1895, Ford, third from the left, is accepting delivery for the company of a new vacuum pump. Ford's future in the power industry would appear to have been a bright one had he been content to remain in it.

Courtesy: Detroit Edison Company

Courtesy: Ford Archives

Ford, however, after testing his first car in 1896, now devoted more and more of his time to his experiments with cars. In 1897 or early 1898 he completed this second car, which was a considerable improvement over his first, and like the first is now preserved in the Henry Ford Museum.

Courtesy: Ford Archives

With the contacts he had made in Detroit and his growing reputation as a builder of horseless carriages that actually ran, Ford in 1899 was able to obtain the support of some of Detroit's wealthiest men, including Frank J. Hecker and William McMillan, son of the senator, in organizing the Detroit Automobile Company. Ford was hired by the company as its mechanical superintendent. His job and that of his men who worked in the company's factory at 1343 Cass Avenue, Detroit, was to design a car that could be put on the market. Ford, who was a perfectionist, was never satisfied enough with the car he was working on to put it into production. Finally, early in 1901, the stockholders, dissatisfied at the lack of progress, voted to dissolve the company.

Courtesy: Ford Archives   *Courtesy: Ford Motor Company*

Not all of Ford's backers had lost faith in him, however, and they continued to support him in his experimental work. On October 10, 1901, Ford took to the racetrack to win publicity and to learn more about automobiles. In an event at the Grosse Pointe Race Track that was billed as the world championship, Ford first trailed Alexander Winton, the Cleveland auto manufacturer and one of the greatest racers of the day. Then, as Ford mastered the unfamiliar technique of taking the turns, he moved ahead, leaving Winton, who was plagued by engine trouble, far behind at the finish. The enthusiasm Ford's triumph aroused among his backers led them to form the Henry Ford Company.

When Ford still failed to settle upon one design and place it in production, his disillusioned backers gave up on him, and in the summer of 1902 they reorganized as the Cadillac Automobile Company and turned to Henry M. Leland, who had been manufacturing parts for Oldsmobile, to produce a car that would bring money into the investors' pockets. The experienced Leland, twenty years older than Ford, wasted no time. By October he had assembled the first Cadillac in his Leland and Faulconer shop. The blurred figure of a tall, bearded man at the right in this picture may be Leland. If so, the camera that took the picture was somewhat prophetic, since time has tended to blur or obscure the great contribution Leland made to the development of the automobile industry.   *Courtesy: Automotive History Collection*

Leland's first Cadillac, a one-cylinder ("one-lunger") car, was an inexpensive vehicle, priced only slightly higher than the curved-dash Olds. It is shown here being road-tested by Alanson P. Brush, an engineer at Leland and Faulconer who had been one of the designers of the car's engine. The passenger is Leland's son Wilfred, who was always closely associated with his father in the automobile business. Production of this first Cadillac model began in 1903 with an initial shipment of 1,895 automobiles, a sizable figure for that period.

The PENALTY OF LEADERSHIP

IN every field of human endeavor, he that is first must perpetually live in the white light of publicity. ¶ Whether the leadership be vested in a man or in a manufactured product, emulation and envy are ever at work. ¶ In art, in literature, in music, in industry, the reward and the punishment are always the same. ¶ The reward is widespread recognition; the punishment, fierce denial and detraction. ¶ When a man's work becomes a standard for the whole world, it also becomes a target for the shafts of the envious few. ¶ If his work be merely mediocre, he will be left severely alone—if he achieve a masterpiece, it will set a million tongues a wagging. ¶ Jealousy does not protrude its forked tongue at the artist who produces a commonplace painting. ¶ Whatsoever you write, or paint, or play, or sing, or build, no one will strive to surpass or to slander you, unless your work be stamped with the seal of genius. ¶ Long, long, after a great work or a good work, has been done, those who are disappointed or envious continue to cry out that it can not be done. ¶ Spiteful little voices in the domain of art were raised against our own Whistler as a mountebank, long after the big world had acclaimed him its greatest artistic genius. ¶ Multitudes flocked to Bayreuth to worship at the musical shrine of Wagner, while the little group of those whom he had dethroned and displaced, argued angrily that he was no musician at all. ¶ The little world continued to protest that Fulton could never build a steamboat, while the big world flocked to the river banks to see his boat steam by. ¶ The leader is assailed because he is a leader, and the effort to equal him is merely added proof of that leadership. ¶ Failing to equal or to excel, the follower seeks to depreciate and to destroy—but only confirms once more the superiority of that which he strives to supplant. ¶ There is nothing new in this. ¶ It is as old as the world and as old as the human passions—envy, fear, greed, ambition, and the desire to surpass. ¶ And it all avails nothing. ¶ If the leader truly leads, he remains—the leader. ¶ Master-poet, master-painter, master-workman, each in his turn is assailed, and each holds his laurels through the ages. ¶ That which is good or great makes itself known, no matter how loud the clamor of denial. ¶ That which deserves to live —lives.

Cadillac Motor Car Co. Detroit, Mich.

Literary Digest, January 30, 1915

Under the leadership of Leland, who became general manager of Cadillac in 1904 and later was named president, the company acquired a well-earned reputation for the superior craftsmanship of its products. It moved up into the high-priced field where it pioneered in the development and use of standardized interchangeable parts, the electric starter, and, in 1914, the V-8 engine, innovations that were soon copied by other manufacturers, leading to this famous Cadillac advertisement in 1915.

Meanwhile, although Henry Ford's original backers had abandoned him, his newly acquired fame as a race-car driver brought an order from a wealthy fellow racer for Ford to design a new racing car. The result was the famous "999," the largest, most powerful car thus far built in the United States. Hesitant about racing the monster himself, Ford, who had now shaved off his mustache, brought in the daring bicycle-racing champion, Barney Oldfield, who reportedly told Ford as he grasped the tiller:

"Well, this chariot may kill me, but they'll say afterward that I was going like hell when she took me over the bank." In October, 1902, Oldfield set an American record of nearly a mile a minute in a five-mile race at Grosse Pointe, defeating Alexander Winton, among others.

Again Ford's racing success attracted new financial support. In June, 1903, the Ford Motor Company was organized. A group of men, led by a Detroit coal dealer, Alexander Malcolmson, shown here seated on a stool in his office at the coal yard, scraped together $28,000 in cash. More than a third of this money came from Malcolmson's uncle, John S. Gray, a Detroit banker, seated at the left. Most of the rest of the investors were also connected with Malcolmson, either as employees or associates. The

Courtesy: Ford Archives

most important of them was Malcolmson's clerk, James Couzens, second from the right, whose contributions to the success of the Ford Motor Company would be second only to Ford's. Ford himself put in no money but was named vice-president and general manager.

For $75 a month the new company rented quarters in a former icehouse on Mack Avenue, and Henry Ford was finally persuaded to give up experimenting and to begin manufacturing a car. In July, 1903, the company made its first sale.

Courtesy: Michigan Historical Commission

Country Life, May, 1904

This early Ford advertisement is one of many in which Ford lashed out at what he called "The Trust," meaning the Association of Licensed Automobile Manufacturers. This was an organization that had grown out of the claim by the holders of a patent issued in 1895 to George B. Selden that all cars powered by gasoline engines were based on Selden's work and their manufacturers must therefore pay a royalty on each such car to the patent holders. In order to avoid costly litigation, some of the leading auto makers in 1903 formed the A. L. A. M., the members of which recognized the validity of the Selden patent and were licensed to manufacture cars in return for the payment of a small royalty on the sale price of each automobile. Ford refused either to join the association or to acknowledge that the Selden patent applied to the cars he was manufacturing. The association then brought suit against Ford, charging him with patent infringement.

107

Country Life, *May, 1904*

The Electric that is Making History

THE two *greatest* chapters in the story of the electric vehicle have been written this year by the Detroit Electric.

The introduction of our new "Chainless" Direct Shaft Drive, *a straight path of power* from motor to adjustable beveled gear in rear axle—without chain or gear reductions; friction or noise.

And the establishing in Detroit, October 5, 1910, of a *new world's record* for mileage in an electric vehicle: 211.3 miles on a single battery charge.

Accomplished by a regular stock Detroit Electric. That's the greatest triumph yet for the Detroit Electric-Edison System of Motor and Battery.

The Detroit Electric is the *last word* in luxury and beauty, as well

as efficiency; distinguished by its stunning lines, its quiet elegance without show; its rich upholstering and air of genuine refinement.

In point of design and the infinite perfection of finish and equipment it is this year, as always, a style creator.

To the well-bred woman—the Detroit Electric has a particular appeal. In it she can preserve her toilet immaculate, her coiffure intact.

She can drive it with all desired privacy, yet safely in constant touch with traffic conditions all about her.

New Car for "Him"

A brand new extra low and rakish Detroit Electric model for *men* is our Gentlemen's Underslung Roadster—lines of a thoroughbred and extra-long wheel base. Pneumatic tires only.

Ten 1911 Models combine Victorias, Coupes, Broughams—beautifully uphol-

stered in imported goatskin, and other de luxe leathers, all hand-buffed rich satins, broadcloths, English whipcords, etc.,—and the Gentlemen's Roadster.

Three optional drives—" Chainless" Direct Shaft Drive, our successful double chain and Renolds Tandem Silent Enclosed Chain Drives. You have your choice, as well, of Special Electric cushion or pneumatic tires; Edison or lead batteries.

Be *informed*—before you purchase any electric. We ask the privilege of explaining all that the special features of the Detroit Electric *really mean.*

Our dealer in any of the larger cities will gladly wait on you with a demonstrating car. Or write direct for catalog and full details.

The Detroit Electric

Anderson Carriage Co.
Department s   Detroit, Michigan

BRANCHES: New York, Chicago, Kansas City
Detroit, Buffalo, Cleveland.
Selling Representatives in all Leading Cities

Literary Digest, *November 19, 1910*

The same magazine that carried the Ford advertisement in 1904 also had an ad two pages away that was paid for by "The Trust" itself. Threats of legal action were made not only against manufacturers of unlicensed cars and dealers who sold them but even against those individuals who bought such vehicles. This pressure ultimately forced most holdouts, such as Ransom Olds' Reo Motor Car Company, to join the association and pay their royalties, but Ford stubbornly held out. He was vindicated in 1911 when a federal court ruled that the engine Ford and most American manufacturers used was of an entirely different design than Selden's, and thus Selden's patent did not apply to them.

Motor vehicles, of course, did not have to be powered by a gasoline engine, and Ransom Olds, in fact, once threatened to return to producing a steam car rather than buckle down and pay royalties to the Selden patent owners. Although he did not carry out his threat, other Michigan manufacturers at this time were producing electric cars. The Detroit Electric is the best remembered of these, with models appearing first in 1906 and continuing to 1923. Appealing "to the well-bred woman" in an industry whose advertising was geared more and more to a masculine audience may have been one reason for the ultimate disappearance of electric cars from dealers' showrooms. This 1910 ad's claim of 211.3 miles on a single battery charge is an impressive one today, as renewed attention is being given to electric vehicles as a possible means of eliminating some of the air pollution created by the exhaust from gasoline engines in heavy city traffic.

Scribner's Magazine,
Vol. 35 (1904)

Courtesy: Michigan Historical Collections

Among the members of the Association of Licensed Automobile Manufacturers in 1904 were several Michigan companies, including such familiar names as the Olds Motor Works and the Cadillac Automobile Company. Not so familiar is the Northern Manufacturing Company of Detroit, which was formed in 1902 and manufactured the "Silent Northern," a car of rather advanced design developed by Charles B. King and Jonathan D. Maxwell, the namesake of the later Maxwell automobile. Like virtually all of the more than three thousand different makes of cars that have appeared on the market in the United States, the Northern survived only a short time before it was absorbed by a larger company in 1908.

Also gone from the scene today but still fresh in the memories of many is the Packard. Originally a product of an Ohio company that began operations in 1899, the Packard was seen in New York in 1901 by two young and wealthy Detroiters, Henry B. Joy and his brother-in-law, Truman Newberry, who had come to attend the annual auto show. Impressed by the car, Joy hurried to Ohio and in a short time had acquired control of the company and moved it to Detroit — a move that helped draw attention to the increasingly important role this city was playing in the automobile industry. Many years later, Joy had this picture of himself taken, seated in the Packard model that had caught his fancy in New York City.

Joy hired a young Detroit architect, Albert Kahn, to design the complex of buildings comprising the Packard plant on East Grand Boulevard, Detroit, that began to rise in 1903. Kahn

Courtesy: Automotive History Collection

shortly revolutionized industrial architecture by employing reinforced concrete to build bright, relatively fireproof factory buildings characterized by vast expanses of windows and floor space inside with widely spaced supporting columns providing a dramatic contrast with the dark, dingy, cluttered, and hazardous working conditions under which workers labored in the traditional industrial plants of that day. Kahn's ideas quickly became the accepted standard, and during the next forty years he and his associates designed one out of every five industrial buildings erected in the United States, as well as many in foreign countries.

Since the cessation of Packard automobile production in the late 1950's, the Packard plant, shown here in the 1920's, has been adapted for warehouse and other use and has undergone extensive change that has tended to obscure, if not obliterate, much of Kahn's work.

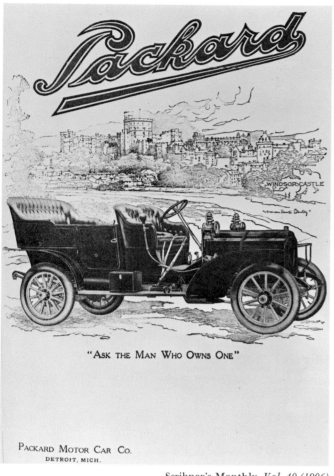

"ASK THE MAN WHO OWNS ONE"

PACKARD MOTOR CAR CO.
DETROIT, MICH.

Scribner's Monthly, *Vol. 40 (1906)*

Henry Joy, although somewhat
eccentric, was a man of
considerable ability who had
had both the business
experience and the
technological training that
were so important to success
in the highly competitive
automobile industry.
Following his own judgment,
Joy scrapped the one-cylinder
Packard and went instead into
the production of a much larger,
and much more expensive, car.
By 1906, through understated
snob-appeal ads such as this,
with the famous slogan, "Ask
the Man Who Owns One," the
Packard was well on its way to
becoming the leading luxury car
of its day, with a price tag
of $3,500 and up.

Courtesy: Automotive History Collection

Although Cadillac, Ford, Packard, Northern, and the early
Oldsmobiles were attracting increasing attention to Detroit,
the importance of automobile manufacturing to the economy
of Michigan as a whole was already being suggested by the
rise of manufacturers in other cities, such as Grand Rapids,
where Walter S. Austin began manufacturing the first car
bearing his name in 1903. This is a photograph of that first
Austin, a car that sold for $2,000. Austin's company,
which is not to be confused with the British manufacturer,
Austin Motors, or the later American Austin Car Company
that manufactured the tiny Austin Bantam in the 1930's,
continued in production until 1920. Walter Austin himself
was around for many more years, and at the time of his death
in Grand Rapids in 1965 he had reached the age of ninety-
nine. He had shared with his fellow automotive pioneers the
successes and defeats that characterized their lives, and he
also epitomized a tendency among many of them to enjoy
an unusually long life span.

You can see the superb value in Jackson cars.

No hill too steep
No sand too deep

You see it in their size—their power—the ease with which they ride.

In the instant and willing response of their powerful motors —in their ability to cope with a difficult situation.

Fifty horsepower—which usually means $3000 or more— is yours in the Jackson "52" for $1800, supplemented by the long wheelbase (124 inches) and the big wheels and tires (36 x 4 inches) so necessary to comfort in a high-powered car.

Instead of the 30 horsepower that a price of $1500 has always implied—40 horsepower in the Jackson "42" at that price; with wheelbase of 118 inches; 34 x 4 inch tires; and complete equipment of top, windshield, gas tank, lamps, etc.

And in the Jackson "32"—our $1100 car—30 horsepower, 32 inch wheels, 110 inch wheelbase. Of the same high quality, in every detail, as the larger Jacksons.

Full elliptic springs, instead of the usual half or three quarter elliptic, on every Jackson car—simply another proof of the value already apparent.

A generosity of power and size and riding ease that, as a rule, is the especial attribute of the costliest cars.

And back of it all a progressive experience of more than ten years in the manufacture of good automobiles.

All we ask you to do is to go to the Jackson dealer and confirm what we have told you.

Let us send you our complete catalog, illustrated in two colors.

JACKSON AUTOMOBILE COMPANY
1205 E. Main St.   **Jackson, Mich.**

Jackson cars exhibited in space No. 111, on the elevated platform—Madison Square Garden Show, New York, January 6-13.

Model Forty-two—$1500
Forty horsepower, four cylinder motor; 118 inch wheelbase; full elliptic springs, front and rear; 34x4 inch tires. Roomy five-passenger body. Price includes full equipment of top, windshield, gas tank, etc.

Model Thirty-two—$1100
Thirty horsepower, four cylinder motor; 110 inch wheelbase; 32 inch tires; five-passenger torpedo type. Gas lamps and oil lamps, tools, etc.

Model Twenty-eight—$1000
Two-passenger roadster. Gasoline tank and luggage box at rear. Four cylinders, 30 H.P.; 100 inch wheelbase. Gas lamps and oil lamps, tools, etc.

Model Twenty-six—$1100
Two-passenger torpedo roadster. Gasoline tank and luggage box at rear. Four cylinders, 30 H.P.; 110 inch wheelbase. Gas lamps and oil lamps, tools, etc.

Model 52 (below) $1800
Fifty horsepower, 4 cylinder motor; 124 inch wheelbase; full elliptic springs, front and rear; 36 inch wheels. Extra roomy five-passenger body. Price includes demountable rims, gas tank, horn, tools, etc.

Harper's Weekly, *January 6, 1912*

Among other outstate cities, Jackson for a time seemed about to challenge Detroit for the title of Motor City. Several companies manufactured cars in Jackson in the early years of the century, including such names as the Imperial, the Earl, the Cutting, the Briscoe, and the Clarke-Carter. The Jackson, produced from 1902 to 1923, was the most successful of these automobiles in terms of the length of time the various models bearing this name were offered to the public. Although the city of Jackson did become an important producer of auto parts, it muffed its greatest opportunity to become a major center of automobile manufacturing in 1905 and 1906 when it failed to persuade the Buick Motor Company to remain in Jackson, rather than to move its offices and assembly operations to Flint.

Courtesy: Crooks Studio

Flint in 1905 celebrated the fiftieth anniversary of its incorporation as a city. Signs arching over the streets of the community of fifteen thousand people publicized the fact that it was known as the "Vehicle City," but the vehicle referred to was not the automobile.

Flint had earned its nickname because of the position it had attained as the hub of the buggy and carriage industry. Since the early 1870's, when this photograph was taken of Sam Randall's Buggy Works at North Saginaw and Third Avenue, various types of horse-drawn vehicles had been manufactured in the county seat of Genesee County.

Courtesy: Crooks Studio

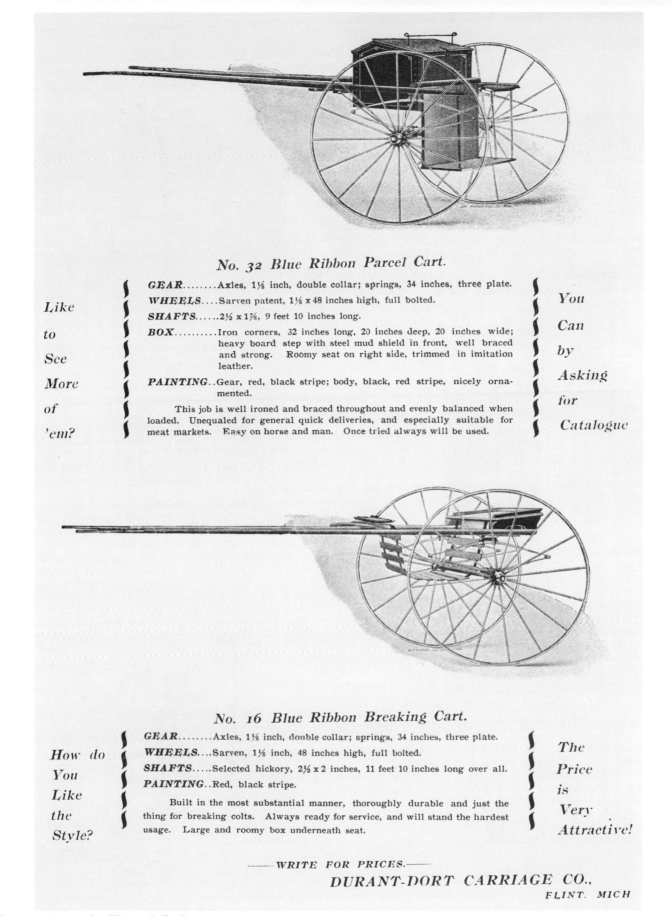

No. 32 Blue Ribbon Parcel Cart.

GEAR........Axles, 1⅛ inch, double collar; springs, 34 inches, three plate.

WHEELS....Sarven patent, 1⅛ x 48 inches high, full bolted.

SHAFTS......2½ x 1⅞, 9 feet 10 inches long.

BOX.........Iron corners, 32 inches long, 20 inches deep, 20 inches wide; heavy board step with steel mud shield in front, well braced and strong. Roomy seat on right side, trimmed in imitation leather.

PAINTING..Gear, red, black stripe; body, black, red stripe, nicely ornamented.

This job is well ironed and braced throughout and evenly balanced when loaded. Unequaled for general quick deliveries, and especially suitable for meat markets. Easy on horse and man. Once tried always will be used.

Like to See More of 'em?

You Can by Asking for Catalogue

No. 16 Blue Ribbon Breaking Cart.

GEAR........Axles, 1⅛ inch, double collar; springs, 34 inches, three plate.

WHEELS....Sarven, 1⅛ inch, 48 inches high, full bolted.

SHAFTS.....Selected hickory, 2½ x 2 inches, 11 feet 10 inches long over all.

PAINTING..Red, black stripe.

Built in the most substantial manner, thoroughly durable and just the thing for breaking colts. Always ready for service, and will stand the hardest usage. Large and roomy box underneath seat.

How do You Like the Style?

The Price is Very Attractive!

——WRITE FOR PRICES.——

DURANT-DORT CARRIAGE CO.,
FLINT. MICH

Courtesy: Automotive History Collection

The giant among these Flint manufacturers was the Durant-Dort Carriage Company, which was founded in 1886 and within a short time was selling its road carts through dealers scattered over the country. In terms of numbers of vehicles sold it was the largest such manufacturer in the country, although the Studebaker Company of South Bend, Indiana, earned more money due to the larger, more expensive carriages it marketed.

At the beginning of the twentieth century some of the Flint carriage manufacturers, foreseeing that automobiles might soon put them out of business, sought to make their futures more secure by acquiring control of an automobile company. The opportunity came in 1903 when a struggling Detroit company, the Buick Motor Car Company, was put up for sale. Flint investors raised the small amount of money needed to buy the company and move it to Flint. The Buick, designed by David Buick, a successful Detroit manufacturer of bathtubs and other plumbing equipment, had some excellent features, but lack of sufficient capital and business acumen had made it impossible for Buick

Courtesy: Automotive History Collection

to succeed in putting the car on the market. The new Flint owners were not much more successful, since they were able to turn out only sixteen of this model manufactured in 1903.

Courtesy: Michigan Historical Commission

In 1904, the Buick owners sought help from William Crapo Durant, the promotional genius responsible for the great success of the Durant-Dort Carriage Company. Durant, a grandson of Henry Crapo, who had made a fortune in the lumber business in Flint in the middle of the nineteenth century and had then gone on to become governor of the state from 1865 through 1868, is one of the most amazing figures in American business history. Possessed of a remarkable ability to forecast the future demand for a product and an even more remarkable ability to convince potential investors of the wisdom of his judgment, Durant ultimately would fail because he never knew when the time had come to settle down to consolidate and administer the fruits of his speculation.

Courtesy: Automotive History Collection

Although Durant knew nothing about an automobile's mechanical workings, his business instincts told him that the Buick was a good car and that what was required to make it a commercial success was additional capital and plant facilities to put it into large-scale production. He took charge of the company, sold half a million dollars worth of stock in one day to Flint acquaintances, moved the assembly of the Buick to a larger factory that was available in Jackson, and began promoting the car with the same vigor and success as when earlier he sold road carts. This ad appeared in the auto weekly, *Motor Age,* on February 8, 1906. Note the Jackson address, so unfamiliar to Buick owners of later generations.

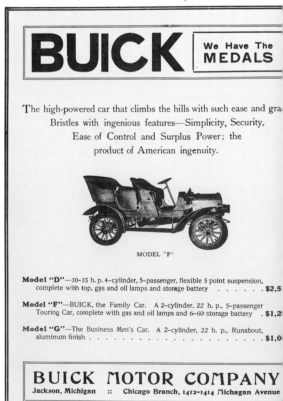

In a time when the total United States automobile production was only a few thousand a year, Durant predicted that the demand for cars would soon push production up into the hundreds of thousands. In order to gain a larger share of that potential market, Durant built what was then the world's largest automobile plant on a 220-acre tract of farmland he had purchased at the north end of Flint and transferred manufacturing operations back to that city from Jackson. (Had Durant been able to raise the necessary capital in Jackson, he might have left Buick in that city.) Flint's population in a few years doubled as workers

poured into the city to meet the mushrooming manpower needs of Buick. A temporary tent city was set up in the Oak Park subdivision Durant was developing near the Buick factory.

By 1908, when this Buick model appeared on the market, Buick had become the leading automobile manufacturer in the country. The company's production that year reached 8,487 cars. But Durant was not satisfied. Realizing that changes in tastes might cause buyers to turn from Buick to some other car that captured the public's fancy, he conceived of organizing many different automobile companies, offering cars in a variety of styles and prices, under one corporate management. Such a merger, if he could bring it off, would immediately increase Durant's share of the market while it lessened the risks by offering the public a broad range of choices.

IT WILL NOT DOWN

REPORT CONCERNING MERGER OF AUTO CONCERNS.

Understood in New York Automobile Circles That Buick Will Be in Consolidation.

(Special to The Daily Journal.)

New York, Dec 28.—The announcement of the formation of the General Motors company for the purpose of absorbing all the principal concerns manufacturing low-priced automobiles, has created a flurry here. It is said that three-quarters of the stockholders of the Olds company, of Lansing, Mich., and a fair-sized proportion of the stockholders of the Buick Motor company, of Flint, Mich., have already assented to the proposed merger. The stockholders of various other automobile concerns, it is understood, will also be approached, and if the plans of the promoters bear full fruition there will be a practical consolidation of the leading companies engaged in the manufacture of low-priced cars.

The General Motors company has been incorporated under the laws of New Jersey with a capital stock of $12,500,000, of which $7,000,000 is preferred and $5,500,000 is common. The shares are of a par value of one dollar, and it is said that the preferred stock will pay a seven per cent accumulated dividend.

When seen in regard to the foregoing dispatch today, W. C. Durant, general superintendent of the Buick Motor company, said there was nothing in regard to the matter which he could give out for publication.

Using his profitable Buick operations as the base, Durant on September 16, 1908, chartered the General Motors Company, an event of enormous importance from the perspective of later years, which, however, received no attention at the time. Even three months later, little word about this business development had leaked out.

Courtesy: Automotive History Collection

Within the next two years, Durant acquired control, usually through stock exchanges, of ten automobile companies, plus assorted truck and auto parts companies. Among the automobile companies that were brought into the GM fold were Durant's own Buick, Oldsmobile, Cadillac, and Oakland. The latter had been formed in 1907 by Edward M. Murphy, a Pontiac buggy manufacturer, who followed the example of the Flint carriage industry by turning his attention to automobiles. He formed the Oakland Motor Car Company and began producing a car that had originally been designed for Cadillac but then had been rejected by that company. In later decades, Murphy's 1907 Oakland, named for the county in which Pontiac is located, would become a much-sought-after and prized possession of antique car buffs, one that would be carefully restored and driven on special occasions in appropriate period costumes.

Oakland (the future Pontiac Division of General Motors) was one of the smaller companies acquired by Durant. By greatly expanding its production facilities, Oakland by 1912 had become a much more important factor in the middle-price-range car market. But the money that was sunk into this expansion program also contributed to financial difficulties for General Motors in 1910, which led to a more conservative leadership taking over control of the company, replacing Durant.

Durant's career in the automobile industry was only beginning, however. He gained control of new automobile companies, most notably Chevrolet, which had been formed in 1911 to produce a car designed by Louis Chevrolet, a Swiss racing-car driver who had previously worked for Durant at Buick. Here, in 1912, Durant's son Cliff sits at the wheel of the first Chevrolet, while his father (at the far right among those standing on the sidewalk) admires the six-cylinder car with its folding top and adjustable windshield. Only 2,999 Chevrolets were manufactured at the company's plant in Detroit in 1912, but the following year Durant moved the company to Flint. By 1916 he had pushed its annual production up to seventy thousand and had used this new success to enable him to talk and buy his way back into control of General Motors.

By the second decade of the twentieth century, automobiles were becoming more advanced and complex in design and buyers were becoming more knowledgeable about cars. These developments combined to make it more difficult for a new manufacturer to break into the industry and to achieve the success that had come to such pioneer companies as Olds, Cadillac, Ford, and Buick only a few years earlier. In addition to Durant's Chevrolet, another one of these entries that made good was Hudson. It was named after the Detroit department store owner J. L. Hudson, who provided the money needed to put the Hudson Motor Car Company in business. But the president of the company that was organized in 1909

was Roy D. Chapin, who, when he posed for this photograph in one of the first Hudsons, had come a long way from the youth in 1901 who had made automobile history by driving an Oldsmobile from Detroit to New York. By 1904, Chapin had become sales manager of the Olds Motor Works. In 1906 he and several other executives began to take the first steps in putting out their own car. The Hudson was the ultimate result.

117

Courtesy: Michigan Historical Collections

Why did the Hudson Motor Company, like so many other auto manufacturers, locate its plant in Detroit? These men, some of the original employees at Hudson in 1909, were an important part of the answer. Many of these men had learned the mechanics of assembling an automobile from previous service with one of the older automobile companies in Detroit or elsewhere in southeastern Michigan. By 1909, Roy Chapin would have found it impossible to locate as large a pool of skilled auto workers to draw upon anywhere else in the country.

Literary Digest, *July 24, 1915*

Although Chapin and his associates no doubt hoped for more when they started out, the slow rise in sales of Hudsons — up to only 7,199 a year after five years of effort — soon made it evident that the company would never become one of the giants of the industry.

Nevertheless, like other smaller auto manufacturers, Hudson could and did attract much attention with some of the models that appeared under that name during nearly half a century. (The practice of introducing the new models well in advance of the model year is demonstrated by this advertisement in July, 1915, for the new 1916 Hudson Road Cruiser — priced with the familiar notation: "F. O. B. Detroit.")

HUDSON
Rides the Crest

POPULARITY

1041 Sold in Two Days

On Monday and Tuesday, June 14th and 15th—Opening Days for the New Model—Dealers Sold to Users 1041 Hudsons

On June 13th, all the country's big newspapers announced that the HUDSON new model was ready.

They announced these innovations:

The Yacht-Line Body
The Lustrous Finish
More Room and Luxury
A $200 Price Reduction

We knew that thousands waited this announcement. To prepare for them, we had shipped for some time more than 100 new models daily. But this avalanche amazed us. Nearly one-half of our first month's production was sold on the opening day.

In Detroit, our home city—the very center of Motordom—our dealers had 42 orders at the close of the first day's business. And they have placed with us orders for 750—right here in this vortex of motor car rivalry.

Thousands Turned Away

But the first two days' sales—1041—merely touched the fringe of the waiting demand for this HUDSON. Men who bought on those days were already converted. The crowds were too heavy to give demonstrations, and thousands were turned away.

By the time this appears we shall have built at least 4500 of these new-model HUDSONS. We are shipping 115 per day. And, beyond any question, every one will have gone to a waiting buyer.

So it has been almost constantly since this new-type car appeared. That was 22 months ago. We have quadrupled our output, but only at rare times have there been HUDSONS enough.

No Second Choice Now

This HUDSON Six, when it first came out, stood alone in this new-day class. It brought the era of lightness to high-grade cars, and the end of over-tax. Only Howard E. Coffin, our famous designer, dared venture in this field then.

But HUDSON popularity brought dozens of followers. And many a man who could not get HUDSON found what seemed a fair second choice.

Not so today. HUDSON engineers have worked out many refinements. In 20 months they made 51 improvements. And the price, which started at $1750, has dropped to $1350, through mammoth production. So the HUDSON today finds no rival in sight of it. You'll find no second choice.

New 1916 Features

Now this HUDSON has the Yacht-Line body. It has the Lustrous finish, whose every coat is baked on in enormous ovens. It has a roomier tonneau, a wider rear seat. It has disappearing extra seats to double the tonneau room.

It has enameled leather upholstery. It has deep, luxurious cushions.

And it has, above all, the approval of owners. Many thousands of men have proved out this HUDSON on millions of miles of road. Go see it before our summer's output is sold. Your dealer will get you an early delivery.

7-Passenger Phaeton or 3-Passenger Roadster, $1350, f. o. b. Detroit. Also a New Cabriolet, $1650

HUDSON service is one of our finest developments. Ask our dealer to explain it to you.

HUDSON $1350 F.O.B. DETROIT

HUDSON MOTOR CAR COMPANY, Detroit, Mich.

118

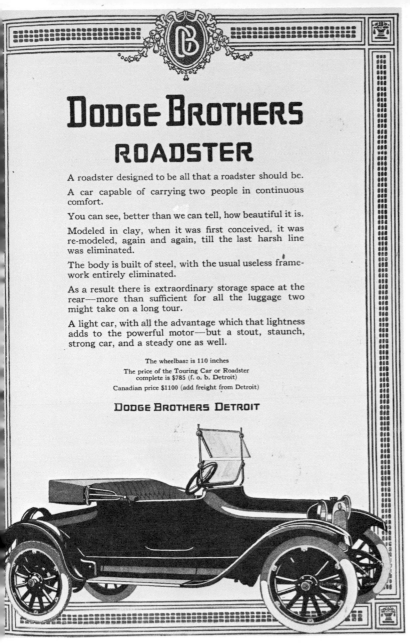

DODGE BROTHERS
ROADSTER

A roadster designed to be all that a roadster should be.

A car capable of carrying two people in continuous comfort.

You can see, better than we can tell, how beautiful it is.

Modeled in clay, when it was first conceived, it was re-modeled, again and again, till the last harsh line was eliminated.

The body is built of steel, with the usual useless framework entirely eliminated.

As a result there is extraordinary storage space at the rear—more than sufficient for all the luggage two might take on a long tour.

A light car, with all the advantage which that lightness adds to the powerful motor—but a stout, staunch, strong car, and a steady one as well.

The wheelbase is 110 inches

The price of the Touring Car or Roadster complete is $785 (f. o. b. Detroit)

Canadian price $1100 (add freight from Detroit)

DODGE BROTHERS DETROIT

Literary Digest, *August 28, 1915*

An even newer company than Hudson that was also competing with several score other car manufacturers for a share of the automobile market in 1915 was the Dodge Brothers Company. Innovations such as the all-steel body help to explain why the Dodge, unlike Hudson, quickly advanced to a point where by 1917, only three years after the formation of the company, it ranked fourth in the industry in volume of production.

Courtesy: Michigan Historical Commission

In the Dodge factory at Hamtramck, workers, using hand-operated chain hoists, began assembling the first Dodge cars in November, 1914. The modern plant, designed by Albert Kahn and built in 1910, was easily adapted to the large-scale production of the complete car, rather than the parts of cars for which it had originally been intended. But for the perfection of mass-production techniques, Dodge would soon follow the example set at the nearby Ford plant in Highland Park.

Courtesy: Ford Archives

It was, in fact, the Ford Motor Company, not General Motors, Dodge, Hudson, or any of the other Michigan automobile manufacturers in the second decade of the twentieth century, that was the pace-setter and unchallenged leader in the industry. This position began to be achieved in October, 1908, when Henry Ford, now in complete control of the company, came out with his Model T, destined to be the most famous car ever manufactured. This is reportedly the first Model T, driven off the assembly line by Ford himself. He now proceeded to scrap all other models and concentrate solely on the production of this sturdy vehicle, which could stand up under the worst road conditions of the day and could be easily repaired by anyone with the most rudimentary knowledge of automotive workings. These were qualities Ford had been seeking in a car. He had also been seeking to produce a cheap car, within the reach of the masses, not the high-priced models some of his directors had favored. The price tag on the first Model T's was $850, making it actually considerably more expensive than earlier Ford models.

To bring down the price of the Model T, Ford called in the ubiquitous Albert Kahn to design a great new assembly plant in Highland Park. These quarters, which the company began to move into in 1910, provided thirty-two acres of factory space in contrast with the 2.65 acres Ford had had available in 1908. Car production increased nearly six times at much less cost per car, so that by 1911 the Model T runabout was selling for less than $600. The working force was more than doubled between 1908 and 1911. The small Detroit suburb now became accustomed to the sight of long lines of men at closing time streaming out of the big factory on Woodward Avenue and queuing up to board the waiting trolley cars.

But Ford did not rely solely on larger facilities and more employees to increase his output of cars. Drawing upon the work of others before them and adding new touches of their own, Ford and his able crew of assistants incorporated into the Highland Park plant new concepts of assembling the automobiles. The operation was designed to move logically step by step along the production line, with each workman assigned a specific task, which, ideally, he could perform in each case in the shortest possible time with the least possible motion.

121

Courtesy: Michigan Historical Commission

Finally, in 1913, the ultimate in mass production for that day was achieved with the introduction of the moving assembly line, bringing the work by mechanical means to the workers and eliminating much of the time and physical labor previously expended on moving the parts of the car through the various stages of its assembly. By September, 1913, when this photograph was taken, the time it took to assemble the chassis had been cut in half.

Near the end of the assembly operations in 1913, the bodies were skidded down this ramp, landing on the chassis that was moved into place at the bottom. As improvements were made in the assembly line, more and more time was saved. Ford, which had already become the leading producer of cars in the country, now increased its share of the market, so that from 1913 until the mid-1920's there was not a year in which at least two out of every five cars sold in the United States were not Ford Model T's.

Courtesy: Automobile Manufacturers Association

122

Ford Company to Divide $10,000,000 Among Employes

Profit-Sharing Plan Announced Whereby Minimum Wage for Males Is Advanced from $2.34 to $5 a Day—Hours Decreased from 9 to 8 Daily

SECRETARY OF COMMERCE REDFIELD PRAISES FORD'S GENEROSITY

Washington, D. C., Jan. 6—Special telegram—A "social advance" and a "recognition of the value of a man in industry," were Secretary of Commerce Redfield's characterizations today of the Ford Motor Co.'s plan to distribute $10,000,000 to its employes.

"Some people will say Ford can't afford to do that," said the secretary. "That kind of talk is foolish. It doesn't depend on whether he can afford it or not. I see in this, as in the removal of Morgan members from directorates, a great step forward. It is a social advance, recognizing the value of men which may be, and I hope is, epochal.

"One must not discuss the details of such a plan, because this may only be done by one who knows the details of the business; but the broad principle involved of recognition of the essential value of the men and the equity of appraising that value at its true worth is entirely sound."

DETROIT, Mich., Jan. 5—Twenty-two thousand, five hundred employes of the Ford Motor Co., working in the main plant here and in the several assembling branches throughout the world, came to the happy conclusion that 1914 is to be a year of promise and prosperity for them today when Henry Ford, founder and president of the concern that bears his name, announced that approximately $10,000,000 will be divided among them during the next 12 months under a profit-sharing plan of his own conception.

In announcing that almost one-half of the annual earnings of the company in the future would be given to his army of employes, President Ford outlined the features of his altruistic plan, which are as follows:

Raises minimum wage for male employes of more than 22 years of age from $2.34 to $5 a day, new wage scale to go into effect January 12 and will affect over 90 per cent of the men immediately.

Workers receiving more than the minimum wage at the present time also will be given their share of the profits.

Younger men, having relatives dependent upon them, will be included when the new wage scale is made out.

Reduction of the number of working hours per day from 9 to 8 and the addition of 4,000 to 5,000 employes so that three shifts can be worked.

Under the new system of remuneration, two classes of workers are provided for—one including the average workmen whose daily wages will be more than doubled and the other taking into consideration the more skilled employes who now receive from $6 to $7 a day but will be given an increase as befits their services as experts. Another plan is being devised that will swell the earnings of the 300 women employes who now receive a minimum wage of $40 a month.

The increased wages are to be paid monthly instead of yearly. No increase in the price of the company's product will be made in order to secure funds to make the profit-sharing plan possible. The $10,-000,000 will be deducted from the dividends of the seven stockholders.

In addition to raising the pay of his workers, Mr. Ford hopes to so arrange the work at his plant that if it becomes necessary at any season of the year to lay off men, the layoff shall come in July, August and September when the employes can readily obtain work in the harvest fields and lose little by the temporary cessation of production.

"Henry Ford is the originator of the plan," said James Cousins, general manager, speaking for the manufacturer and chief owner of the plant which bears his name. "He believes there has been too big a division between capital and labor and that labor has not shared to the extent it should. Therefore we began to devise a profit-sharing scheme. It is not an increase in pay, to put it in those terms, but it is a plan whereby every employe in the plant will share in what the plant and its branches produce. It will bring their monthly pay check up, and we believe will help improve the standard of our employes."

In explaining the plan Mr. Ford says that it is one of "social justice." The employes will not be subject to preemptory discharge by the foreman but in case a foreman feels that a man is unfitted for work in his department he will be transferred to another department until it is definitely established that he is entirely inefficient. Along this line a new department will be created, known as the sociological department. Just what the duties of this department will be cannot at this time be definitely stated, but it's functions will be very broad. Not only will it include the work of transferring or placing men in the departments in which they are the most efficient, but it will also look to the conduct of the men outside of working hours. It will attempt to guide these men so that the new prosperity will not result in their own injury. If a man cannot be brought to a realization of his economic duties there is no question but that after a reasonable trial his place will be given to a man who will.

The announcement brought some 10,000 men looking for work at the Ford plant this morning. The company, however, announced that no men would be hired at present.

CHANGE IN KEETON PLANS

Detroit, Mich., Jan. 5—The Keeton Motor Co., which has been manufacturing Keeton cars for the past year, has just completed arrangements whereby the American Voiturette Co. of Detroit, manufacturer of the Carnation, also will manufacture and sell the Keeton car. Charles B. Shaffer, president of the American Voiturette Co., states that, owing to the field for a car of the class and type of the Keeton being somewhat limited, it has been decided best to have the Keeton car made in conjunction with the Carnation.

The officers of the American Voiturette Co. are as follows: C. B. Shaffer, president; H. H. Newson, vice-president and general manager; C. B. Lewis, secretary and treasurer; C. P. James, assistant secretary and treasurer.

The outward appearance and name of the Keeton remain unchanged, while the mechanical construction and details have been refined, and the personnel of the organization has been completely revamped.

INCREASE OF CAPITAL BY G & J

Indianapolis, Ind., Jan. 5 Notice has been filed with the Indiana secretary of state that the G & J Tire Co., which is the Indianapolis branch of the United States Tire Co., has increased its capital stock from $1,000,000 to $2,000,000. The additional capital is in preferred stock. The Western Motor Co. of Marion, Ind., has filed notice that its capitalization has been reduced from $400,000 to $1,000. The Rutenber Electric Co., Logansport, has issued $35,000 worth of preferred stock.

WIRE WHEEL SUIT STARTED

Philadelphia, Pa., Jan. 6—Rudge-Whitworth, Ltd., of England, and the receivers of the Standard Roller Bearing Co. of Philadelphia have brought suit against

Courtesy: Automotive History Collection

In order to get and to hold the army of workers needed to make full use of the revolutionary new production facilities that had been developed, Ford on January 5, 1914, made an announcement that startled the nation. At a time when the average American worker's pay was only a few pennies an hour and the ten- or twelve-hour workday was still common, Henry Ford declared he would pay his men five dollars for an eight-hour day. The question of whether Ford or James Couzens (whose name is misspelled here by the trade magazine, *Motor Age*) deserves credit for this decision is a subject of continuing debate, and the actual implementation of the policy was not nearly as utopian as the announcement may have indicated it would be. Yet there can be no doubt that the $5 day solidified Ford's reputation as the most innovative, forward-looking firm on the American industrial scene.

Henry Ford, Miracle Maker

Second article in The Independent's Industrial Series on the big plants that are finding a successful answer to the problems of labor unrest

By Professor John R. Commons, of the University of Wisconsin

In collaboration with A. P. Haake, O. F. Carpenter, Malcolm Sharp, Jennie McMullin Turner, Ethel B. Dietrich, Jean Davis, John A. Commons

"THE industrial miracle of the age," John D. Rockefeller is reported to have said of the Ford Motor Company. He might have added, the psychological miracle of the age. The industrial end is amazing enough. Three completed cars moving off every minute on their own gasoline. The bread-winners of a city of two hundred and fifty thousand at work in one factory.

But the psychological miracle is equally miraculous. Ford reversed the ordinary psychology of industry. Instead of sharing profits with employees at the end of the year he shared them before they were earned. Instead of carefully selecting employees at the gates he takes them as they come—gets a cross-section of the community—has a theory that he must carry his share of the maimed, blind, and criminal, because somebody has to do it anyhow—believes in ordinary plain people as they come along.

This is not scientific and is not business. According to the usual ideas Ford ought to break. They tried to prove in court that he was a very ignorant man and could scarcely even read and write. He needs somebody to protect him against himself. And that is what his employees are doing.

Ford says, in effect, to anybody who gets into his works, "How much do you think you are worth?" Well the man thinks he is worth a little more than he has been getting elsewhere. "Why," says Ford, "that's nothing. Here is the biggest thing in the world. We are going to sell a million cars a year and give every family in America a 'Lizzie.' If you get into the game you are worth twice as much, ten times as much, as you have been getting. We will pay you that in advance. Now go to it."

And just the ordinary, everyday man rises up out of himself and sees himself twice as big, ten times as big, as he had ever thought possible. He goes to it.

That is why even men with a prison record have done big things at Ford's. There are 400 of them and the majority making good.

Two thousand men go around with labels, "For light work only." A blind man does the work of three men. The fact is, everybody turns in and protects Ford against himself. He is positively too democratic for this world. One man is just as good as another, he thinks. That certainly is not business. But behold, you see or-

160

Henry Ford is really a plunger—a plunger in social psychology. Instead of sharing profits with employees at the end of the year, he shares them before they are earned. Instead of carefully selecting his men at the gates, he has a theory that he must carry his share of the maimed, the criminal and the blind. And his employees protect him by reducing the labor turn-over in his plant to such an extent that real team work is possible

dinary, common men doing big things at Ford's.

Of course, they make mistakes. Ford took his sociologists out of the ranks, and they certainly did raw work for a while. Ford somewhere had gotten an idea that what he wanted as workers in his factory were men who were living clean and wholesome and constructive lives. So he did not care to have employees examined as to their efficiency—efficiency was to be a by-product of the clean and wholesome life. He was going to share his profits, not with those who got out the work, but with those who led a clean and wholesome life. So he picked out his sociologists from the ranks to investigate and find out. And they went into the homes, investigating and re-investigating everybody. They had an idea that that was the clean, wholesome and constructive life.

Well, after about three years, Ford called in Dr. Marquis, Dean of the Episcopal Cathedral, and spoke in this wise: "There is too much of this snooping around in private affairs. We'll change this from a Sociology department to an Education department—you take charge. You know what I want—clean and constructive life—but cut out all except those that really need further assistance and advice."

And that is what Dr. Marquis has been doing. He has about fifty men on that job.

Then about the 400 with prison records. Ford had an idea that if he could save men from the penitentiary they would make good. All they needed was a chance. But the idea did not work. They had a different idea. This was just another chance to get off, and so they took advantage of it and went on with their criminality. Now this has been changed. The Education department takes on no convicted delinquent until after he has served his term, or at least an appreciable part of it. He must take his medicine. Then he may have his chance to make good. These four hundred are assigned to a confidential adviser—a kind of unofficial parole officer attached to the Education department of the factory. So Ford tried out his theory of faith in human nature, and his Education department learned how to protect Ford against himself.

People say, "Oh yes, Ford can do these things because he has such an enormous business. There is nothing at Ford's that can teach other employers anything in any ordinary business subject to competition."

The Independent, *May 1, 1920*

No matter how influential James Couzens and other officials in the Ford Motor Company were in the decisions that had placed that firm far in advance of any other automobile manufacturer, it was generally accepted by the public that Henry Ford was responsible for everything his company had achieved. Although criticisms of Ford did appear in print, "Henry Ford, Miracle Maker," the title of this article by the great economist John R. Commons, summed up the view shared by most people, a view that transformed Ford into the great folk hero of the twentieth century. If anyone else from Michigan had ever done as much for the benefit of mankind as Henry Ford had done, there would have been very few who could have been convinced that such was in fact the case.

The Progressive Era

The death of Senator Russell A. Alger in 1907 removed from the scene one of the last of the leaders who had emerged from the Civil War to dominate the business and political activities in the state during the remainder of the nineteenth century. But now a new century had arrived, and to men of the twentieth century, the Alger name on the fountain in Detroit's Grand Circus Park, unveiled in 1921 as a memorial to the late senator, struck as little response as did the symbolism of the Daniel Chester French statue.

Courtesy: Detroit Historical Museum

(See opposite page)

In more ways than one, the year 1907 promised to be a milestone in Michigan's political development, dividing the politics of the nineteenth century from those of the twentieth. During the year, delegates assembled in Lansing to write a new constitution that would be more in tune with the times than the existing state charter that had been adopted in 1850 when Michigan was still little more than a raw frontier state. The delegates included some very distinguished men, such as Clarence M. Burton, founder of the famous abstract company and indefatigable collector of books and documents on the history of the state, who served on the education committee, along with the committee chairman, former state superintendent of public instruction Delos Fall, University of Michigan regent Levi Barbour, State Library commissioner Fred Baldwin, and state legislator Horace Barnaby, Jr. But the membership of the convention was also overwhelmingly Republican in party affiliation and conservative in temperament. Although some improvements were made in the new constitution that was adopted in 1908, much of the wording and philosophy of the old mid-nineteenth-century constitution was retained and was left for a later convention to discard.

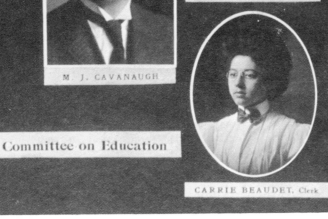

C. M. BURTON

F. J. BALDWIN

L. L. BARBOUR

DELOSS FALL, Chairman

A. L. DEUEL

M. E. LOUISELL

H. T. BARNABY, Jr.

G. R. CAMPBELL

H. H. WOODRUFF

M. J. CAVANAUGH

G. J. WICKSALL

Committee on Education

Constitutional Convention

CARRIE BEAUDET, Clerk

Courtesy: *Michigan Historical Commission*

In spite of the stand-pat attitude of the 1907 Constitutional Convention, new political ideas were sweeping the nation in this period known as the Progressive Era. The national leader around whom the supporters of these ideas rallied was President Theodore Roosevelt, who came to Lansing in 1907 to participate in the fiftieth-anniversary celebration of Michigan Agricultural College.

Roosevelt was of the new generation of political leaders, since he had not even been born when the first students enrolled at the college in 1857. He was driven out to the college campus in a Reo, with Ransom E. Olds himself at the wheel. Dr. Jonathan L. Snyder, president of the college, rode in the back seat with Roosevelt. (In order not to show any partiality, Roosevelt returned to Lansing in an Oldsmobile.)

Michigan's governor at the time was Fred M. Warner, shown here at the wheel of his 1908 Jackson. (Placement of the steering wheel on the right side was standard on virtually all American cars at the time and continued in use on the majority of cars manufactured in the United States until 1914.) The cheese factory at Powers Station in Oakland County was one of a dozen such plants that Warner had established since 1889, making a fortune for himself and his family in the dairy industry. One of the state's most underrated chief executives, Warner was a shrewd and capable politician, who had originally been put into office in 1905 by the McMillan machine. Sensing the growing support for the Progressives' demands for better, less boss-ridden government, Warner subsequently abandoned the old guard and took up the cudgel for such reforms as an effective direct primary law, which, when adopted in 1907, gave party voters, not convention delegates, the chance to select their party's candidates for governor and many other offices.

Courtesy: Michigan Historical Commission

Courtesy: Michigan Historical Collections

Courtesy: Michigan Historical Collections

Although Warner, in three consecutive, precedent-shattering terms as governor, secured the adoption of some major reforms, he won few friends among the liberals in the Republican Party, who turned instead to Chase Salmon Osborn. In his love of the outdoors and of travel, as typified here in a duck-hunting trip to Saskatchewan in 1906, in his interest in conservation and certain other reforms, and in his personal egotism, Osborn equaled — if he did not surpass — the same qualities in Teddy Roosevelt, whom he greatly admired.

Osborn in 1910 launched a vigorous campaign to obtain the Republican nomination for governor in the primary election, a nomination that was at that time, in the predominantly Republican Wolverine State, virtually tantamount to being elected to the office itself. Osborn promised that if he were elected he would wipe out what he termed the evils of Warrenism — as shown in this cartoon. His campaign slogan was "Osborn, Harmony, and a New Deal."

Courtesy: Michigan Historical Commission

Osborn won his campaign, both in the primary and in the general election, and as a resident of Sault Ste. Marie he became the first and only man from the Upper Peninsula to be governor of the state. Osborn was a strong-willed man who had been a newspaper editor and publisher, first in Florence, Wisconsin, and then at the Soo, before becoming wealthy from the development of iron ore deposits he had discovered on prospecting trips in the Lake Superior area. As governor in 1911 and 1912, he pressed for programs of positive reforms and was able to point to some impressive achievements, especially in the area of labor legislation. He is shown here at his desk in the executive office in 1911, affixing his signature to one such bill that had been passed by the legislature.

129

Despite Osborn's success and his considerable popularity with the electorate, the conservative element in the Republican Party remained hostile. In 1912 the split between this faction and the Osborn progressives came out in the open at the Republican State Convention in Bay City. The old-guard element, which supported the renomination of President William Howard Taft, gained control of the convention hall and forcibly ejected the progressive faction that supported the rival candidacy of Theodore Roosevelt. The progressives, shown here milling about the hall, selected a separate slate of delegates, which went to the national convention and unsuccessfully challenged the seating of the delegates chosen by the Taft forces.

Courtesy: Michigan Historical Collections

When Taft was renominated by the Republican National Convention, many Republicans bolted their party to support the third-party candidacy of Teddy Roosevelt, shown here campaigning in Marquette on October 9, 1912. From the expression on many of the faces, it would appear that something had happened that amused the spectators and two of the men on the platform. Roosevelt does not seem to find the incident amusing, however, and neither did most Republican politicians who looked upon the division between the Taft and Roosevelt factions in the party as simply insuring a Democratic victory.

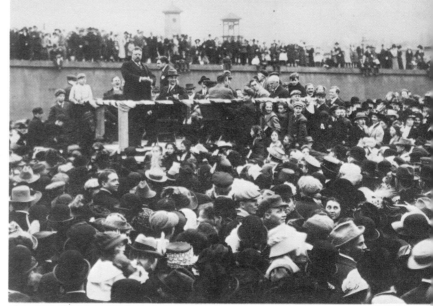

Courtesy: Michigan Historical Commission

Courtesy: Michigan Historical Commission

In the confusing 1912 election, Michigan voters showed a remarkable streak of independence, a trait for which they would become increasingly noted in the twentieth century. While Roosevelt demonstrated his popularity in the state by winning Michigan's electoral votes, he did not carry into office many of his fellow Progressive Party candidates in Michigan. The Republicans won a majority in both houses of the legislature and all executive offices save one. On January 1, 1913, that one, the office of governor, was filled by a tall Democrat, Woodbridge N. Ferris, founder and head of Ferris Institute in Big Rapids. His election was not only an indication of the willingness of many voters to cross party lines but was also a tribute to the personal popularity Ferris had achieved throughout the state because of his educational philosophy. Ferris Institute opened its doors to many who, for economic or other reasons, could not have enrolled in other colleges or universities.

130

If the Progressive Era is usually thought of as a period of change, the changes that resulted from the reforms enacted under the leadership of Warner, Osborn, and Ferris were overshadowed by those which were brought on by technological advances, particularly those related to the automobile. These early motor sight-seeing buses, amusing as they may seem to have been to the women passengers, clearly forecast the extent to which the old patterns of transportation would become obsolete.

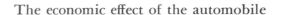

The economic effect of the automobile extended into many areas besides that of the manufacturing and selling of cars. New businesses sprang up to serve the motoring public. This was Flint's first gas station as it looked in 1910. Air was free and another sign indicates a concern even at that early day with motoring safety. The corrugated metal structure stood at the corner of First Avenue and Saginaw Street, on the site where the Pick-Durant Hotel now stands. Oddly enough, no one has ever evidenced much interest in preserving old gas stations, perhaps because the styles used in their construction have changed almost as often as those of the cars that use them.

The Riverside Garage and Paint Shop on West Maumee Street in Adrian, shown in this photograph, which is also from about 1910, was another kind of enterprise that was a direct offspring of the automobile. The mechanics standing in front of this garage, together with others like them who worked in similar garages in every town of any size across the state, added up to a sizable number of breadwinners whose jobs depended on the continuing popularity and use of automobiles fully as much as those of the workers in the automobile plants in Highland Park, Flint, Lansing, or Detroit.

131

Courtesy: Automobile Manufacturers Association

The leisurely pace of traffic in the horse-and-buggy age was rapidly becoming but a memory when Detroit in 1914 installed what was reportedly the first stop sign to direct the greatly increased traffic on the city's streets. More and more members of the police force would now have to be assigned to traffic control duty, while pedestrians would learn the necessity of remaining on the curb when the cars were given the green light.

Courtesy: Automobile Manufacturers Association

The condition of the streets and roads of the day was of great concern to automobile owners and manufacturers alike. One of the purposes of the organized tours that were conducted by various motoring groups was to point up the need for road improvements to meet the needs of this new age. The most famous of these was the Glidden Tour, an annual affair between 1905 and 1913, which was held in different parts of the country. The ambitious tour of 1909 began here at the Pontchartrain Hotel in Detroit and continued all the way to Denver and back to Kansas City. (The Pontchartrain had been built in 1907 and soon became the favorite gathering place for Detroit's automobile men — but not for long. In 1920 the hotel was torn down, only four years after much money was spent to enlarge the building.)

Courtesy: Michigan Historical Collections

One of the most active champions of better roads among the Michigan automobile men was Henry B. Joy of Packard. Among other interests, Joy became president of the Lincoln Highway Association, which sought to promote a coast-to-coast surfaced highway and thereby demonstrate the advantages of this type of road to the entire country. On May 27, 1915, Joy, on the right, with two associates, prepared to leave Detroit and drive a Packard to San Francisco over the various roads that then made up the Lincoln Highway.

Joy soon found that it would be some time yet before the dream of an all-weather Lincoln Highway became reality. On May 30, Joy was struggling through the mud in Tama, Iowa, and making slow progress, even with chains on the rear wheels.

On the outskirts of Lodge Pole, Nebraska, on June 7, Joy's Packard slid off the muddy Lincoln Highway into the ditch. It took the combined efforts of Joy's two companions, several farmers, and a team of horses to get the car back on the road. Joy finally did reach San Francisco, but his difficulties along the way, with the photographs to prove it, helped to stir some laggard communities to take better care of their sections of the highway.

It was not necessary to leave Michigan, however, to illustrate the need for better roads. This photograph was taken in Port Huron, probably at the end of the nineteenth century. In a day when the dirt road was the standard, and macadam, gravel, brick, or other forms of surfacing were the exception, most roads and streets in Michigan became virtually impassable during long periods, especially in the spring and fall.

133

Courtesy:

Detroit News

The faster speeds of automobiles forced highway engineers to revise their ideas about road construction. What had been regarded as the ideal or even simply as adequate roads for horse-drawn vehicles did not stand up under motor traffic. This stretch of Woodward Avenue in Detroit, between Six and Seven Mile Roads, became a testing ground for a new type of road surfacing. The road looked like this in 1908.

Courtesy: Detroit News

A year later, road-building crews and machines were paving this stretch of Woodward Avenue with concrete. When they had finished, they had laid the first mile of concrete highway in the United States. The success of the test strip helped to establish concrete as the ideal type of all-weather surfacing material. From such modest beginnings as this arose the twentieth century's enormous highway-construction industry, a product of the automobiles and their owners who demanded roads that fit the needs of the new motor age.

Courtesy: Michigan Historical Collections

In the summer of 1914, Michiganians followed with great interest the news from Europe as the nations of that continent drifted into what the Marshall *Weekly News-Statesman* quite accurately described as the "greatest war of history." Whatever their philosophical views may have been regarding the causes of the war, the farmers who read the Marshall paper undoubtedly paid special attention to the prediction by unnamed "authorities" at Michigan Agricultural College that the war between Austria-Hungary and Serbia alone would "fatten the pocketbooks of Michigan farmers by at least $1,105,000."

136

Earlier wars had had an important effect upon Michigan's economy, but with the state's emergence as a major source of manufactured items, the potential economic impact of World War I on Michigan was much greater than that of previous wars. This advertisement, which appeared within five months after the outbreak of war in Europe, is an interesting example of how one of Bay City's pioneers in the manufacture of prefabricated housing sought to direct attention to the wartime application of its product.

The advertisement below from the back cover of the *Literary Digest* was an indication that Michigan automobile manufacturers were not unaware of the market for their product among the armed forces. The United States Army at this time was far behind the times in its use of motorized vehicles, but as the war in Europe demonstrated the value of such vehicles, even the smaller Michigan car manufacturers, such as King, hoped to grab off a share of the orders that would be forthcoming as the American military forces were modernized. (The automotive pioneer, Charles B. King, was for a time vice-president of the company that bore his name, but by World War I, King, more interested in learning what made machines operate than in their production, had left the firm and had turned his attention to airplane engines.)

Literary Digest, *November 20, 1915*

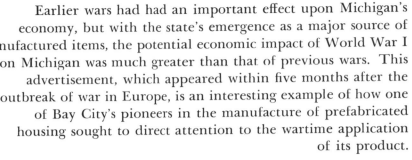

American entry into the war in April, 1917, did not mean the complete curtailment of automobile production, as happened during World War II, but nevertheless, Michigan's automobile manufacturers devoted more and more of their production facilities to filling war orders, clearly foreshadowing the awesome uses the armed services would make of these same facilities during that later war. The Packard Motor Car Company began receiving military orders for trucks shortly after the war broke out in 1914. By 1915, in fact, Packard was producing more trucks than passenger cars.

Literary Digest, *July 21, 1917*

"Packards for Pershing" the sign proclaimed on the side of this truck which was negotiating the hairpin turn outside McConnellsburg, Pennsylvania. It was part of a convoy of trucks that left Detroit for France on December 12, 1917, via Monroe, Toledo, Pittsburgh, and Baltimore. Despite the wartime fame of its trucks, however, Packard did not gain a larger share of the civilian market for trucks after the war. Instead, it shortly ceased truck production entirely as an economy measure during the postwar slump.

Courtesy: Michigan Historical Commission

Packard also played a major role in the field of wartime aviation. One of its engineers was one of the two men credited with designing the Liberty Motor. This Packard airplane engine, mounted on a Packard truck early in 1917, was part of this experimental work which led to Packard and other Michigan automobile companies manufacturing most of the Liberty Motors used by the United States and its allies in the war.

Courtesy: Automotive History Collection

Courtesy: Michigan Historical Collections

Buick, which manufactured some Liberty Motors, also turned out ambulances, such as this one, for the United States Army Medical Corps.

138

Henry Ford's actions after war broke out in Europe were typical of the eccentric manner in which he often reacted to events. He expressed his opposition to the war in strong enough terms to interest pacifist groups, leaders of which persuaded Ford to sponsor a peace mission to Europe late in 1915. Ford plunged into the project with enthusiasm. He and assorted pacifists and newspapermen sailed from New York for Norway early in December, with the announced intention of bringing the heads of the warring nations together and "getting the boys out of the trenches by Christmas." By the time the ship reached neutral Norway, however, Ford had lost much of his interest in the campaign, and he almost at once returned to the United States.

By 1916, Ford was quietly preparing his plants for war production, at the same time that he continued to voice his opposition to the war. With the American entry into the war, the Ford Company produced, among other war items, submarine-chasing Eagle boats at the huge new manufacturing establishment Ford was building on the River Rouge.

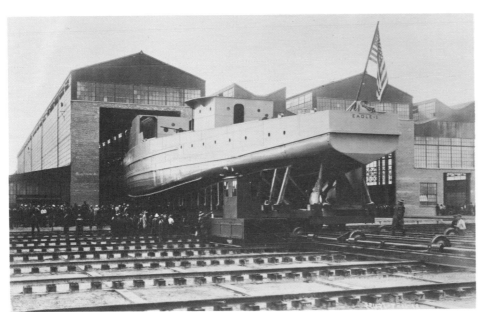

The merchant steam vessel *Lake Lilicusun* being launched here by the Michigan Shipbuilding Company in Saginaw was one of seventy-three such vessels in the "Lake" series, each of around 2,500 gross tons, which were built during the war period at shipyards in Wyandotte, Ecorse, and Saginaw as part of the enormous shipbuilding program instituted by the United States Shipping Board. Like five out of every six of the more than three thousand ships built under this program, the *Lake Lilicusun* was not delivered to the federal government until after the armistice of November, 1918, that ended the war.

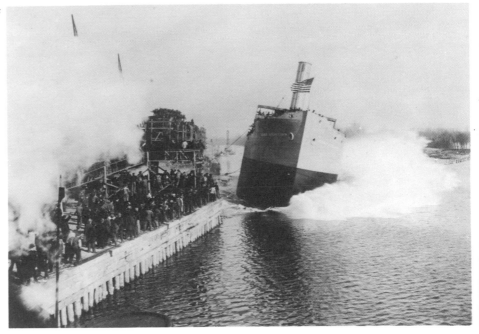

139

When the United States entered the war on April 6, 1917, many, including Governor Albert Sleeper, thought that the military manpower needs of the nation could be filled through voluntary enlistments, as they had been in the nineteenth century. Recruiting stations were set up, such as this one, which sought volunteers for the United States Army and also promoted the Michigan State Troops, a home force that was formed to protect installations and areas in the state deemed to be of vital importance to the war effort.

Courtesy: Michigan Historical Commission

The 32nd Division in the World War

At the start of the war, one regiment of the Michigan National Guard, peacetime volunteers, was already in federal service, having been mustered in the previous year for service along the Mexican border to fight Pancho Villa. The remaining guard units were now also called up and, together with the Wisconsin National Guard, formed the 32nd or Red Arrow Division. By early 1918 this division had arrived overseas in France and was in active combat by May. In July, these soldiers from Michigan and Wisconsin became the first American troops to set foot on German soil as they marched into Alsace past the striped pole that marked the boundary between France and Germany.

The 32nd Division in the World War

Near Sentheim in Alsace, the commander-in-chief of the American Expeditionary Force, John J. Pershing, inspected the division, some of whose members from Michigan he had led two years before when he commanded the expedition against the Mexican raiders.

140

The 32nd Division in the World War

From May, 1918, through to the end of the war, the Red Arrow Division saw almost continuous combat action in the brutal trench warfare along the Western Front. Here on October 14, following an artillery barrage, members of the division surge across the desolate no-man's-land to attack German entrenchments near Romagne as part of the great Meuse-Argonne offensive.

Near the end of October, the division had a short respite after twenty days of fighting in rain and mud. The division's commander, Major General William G. Haan, a regular army officer, addressed the men, telling them: "You have just been through perhaps the greatest battle that has ever been fought in the world, and you were in the very center of that, and every one of you is glad of it." But 1,232 members of the Red Arrows who were killed in this battle of the Meuse-Argonne did not hear him, nor did many of the 4,573 wounded men. A few more would die in the fighting that lay ahead before the armistice on November 11 silenced the guns. All told, the 32nd Division, which had left the United States less than a year before with some 27,000 men, suffered casualties of 2,671 killed, 10,242 wounded, and 103 captured during the war.

Courtesy: Michigan Historical Collections

The 32nd Division in the World War

Although a third of the 135,485 men Michigan furnished to the armed forces in World War I were volunteers, the country this time, as in all subsequent twentieth-century wars, relied primarily on the draft to fill the ranks. Within two months after the American declaration of war, some 380,000 men between the ages of twenty-one and thirty-one registered in Michigan for the draft.

Later in the summer of 1917, the first men were called up for their examinations. This group of draftees, stepping along in a rather unmilitary fashion, paraded through the streets of Owosso. Some Michiganians may have regretted that volunteers were not relied on to fill the ranks as they had been in the Civil War, but none could deny that the manner in which the draft was administered during World War I and the manner in which it was accepted was a vast improvement over the practices in the Civil War when it was generally regarded as a social disgrace to have been conscripted.

Courtesy: Michigan Historical Collections

Courtesy: Michigan Historical Commission

In the summer of 1917, Camp Custer was built west of Battle Creek to serve as the training center for draftees from Michigan and Wisconsin. In September, the first men arrived, wending their way across the rolling terrain of what had once been the site of a peace-loving experiment in communal living.

Courtesy: Michigan Historical Commission

In the months ahead, the men at Camp Custer were put through intensive training in the grim techniques of trench warfare. Veteran British army officers who had survived the campaigns in Flanders stood and observed the trainees in the trenches and pointed out what they might expect under actual combat conditions.

(See also pictures on opposite page)

(For description, see last caption on opposite page)

Courtesy: Michigan Historical Commission

By April, 1918, when the men at Camp Custer marched in review, this first group of draftees was rapidly rounding into shape. In July, 1918, the various units were shipped overseas, and a new batch of draftees moved into camp to begin their training.

To maintain the morale on the home front in the face of fuel and food shortages and other wartime hardships, patriotic ceremonies were held constantly. Here in Battle Creek's Monument Square, soldiers and civilians gather around the monument, which had been erected to honor those from the city who had served in the Civil War. The occasion may be the Memorial Day services in May, 1918.

Courtesy: Michigan Historical Commission

During the course of the war, four bond drives were staged to raise some of the money needed if victory was to be won. Here members of a battalion from Camp Custer come to Vicksburg to stimulate local interest in subscribing to the fourth Liberty Loan drive in the fall of 1918. By 1918, this tiny western Michigan rural community had seventy-seven stars on its service flag, which can be seen in the upper right-hand corner of the photograph.

Courtesy: Michigan Historical Commission

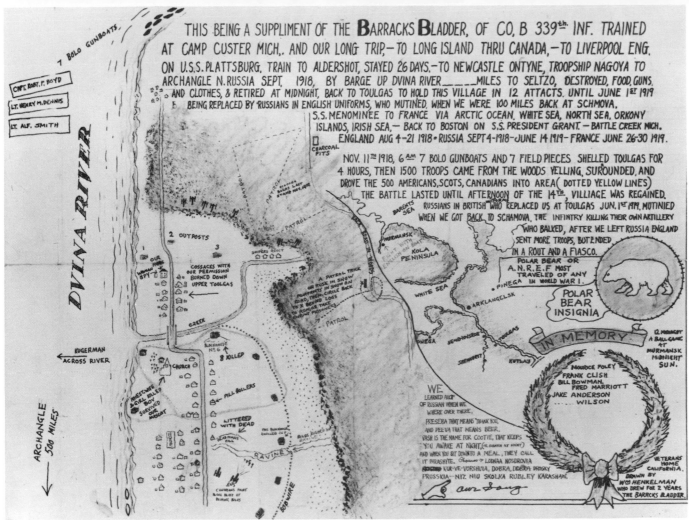

Courtesy: Michigan Historical Collections

The most unusual wartime experiences of any Michigan men happened to those who were among the several units of the first division of draftees to be sent overseas from Camp Custer. They landed, not in France with the rest of the division, but in northern Russia. There, at Archangel, they were part of a futile Allied attempt to help White Russians overthrow that country's new Communist regime. A veteran of this Polar Bear expedition, as it was soon nicknamed, later recorded, in this picturesque fashion, some of the things that happened when he and his comrades unexpectedly found themselves fighting not Germans but Bolos, as they called the Bolshevik soldiers.

Courtesy: Michigan Historical Collections

The 339th Infantry Regiment, which contained a large proportion of men from Michigan, constituted the most sizable group among the 5,500 Americans assigned to the north Russian front. The coats buttoned up to the neck, collars pulled up around the ears, and the scattering of fur hats are signs of the near-Arctic weather conditions these men had to face in the winter of 1918-19.

Courtesy: Michigan Historical Collections

In the summer of 1919, the American troops returned from Russia to the United States, and on July 4, some eleven hundred members of the 339th Infantry Regiment paraded on Belle Isle before spectators who included many relatives and friends of these men. The war was over and the uniforms would soon be laid aside for civilian dress.

Courtesy: Michigan Historical Collections

In 1929, a special commission supervised the return of the bodies of Michigan men who had died in the Polar Bear expedition and had been buried in Russia. Fifty of the eighty-six bodies were interred in a special section of the White Chapel Memorial Cemetery in Troy. An impressive monument was also erected in the memory of these men who had served in the first of the nation's major wars of the twentieth century.

The Roaring Twenties

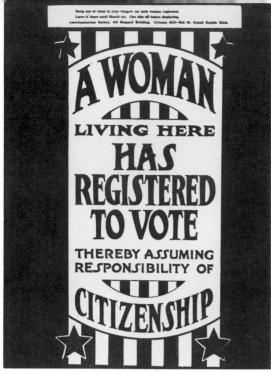

STATE TICKET.

For Governor,
AZARIAH S. PARTRIDGE.

For Lieutenant Governor,
HENRY I. ALLEN.

For Secretary of State,
EDWIN S. PALMITER.

For State Treasurer,
ANSEL P. CODDINGTON.

For Auditor General,
LUCIUS H. IVES.

For Commissioner of the State Land Office,
CARLTON PECK.

For Attorney General,
JAMES R. ADSETT.

For Superintendent of Public Instruction,
DAVID HOWELL.

For Member of the State Board of Education,
CHARLES SCOTT.

For Associate Justice of the Supreme Court, to fill vacancy,
NOAH W. CHEEVER.

CONGRESSIONAL TICKET.

For Representative in Congress, Fifth District,
EDWARD L. BRIGGS.

LEGISLATIVE TICKET.

For Senator in State Legislature, Twentieth District,
CHARLES S. FIELD.

For Representative in State Legislature, First District,
JAMES H. THAW.—Two Votes.

COUNTY TICKET.

For Sheriff,
KING S. DAVIS.

For County Clerk,
HOMER R. BRADFIELD.

For County Treasurer,
JOHN I. CUTLER.

For Register of Deeds,
JAMES H. MARTIN.

For Prosecuting Attorney,
WILLIAM C. SHEPPARD.

For Circuit Court Commissioners,
CHARLES G. HYDE.
WILLIAM F. SHEDD.

For Surveyor,
ASA W. SLAYTON.

For Coroners,
MELLE VEENBOER.
JOHN G. COWEN.

Printed by Authority: Gilbert R. Osmun, Secretary of State.

The so-called Roaring Twenties actually could be said to have begun in 1919 as the nation strove to get back to peacetime conditions following the war. Ironically, however, the dream of a "return to normalcy," as Warren G. Harding phrased it in 1920, if it meant a return to prewar conditions, was shattered from the outset by dramatic changes that made such a return impossible. In 1920, following the ratification of the Nineteenth Amendment to the United States Constitution, Michigan's constitution was amended to give women the vote, which was the climax of a long struggle.

Among the foremost leaders of the drive for woman suffrage was Dr. Anna Howard Shaw, who had grown up on a farm near Big Rapids. She had graduated from Albion College and begun her work in the Methodist ministry at Ashton, Michigan, before leaving the state to work for various reforms, most notably that of obtaining the vote for women, which for her became the Cause, with a capital "C."

Dr. Shaw had also been active in the temperance movement, which also was climaxed after World War I by the adoption of the Eighteenth Amendment, which prohibited the sale of liquor in the United States. The Prohibition Party, which advocated this step, had been active in Michigan since 1872, and although it never achieved much success at the polls (Azariah S. Partridge led this slate of candidates in the election of 1890, receiving 26,681 votes out of nearly 400,000 that were cast for governor), it kept the issue alive. A local-option law passed in 1889 permitted counties, if they so chose, to become dry.

Here around 1907, citizens of Kalamazoo gathered in all their finery to observe the triumph of the Prohibition spirit in a ceremonious "dumping of the booze."

Courtesy: Western Michigan University Archives

In 1916, the Anti-Saloon League, Michigan Dry Campaign Committee, and other groups favoring prohibition rallied sufficient support to secure adoption of an amendment to the state constitution authorizing legislation to prohibit the sale of liquor in the entire state. Such legislation was passed and went into effect in 1918, two years before the adoption of the Eighteenth Amendment paved the way for national prohibition.

Courtesy: Michigan Historical Collections

Enforcing prohibition in Michigan, as elsewhere, proved to be a difficult task. The Detroit River area became a center of bootlegging operations because of the relative ease with which liquor could be brought over from Canada. A Detroit *News* photographer, hiding in a warehouse, took this dramatic picture in 1929 of rum runners transferring suitcases of liquor from a boat to their car, parked at the foot of Riopelle Street in Detroit.

Courtesy: Detroit News

STATE WIDE ORGANIZATION RALLY!
WASHTENAW COUNTY AT
ANN ARBOR
THURSDAY MAY 4
ALL DAY SESSION
Organization Meetings for Men and Women
— AT 2:00 p.m. —
IN THE PRESBYTERIAN CHURCH
REV. EDWIN SIMPSON
Detroit Superintendent of the Anti-Saloon League
DR. LUCY KIRK PEEL IN CHARGE OF
The Safety and Efficiency Department of the
Michigan Dry Campaign Committee.
BANQUET
AT 6:00 O'CLOCK IN THE
Y. M. C. A.
CITY
Address By
HON. J.T. BOTKIN
EX-CONGRESSMAN FROM KANSAS
SPECIAL MUSIC
in charge of
Mr. J. A. Carroll of California
Come. Invite your friends. Bring enough "pep" to last all day
Now altogether, to make it State-wide November 7th, 1916.
MICHIGAN DRY CAMPAIGN COMMITTEE
410, 418-22 TUSSING BUILDING
LANSING, MICHIGAN

149

These men in Detroit were photographed in 1931 enjoying an illegal glass of beer in a blind pig on East Columbia Street. Such obvious lack of enthusiasm for the law and the Constitution led to the end of the "Noble Experiment" in 1933.

The beginning of the Twenties saw the inauguration of a new medium of communication, the radio. A station owned by the Detroit *News* (the call letters WWJ were adopted in 1922) began to transmit regularly scheduled programs in August, 1920, making it a pioneer in the field of broadcasting. Here, Wendell Hall, the "Red-headed Music Maker," performs on one of these early radio shows in a period when owners of radio receivers were more excited about picking up any station than in the contents of the program or lack thereof.

Other radio stations were soon licensed in Michigan. Along with the commercial stations, one noncommercial station emerged from the early experimental years, WKAR, owned and operated by Michigan State College in East Lansing. Its programming, some of it of a type especially useful to farmers and much more of it presenting educational and cultural features lacking in commercial radio, did much to enhance the reputation of the college.

The airplane, still a relatively new form of transportation, began receiving increasing use in the 1920's. William B. Stout, who had been chief of the aircraft division of Packard during World War I, in 1925 developed the famous Ford Tri-Motor airplane, which the Ford Motor Company manufactured for several years, and a number of which are still in active service forty years later. Stout also established the Stout Air Service, which pioneered in regular air passenger service between Detroit and Grand Rapids in 1926 and between Detroit and Cleveland in 1927. Stout's airline, which employed the tri-motor, subsequently became part of United Airlines. The planes operated out of the Ford Airport at Dearborn.

In June, 1920, Mrs. Julia A. Moore, the "Sweet Singer of Michigan," died at her home near Manton, Michigan. Virtually forgotten at the time of her death, Mrs. Moore had created something of a sensation in 1876 with the publication of a volume of her poems. The critics were unmerciful in their analysis of the literary qualities of Mrs. Moore's verses, while the humorist Bill Nye, examining the horribly crude portrait that appeared in the book, observed that Mrs. Moore's "brow is slightly drawn . . . , as though her corns might be hurting her. Julia wears her hair plain, like Alfred Tennyson and Sitting Bull." Although Julia Moore's work was so bad that it might be considered "camp" today, it clearly had no relationship to the kind of literature for which the decade following her death became famous.

151

Courtesy: National Park Service

Three years after Julia Moore's death, a collection of stories and poems appeared from the pen of Ernest Hemingway, a native of Illinois who was then one of a large group of American expatriates living in Paris, France. Hemingway's early stories had a northern Michigan setting, which reflected the many months the author had spent as a boy and young man at the family's summer home on Walloon Lake, near Petoskey, a home that is now a national historic landmark. Hemingway became the leading spokesman of the writers of the "lost generation," who helped to make the 1920's one of the most exciting and genuinely creative periods in America's cultural development. The rather tenuous link of Hemingway and his writings to Michigan is one of the means by which overly enthusiastic Michiganians sometimes try to enhance their state's cultural image during these years.

Courtesy: Michigan Historical Collections

Another major figure on the literary scene of the twenties was Ring (short for Ringold) Lardner, who was born in Niles in 1885. The home of the well-to-do Lardner family is still preserved in that southwestern Michigan city where Lardner grew up and worked at various odd jobs before leaving to become a leading sportswriter and then one of the great practitioners of the art of the short story. But aside from an occasional reference to excursion trips from Chicago to St. Joseph, Lardner's fiction reflects little of his native state, which he abandoned permanently for the more intellectually stimulating atmosphere of Chicago and New York.

The YOUTH'S COMPANION combined with
American Boy
Founded 1827

Volume 105   April, 1931   Number 4

Price: 20 cents a copy; $2.00 a year, $3.00 for three years in the United States and its possessions; 25c a year extra in Canada; 50c a year extra in foreign countries.

We took the map along—and at least fifty times afterwards I wished we hadn't!

Mark Tidd Back Home

By Clarence Budington Kelland

Illustrated by R. M. Brinkerhoff

Chapter One

MY name is Tallow Martin and I am one of the three fellows who went all over Europe and Asia and Africa and places with Marcus Aurelius Fortunatus Tidd. The other two were Binney Jenks and Plunk Smalley, but they don't amount to much, and never did, and as far as I can see, they never will. Mark Tidd is different. He amounts to a lot—about two hundred and twenty pounds or maybe more after a square meal.

Well, we spent a good many months on the other side of the ocean and had quite a time of it, but we got tired of it after a while and were pretty glad to get back to Wicksville again and see our folks and be around among people that talked English and wore regular clothes. We got home just the time vacation was starting; so we didn't have to go back to school, and Mrs. Tidd said we ought to be put right smack to work before we got into mischief.

But Mrs. Tidd barks worse than she bites, and Mr. Tidd doesn't do anything but read about the Decline and Fall of the Roman Empire and invent gadgets. And our own folks were so glad to see us back that they didn't get around to doing anything disagreeable till it was too late.

And that's how we happened to have a whole summer vacation on our hands after being abroad and getting our minds cultivated by foreign travel and all.

The rest of the kids around town admired us a lot on account of where we'd been and what we'd seen, but they tried not to let on. We acted just as if we'd never been anywhere at all and never bragged, only when somebody'd say that Wicksville had a fine standpipe we'd say, "Yes, it has, but you ought to see the Pyramids." You know, like that. Just dropped it in casual-like, as if it didn't mean a thing to us and Pyramids were our regular breakfast food. But we always told people we were glad to be back home again, and we were.

I don't know if you ever were in Wicksville, but it's a great town, probably the finest town of anywhere near its size that there is in the world. About twelve hundred people live there, but they seem like a lot more on account of their being such busy people and all. The town is on a river that cuts it in two in the middle, and there is a dam when the spring floods haven't taken it out, and a gristmill and a planing mill and the waterworks. And there's the island in the river and our cave and what-not—plenty to do with.

And so, about a day after we got home, we were all over at Mark Tidd's house in the afternoon, and Mark hollers in and says, "Ma, can we have some p-p-pie?"

And Mrs. Tidd calls right back, "No you can't have any pie—it'll ruin your stummicks."

And Mark says, "Ma, we're awful hungry."

And she says, "If you ate at mealtimes you wouldn't always be piecin'."

And then out she came with a whole apple pie and a pitcher of milk, kind of grumbling away as she always does, and she set it on the back stoop and said she never saw such boys and why didn't we stay at home where we belonged.

BUT we didn't mind a bit because we knew Mrs. Tidd and that was just her way, and she always said you couldn't when you

On quite a different level from the works of Hemingway and Lardner were those of Clarence Budington Kelland, a native of Portland, Michigan, whose innumerable stories about Scattergood Baines and other characters Kelland created were read by millions in the pages of the *Saturday Evening Post* and other strictly non-avant-garde publications. But to hundreds of thousands of boys during these same years, Kelland was known as the author of stories about fat Mark Tidd and other fictional people that appeared in the pages of *The American Boy*.

153

Although Kelland had long since left Michigan, where he had begun his career as a newsman in Detroit, he continued to serve in an editorial capacity with the best-known magazine ever published in Michigan. Legions of men now fondly remember those fat issues of *The American Boy*, published in Detroit, with their clean-cut, all-American adventure and sports stories, their superb artwork, their jokes, which somehow seemed funnier to a ten-year-old boy than they would to that boy grown into manhood thirty or forty years later, and their ads, which always included a lot of publications that could be obtained simply by mailing in a postcard. The magazine ceased publication in the early 1940's, but its long-time managing editor, George F. Pierrot, went on to become a familiar figure to many thousands of television viewers in the Detroit area as the host of a daily travel show that has been running for many years and as the promoter of a popular series of travel films shown weekly at the Detroit Institute of Arts.

(See also illustration on opposite page)

FUNNYBONE TICKLERS

Cutting Expenses

A man running after a taxicab panted to the driver, "How much to the station from here?"
"Fifty cents," replied the driver.
The man continued to run, and after having covered another stretch asked breathlessly, "How much now?"
"Seventy-five," retorted the driver. "You're runnin' the wrong way."

Very Discriminating

Mrs. Smith hired a Chinese servant, and tried to teach him how to receive calling cards. She let herself out the front door, and when the new servant answered her ring she gave him her card.
The next day two ladies came to visit Mrs. Smith. When they presented their cards, the alert Chinaman hastily compared them with Mrs. Smith's card, and remarked as he closed the door: "Tickets no good; can't come in."

Roll Over

Nurse: "Good morning. I'm the new nurse."
Grouchy Patient: "You a trained nurse?"
Nurse: "Yes, of course I'm a trained nurse."
Grouchy Patient: "Then let's see you do some tricks."

You've Got to Watch 'Em

Notice in village paper: "I have been instructed by the Village Council to enforce the ordinance against chickens running at large and riding bicycles on the sidewalk."

They Love the Woods

"Isn't this an ideal spot for a picnic dinner?"
"It must be. Fifty million insects can't possibly have made a mistake."

Tattooer Maybe

"He may be a great artist," said the young thing, "but he certainly has a peculiar way of working. When I visited his studio recently and asked him about his work, he told me that he painted his best pictures on an empty stomach."

Tie That One

Smart Aleck: "I can tell you the score of the game before it starts."
I. L. Bite: "What is it?"
Smart Aleck: "Nothing to nothing—before it starts."

After Monkeys—Man

Comedian: "Look here, I object to going on right after that monkey act."
Manager: "You're right. They may think it's an encore."

Concentrated Composition

Teacher: "How is it that you have only written ten lines on 'Milk' and the others have written pages?"
Pupil: "I wrote on 'Condensed Milk,' sir."

Painless?

Willie: "Hey, Mama! That dentist I went to wasn't painless."
Mother: "Why, did he hurt you?"
Willie: "Naw, but he yelled just like any other dentist when I bit his finger."

Pluck, Too!

"That's a swell job Joe's got playing the guitar."
"Yeh, he got it by pulling strings."

Silly Question

And then there's the college girl who, when asked if she were going to include bacteriology in her course of study, chirped, "Oh, don't bacilli."

Prompt Punctuation

Rhetoric Teacher: "How would you punctuate this sentence: 'A pretty girl, walking down the street, turned a corner just as I saw her'?"
Bright Boy: "I would make a dash after her."

Hard to Tell

"I want an E string, please," said the violinist to the London music seller.
"I'm a new 'and at this business, sir," explained the clerk as he took down the box. "Would you mind picking it out for yourself? I 'ardly knows the 'es from the shes."

He Aimed but Didn't Please

Hubby: "I miss the old cuspidor since it's gone."
Wifey: "You missed it before. That's why it's gone."

Read All About It

Cora: "What's the matter?"
Student: "Nothin'. Just a bit dizzy from reading a circular letter, that's all."

But She Loved Him

She came to the police station with a picture in her hand.
"My husband has disappeared," she sobbed. "I want you to find him. Here is his picture."
The inspector looked up from the picture. "Why?" said he.

Les Femmes Incorrigibles!

"Will you give me ten cents to help the Old Ladies' Home?"
"What! Are they out again?"

Method in His Mudness

Mother: "Freddy, Aunt Mary will never kiss you with that dirty face."
Freddy: "That's what I figured."

Ample Proof

Mistress: "You say you worked for the Van Twillers. Can you prove it?"
Maid: "I can show you some spoons and things with their initials on them!"

Reincarnation

"By the way, where did you get the plot of your second novel?" asked the publisher of a successful novelist.
"From the film version of the first," was the reply.

A Curio Father

Dick: "My dad is an Elk, a Moose, a Lion, and an Eagle."
Nick: "How much does it cost to see him?"

Vegetarian Love

"Do you carrot all for me? My heart beets for you and my love is as soft as squash. But I'm strong as an onion for you're a peach. With your turnip nose and your radish hair you are the apple of my eye. If you cantaloupe with me, lettuce marry anyhow, for I know weed make a pear."

Courtesy: Jordan Humberstone

(For description, see caption on opposite page)

The rugged outdoor life was the most important influence exerted by Michigan on its authors, giving rise to a he-man school of writing. The foremost of these was Stewart Edward White, who was born in Grand Rapids and whose early works reflected his experience in Michigan's lumbering country. The works of Attwood's Rex Beach and James Oliver Curwood were also immensely popular among men who had outgrown the juvenile outdoor stories of *The American Boy.* White and Beach left their home state, but the eccentric Curwood continued to live in his birthplace of Owosso, where he built a weird house on the banks of the Shiawassee River. Nicknamed "Curwood's Castle," it continues to be a major tourist attraction four decades after the author's death in 1927.

Courtesy: Michigan Tourist Council

In addition to Curwood, other Michigan-born authors also resisted the temptation to move elsewhere. One of these, Arnold Mulder, a native of Holland, used his knowledge of western Michigan effectively in his novels, such as *The Sand Doctor,* published in 1921. Although his books won some critical acclaim, they were scarcely major literary successes. Mulder also became a highly popular teacher of English at Western State Teachers College and Kalamazoo College.

Courtesy: Netherlands Information Service

Courtesy: Michigan Historical Commission

In the field of nonfiction, Michigan writers enjoyed considerable success, both popular and critical. Most notable of these was Paul de Kruif of Zeeland, who taught bacteriology at the University of Michigan before becoming the best-selling author of such popularized works on science as *Microbe Hunters,* his first big success, published in 1926. De Kruif, who, like Mulder, came from a Dutch-American background, also continued to maintain a residence in his native western Michigan where this photograph was taken around 1960.

156

But unquestionably the most famous and widely read resident Michigan writer in the 1920's was Edgar Guest, shown here a few years earlier with his son, Edgar, Jr., better known as Bud, who would go on to become one of Michigan's most popular radio personalities. Born in Birmingham, England, in 1881, Edgar Guest had been brought to Detroit as a boy of ten, and it was here that he would remain the rest of his life. He began working for the Detroit *Free Press* in 1895 and published his first poem in that paper three years later. From 1904 until his death in 1959, an Edgar Guest poem was a daily *Free Press* feature, and after 1916 it became a syndicated feature carried by some three hundred papers around the country. Periodically these poems were collected and published in volumes

Courtesy: Burton Historical Collection

whose sales mounted into the hundreds of thousands. Critics scoffed at his work, but actually Guest never claimed to be a poet, only a newspaperman who wrote sentimental verses.

Courtesy: Michigan Historical Collections

Occasionally, Michigan's colleges and universities took steps to try to improve the literary image of the state. The University of Michigan in 1923 brought in Robert Frost, to be resident poet on the campus for a full year. Arnold Mulder later compared the university's action in importing Frost from New England in an effort to put poetry in the state back on its feet to the subsequent move that called in Fritz Crisler from Dartmouth when the fortunes of the university's football team had reached an equally low ebb.

Although Michigan's contributions to the world of literature may have been rather spotty, its contributions to certain other areas of culture were often distinguished. In the summer of 1928, a music camp for talented high-school musicians was opened in a beautifully wooded setting between two lakes at Interlochen, a few miles from Traverse City.

The father of the idea was Professor Joseph E. Maddy of the University of Michigan, shown here on the left. Visiting the camp that first summer were Ossip Gabrilowitsch (second from the left), who, as conductor of the Detroit Symphony Orchestra, had built that group into a respectable musical organization, and Dr. Howard Hanson (third from the left), long-time head of the Eastman School of Music in Rochester, New York. On the right is Thaddeus P. Giddings, Maddy's associate in earlier programs to encourage high-school musicians from around the nation.

Courtesy: Michigan Historical Collections

157

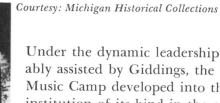

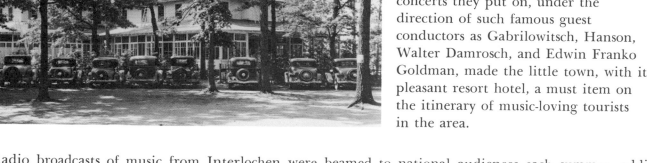

Under the dynamic leadership of Maddy, ably assisted by Giddings, the National Music Camp developed into the leading institution of its kind in the country. Not only did hundreds of young musicians come to Interlochen, but the concerts they put on, under the direction of such famous guest conductors as Gabrilowitsch, Hanson, Walter Damrosch, and Edwin Franko Goldman, made the little town, with its pleasant resort hotel, a must item on the itinerary of music-loving tourists in the area.

Radio broadcasts of music from Interlochen were beamed to national audiences each summer, adding to the fame of the camp. The success of this summer program, whose best-known graduate is the pianist Van Cliburn, led Dr. Maddy in the 1960's to establish here a school to offer training in music and the arts on a year-round basis.

Courtesy: Burton Historical Collection

Equaling the achievements of Maddy in the field of music were those in the field of drama by Jessie Bonstelle, who created one of America's greatest civic theater groups. Miss Bonstelle had organized a stock company in Rochester, New York, which she had begun bringing to Detroit in 1910. The support Detroit gave her ultimately encouraged her to locate her company permanently in that city. There, between 1925 and Miss Bonstelle's death in 1932, she gave to Detroit and Michigan theatrical productions that, in their variety and high caliber of performance, have rarely, if ever, been matched in the state.

Miss Bonstelle lent encouragement to other theater groups in Michigan, such as the Ypsilanti Players, an organization that pioneered the little-theater movement in the state in 1914. Performing on a tiny stage in a remodeled barn, the Ypsilanti Players attracted national attention with its lively programming of dramas that were frequently of an experimental character. Daniel Quirk, Jr., owner of the local paper mill, acted both as director and financial angel for the nonprofit organization. Among the players at this time was a future Michigan secretary of state and Republican state chairman, Owen Cleary, who, like some other politicians, may have found the make-believe of the stage good training for the oratory of the campaign platform.

Melvyn Douglas, Gale Sondergaard, Jessie Royce Landis — these were a few of the stars of the future who got their start in the Bonstelle Company. Miss Bonstelle's ambition, however, was not simply to present drama, but to enrich the cultural life of the community through an educational program and through activity in the related fine arts, as exemplified by the Bonstelle-Garagusi Concert Trio.

Beginning Monday Night, June 14th, 1926

Matinees—Tuesday, Thursday and Saturday

First Time in Detroit—As Presented in New York by Ann Nichols

THE BONSTELLE COMPANY PRESENTS

"White Collars"

A Comedy in Three Acts by Edith Ellis

Characters in the order of appearance

William Van Luyn..............................Donald Cameron
Joan Thayer..................................Jessie Royce Landis
Cousin Henry......................................Neill O'Malley
Helen Thayer................................Carolyn Humphries
Mr. Thayer.......................................Walter Sherwin
Mrs. Thayer..Nina Moise
Frank Thayer.....................................Thayer Roberts
Sally Van Luyn..................................Gale Sondergaard
Tom Gibney.......................................Melvyn Douglas

SYNOPSIS OF SCENES

ACT   I.   SCENE I.   Portion of William Van Luyn's private office.
           SCENE II. Dining room in the Thayer flat. Same day.
ACT II.   Parlor in the Thayer flat; a month later.
ACT III.   SCENE I.   Dining room of the Thayer's, ten days later.
           SCENE II. The same. Evening.
           PLACE: New York City.
           TIME: The present.

Directed by Adams T. Rice

All productions under the personal direction of Jessie Bonstelle.

STAFF FOR MISS BONSTELLE

ADAMS T. RICE—*Director.*
MARGARET STOREY—*Stage Manager.*
THAYER ROBERTS—*Assistant Stage Manager.*
DOROTHY RICHEY—*Technical Assistant.*
SCENIC ARTIST—*Steven Nastfogel.*
MASTER CARPENTER—*James O'Dea.*
MASTER OF PROPERTIES—*William Strachan.*
MASTER ELECTRICIAN—*Alvin Anderson.*

THE BONSTELLE-GARAGUSI CONCERT TRIO

Nicholas Garagusi, Violin———Lucienne Paquet, Piano———Jacob Holskin, Cello

1.   Selection from "The Firefly"..............................Friml
2.   Suite Carnavalesque...............................Gabriel-Marie
3.   I.   Les Gardes Francaises
        II. Reverie de Columbine
        III. Sabotiere
        IV. Final-Valse
3.   (a) Serenade...................................A. Oelschlegel
     (b) Czardas..Monti
     (c) Song. "Oh, That We Two Were Maying".................Nevin
4.   "The Blue Room," from "The Girl Friend".................Rodgers

---

MISS JESSIE BONSTELLE

invites

THE YPSILANTI PLAYERS

Under the Auspices of Detroit Alumnae of Collegiate Sorosis

to present

An Afternoon of Staged Modern and Classical Poetry

at

THE BONSTELLE PLAYHOUSE

Detroit

May 8, 1925, 3:30 O'Clock

TWO SLATTERNS AND A KING

A FANTASTIC INTERLUDE

Edna St. Vincent Millay

Chance.................................Owen Cleary
King...................................Stuart Lathers
Tidy..................................DeLynn Whitmire
Slut..................................Gertrude Lamb

Intermission ten minutes

Followed by

THE ANCIENT MARINER

A Dramatic Arrangement of

Samuel Taylor Coleridge's Poem

A fantastic illusion for those who abandon themselves to its spell, to feel its movement, to see its sights, to hear its sounds.

The Ancient Mariner.................Richard Forsyth
First Wedding Guest.......................Carl Smith

Second Wedding Guest....................Charles Lamb
Third Wedding Guest......................Orlow Owen

Sailors:—Burns Fuller, Plynn Matthews, Joseph Metcalf, Theodore Schaible, Clemens Steimle, Philip Tuefer, Leo Whitmire.

Spirit in the Sea..................Kathrina McCulloch
Death...................................Grace Ford
Life-in-Death.......................Gladys Newton
Pilot—First Spirit.......................Carl Smith
Hermit—Second Spirit....................Gaylord Kerr

Incidental music arranged and directed by Russell Gee
Costumes from the illustrations of Gustave Dore
Boat designed by Edward C. Cornwell
Masks by James Light

The curtains will close between the parts. The Playhouse will remain dark throughout. Kindly reserve applause until the end.

A NOTE ON THE STAGING OF

THE MARINER

In bringing Coleridge's famous and beautiful rime to the Bonstelle Playhouse we hope to bring one of the greatest long poems to life in the sight of many by whom it has long been forgotten. By the pantomime of grouped bodies and changing lights and rythms of music while the Ancient Mariner describes the story of the voyage we aim to give to this old poem an immediacy.

DANIEL L. QUIRK, JR., *Director*

PLAYS STAGED BY PAUL STEPHENSON

Courtesy: Detroit Public Library

Courtesy: Detroit Public Library

These draftees moving into Camp Custer in 1918 were indicative of changes in the composition of Michigan's population that became much more evident in the postwar decade. Negroes, who had constituted a small, relatively unchanging fraction of the state's population in the last half of the nineteenth century, began to increase in numbers rapidly after 1910 as Negroes from the South flocked to Michigan in search of jobs and increased economic opportunity.

Since the arrival of the French in the seventeenth century in a Michigan previously inhabited solely by Indian tribes, the coming of new peoples and their acceptance — or rejection — by the old has been a continuing part of the story of Michigan's development. It had been a part of the life of thousands of poor Irish immigrants in the nineteenth century — whose descendants only a few decades later, although still proud of their Irish ancestry, were thoroughly Americanized members of a club sponsoring an athletic event on such a thoroughly American holiday as Thanksgiving.

COMPETITORS' INFORMATION BLAN

Fourth Annual **Ten Mile Run** Fernda to Detro

Under the Auspices of

IRISH-AMERICAN ATHLETIC CLUB
DETROIT, MICH.

THURSDAY, NOVEMBER 30th, 192
(THANKSGIVING DAY)

Sanctioned by the Central Amateur Athletic Association of the U. S.   Official Sanction No. 2

COMPLIMENTARY DINNER
The Irish-American Athletic Club has arranged to tender a complimentary dinner to competitors a officials at Hotel Statler following the race. The dinner will be at 3 p. m. and all prizes will be awarded that time.

All competitors must show their registration cards when securing their number from the number cle
TIME OF START 12:00 M SHARP
ROUTE—Starting at Ferndale, down Woodward Ave. to Geneva Ave., turn right one block to Seco Blvd., turning left down Second Blvd. to Grand Blvd. left turn to Cass Ave., then right on Cass Ave finish line at the Moose Temple, corner of Elizabeth St.

PRIZES
TEN HANDSOME PRIZES will be awarded to the first ten men to finish. A souvenir medal to all m who finish after the prize winners.
POINT TROPHY—Silver loving cup donated by Sheriff Irving J. Coffin to the club having the fi three men to finish, scoring the lowest number of points. Points will be counted according to the order finish.

OFFICIAL PHOTOGRAPHS
for the run
SPENCER & WYCKOFF
714 Peter Smith Bldg.
Who will take photographs of the Officials, in front of the Ferndale Police Department, at 11 A. also a photograph will be taken on the start of the race.
Proofs of these pictures will be shown at the dinner, at the Hotel Statler, where orders will be tak for copies, the price each will be $1.50

Intending competitors must realize that a course of training is necessary for such a long distance, and th it would be unwise to attempt to run in this race without preparation.

The start will be made at Ferndale, Mich., at 12:00 M. Arrangements will be made for the Compe tors at a hotel near the start.
START AT EXACTLY NOON
No athlete under 18 years of age will be allowed to compete.

Definition of an Amateur.
An amateur sportsman is one who engages in sport solely for the pleasure and physical, mental or social benefits he derives therefrom and to whom sport is nothing more than an avocation.

Registration cards can be secured from the D troit Amateur Athletic Association, Room 35 Equity Building, corner Griswold and Larned St

All Competitors MUST be registered.

Would like to have photographs of competitors in running costume, and club teams, to be used in th newspapers. Mail in when making entry.

FOURTH ANNUAL **Auto City Marathon, Saturday,** APRIL 192

Courtesy: Netherlands Museum

Courtesy: Michigan Tourist Council

Likewise, in the twentieth century the Dutch and the Germans whose fathers had settled in Michigan were as American as the sons of the Yankee settlers of the same era. At the same time, however, they retained an affection for their European heritage and eventually capitalized upon it, as in Holland's Tulip Festival, with its Klompen Dancers, and Frankenmuth's Bavarian Festival.

161

ZEP	150	ZUC

Zeppala Peter, saloon, 210 E. Bonnie, res. same.
Zeppala Sam, miner, res. 210 E. Bonnie.
Zeppenfelt William, res. 211 Bundy.
Zeppenfelt William Jr., driver, res. 211 Bundy.
Zianone Martino, miner, res. 836 E. Ayer.
Ziechto Martin, lab., res. 122 Luxmore.
ZIEGELMAIER HENRY J., salesman The Leader, res. New St. James.
Zieno Dominic, miner, res. 359 Ashland loc.
Zimmer Andrew, clerk, res. 209 S. Mansfield.
Zimmer Franz, miner, res. 831 E. Ayer.
Zippa John, miner, res. 301 E. Pine.
Znorowski John, lab., res. 316 S. Marquette.
Zuca James, miner, res. 201 W. Aurora.
Zucali Louis, miner, res. 846 E. Ayer.

Wright's Directory of Ironwood, 1893-94

Before the end of the nineteenth century, immigrants from eastern and southern Europe were entering in large numbers, bringing with them cultures and traditions different from the earlier immigration from northwestern Europe. This last page from the city directory of Ironwood in 1893-94 reflects the appearance of these new elements that helped to make Michigan's mining towns the most cosmopolitan communities for their size in the state.

Courtesy: Michigan Historical Collections

Immigrants from Finland came to work in the iron and copper mines of the Upper Peninsula or to farm this area where conditions were often so similar to those they had known in their homeland. Mrs. Mary Kangas, photographed here in 1940 when she was seventy-five years old, had come to the Copper Country in the 1890's. In her old age she still felt most at home speaking her native language and weaving a "matto," or rag rug, as she had learned to do as a child in Finland. Although she and thousands of other Finnish immigrants had had to change many of their ways to adapt themselves to life in this new land, the area in which they settled had also had to adapt itself to these new peoples, with the result that in many parts of the Upper Peninsula the Finnish influence became as noticeable as that of the Dutch in western Michigan or the Germans in the Saginaw Valley.

162

To the predominantly Protestant, so-called native American element, the ways of the new immigrants of the twentieth century were strange indeed. A Polish funeral procession in Detroit, with the seemingly unpronounceable words embroidered on the banners carried by the mourners, or the bearded leader of the Orthodox Church being helped with his vestments prior to conducting a service for members of this faith on the occasion of the 250th anniversary of Detroit's founding — these were symbols of the wide gulf that existed between the New England heritage of so many of Michigan's residents whose roots in the state went back several generations and the heritage of a large percentage of the new arrivals. For many on both sides, the gulf could not be bridged, and they lived apart in their separate communities, not knowing or understanding each other.

In some cases, the treatment accorded those who were different from what many regarded as the norm resulted in discriminatory practices on the part of the majority towards these minorities. Among those who suffered were the Mexican laborers, who, in the 1920's, began to be brought in to work as field hands on the sugar-beet farms of eastern Michigan and, somewhat later, as fruit pickers in the western part of the state. The fact that these migrant workers performed menial tasks for pitifully low wages that resident laborers would not accept caused some people to despise them all the more and to feel that these workers and their families could be forced to live and to work under conditions that most other workers likewise would find unacceptable.

163

The special manner in which Michigan's Negroes were treated and which served to set them apart from all the other minority groups is summed up in this photograph of Negro soldiers in World War I, segregated into an all-Negro unit and assigned to separate "colored" barracks at Camp Custer. Different as the eastern or southern European might be from the native-born white American, the two groups were regarded as compatible enough to be thrown together in the same company in the army, but mixing black soldiers with whites was not permitted.

Separation of the races was not a condition found only in the armed services and the South at this time. It existed in Michigan as well. In October, 1919, the National Urban League, which had been formed in 1910 to seek to improve the status of the Negro, held its annual meeting in Detroit, the first time this national organization met outside of New York. The Negro members attending the conference stayed with Negro families in Detroit since local hotels would not admit them. As a result, the president of the league, Hollingsworth Wood (seated front row center), and some of the other white delegates also stayed in Negro homes rather than accepting the quarters that the color of their skin would have obtained for them in the hotels of this Michigan city.

164

A local chapter of the Urban League was formed in Detroit in 1916, and in 1918 John C. Dancy, a native of North Carolina, came in to head the organization. Dancy, shown here in 1949 with his wife Malinda, continued as director of the Detroit Urban League until his retirement in 1960. During that period, when Detroit's Negro population increased more than twentyfold, Dancy and his fellow Negro leaders were faced with a monumental task in seeking to improve the economic and social condition under which these Negroes worked and lived and to accomplish these goals in the face of a generally hostile white majority.

Jobs and housing were the basic concerns of these leaders in this period, but other interests, in some respects even more important, could not be overlooked. Medical facilities available to Negroes were inadequate. With rare exceptions, Negro doctors were not permitted to practice in Detroit's white hospitals. Negroes who were coming up from the South had had little contact with trained medical personnel, and for many the only ideas they held about medical care were rooted in superstition. The baby clinic established in 1919 at the Detroit Urban League's community center at 553 East Columbia Street attempted to deal with some of these problems by providing trained personnel to instruct mothers in better methods of caring for their children.

The league's community center was also designed to provide much-needed recreational facilities for Detroit's Negroes, such as this reading room. Negroes were not welcomed as members in Detroit's YMCA, although a few token Negro memberships had been granted. Rather than submit to complete integration, the white directors encouraged the development of a separate YMCA organization in the city for Negroes only.

This was an era when Negro organizations did not hesitate to accept the help of white men of good will who desired equal opportunities for Negroes. When these three socially prominent Detroiters, including Henry Williams (center), the father of the future Michigan governor, learned that no summer camps would accept Negro youths, they assisted the Detroit Urban League in obtaining land near Jackson where a Negro camp could be established.

In the summer of 1931, the flag was raised over the new camp, which was named Green Pastures, after the popular Broadway production of that day with a Negro theme and a nearly all-Negro cast. Streets and buildings in the camp were given the names of prominent American Negroes of the past, to acquaint the campers with their own heritage. At a time when the more militant Negro leadership was fighting to get white organizations to drop their discriminatory practices towards Negroes, the answer of the more conservative Urban League to this problem was frequently to sponsor a Negro counterpart to the all-white organizations. Forty years later, the most militant Negro leaders had adopted these same separatist views and those who advocated complete integration were now regarded as the conservatives.

The rapidly changing character of Michigan's population was but one manifestation of the ways in which the state was being refashioned by the economic boom that had been underway, with only brief setbacks, since the beginning of the century. In the late 1920's, the Great Lakes Steel Mill, the open hearth section of which is seen here in process of construction, rose at Ecorse, helping to fulfill the promise that the down-river Detroit area had held as a major iron and steel center since the heyday of Eber Brock Ward's Eureka Iron and Steel Company in the mid-nineteenth century.

Courtesy: Transportation Library

In the same period, the strong reemergence of Michigan as one of the nation's leading shipbuilding centers was made very visibly evident to those spectators who witnessed the 1929 launching at the Great Lakes Engineering Works in River Rouge of the *Myron C. Taylor*. The ore carrier, the equivalent of two football fields in length and with a carrying capacity of twelve thousand tons, seemed huge at that time, but within two decades new and larger ore boats would be appearing on the lakes with double the capacity of the *Myron C. Taylor*.

In central Michigan, where economic progress had stagnated since the days of the lumber boom, a new boom in a previously untapped resource developed in the twenties with the discovery of vast amounts of oil and gas at numerous points across the lower peninsula. Oil derricks, such as these near Clare in an oil field developed in the 1930's, and this refinery at Alma became familiar sights. To the residents of the area the smell of oil was a most pleasant one, as Michigan became one of the leading petroleum producers in the eastern United States.

Courtesy: Michigan Historical Commission

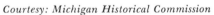

Courtesy: Michigan Historical Commission

Courtesy: Ford Archives

It was appropriate that Michigan began to furnish some of the fuel and lubricants needed for the cars it produced. The state's dominance of the auto industry, in fact, became ever greater during the twenties, and the unchallenged leader of this industry, in the public's eyes, continued to be Henry Ford, shown here in the Upper Peninsula in 1923 on one of his well-publicized camping trips with his friends Harvey Firestone and Thomas A. Edison (on Ford's right and left, respectively).

In the 1920's, Ford completed his enormous new plant on the River Rouge in what became a part of Dearborn in 1928. Hailed as the "greatest industrial enterprise since the Pyramids," the Rouge plant was an attempt to combine all the operations involved in the production of automobiles. Iron ore, coal, limestone, soda ash, and other raw materials were brought in in Ford's own boats and railroad cars, transformed on the site into iron and steel and glass, which were then fashioned into cars in the manufacturing section of the huge complex, which occupied some 1,100 acres of land. At its peak, the Rouge plant employed 88,000 men.

Courtesy: Michigan Historical Commission

But Ford's operations were not confined solely to Dearborn. The body plant outside Iron Mountain was part of a growing series of activities by Ford in the Upper Peninsula in the twenties, which held out the hope that manufacturing might revitalize the economy of this area of frigid winters and declining revenues from the exploitation of its mineral and timber resources. Elsewhere, the economics of the auto industry had long since dictated the establishment of a network of assembly plants to reduce the cost of shipping cars and trucks from Dearborn and Highland Park to the more distant parts of the nation and the world.

With the exception of the luxury car, the Lincoln, which Ford began to produce in limited numbers after acquiring the company from the Lelands in 1922, the Ford Motor Company in the 1920's continued to produce only one model, the Model T. On May 26, 1927, Henry Ford, with his son Edsel at the wheel, rode in the fifteen millionth Model T to be assembled. Although the car had been dressed up a little over the years, it was still basically the same car that had first appeared nineteen years earlier. But the tastes of the public had changed, and so this scene also marks the end of Ford's production of the Model T.

For months automobile production at the Ford plants halted while the company developed the new model that would replace the familiar old Tin Lizzy. Early in 1928, the long-awaited new Ford, the Model A, began to move down the assembly line at the Rouge plant and into

the dealers' show windows. The public, which still had unbounded confidence in Henry Ford's ability to outdo his competitors, eagerly snapped up the new Ford and temporarily gave the company the lead in the low-priced-car field it had lost in the last year of Model T sales. But 1928 was not 1908, and the Model A did not have the same impact on the market the Model T had had. Henry Ford was now sixty-five years old and set in his ways. Other companies, under younger, more imaginative leadership, now challenged or surpassed Ford's auto sales.

In the late twenties, Ford faced a major challenge from a new company put together by one of the major figures in modern American business history, Walter P. Chrysler, shown here taking a practice swing with a golf club, a sport that became increasingly popular in the twenties. The manner in which Chrysler is dressed, however, indicates that this hard-working, hardheaded businessman was not intending to spend much time on the links. A native of Kansas, Chrysler had risen to a top position in the railroad-car industry before joining the Buick organization in 1911. In a short time he had risen to the presidency of the company and had made it the strongest unit within General Motors. His services were deemed to be so essential that William C. Durant upped Chrysler's annual salary to a fantastic $500,000 in 1916 to keep him from accepting an offer from the Nash Motor Company.

Courtesy: Automotive History Collection

Literary Digest, *November 5, 1910*

After Chrysler resigned from General Motors in 1920 because of disagreements with Durant, he was in great demand as a troubleshooter who might put life back into automobile companies that were on the verge of going under. Late in 1920 he was called in to try to save two old and familiar Detroit-made cars, the Chalmers and the Maxwell. The two firms had been operating under the same management since 1917, although a formal merger had not taken place. In the postwar depression the companies were driven to the wall. Over a period of five years, Chrysler directed a series of complicated moves designed to create a financially sound new organization out of the wreckage of the bankrupt Chalmers and Maxwell companies. (*See also top illustrations on opposite page.*)

170

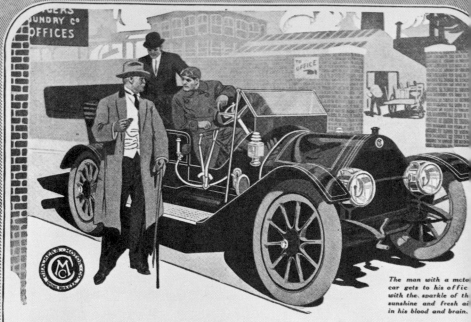

The man with a motor car gets to his office with the sparkle of the sunshine and fresh air in his blood and brain.

You're Paying for a Motor Car

You may think you don't *want* a motor car. But there isn't any question about your *needing* one.

If you need a car you are paying for it. Paying in the time that a car would save you. In the opportunities that get away. In the fresh air and recreation which now you do not get.

Whatever we really need we pay for, whether we actually own it or not. You could get along without an overcoat this winter, but you would pay for one with discomfort and bad colds.

The motor car didn't create its demand after it arrived. The demand has been waiting for forty centuries.

When the steamship, the railroad and trolley took care of the problem of public transportation, the world took a long step ahead.

When the automobile took care of the problem of individual transportation, the world took another long step ahead.

The man with a motor gets down to his business in the morning quickly, cleanly and with gladness—the sparkle of the sunshine and fresh air in his blood and brain.

He is able to take up his business problems with clearer vision and greater energy than the man who has been worried and doped by the rush and jam and the bad air of a crowded car.

At noon he can use his car to entertain a business associate with a ten mile ride to a pleasant luncheon place. He can send it out in the afternoon to entertain guests while he goes ahead with his business.

After the day's work, he drives home again, arrives with weariness and worry air-sprayed from his brain; with a keen appetite and good humor for dinner.

In the evening he may use his car for a spin into the country with family and friends.

The man with the motor car lives a fuller life than if he didn't have one. He has more experience—more sensations. He lives twice as long in the same length of time as the man who hasn't a car.

There are many good cars made nowadays, and any good car is a good investment. Yet we honestly believe that Chalmers cars offer the best value for the money of any on the market. We ask you to see the Chalmers before you buy. Compare them with others. Comparison has sold more Chalmers cars than all our advertising. The new models are now on exhibition at all dealers' show rooms. We have a brand new catalog "BK"—write for it.

How the Family Benefits

Head of the Family:—Going to and from business in fresh air. Making business calls. Entertaining customers and business associates. Tours in the country. More knowledge of the country. Mental and physical exercise of driving. Good appetite—better digestion—better humor—better health. Prestige.

Wife and Daughter:—Social calls. Entertaining. Plenty of fresh air to drive away "nerves." More time with husband and father.

Sons:—Educative value of understanding and caring for a wonderful piece of machinery. Training of mental and physical faculties in driving. Clean, fresh air recreation and decent entertainment in company of other members of family.

Chalmers Motor Company (*Licensed under Selden Patent*) **Detroit, Mich.**

(For description, see bottom caption on opposite page.)

Maxwell

You will have only yourself to blame if you are "talked into" buying an "unsuitable" or a "theoretical" car

The two commonest mistakes made in buying an automobile are—*First*, Buying a car not suited to your needs.—*Second*, Buying a car that has not passed the theory stage.

The first mistake—buying an "unsuitable" car—is perhaps made even less often than the second.

The second mistake—buying a "theoretical" car—is perhaps the sadder mistake of the two—because when you have made this mistake, you have on your hands some engineer's or designer's untried theory, instead of a tried, known, successful car. Study your needs sensibly, just as you study your household needs, and buy a car you *can afford* to enjoy.

38,000 happy, satisfied Maxwell owners are driving 38,000 handsome stream-line Maxwell cars to-day—at an up-keep cost that any man of any standing can afford, and at an original cost that is simply a practical investment.

The Maxwell Company's Guarantee of Service to Maxwell Owners

No other automobile is backed by a more reliable service than that guaranteed every Maxwell owner. More than 2,000 Maxwell dealers—located in every part of this country and Canada—are always ready to give expert advice, make adjustments, and supply or secure new parts at reasonable prices.

And this splendid dealer service organiza-tion is perfected and completed by sixteen great Maxwell Service Stations which are so located throughout the country that a Max-well dealer can get, within a few hours, any part that he has not in stock.

Order a Maxwell from us now, and when you want it delivered, we will give you your car—not an excuse on delivery day.

Maxwell Five-Passenger Touring Car, $695, f.o.b. Detroit.   In Canada, $ 925.
Maxwell Roadster,   -   -   -   670, f.o.b. Detroit.   In Canada,   900.
Maxwell Cabriolet,   -   -   -   840, f.o.b. Detroit.   In Canada, 1,105.
Any model equipped with electric self-starter, $55 extra.   In Canada, $70 extra.

Write for beautiful 1915 Maxwell Catalogue. Address Department A. L.

MAXWELL MOTOR COMPANY, Inc.,   Detroit, Michigan

"Every Road is a Maxwell Road"

Literary Digest, April 3, 1915

Courtesy: Michigan Historical Commission

By 1925 Walter Chrysler had achieved his goal. He had put together a new automobile company, had secured the necessary financial backing, and had put on the market a new car, such as this roadster model, which, like the company, bore Chrysler's own name.

171

Drawing upon his earlier experience with the diversified lines of automobiles produced at General Motors, Chrysler soon acquired the Dodge Brothers Company, and by 1928, with the introduction of the Plymouth, he was offering cars in the high, medium, and low-priced fields. At a time when the number of car manufacturers was steadily being reduced, Chrysler had succeeded in establishing a new company that overnight became the third largest manufacturer of automobiles and was threatening to move ahead of Ford into second place.

Courtesy: Automotive History Collection

In the twenties, General Motors finally achieved the preeminence in the industry that its power-packed lineup of cars had always indicated it should have. The man who had assembled the stars of the GM organization, however, was no longer running the team. The depression of 1920 almost spelled the end of General Motors, and for the second time in a decade William C. Durant's departure from the company was deemed to be essential to the success of efforts to save the firm from collapse. Years later, when this photograph was taken and Durant was no longer a controversial figure, the giant corporation made room for the man from Flint in the ceremonies marking the production of its twenty-five millionth car in 1940.

Courtesy: Michigan Historical Collections

Courtesy: Michigan Historical Commission

Succeeding Durant as the dominant figure in General Motors was Alfred P. Sloan, Jr., the brilliant, coldly efficient graduate of Massachusetts Institute of Technology, who developed the organizational plan that was needed to bring order to the undigested collection of manufacturing units, each operating very largely autonomously, that comprised the empire Durant had built.

172

It was not Sloan's organizational charts, however, that pushed GM to the top in the twenties, but the sales of its cars. Oldsmobile and Oakland, with that division's new entry, the Pontiac, grabbed a larger share of the market, taking some of the pressure off Buick and Cadillac, which had always been the strongest entries out of the GM stable. It was, however, the spectacular rise of Chevrolet that finally accounted for the triumph of General Motors over its competitors. After whittling away for several years at the once enormous lead of the Ford Model T in the low-priced field, the 1927

Courtesy: Automotive History Collection

Chevrolets, such as this shiny little roadster, with the rumble seat in the back, forged ahead. Chevrolet was rarely less than number one in the years that followed.

Courtesy: Michigan Historical Collections

During 1919 and 1920, General Motors built what was at the time the largest office building in the world. Nearly fifty buildings that had occupied the area along West Grand Boulevard between Cass and Second in Detroit were torn down or removed to make way for this Albert Kahn-designed, $20,000,000 structure. Not only did it house the offices of the automobile firm, but, as the card accompanying this photograph of the completed building stated, office space was also leased by other companies —"discriminating tenants — the kind you would welcome as neighbors and business acquaintances."

Wayne County Manual, 1926

The changes the erection of the GM building brought to one block of downtown Detroit were no greater than the changes that occurred throughout Michigan's largest city, whose growth in area, as well as population, had been steady in earlier decades but had become spectacular in the years after 1910, when the city became a mecca for hordes of workers seeking employment in the auto plants. Detroit's city limits were pushed further and further out by a rapid succession of annexations that left the cities of Highland Park and Hamtramck as isolated pockets, completely surrounded by Detroit.

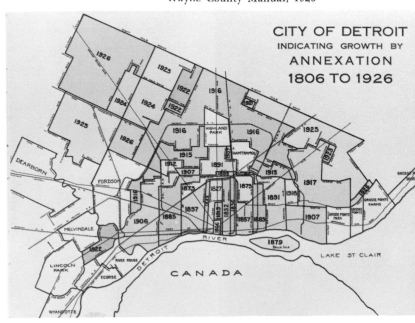

CITY OF DETROIT
INDICATING GROWTH BY
ANNEXATION
1806 TO 1926

Courtesy: Burton Historical Collection

Courtesy: Burton Historical Collection

As Detroit's population increased from under half a million in 1910 to about a million in 1920 and 1,568,662 in 1930, the city's physical appearance began to conform more nearly to that of a big city, the fifth largest in the country. Skyscrapers, the tallest of which, the Penobscot Building, is shown here going up in the late twenties, now dwarfed such older structures as the stately, but doomed, Detroit City Hall, and the little Bagley Memorial Fountain in the foreground, Michigan's only surviving example of the work of the great nineteenth-century American architect Henry Hobson Richardson.

In 1928, the same year that the Penobscot Building, designed by the Detroit architectural firm of Smith, Hinchman and Grylls, was completed, the Fisher Building, with its golden tower, was opened, the second in the complex of office buildings in the West Grand Boulevard area designed by Albert Kahn. Like the General Motors Building across the street, the Fisher Building, named for and financed by the brothers who founded the body division of GM, revealed Kahn's great skill in creating buildings other than the functional factories for which he is most famous.

Courtesy: Michigan Historical Commission

"Going out of business" signs became commonplace, ironically, as Detroit grew and business as a whole increased. These merchants along Woodward Avenue in May, 1914, were selling out their stocks at what one of them termed a "tremendous slaughter in prices" because the site was desired by the J. L. Hudson Company....

174

...In this block now arose the huge new store building in which Hudson's was able to offer residents of southeastern Michigan the services of a department store that equaled, if they did not exceed, those of Macy's, Gimbel's, Marshall Field's, or any of America's other famous stores.

Courtesy: Michigan Historical Commission

At the same time that its skyline became more big-time, some other features of Detroit were also altered, as befitted a city of its size. In 1921 the first stage in a carefully planned city cultural center was completed with the opening of the main Detroit Public Library building. Early in the twentieth century plans for the development of this center, far removed from the crowded downtown business section, began to materialize with the acquisition by the boards governing the city's library and its art museum of large tracts of land on either side of Woodward Avenue at Kirby and Farnsworth. The new library building was an impressive white-marble structure of the Italian Renaissance style, designed by the New York architect Cass Gilbert to house the collections of the library that dated back to the first purchases that had been made in 1819.

Courtesy: Michigan Historical Commission

Across Woodward from the new library the new quarters of the Detroit Institute of Arts were opened in 1927. Designed by the Philadelphia architect Paul Cret, in a style that harmonized with the library building, the structure provided what was for that time ample space in which to display the art treasures that had been accumulated under the direction first of private groups and then, after 1918, of a public arts commission.

Courtesy: Michigan Historical Commission

The great building boom that characterized this era in Detroit did not leave the rest of the state untouched. Nor was Albert Kahn's influence confined to the Detroit area. This sketch of the man who was one of the major figures in twentieth-century architecture is inscribed by Kahn to Mr. Shirley Smith, an official of the University of Michigan, where Kahn had a hand in most of the many new construction projects that were completed during the twenties as the Ann Arbor school underwent great expansion.

Among the buildings at the University of Michigan that went up in this period, one that would house the William L. Clements Library is said to have been Kahn's favorite of all the buildings he designed. Here, as in a number of Kahn's other creations, such as the General Motors Building, he adopted the Italian Renaissance style, which enjoyed somewhat the same popularity in the public buildings constructed in this period as the Greek Revival style had enjoyed a century earlier.

Courtesy: Michigan Historical Collections

Courtesy: Michigan Historical Collections

Courtesy: Michigan Historical Collections

Meanwhile, at East Lansing, the Beaumont Memorial Tower, completed in 1928, marked the site of the first college building in the country that was devoted to the scientific teaching of agriculture. But its construction came at a time when Michigan's agricultural college was being changed to a school where other sciences and the arts were receiving more attention, as was partially indicated by the change of the institution's name in 1925 to Michigan State College of Agriculture and Applied Science.

In Lansing itself, the new State Office Building, constructed between 1920 and 1922, with Kahn acting this time as a consultant on the project (Bowd-Munson of Lansing were the architects), reflected the needs of the ever-expanding state government, whose many departments, agencies, and bureaus could now be collected under one roof to a greater degree than had been possible for many years. The building, which, as in the case of the nearby State Capitol, conformed to what Americans have always seemed to think a government building should look like, underwent extensive interior and some exterior alterations in the 1950's, following a fire, and it was then renamed the Lewis Cass Building.

Dramatic evidence that the state government no longer exerted quite the same power in Lansing as it once had done, however, came at the beginning of the decade following the twenties when the Olds Tower rose at the corner of Allegan Street and Capitol Avenue. The 345-foot skyscraper, the tallest building in Michigan outside Detroit, now loomed up over the domed capitol across the street, which had previously dominated the landscape. Just down the street from the Olds Tower was the Hotel Olds, built a few years earlier during the twenties, its name, too, reflecting the prominent new role of the auto industry in Lansing, as a result of the activities of Ransom E. Olds. (Olds's fame, even in his hometown, was a fleeting one, however, and by the 1960's both buildings bore entirely different names.)

177

A few blocks from the Olds Tower, Ransom E. Olds built this home in 1904 at the corner of South Washington and Main. The exterior design, shown here in 1965 following certain alterations that were made in 1952, was unattractive. Within, the stairway at the far end of the hall led up to the second floor with its opulent music room, complete with pipe organ and grand piano. A television set had been added by the time these photographs were made, by which time Ransom Olds had been dead for fifteen years and his mansion would soon be torn down, destroyed, appropriately enough, to make way for an expressway.

178

Fair Lane, Henry Ford's mansion built in 1914-15 in Dearborn, has enjoyed a happier fate than that of the Lansing home of Ford's fellow auto pioneer. The sprawling mansion with its fifty-six rooms was home for Henry and Clara Ford from the time of its completion until their deaths over thirty years later. Its secluded location along the River Rouge, with a huge surrounding wooded estate, was striking testimony to the dominant independent streak in Ford's personality — especially in a period when Grosse Pointe, not Dearborn, had become the socially acceptable address for Ford's fellow multimillionaires in the Detroit area. In 1956, Fair Lane was turned over to the University of Michigan to serve as the nucleus for the university's Dearborn center.

Courtesy: Allen Stross

Courtesy: Allen Stross

Of greater aesthetic interest than either the Olds or the Ford home, however, are two brick houses in Grand Rapids that were built for Meyer S. May, a young retail merchant, and his father-in-law, David Amberg, in the early part of the twentieth century, which were forward-looking in their architectural design, rather than representing an attempt to return to some earlier style. Both houses reflect the influence of America's greatest architect, Frank Lloyd Wright. Wright designed the May house (left) at 450 Madison Avenue, S.E., which was built in 1909, while the Amberg house (right) at 505 College Avenue, S.E., which was completed in 1910, although finished by other architects, followed the general ideas of Wright, who had obtained the original commission.

Courtesy: Detroit News

The imagination and individuality represented in the May and Amberg houses were qualities sadly lacking, however, in residential construction in Michigan for many years. The result of this deficiency, together with poor city planning, totally unprepared to deal with the problem of the mushrooming industrial metropolis, was the rise in the twenties of block after block, mile after mile of identical, or nearly identical, houses, crowded on narrow lots. The undistinguished character of these houses is graphically demonstrated by this aerial view of a typical Detroit residential section.

A school building in the small rural central-Michigan town of Bath dates in part from the twenties, as does such a large proportion of Michigan's buildings, both public and private, today. But it represents much more than simply another construction project to be completed during the booming twenties. It recalls one of the most bizarre and tragic events of that decade and the response to that event by one of Michigan's most famous public figures in the twenties.

On May 18, 1927, an explosion, set off by a maniac, destroyed part of the public school building at Bath, killing thirty-eight children and injuring many more. The cost of rebuilding the school was handled by James Couzens, and a charitable fund he had established helped to defray the medical expenses of the injured. The citizens of Bath did not forget this help. When Couzens died nine years later in the midst of the Great Depression, the schoolchildren of the town pooled their pennies to pay for a floral tribute to their benefactor. The school building itself is now the James Couzens Junior High School.

The actions James Couzens took in the case of the Bath tragedy were indicative of a generous humanitarian side of his personality, which had been little evident in his days with the Ford Motor Company when his hard-driving business-management techniques had been credited with a large share of the responsibility for that company's success. After parting company with Henry Ford in 1915, Couzens entered public service, and as police commissioner and then mayor of Detroit he showed the same independent qualities that had characterized that earlier businessman-turned-politician, Hazen Pingree. In 1922, Governor Alex Groesbeck appointed Couzens to fill a vacancy from Michigan in the United States Senate. Although nominally a Republican, Couzens during his fourteen years in the Senate was the prototype of the maverick in politics. Uncompromising and outspoken in his advocacy of a variety of measures that would benefit those in the low-income brackets, some of them foreshadowing the New Deal reforms of the following decade, Couzens, as this photograph taken in the summer of 1929 suggests, enormously enjoyed his new role. Observers of the Washington scene gave him a far higher rating than has been accorded to most Michigan congressmen and senators over the years.

The man who originally appointed Couzens to the Senate, Alex J. Groesbeck, was the state's chief executive from 1921 through 1926. Groesbeck was that rarity in Michigan politics, a top political figure who had been born in the state and, even rarer, one whose family harked back to Michigan's French period. Groesbeck left a prosperous Detroit law practice to serve as the state's attorney general during the period of World War I, and in 1920 was elected governor. A bachelor, Groesbeck gave his complete attention to the job, working long hours weekdays and weekends at his desk in the capitol and expecting the same devotion from his associates.

Courtesy: Michigan Historical Commission

Like Senator Couzens, Groesbeck was something of a loner in politics, a man with an independent mind who achieved great popularity with the voters, such as those in this group at Bay Port whom he addressed during his campaign for reelection in 1924. Unlike Couzens, however, Groesbeck was basically a conservative, whose primary interest was in modernizing the antiquated structure of the state government in the interest of achieving greater efficiency. His success was remarkable, establishing him as probably the most capable administrator ever to hold the office of governor in Michigan. But his desire to strengthen this office and to make its holder truly the chief executive of the state caused him to lose support among important Republican leaders, whose toes he stepped on too often.

Courtesy: Michigan Historical Commission

Politically, the independents, Couzens and Groesbeck, were atypical of the twenties, for in matters of politics, if in nothing else, Michigan did "Return to Normalcy," and with a vengeance. The decade marked the all-time zenith of Republican power in the state. In January, 1923, Lieutenant Governor Thomas Read of Shelby stood in front of the steps of the State Capitol. Behind him were the thirty-two members of the state Senate over which he would preside during the next two years. Read and every one of the senators were Republicans. A lock of hair that projected beneath the brim of Read's hat was almost the only touch of the unconventional visible in the entire group. In the lower house, only five of the one hundred members were Democrats, and two years later, even those five votes were wiped out as the Republicans won complete control of the entire legislature. Strongly rural in their orientation at a time when an ever growing majority of the state's residents were city dwellers, these legislators were ill-prepared to recognize and deal with the problems of an urbanized, industrialized society.

Thoroughly in keeping with the complacent political philosophy in the twenties was Fred W. Green, seated at the left. Green, onetime member of Governor Pingree's military staff, successful Ionia businessman, and one of the shrewdest politicians in Michigan history, had thwarted Groesbeck's ambitions to become the state's first four-term governor and had won the job for himself in 1926. Seated with Governor Green in this formal picture in 1927 are the other members of the State Administrative Board—conservatively dressed, generally older men, who were the epitome of respectability and of the conservative elements of the GOP that dominated the state. On Green's left is Oramel Fuller of Delta County, nearly seventy years old, who had been auditor general since 1908. Next to Fuller is State Treasurer Frank D. McKay of Grand Rapids, the youngster of the group, and the most powerful Republican in the state during the next decade and a half. At the other end of the table from Green is Luren D. Dickinson, staunch Prohibitionist and Methodist from Charlotte, now in his fourth term as lieutenant governor. Nearly seventy years old at this time, Dickinson would become governor eleven years later. The man with the glasses at the far right is John Haggerty of Detroit, a former bosom friend of Groesbeck until they had a falling out and Haggerty was rewarded by Green with the nomination for secretary of state.

The distinguished man with the white mustache is Frank F. Rogers, sixty-eight, completing his fourth four-year term as state highway commissioner.

Courtesy: Michigan Historical Commission

In 1928, Arthur W. Vandenberg, editor of the Grand Rapids *Herald,* was named by Green to fill the vacancy left by the death of Senator Woodbridge N. Ferris, the only Democrat in the first three decades of the century to win a state-wide election. Although Vandenberg would ultimately reveal a streak of independence, the immediate effect of his appointment was to increase the strength of the conservative element in the Republican Party that was represented by Fred Green and most of the other elected officials, with the notable exception of Senator Couzens.

Courtesy: Michigan Historical Commission

In his public pronouncements, Green, during his four years as governor, reflected the satisfied, stand-pat mood of the times. On the golf links of Mackinac Island, with his wrinkled plus fours and his broad grin, the fun-loving governor just as accurately mirrored the carefree attitude for which the Roaring Twenties are now best remembered.

184

At the end of the 1920's two major construction projects were completed, linking Detroit and its sister city, Windsor, across the international boundary. Financed by private companies, the Ambassador Bridge was completed in 1929 at a cost of $16,821,000, ...

Courtesy: Michigan Historical Commission

Courtesy: Michigan Historical Commission

... while the $22,000,000 Detroit-Windsor Tunnel, the first public vehicular tunnel between two countries, was opened in 1930. The traffic at the time was insufficient to support two competing toll facilities, and this fact, plus the Depression that shortly broke over the country, soon plunged the operating companies into bankruptcy and receivership. Nevertheless, the two represented the boundless optimism of the twenties, an optimism that scoffed at practical considerations and that was in strange contrast with the cautious attitudes expressed in the speeches of the political leaders of the period. But years later, when Fred Green and Oramel Fuller, and, for that matter, Alex Groesbeck and James Couzens, are dimly remembered, a constant stream of traffic pours over and under the Detroit River via a bridge and a tunnel, tangible mementos of one of the most productive decades in Michigan's history.

The Depression Years

Courtesy: Burton Historical Collection

In the last week of October, 1929, the bottom dropped out of the stock market. In brokers' offices in Detroit and elsewhere, stockholders watched in growing panic as their losses mounted with each new report from the ticker tape. Auto stocks, which for several weeks had fallen off sharply from their high quotations for the year, were among the most closely watched as everyone, both amateurs and professionals, tried to figure out what had happened to the market. General Motors common stock dropped from 57⅜ at the opening on October 24 to 33½ at the market closing on October 29, while Chrysler, which sold for 51 at the beginning of October 24 (its high during the year had been 135), reached a low point during the panic of 26.

188

The third member of the automotive Big Three, Ford, whose stocks were wholly owned by the Ford family and were not listed or traded, reacted quickly to the changing economic conditions. On November 1, this advertisement appeared in newspapers across the country, announcing a reduction in the prices of the various Ford models, a technique Henry Ford had used a decade earlier to help his company weather the postwar depression. But such efforts to shore up the nation's economy proved unavailing in 1929, and the closing weeks of the year marked not only the end of a decade but also the end of the atmosphere of prosperity, speculation, and optimism that had made the twenties roar.

Courtesy: Automotive History Collection

The auto companies continued with business as usual in the early 1930's, coming out with their new models and displaying them at the annual New York auto show. The Cadillac exhibit in 1932 included the twelve-cylinder and sixteen-cylinder models that it had added in 1930 to its already lavish lines.

Courtesy: Automotive History Collection

But auto sales declined. By 1933, auto production was down to 1,331,860 units, in contrast with the five million cars produced in the banner year of 1929. The Big Three manufacturers were able to weather the storm, but the depression killed off a number of the smaller manufacturers. Among this latter group was Durant Motors, formed by the irrepressible William C. Durant after he had been removed from General Motors in 1920. During the great bull market of the 1920's, Durant, besides directing his new automobile company, had returned to his first love, the stock market, and by 1929 had reportedly built up a fortune of $100,000,000 through his dealings. The crash ruined him and, despite the brave showing of the new Durant models at the New York auto show in 1931, his company was on the rocks by that time, with final liquidation coming in 1933. This time the aging Durant made no spectacular comeback from defeat. Instead, in 1936, when he was seventy-five years old, he declared bankruptcy, listing liabilities of $914,000 and assets of only $250.00 — the clothes on his back.

Courtesy: Michigan Historical Collections

By 1930, one out of every five industrial workers in Michigan was unemployed. Their distress, which was felt most severely in the heavily industrialized Detroit area, led to demonstrations, such as this one near Detroit's City Hall in March, 1930. The use of the city's mounted police to disperse the demonstrators was blamed on Mayor Charles Bowles, whose growing unpopularity because of this and other actions led to a rare use in Michigan of the recall procedure to remove Bowles from office in July, 1930.

Courtesy: Detroit News

With no work and no income, hungry men were forced to accept charity and to get a free meal of bread and soup at places such as the St. Francis soup kitchen in Detroit's Tertiary Hall. This photograph was taken in December, 1930.

Courtesy: Detroit News

A year later, at Thanksgiving, by which time Michigan's unemployment rate had risen to 29 percent, these men, still proudly wearing suits and neckties, lined up for a hot meal ladled out by Detroit firemen.

Courtesy: Michigan Historical Commission

Courtesy: Michigan Historical Commission

Courtesy: Michigan Historical Commission

But the hard times of the thirties did not affect only the city residents. These people, photographed during these years, were residents of rural Manistee County whose plight demonstrated how the tragedy of the Great Depression left no economic or social group untouched.

191

In September, 1930, Frank Murphy took office as mayor of Detroit after winning the special election that was held following the recall of Mayor Bowles. As Murphy stood in his shirt sleeves and addressed the Common Council in the crowded council chambers, he realized that his political future depended on how successful he was in dealing with Detroit's depression-born problems.

Murphy soon became aware that the resources of local governmental units, such as Detroit, were entirely inadequate to finance the programs that were needed to help the unemployed and the hungry. As chairman of a special committee representing mayors of some of the nation's larger cities, Murphy led an effort in June, 1932, to secure Congressional approval of a five-billion-dollar federal work relief program and federal refunding of municipal debts. Murphy is shown here conferring with Speaker John Nance Garner of the United States House of Representatives (second from left), together with such other mayors as James Curley of Boston (fourth from left) and Dan Hoan of Milwaukee (far right), and the veteran Republican politician, George Welsh, city manager of Grand Rapids (third from right). But the appeal of the mayors did not convince President Herbert Hoover, who continued to favor more conservative measures and vetoed large-scale work relief programs.

Murphy was a small-town boy who had made good as a lawyer and judge in the big city of Detroit. In Harbor Beach, where Murphy's father John had been an attorney, the house in which Frank was born in 1890 is preserved today as a historic museum in memory of the man who in the 1930's was one of the bright stars among the liberal, humanitarian forces who felt that government had a responsibility to do all it could to aid the people in combating the ravages of the depression.

Courtesy: Michigan Historical Collections

George Welsh had warned that if massive aid was not forthcoming in 1932, when nearly one out of every two nonagricultural workers in Michigan was out of work, "Communism and Bolshevism . . . will undermine the morale of our people." Actually, as early as the fall of 1930, a Communist-led rally in Detroit's Grand Circus Park gave striking evidence that many people were looking for radical solutions to the problems of the day. In addition to revealing how uncommon a hatless or capless man was in that period, the demonstration, with the escapist motion picture classic *Trader Horn* playing on the other side of the park, foretold trouble for the incumbent Republican administrations, both national and state.

Courtesy: Detroit News

President Hoover, running for reelection in 1932, managed a smile as he prepared to return to Washington after speaking at Detroit's Olympia Stadium on October 30. Behind Hoover and his secretary, Lawrence Richey, stands Henry Ford, whose presence was intended to add luster to Hoover's campaign. (Mrs. Hoover, at the right, towers over Clara Ford.)

Courtesy: Michigan Historical Commission

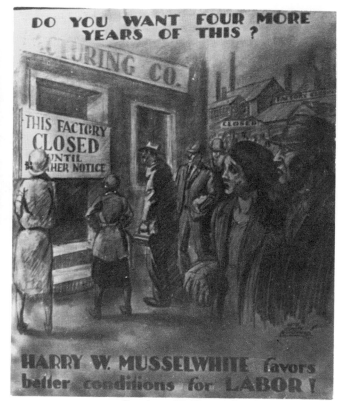

Courtesy: Michigan Historical Commission

By the end of October, however, it was becoming increasingly apparent that 1932 would be a Democratic year. In areas previously regarded as Republican strongholds, many voters looked with favor on election posters urging support for the Democrats. Harry W. Musselwhite of Manistee, Democratic candidate for Congress in the Ninth District (eleven west Michigan counties from Muskegon on the south to Leelanau in the north), sensed that issues raised by the Depression gave him a chance for victory. His Republican opponent, James C. McLaughlin of Muskegon, had been representing the district in Congress continuously since 1907 and in that time had had only one reasonably close contest for reelection. In 1928 he had had no opposition at all, and in 1930 he had swamped his Democratic opponent by a three-to-one margin. Yet in 1932 McLaughlin suddenly found his support among the voters melting away and in November he went down to defeat. (He died at the end of the month, and Musselwhite himself served only one term before being retired in 1934 when a majority of voters in the district returned to the Republican fold.)

On the state level, Democrats, long conditioned to defeat, also glimpsed the prospects of victory in 1932. This faithful Oakland County Democratic group hauled out the banner they had displayed every two years since 1926 for the wealthy party leader, William A. Comstock, who had allowed his name to be entered in the race for governor in 1926, 1928, and 1930, losing by margins of 172,000, 557,000, and 126,000 votes. But 1932 would be different, and most Democrats felt that good sport Comstock deserved the chance to show that he could be a good winner as well as a good loser.

Courtesy: Michigan Historical Collections

194

Democratic hopes were buoyed even more by the appearance of a magnetic new political leader as the Democratic presidential candidate, Governor Franklin D. Roosevelt of New York, campaigned in Michigan and promised that if elected he would inaugurate a New Deal, thereby borrowing a slogan used by Chase Osborn in his successful gubernatorial campaign of 1910.

On Wednesday, November 9, results of the election were reported by the Grand Rapids *Press,* which had been founded in 1890 as that city's first penny newspaper and in 1932 still cost only three cents. Roosevelt had carried Michigan, the first Democratic presidential candidate since 1852 to win all of the state's electoral votes. On the state level, Comstock, as the headlines indicate, was an "easy victor," winning the governorship with an even larger vote than that for Roosevelt. Even more startling, when the official count was completed, every other executive office on the ballot, save one, a majority of both houses of the legislature, and a majority of the state's congressional delegation had been won by Democrats.

After taking office in 1933, the state's new Democratic administration found itself faced with a banking crisis. Since 1929 nearly two hundred Michigan banks had failed, and when it appeared impossible to prevent the collapse of the state's two largest banking groups, Comstock on February 14 proclaimed an extended bank holiday. While the banks remained closed, Comstock conferred with Jesse Jones (on the right), head of the Reconstruction Finance Corporation, seeking the financial aid that would enable the more stable banks to reopen.

On March 24, the new National Bank of Detroit, formed with help from the RFC and General Motors, opened its doors. It had taken over the good assets of two of Detroit's largest banks that had failed to survive the emergency. Depositors in the defunct banks waited anxiously to learn the fate of their deposits. Although some had to wait a good many weeks, ultimately all received their money.

Although the state and local governments did what they could, the task of providing relief for the unemployed was so great that only the federal government had the necessary resources and powers to deal with it. Roosevelt's New Deal programs began to funnel millions of dollars for relief into Michigan beginning in 1933. The most famous of these programs were those of the Works Progress Administration, which between 1935 and 1943 spent over half a billion dollars in Michigan. At various times about two million people in the state depended solely on WPA paychecks for their support. Here, at least seventy-five men worked in the block at Grand River and Lothrop Avenues, Detroit, in 1936, engaged in a street-repair project.

In February, 1936, a score of WPA workmen on Gratiot Avenue, Detroit, leaned on their shovels, doing nothing, an attitude critics of the New Deal claimed characterized most of these work-relief activities.

Nevertheless, many public works of enduring value were built by WPA employees. These men, pouring concrete for a pavilion in Lansing's Comstock Park in the summer of 1936, once again knew the pride of earning a paycheck and at the same time having a part in something that would be worthwhile to their community.

In northern Michigan, the more than one hundred Civilian Conservation Camps that were set up provided not only relief, but training and, again, a sense of accomplishment to thousands of unemployed young men who were put to work at many tasks in state parks and state and national forests. The pleasure many thousands of people have had from the bathhouse at Ludington State Park, with its superb veranda overlooking Lake Michigan, has long ago justified the tax dollars that financed this CCC project in the 1930's.

197

These boys were learning the use of a motor tester as part of a National Youth Administration program at Detroit's Cass Technical High School.

This sewing project was part of the welfare relief program in Manistee County.

By 1934, economic conditions were showing signs of improvement. Automobile production was moving upwards again, although it would be a decade and a half before the production figures would reach the level achieved in 1929. This posed photograph, as important today as a record of the fashions of the period as it is of the new Hudson it was intended to promote, illustrates still another point. In the midst of the gloom and despair of the nation's worst

depression, businessmen, even the leaders of Hudson, one of the hardest hit of the smaller auto manufacturers, sought to carry on as if nothing unusual were happening. The company appealed not to the fifty percent of the working population that was out of work, but to the other half that had jobs and an income, which, if reduced, still might be sufficient to enable the wage earner to purchase costly items, such as a new car.

The sagging spirits of many Michiganians in the mid-thirties received a boost as a result of achievements in the area of sports. Michigan, in fact, and particularly Detroit, was for a time the sports capital of the nation. The Detroit Tigers, a team that had fallen on hard times since the great days of Ty Cobb, came back to win the American League pennant in 1934 and 1935 and in the latter year also won the World Series. That same year the Detroit Red Wings were the champions of professional hockey, while the Detroit Lions were crowned champions of professional football when they defeated the New York Giants 26 to 7 on December 15, 1935, before 15,000 spectators in the University of Detroit stadium. The players of 1935 were smaller and there were fewer of them than on the teams of a later era. The substitution rules being what they were, most of the regulars had to be ready to play nearly the entire game, on offense and defense. Detroit's star was the great Earl "Dutch" Clark, number 7, an authentic triple-threat player who had quarterbacked the team since its earlier career in Portsmouth, Ohio. The owner of radio station WJR, G. A. Richards (seated between Clark and fullback Ace Gutowsky, number 5), bought the team in 1934 and moved it to Detroit. Young Raymond "Buddy" Parker, number 4, a substitute on the 1935 team, would return to coach the Lions during their great championship years of the 1950's.

199

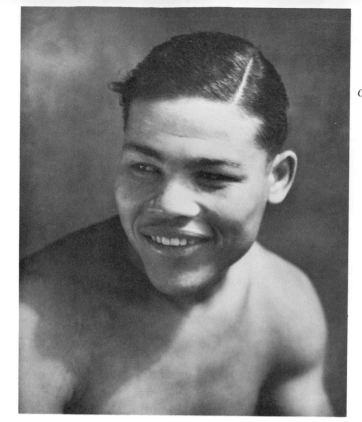

Professional sports at that time, especially organized baseball, were largely if not exclusively the domain of white performers. Boxing was one of the exceptions, and in 1934 a young Negro from Detroit made his first appearance as a professional boxer. Joe Louis Barrow (he would drop the last name when he began his boxing career), like the majority of Michigan's nearly two hundred thousand Negroes, was not a native of the state but of the South, which his family had left to seek greater economic opportunities in the North. Joe Louis found that opportunity with his fists. By 1937 he was heavyweight champion of the world, a title he would hold until 1949. Although most of his fights were held outside of Michigan, his exploits gave an important lift to the morale of his fellow Negroes in Detroit and elsewhere, whose economic and social position, never very favorable, had been made even worse by the deprivations of the 1930's. But equally significant was the fact that Louis, whom sportswriters at once tagged the "Brown Bomber," was as great a hero to white boys as he was to blacks.

Joe Louis was not the only Michigan Negro who found that athletic talents might be a means to opportunities that would otherwise be denied to him. Eddie Tolan's exploits as a Detroit high-school track star induced the white Detroit businessman Clarence M. Burton to pay Tolan's expenses at the University of Michigan, where the bespectacled young Detroiter became probably the greatest sprinter in the history of track at the Ann Arbor school. Tolan capped his career by winning gold medals in the 100 meter and 200 meter dashes at the 1932 Olympic games, establishing new Olympic records in both instances, with his time for 100 meters not being surpassed until the 1960 games.

But even a Joe Louis or an Eddie Tolan found many doors that remained closed to them simply because of their color. To the multitudes of Detroit's Negroes who were not world-famous sports figures, the depression years were years in which the lack of jobs made the other discriminatory practices of the city's white population even more difficult to endure. Thomas P. Danahey, president of the Detroit Housing Commission, pointed out to two prominent white business leaders in 1938 the obvious need for better housing in the city's Negro ghetto. Pitifully little low-cost housing was provided for Detroit Negroes, however, and with no change in the real-estate practices that confined Negroes to a few crowded, segregated areas of the city, adequate housing continued to be one of the frustrations to which the Negro must submit. Danahey and his companions in 1938 unfortunately could not foresee the tragedy that lay in the future when some of Detroit's black population would finally refuse to accept any longer the white man's terms without a fight.

The year 1934 witnessed a resurgence of the Republican Party in Michigan. Capitalizing on the dissension that developed in the ranks of Democrats who could not agree on how to share the fruits of their unaccustomed victory in 1932, Secretary of State Frank D. Fitzgerald of Grand Ledge (shown here in his office in the State Capitol), who had been the only Republican state officeholder to win two years earlier, now in 1934 recaptured the governorship for his party, while the GOP also regained much lost ground in the legislature.

201

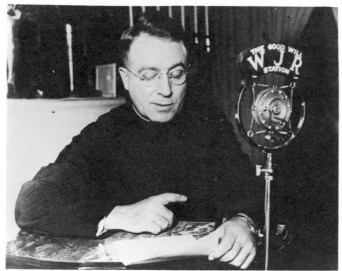

Courtesy: Detroit *News*

The Republicans were now joined in their criticism of the Roosevelt administration by the powerful voice of Father Charles E. Coughlin, Catholic priest of Royal Oak, who had built up a national following with his weekly radio broadcasts emanating from station WJR in Detroit. Originally a strong supporter of Roosevelt in 1932, Coughlin, by the time this photograph was taken in 1935, had become an outspoken, oftentimes vituperative opponent of Roosevelt and what Coughlin felt Roosevelt stood for.

Courtesy: Michigan Historical Collections

In 1936, Coughlin joined with the equally demagogic Protestant preacher, the Rev. Gerald L. K. Smith, and Dr. Francis Townsend to form a third party, which ran Congressman William Lemke of North Dakota as its candidate for president. Father Coughlin now supplemented his radio messages with a weekly paper that carried his extremist views to his followers for several years, until it was barred from the mails in World War II as a subversive publication.

Courtesy: Michigan Historical Collections

Roosevelt, who, as it turned out, was unduly concerned about his chances for reelection in 1936, made a campaign swing across southern Michigan in a special train on October 15. From the rear of his Pullman car he addressed a crowd of people at the Grand Trunk station in Lansing.

Many thousands more turned out in Flint's Atwood Stadium, where Roosevelt, speaking from an open car, was flanked on his right by Frank Murphy, whom Roosevelt had persuaded to return from the Philippine Islands, where Murphy had been serving as High Commissioner, to run for governor, in order to strengthen the Democratic ticket in Michigan. Fifth from the left is Congressman Prentiss M. Brown of St. Ignace, the Democratic candidate for the United States Senate. Mrs. Roosevelt is seated in the car with her husband.

Courtesy: Michigan Historical Collections

That evening in Hamtramck, Roosevelt dedicated a stadium that had been built as a New Deal work-relief project. Before the program began, a WPA photographer captured a dramatic moment. In the picture with Roosevelt and his wife is the incumbent Republican Senator James Couzens, at the left, who, although he was gravely ill, had gotten out of his hospital bed to keep his appointment as chairman of the local committee that greeted the President. Couzens, always independent, had publicly supported Roosevelt for reelection, even though it had meant political suicide for him. A week after this last public appearance, the distinguished business and political career of James Couzens was ended by death.

Courtesy: Michigan Historical Collections

On the completion of Roosevelt's tour, Frank Murphy bid the President farewell in another dramatic and well-publicized moment in the campaign of 1936. As it turned out, Murphy needed all the help he could get through being identified in the voter's mind with FDR, for when the votes were counted, it was clear that Murphy owed his victory in the gubernatorial race to the enormous popularity of Franklin D. Roosevelt, who secured reelection by the most decisive margin in American history.

Courtesy: Detroit News

During the next two years, Governor Murphy sought, with considerable success, to duplicate on the state level some of the social and economic reforms of the New Deal. One landmark act passed by the legislature with Murphy's backing was one that placed most state employees under civil service, where previously their jobs had been political plums awarded to loyal party members. Watching Murphy sign the measure in 1938 are members of the merit system commission, appointed by Governor Fitzgerald, which had recommended the reform. The balding man with the colorful tie on Murphy's right is Professor James K. Pollock of the University of Michigan, one of the principal leaders of the fight for civil service who would in the years ahead continue to battle to protect the system from those who wanted to weaken or abolish it.

When he took office in January, 1937, however, Governor Murphy was faced with a major crisis, which had developed late the previous month. Workers at General Motors plants in Flint had sat down on their jobs and seized control of the buildings in a dramatic effort to win recognition of the new United Automobile Workers as the bargaining agent for the GM employees. In the weeks ahead, as Murphy met the equally bushy-browed labor leader John L. Lewis and with leaders of management, the manner in which he brought about a settlement won him both praise and criticism and largely determined the fate of his political career in Michigan.

Labor unions as such were nothing new in Michigan in the thirties. Scattered efforts of Michigan workers to organize went back to territorial days, and success began to be achieved by some in the 1860's. This marker in Marshall notes that the Brotherhood of Locomotive Engineers grew out of a meeting held in that city in 1863 with the formal organization of this national labor union taking place at a convention in Detroit a few weeks later.

204

In the late 1870's, Jo Labadie, a native Michiganian whose family roots ran back to the earliest French and Indian phases of the state's history, led in the organization of the state Knights of Labor, a branch of the short-lived national labor organization that sought to organize all workers into one big union and to make their united influence felt in the political as well as the economic arena. Labadie himself, however, was not a militant but a peace-loving anarchist who wrote poems. Shown here as he looked in his later years, he was not a man who would frighten anyone.

Although the Knights of Labor and the kind of union it stood for failed to catch on, efforts to organize particular crafts were more successful. Here in the early part of this century, street-railway employees in Lansing stage a demonstration to win support for a union to represent them.

In these early years of the labor movement in Michigan, the most violent clashes occurred in the lumber and mining industries of northern Michigan. Here the hard and dangerous conditions under which the men had to work and the strong, paternalistic control the companies exercised over the mining and lumbering towns sometimes formed an explosive combination. The added suffering brought on by the depression that followed the Panic of 1893 led to violent eruptions by miners in the iron ranges of the western Upper Peninsula. Here striking workers parade down Division Street in Ishpeming in 1895 as they seek union recognition, higher wages, and better working conditions.

The mining companies crushed the strike, however, as state troops were called in to maintain order and to prevent the union from operating effectively. The power of the iron-mining companies would remain unhampered by the restraints of unions for many more years.

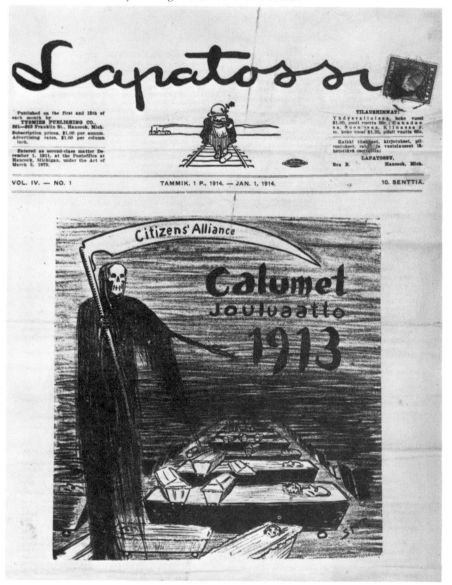

In July, 1913, a strike against the mines in the Copper Country was called by the Western Federation of Miners, which demanded that it be recognized as the bargaining agent for the copper miners and also listed various demands for improvements in wages and working standards. The strike lasted for many months into 1914 and was one of the most bitterly fought in American history. Union efforts had gained much support among recent immigrant groups, many of whom were accustomed to the more radical, class-oriented labor movements of Europe. Here a Finnish-language paper, published in Hancock, blames the pro-management organization, the Citizens' Alliance, for causing a panic at a Christmas Eve party in Calumet that resulted in seventy-three women and children of copper miners being trampled to death.

BIG MASS MEETING

AT KANSANKOTI HALL
January 9th at 2 P.M.

CHAS. H. MOYER

has come back and will speak together with the famous ex-congressman

VICTOR L. BERGER
from Milwaukee and

SEYMOUR STEDMAN
the well known Labor Attorney from Chicago

Everybody Invited.
Admission Free.

Courtesy: Michigan Historical Commission

Despite the personal leadership of Charles H. Moyer, president of the Western Federation of Miners, and the appearance of such nationally prominent figures as the Socialist leader Victor L. Berger, the superior power of the mining companies ultimately enabled them to win. The strike ended in the spring of 1914 with some concessions to the returning miners, but with no recognition for the union. The economic consequences of the long strike were almost irreparable, and the hostilities that had been aroused remained, in many cases, throughout the lifetime of those who were involved in the dispute.

Courtesy: Burton Historical Collection

Automobile Workers!

Attend Your Own
STATE-WIDE PICNIC

Enjoy a Holiday of Fun and Sport for the Entire Family

FOR THE GROWN-UPS—Fishing—Baseball—Boating
FOR THE KIDS—Merry-Go-Round—Teeter-Totters—Swings—Rides. . . . FOR EVERYBODY—Swimming—Races—Contests—Prizes.

SPEAKERS:
FRANK MURPHY
Labor's Candidate for Governor
HOMER MARTIN
President, International Union, United Automobile Workers of America

A Real Workers' Holiday at

DODGE PARK NO. 1, ISLAND LAKE
Two Miles Southeast of Brighton on Route 16

SUNDAY SEPTEMBER 6, 1936
(Sunday Before Labor Day)

ADMISSION FREE
All Automobile Workers Invited

Sponsored by
International Union, United Automobile Workers of America

To the Working Class of Flint!

The working class of Flint and those of the Auto Industries especially are today faced with a condition that gives them a chance to show if they are willing to do something for themselves and their families, or if they are willing to meekly submit to the price raising, wage cutting policies of the parasites, who own and control the industries.

The Automobile cities of Flint, Detroit and Pontiac have always been open shop cities. That is the way the Owners want it. They fear to have the workers organize, unless they can control them, so they try to give us the Company Union. THE INDUSTRIALISTS THEMSELVES ARE ORGANIZED SOLIDLY. If we workers are unorganized, THEY can do as they please with us. Only through an organization built and controlled by the workers themselves, can we fight the class who live by exploiting us, FOR THE CAPITALISTS PROFITS COME ONLY FROM THE WEALTH PRODUCED BY THE WORKING CLASS AND THE FIGURES OF 1929 SHOW THAT FOR EVERY DOLLAR THE WORKERS IN THE AUTO FACTORIES RECEIVED IN WAGES, THE CAPITALISTS RECEIVED THREE DOLLARS IN PROFITS.

The mechanics in the factories of Flint, Detroit and Pontiac are on strike and their battle is the battle of the whole working class. They are standing solid. They have not gone back to work as the lying and treacherous newspapers and radio are trying to make us believe.

Production men, support the members of your class who are on strike. REFUSE TO BE TRANSFERRED TO TOOL AND DIE WORK! DO NOT LET THE BOSSES MAKE SCABS OUT OF YOU. Even bosses despise a scab.

Auto workers, Strike for higher pay and the right to our Own Union.

This is an appeal from The Proletarian Party of America, independent of the Mechanics Educational Society.

THE PROLETARIAN PARTY HAS NO INTERESTS SEPARATE AND APART ROM THE WORKING CLASS AS A WHOLE. IT IS AN INTEGRAL PART OF THE WORKING CLASS. IT SEEKS TO ACCOMPLISH THE IMMEDIATE, THE FUTURE AND THE FINAL VICTORY OF THE WORKERS.

The Proletarian Party of America
LOCAL FLINT

Courtesy: Michigan Historical Collections

The success of the mining companies in keeping out labor organizations was typical of large areas of Michigan industry. Michigan's reputation as an open-shop state was an important factor in persuading automobile manufacturers to locate in Michigan. The high wages received by the automobile workers served for many years to make the majority of them uninterested in the feeble efforts that were made to organize some of the crafts represented in the industry. The depression of the 1930's changed all that. Unemployment, wage cuts, assembly-line speedups, and other problems altered the viewpoint of the auto worker toward the need for a union. When the new administration of Franklin Roosevelt began to encourage the growth of unions as a means of restoring a healthier economy, serious efforts began to be made to organize the workers in the auto plants. Announcements such as this one gave notice that the ideological viewpoint of the movement was far to the left of the conservative approach of the older craft unions.

A new concept, that of the industrial union, developed. The United Automobile Workers of America was formed to organize all of the workers in the automobile factories, regardless of their crafts, into one union. The drive to win support picked up steam in 1936. The union gave its support to Frank Murphy, who addressed union members at a picnic held, ironically, in a park located on land that was originally donated to the state by the auto magnates, the Dodge brothers.

207

Courtesy: Wayne State University

Late in December, 1936, the union made its first big move, tackling the largest auto manufacturer of them all, General Motors. A sit-down strike closed down one of the Fisher Body plants in Flint and soon spread to other GM plants in that city. The action was in part a spontaneous local reaction to rumors of pending moves by the corporation that might be designed to break the union. During the weeks that followed, the striking workers inside the plants organized bands and other activities to maintain their morale while they maintained a close watch on any attempts by the company to regain control of the plants.

Other union members, their families, and union sympathizers brought food to the strikers, as these people are doing on January 12, 1937, for the men inside Fisher Body Plant No. 1.

Courtesy: Detroit News

Courtesy: Wayne State University

Inevitably, as the company enlisted the aid of local law-enforcement agencies to try to evict the strikers, violence broke out, and Governor Murphy sent in National Guard units to restore order. In this case, however, the Guard was under strict orders to remain neutral in the strike. Murphy would not permit it to be used as a force to break the strike.

Finally, Murphy's persistence, and that of federal negotiators and others who were interested in achieving a settlement, resulted in the end of the strike on February 11 — an end that was eminently satisfactory to the men in Fisher Body Plant No. 1 who had been striking since December 30. General Motors had agreed to accept the UAW as the bargaining agent for those employees who belonged to the union. The union had achieved its first big breakthrough against the auto giants.

In the months following the conclusion of the GM strike Michigan continued to be a center of attention in a year in which the new Congress of Industrial Organizations, to which the United Automobile Workers belonged, made great gains throughout the country. Chrysler followed the lead of General Motors in recognizing the UAW, which then tackled Ford. Here on an overpass that carried workers from the River Rouge plant to parking lots and buses on the other side of Miller Road, UAW organizers prepared to hand out union literature to workers on May 26, 1937. Third from the right is Walter Reuther, who had led the

successful strike against General Motors. Second from the right is the heavyset former football player Richard T. Frankensteen, who, before joining the UAW, had taken part in earlier union activities among Dodge workers. Approaching the union men from the left are Ford guards who, moments after this picture was taken, proceeded mercilessly to beat up these and other labor organizers, women as well as men, who had assembled along Miller Road. The Ford Motor Company contended that the union was trespassing on company property, but in actuality the overpass was a public facility. The police in Dearborn, however, did nothing to prevent the Ford security forces from carrying out their attacks. The UAW would not finally win its fight for recognition from Ford until 1941.

Violence was not confined to the auto strikes, but was widespread in the labor disputes of 1937. In June, the efforts of the United Steel Workers (CIO) to organize the Republic Steel plant in Monroe were broken up by two hundred special deputies who used tear gas to disperse pickets. Here one victim of the gas is being led away.

The violence that accompanied the organizational drives in 1937 and the radical views expressed by many of the leaders of the strikes caused many people to fear that class warfare and revolution was about to sweep the state and nation. This conservative reaction to the events of 1937 contributed to the defeat of Frank Murphy in his bid for a second term in 1938, since he was charged with being too liberal and pro-labor. Actually, as this election poster suggests, there were sharp divisions between the more radical elements in the labor movement, which led to some of these factions refusing to support Murphy. At any event, Murphy lost, and in January, 1939, Michigan once again was turned over to a Republican administration.

Why does the Socialist Party OPPOSE the Re-election of Governor Murphy?

Hear...

RICHARD McMAHON

Communist Candidate for State Representative

Answer this Question at...

Dom Polski Hall

3426 JUNCTION AVENUE

2 Blocks South of Michigan

SUNDAY, OCT. 30th

2:00 P. M.

Everybody Welcome :-: Admission Free

Don't miss the big —

Communist Election Rally

WM Z. FOSTER, *Main Speaker*

Tuesday, Nov. 1st, 8 P. M.

ARENA GARDENS

Richard McMahon

210

World War II

By the end of the thirties, life in
Michigan was returning to a more
even keel after the terrible
stresses of the depression, which had
left few if any unscarred. Here at
Lola Valley Park in Wayne County in
August, 1939, families could enjoy
a weekend outing with less
likelihood that the father and mother
would worry about whether they could
afford it than at any time
since 1929.

Courtesy: Transportation Library

Times were once more good. Unemployment
was still a problem and depression-born
relief programs were still in evidence,
but the cars, most of them late models,
that lined the pavement and the sides
of the Middle Rouge Parkway in Wayne
County on July 4, 1940, provided
plenty of evidence that people once
again had money and were spending it.

Courtesy: Michigan Historical Commission

Courtesy: Transportation Library

In September, 1941, Michigan took a nostalgic
trip in time back to the Civil War as Governor
Murray D. Van Wagoner, a Democrat elected in
1940, returned to the Southern states the
Confederate battle flags Michigan regiments
had captured during that war. The ninety-five-
year-old commander of the United Confederate
Veterans was present in the ceremonies on the
steps of the Michigan Capitol to express the
thanks of the South. As Van Wagoner waited,
holding a container in which some of the flags
had been placed, he could hardly have failed
to reflect on a new war, which had engulfed all of
Europe and much of the rest of the world since
1939 and into which the United States was being
drawn to a greater degree every day.

In September, 1940, the nation's first peacetime draft was approved, and in November, Michigan men who had been conscripted began to enter the army, including this group of young men, surprisingly enthusiastic, who assembled at the Michigan Central Station in Detroit on November 22 for the trip to Fort Sheridan, Illinois. These were among the more than 600,000 Michigan men and women who were to serve in the armed forces by the end of World War II in 1945.

Courtesy: Detroit News

Courtesy: Michigan Historical Commission

Great as was Michigan's contribution of manpower, its most distinctive contribution to the American war effort was in the industrial area — one which earned the state the name of the Arsenal of Democracy. The process probably can be said to have begun on May 28, 1940, when William S. Knudsen, president of General Motors, was drafted to become director of industrial production for the National Defense Advisory Commission. In this job and later as head of the Office of Production Management and still later as the director, with the rank of lieutenant general, of production activities for the War Department, Knudsen directed the transformation of American industry from peacetime to wartime output. It was only natural that Knudsen would turn most often to that segment of American industry which he knew best — the auto industry.

Courtesy: Chrysler Historical Collection

In June, 1940, Knudsen asked his old friend and business rival, K. T. Keller, president of Chrysler, if his company would manufacture tanks. "Yes," said Keller, "where can I see one?" Within two months Chrysler had received a federal contract to build and equip a $20,000,000 tank arsenal. Ground-breaking ceremonies took place in September on farmland on Van Dyke Boulevard between Eleven and Twelve Mile Roads in Macomb County. By November, the steel structural work began.

Within a matter of two months, in spite of extreme winter-weather conditions, the steelwork had been completed, the plant was being roofed, portions of the interior were being finished and heated, and machinery was installed.

Meanwhile, plant engineers had been planning the layout of the tank arsenal, which was 500 feet wide and 1,380 feet long. The same mass-production, assembly-line techniques these men had used to produce Chrysler, Dodge, DeSoto, and Plymouth cars now had to be adapted for the production of armored tanks.

On April 24, 1941, barely five months after the steelwork on the plant had started, the first M-3, 28-ton General Grant tank was delivered to the army. By the summer, mass production was well under way. During the course of the war, Chrysler produced more than twenty-five thousand tanks of several sizes at this plant. With production sometimes reaching as many as a thousand tanks a month, the Chrysler Tank Arsenal's record was one of the most spectacular wartime achievements of American industry.

THE KALAMAZOO GAZETTE

EXTRA | EXTRA

109TH YEAR—NO. 17.   ASSOCIATED PRESS   KALAMAZOO, MICHIGAN, SUNDAY, DECEMBER 7, 1941.   UNITED PRESS   PRICE DAILY 3c SUNDAY 5c PER COPY DELIVERED 7 DAYS A WEEK 20c

JAPS OPEN WAR ON U.S.

Bombers Rain Death on Honolulu Killing Many; Hitting Battleship

Surprise Attack Held Stroke to Avert Blockade

Swift Attempt to Break Up Enemy Communications in Pacific Expected to Be U.S. Reply.

By JOHN M. HIGHTOWER

FBI Ready to Prevent Any Jap Sabotage

Consul Offices Throughout Country Started.

Norfolk Plans Arrests

Survey Jap Sections

Radio at Tokio Quiet on Attack

Guard Chicago Consulate

British Boat Sunk by Japs

U.S. Gunboat Nearby Unhurt in Shanghai Attack.

Censor Outgoing Manila Messages

Uncle Sam's Forces Ready in Pacific

The Pacific fleet accompanied by squadrons of fighting planes shown in practice action off...

Army and Navy On War Basis

All Leaves Cancelled and Furloughs Revoked.

Order All Craft Into Home Ports

18,000 Motor Boats, 1,000 Fishing Boats Affected.

'See It Through,' Wheeler's View

Parachute Troops Reported Among Jap Force Attacking Pearl Harbor

Latest Bulletins

Canadian Cabinet to Meet

Alaskan Calls Cancelled

Jap Planes Downed

State of Alert

Several Planes Downed

Call Naval Men to Duty

All Leaves Revoked

German Reaction Withheld

Sudden Assault Comes Without Warning While Hull Talks with Envoys

Pearl Harbor Naval Base Attacked by Sea and Air; White House Reports Heavy Damage in Islands.

(Pictures on Page 12)

Further Extras

In the event of further major developments in the Far Eastern war, The Gazette will issue further editions early Monday morning.

Japan Attacks at Dawn

By The Associated Press

British Ready

Invites Congressional Leaders

Skies Dotted by Dogfights

Attack S0'0 in Progress

Courtesy: *Kalamazoo* Gazette

The furious activity on the part of the thousands of men who built the Chrysler arsenal and put it into production within less than a year all took place at a time when the United States was not even at war. The headlines that told the story of the attack on Pearl Harbor brought a sudden end to that strange period of nonbelligerency. Within a few weeks, civilian industrial production, most notably that of passenger cars, was suspended in order to meet the more urgent military needs of the United States and its allies.

216

More and more attention was now focused on a great tract of land some three and a half miles east of Ypsilanti, where an enormous factory, its dimensions dwarfing those of the Chrysler Tank Arsenal, had begun to rise in the spring of 1941. This was to be the Willow Run Bomber Plant, where the Ford Motor Company would make the most widely publicized contribution to the war effort of any American company during these years of world conflict.

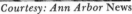

The $100,000,000 bomber plant climaxed the careers of a number of the giants of Michigan's twentieth-century industrial development. The plant was one of the last designed by Albert Kahn, nearly forty years after he had first made his reputation as an architect with his Packard factory.

The general concept of the plant and the special production facilities and layout that would be required to manufacture the bombers was the work of Ford engineers and production men, especially Charles Sorenson, one of the last of Henry Ford's aides from the early days who were still working for the company. The Ford management had been criticized increasingly as being antiquated and unimaginative since the company had lost its leadership in auto production in the 1920's. Now it faced the greatest single challenge in its history.

By September, 1942, the Willow Run Plant was completed. To the rear of the plant was a vast airfield, from which the B-24 Liberator bombers that came off the assembly line were to be flown away. The paving of the runways had been completed three days before December 7, 1941. In the months after Pearl Harbor doubts began to be expressed as to whether Ford would ever produce any significant number of planes. On September 10, 1942, the first bomber was put together at Willow Run, but few others followed it the rest of that year, as Ford workers sought to overcome various production problems.

At least fifty thousand workers were needed to operate Willow Run at capacity. To enable workers hired from the Detroit area to commute to work more easily, Michigan's first expressway was constructed from the Motor City to the bomber plant on the eastern limits of Washtenaw County.

Thousands of spectators assembled on September 12, 1942, as the new highway was formally opened in ceremonies featuring a dedication speech by Undersecretary of War Robert Patterson. What was for its time a most modern facility was outmoded within two decades, necessitating an almost complete reconstruction job in the late 1960's.

Courtesy: Ann Arbor News

To house the many thousands of workers who poured in from more distant parts of Michigan and from elsewhere in the country, particularly the South, the federal government spent $20,000,000 to build various temporary living quarters at Willow Village. Within a little over a decade, virtually all the buildings had been torn down or otherwise disposed of, leaving nothing to show for the money that had been spent but a network of deteriorating streets and sidewalks running through blocks of vacant land.

Finally, in 1943, the efforts of the preceding two years began to jell. The assembly line inside the plant was not quite a mile long, as Sorenson had originally planned, but it was an awesome sight to look down at the bombers moving from the far distant end of the line through the various stages of assembly. Before the end of 1943, production was ahead of schedule, and before production was halted on June 30, 1945, over 8,500 B-24's were assembled at Willow Run. Some of these were shipped out in knockdown units, to be put together at their destination. But the great majority of the bombers were "flyaways," flown directly from the Willow Run airport to army air-corps fields and then to combat overseas.

Courtesy: Michigan Historical Commission

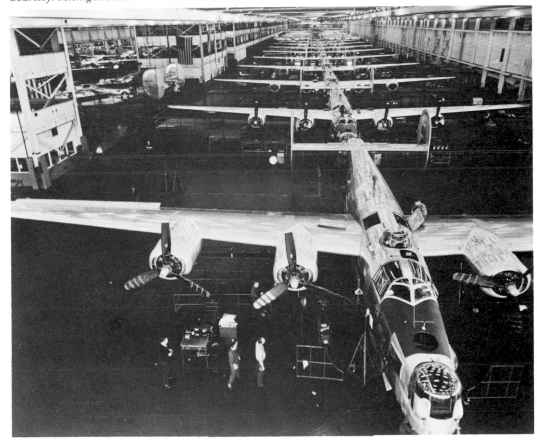

Bombers and tanks and many other kinds of war material were not all there was to World War II in Michigan. Fort Custer, the successor to World War I's Camp Custer, was used in part as a camp for German prisoners of war who are shown here lined up for inspection in what could be mistaken for a scene from a Hollywood war movie or television series but which is a slice of grim, real-life action near Battle Creek, in the early 1940's.

Courtesy: Michigan Historical Collections

Also very real is this photograph of wounded American soldiers convalescing at Percy Jones Hospital in Battle Creek during the war.

Courtesy: Clarke Historical Library

This was the historic Campus Martius area of Detroit in July, 1942. A photographer for a federal agency, Arthur Siegel, took his camera to this busy intersection during World War II, as Jex Bardwell had done to capture several memorable scenes eighty years before during another war. The signs and the navy exhibit indicate the period clearly enough, but the pedestrians and the street traffic scarcely suggest the congestion that developed as tens of thousands of men and women moved into the city and its environs to take jobs in war plants. They placed a heavy burden on the city's transportation and housing facilities, already hard hit by wartime scarcities.

Courtesy: Library of Congress

Courtesy: Detroit News

The housing shortage was most severe among Detroit's Negroes. The restrictions limiting the areas in which Negroes could live in the city were nowhere more baldly stated than in this photograph, which appeared in the Detroit *News* on July 3, 1941, showing an eight-foot-high concrete wall erected by white residents for half a mile from Eight Mile Road to this point on Chippewa to separate their subdivision from the Negro housing area to the right. The whites may have hoped, by blocking them off, that they could forget about their black neighbors. But as more and more Negroes came in during the war, further taxing the already overcrowded ghettos, resentments and tensions mounted.

Then, on the evening of June 20 and throughout June 21, 1943, the thing happend which many in Detroit had feared would happen but which few, including the local communications media, had wanted to admit publicly would happen — racial violence swept the parks and streets of Michigan's metropolis. At the same time American soldiers, both white and black, were fighting the nation's declared enemies in the Pacific, Africa, and Europe, mobs of white men in Detroit were chasing a lone Negro across a street with the intent to inflict on him great bodily harm and possibly death, for no other reason than that he was black.

Courtesy: Detroit News

Senseless violence and destruction raged. Here a car has been overturned and burned. The people crossing the intersection a few feet away seem only casually interested, if at all.

Courtesy: Detroit News

221

Finally, late Monday night, June 21, after it was evident that city and state police were completely unable to gain control of the situation, federal troops were brought into the city and order was finally restored. The great amount of looting that accompanied the rioting is evident here in the Negro section of Farnsworth and Hastings by the debris and by the steel window grill that has been ripped off in order to break into the store.

The governor of Michigan during this tragic moment was Harry Kelly, shown here on a more tranquil and routine occasion in the executive office in Lansing. Kelly's handling of the Detroit race riot was criticized by many at the time, but in the light of how other public officials have reacted to similar situations before and since that time, Kelly can be said to have done as well as most of them. But thirty-four dead and a thousand wounded was a high price to pay for a vivid lesson in the need for an end to racial prejudice.

DETROIT TIMES

Only Detroit Newspaper Carrying Both International News Service and United Press

88TH YEAR
No. 215 — C — Detroit 31, Mich., Tuesday, Aug. 14, 1945 — 5 Cents

JAPS ANNOUNCE SURRENDER!

Acceptance by Japan of the Allied terms of surrender was reported today by Japan's Domei Agency. Washington did not immediately confirm the Japanese report. The Domei account, recorded by the FCC, said that the Japanese government had agreed to the surrender formula as transmitted to Tokyo by the U. S. State Department. The announcement had all the authoritative ring of the first reports from Tokyo last week that Japan was ready to capitulate.

Domei is the agency for transmission of official information and throughout the war was the principal propaganda outlet of Nippon.

The dramatic message, signifying perhaps an immediate end of the war, was recorded by the Federal Communications Commission and the American Broadcasting Co.

It climaxed a series of Japanese radio transmissions which had promised delivery of Nippon's reply to the Allied note "as soon as legal procedure is completed" and said the cabinet in Tokyo had weighed the issue until late Monday night.

Guns Roar 'til Big 4 Gets Tokyo Note

By WILLIAM K. HUTCHINSON

WASHINGTON, Aug. 14 (INS)—The second world war with its frightful toll of human carnage rolled haltingly to an end today as the Big Four awaited official confirmation of Radio Tokyo's declaration that Japan had accepted the Allied terms of unconditional surrender.

This Japanese decision makes their god-emperor, Hirohito, a puppet of the supreme commander of the Allied army of occupation.

There will be no cessation of hostilities, however, until the official imperial message is transmitted from Tokyo to Washington by the Swiss government. The Allied air, land and sea armadas will continue battling the Japs until their own commanders issue a cease firing order.

This will come after the imperial message is received in Washington by President Truman.

Truman to Act for Allies

Mr. Truman has been authorized by Great Britain, China and Russia to accept Japan's offer of surrender.

His first act, on receipt of this message, will be to order the American army and navy to stop fighting. His second will be to notify Britain, Russia and China of Japan's capitulation so those governments, in turn, may issue "cease firing" orders.

The news of Japan's surrender was broadcast to the United States by the Tokyo radio. It was a statement by the Domei official news agency.

Domei, in a wireless dispatch recorded by the FCC, said that Tokyo had agreed to the terms embodied in the note dispatched to Tokyo by the U. S. state department.

"It is learned that an imperial message accepting the Potsdam proclamation is forthcoming soon," the English-language dispatch said, directed to the American zone.

President Truman has announced that the cease firing order will not actually end the "shooting war."

That will come only after the Japanese have formally signed a document of unconditional surrender to the Big Four.

Must Meet Jap Warlords

This act of formal surrender may not come for two or three days because arrangements must yet be made for the Allied commanders in the Pacific and Asia to meet with the Japanese war lords.

The President also said he would not proclaim V-J Day until the Japanese war lords had actually signed a document attesting their unconditional surrender.

The legal end of the war may not come for years if the precedent of the first world war is followed. Germany surrendered on Nov. 11, 1918, but Congress did not declare the war at an end until the year 1921.

Gen. MacArthur will be named promptly the supreme commander of the Allied army of occupation. This will make him the boss of Emperor Hirohito. He was chosen previously by President Truman to head the American invasion of Japan if the Japs had not surrendered.

In this choice, Mr. Truman confirmed the act of the late President Roosevelt in naming MacArthur head of all the American army forces in the Pacific.

The Japanese cabinet reached its decision at a time when American military authorities were pondering whether to force an early verdict by launching a third atomic bomb attack on the enemy homeland.

Official exasperation over Japanese dilatoriness had been mounting hourly in Washington.

President Truman was vexed particularly over the Japanese claim that the Big Four's unconditional surrender note

(Continued on Page 3)

It's Not V-J Day

Despite the Jap radio's announcement of surrender, official V-J Day must await President Truman's proclamation. The President has said that he will not declare the holiday until the Japanese representatives have signed the surrender agreemnt.

Japan's fateful reply to the Allied demand for capitulation, which would permit the emperor to remain on the throne under Allied military supervision, apparently was being transmitted or had been prepared for transmission to Washington through Switzerland.

FCC engineers said that since 9:18 o'clock Monday nght, Pacific war time, a Tokyo code station had been sending long code messages to Switzerland.

News of the momentous development was flashed immediately to the Allied forces on the far-flung Pacific fronts.

The first word from Tokyo on the momentous decision by the Japs was brief.

"It is learned," said Domei, "that an imperial message accepting the Potsdam proclamation is forthcoming soon."

The Domei dispatch was recorded at 1:49 a. m. Detroit time (2:45 p. m. Japanese time).

The Japanese ast Friday announced to the Allies through the Swiss government their willingness to accept the terms of the Potsdam declaration but requested that Emperor Hirohito be permitted to remain on the throne.

In the answer dispatched to Japan by U. S. Secretary of State Byrnes with the approval of the three other principal Allies, it was agreed that Hirohito might remain as the figurehead in Japan subject to the directives of an American Allied commander in chief.

The Allies stipulated also that subsequent democratic elections must be held in the Japanese empire to give the Japanese people an opportunity to decide whether they wished the emperor to be retained.

Hirohito Accepts Allies' Demands

The Domei announcement indicated in its report of the forthcoming imperial message that Hirohito had decided to accept the Allied counter proposals.

The virtual confirmation that the Japs had thrown in the towel to bring to an end the most costly conflict known to mankind came

only a short while after Domei reported the Tokyo government was deliberating on the Allied surrender terms.

Domei at that time said that the Japanese reply to the message from Secretary of State Byrnes probably would be available as soon as "legal procedure" were completed.

Immediately thereafter monitors in America and in Europe reported that a Tokyo code station had been sending long code messages to Switzerland which has acted as go-between for Tokyo and Washington.

These monitors said the Tokyo transmissions to Switzerland had been in progress since 12:48 a. m. (Detroit time).

Accepts Potsdam Promclamation

Although Domei said only that "an imperial message accepting the Potsdam proclamation" was forthcoming, it was believed that the agreement must of necessity comply with the provisions regarding the emperor.

An imperial message would emanate from the emperor himself.

The fact that the government-controlled Domei agency put out a statement of the type issued indicated that V-J Day for the Allies was at hand.

Despite Domei's failure to say flatly that Japan had surrendered, it appeared that this actually was the case.

The Japanese people were not

told even as much as Domei revealed to the allied world.

Radio Tokyo in a Jap language broadcast to occupied Asia at 2 a. m. (Detroit time) the FCC said, made no mention of a forthcoming surrender.

(Continued on Page 2)

Pacific Yanks Wild With Joy Over Peace

GUAM, Aug. 14 (INS)—America's victorious ocean and air fleets rang with cheers and emotional rejoicing today when radio Tokyo's report that Japan had surrendered was flashed throughout the Pacific area.

Pilots of Adm. Halsey's famous Third Fleet, their floating bases still lying in Japanese waters, hardly had rested up from Monday's great attack on the Tokyo area—probably their last blow of the war—when the report came through from Tokyo.

Some 200,000 servicemen have wiped out the Jap fleet and, with other commands, reduced the Jap air force to impotency greeted the flash as genuine assurance that they need not go the way of their buddies and shipmates who have died.

Courtesy: Tom Ketten, Sr.

Finally, after nearly four years of American participation, World War II came to an end with the surrender of Japan on August 14, 1945. President Harry Truman received official confirmation of Japan's surrender a short time after this early edition of the afternoon Detroit *Times* appeared on the streets.

223

The end of the war was greeted by wild celebrations. Here in Detroit's Cadillac Square a fat old man, who had seen wars end before, sits on the front fender of a car piled high with boys for whom this was a new experience. To the rear, others scramble over the Soldier's and Sailor's Monument, a memorial to the Civil War. It is certainly significant that few monuments, and none so elaborate, have been erected in Michigan to those who served and died in this most terrible of all wars, the Second World War.

The Postwar Years

It was a dramatic scene. The auto-industry leaders were assembled in Detroit on May 31, 1946, to celebrate what was called the Automotive Golden Jubilee, harking back to the work of Michigan's pioneers in the industry in 1896. There was the stooped, wizened figure of Henry Ford, now in his eighty-third year, happily reminiscing with his old racing driver, Barney Oldfield, who, with his familiar cigar and his loud tie, still looked the part of a daredevil. Behind him, the youthful, apple-cheeked Henry Ford II, who, the year before, had replaced his grandfather as head of the Ford Motor Company, and a young George Romney, looking somewhat out of place and uncomfortable in his formal attire, personified the new wave of leaders who, in the postwar years, moved in to take charge not only in the business world but also in other areas of Michigan life.

These happy celebrants were workers at the Ternstedt Plant of General Motors in Detroit, who, together with their fellow members of the United Automobile Workers in GM, had gone on strike in November, 1945. Now, nearly four months later, on March 13, 1946, they had just learned that the strike was over and that they would be returning to their jobs. Although the union failed to get all it had asked for, the terms were obviously a satisfactory settlement in a strike that had been regarded as the test of strength in the postwar period to determine if the auto union could hold and improve upon the gains it had won in the years just before the war.

The biggest winner in the General Motors strike was Walter Reuther. The tenacity with which he had conducted the negotiations on behalf of the union was the key factor in Reuther's successful drive to become president of the UAW. Here at the UAW national convention in March, 1946, the newly elected president is hoisted aloft on the shoulders of two of his supporters. The articulate, ideologically oriented Reuther now took his place as one of the major figures in organized labor who would exert great influence on political as well as economic developments in the years ahead. At the left, the grinning man with the glasses and striped tie is Reuther's brother Roy who, like Walter, had helped direct the UAW's first major victory at the time of the Flint sit-down strike nine years earlier.

226

Another Michigan labor leader who rose rapidly to national prominence in the late 1940's and the 1950's was James R. Hoffa, who advanced through the ranks of the Teamsters Union ultimately to head that organization, whose membership was the largest of any American union. Hoffa is shown here being sworn in to testify before a Congressional committee meeting in Detroit in June, 1953, to investigate labor rackets. This became a familiar pose for Hoffa in an endless series of investigations and trials regarding his conduct of union affairs. Eventually, he would be

convicted on another charge and sentenced to federal prison, while the broader accusations made against the Teamsters led to the expulsion of that union from the AFL-CIO. In 1968, Hoffa's Teamsters and Walter Reuther's United Automobile Workers agreed to work together in an alliance of the two seemingly dissimilar unions.

A new automobile company joined the thinning ranks of Michigan's auto makers at the end of World War II. The Kaiser-Frazer Corporation had financial and production resources that would have astounded the founders of the pioneer companies a half-century earlier. But despite the optimism of the banner in this dealer's showroom displaying the 1949 Kaiser convertible ("The Post-War Design Leader does it again!"), times had changed, making it now nearly impossible for a newcomer to succeed in this business. Within two years the company dropped its Frazer models, and by 1955 it was out of the passenger-car field

entirely. The same decade also saw the end of Packard and Hudson, the last of the once numerous group of smaller Michigan automobile companies outside the fold of the Big Three.

The Big Three car manufacturers, meanwhile, successfully weathered a variety of crises as they continued to increase their dominance of the field to a point where competition from other firms was almost negligible. Chrysler, the smaller of the three, continued to enjoy a reputation as the builder of sturdy, dependable cars, such as these 1954 Plymouths coming off the assembly line, but it suffered from serious administrative problems in the 1950's, which seemed for a time to threaten the very life of the corporation. These problems were resolved, however, and in the 1960's the company emerged again as a vigorous, vital force in the industry.

The commanding lead General Motors had maintained over its rivals since the late 1920's was not seriously challenged in the postwar years. GM regularly produced fifty percent or more of all cars sold in the country each year. Although its management made some mistakes, they usually seemed fewer than those of its competitors and it seemed to be able to forecast the course of public tastes in automobiles. The fact that the first Corvette produced in Flint in June, 1953, had a fiberglass body was an interesting evidence of GM's use of new materials. But from the perspective of the late 1960's, the Corvette of 1953 can be seen as an advance agent for the emphasis on speed, sporty appearance, and an appeal to youth, which characterized the cars of the following decade.

At the Ford River Rouge plant, the company's own ore boats continued to unload their cargoes as they had since that classic example of an integrated manufacturing operation was created a quarter of a century earlier. But the new head of the company, after whom the steamship *Henry Ford II,* shown in this painting, was named, made a clean break with most of his grandfather's ideas about how an automobile company should be run. The few remaining oldtimers among the executives were replaced by bright young men who modernized the antiquated administrative organization and helped to reestablish the image Ford had had in its

earlier days as a forward-looking, creative leader of the industry.

Fifty years after Henry Ford and his associates had formed the Ford Motor Company, the firm was still going strong, as evidenced in this photograph of a portion of the huge, 113-acre parking facility provided for employees at the Rouge plant. Hundreds and hundreds of parked cars cover the area in neat rows, stretching far beyond the range of the lens of the noted photographer Philippe Halsman's camera. The packed lot and the fact that nearly all the cars were late models attested to the prosperity of the industry and its workers, but also to the severe impact a prolonged layoff resulting from an economic slump or a strike would have upon the communities in which the owners of these cars lived.

In the political sphere, the immediate postwar years marked the sudden emergence of one of Michigan's veteran political figures to a position of national and international prominence rarely achieved by any Michiganian. On the floor of the Senate in January, 1945, Senator Arthur Vandenberg made a formal public break with his earlier isolationist stand on foreign-policy issues. From that time until his death in 1951, Vandenberg, shown here making a radio address in 1946, was a staunch supporter of the bipartisan, internationalist foreign policy, and was one of the principal architects of the United Nations charter and the North Atlantic Treaty. Many of those who had ridiculed Vandenberg as a bumbling Midwestern political mediocrity in the 1930's were hailing him as a great statesman in these later years of his career on Capitol Hill.

Courtesy: Detroit News

Courtesy: Detroit News

In state politics, the Republican Party in the years right after World War II seemed well on its way back to the kind of dominance it had held in Michigan politics prior to the depression. In 1946, the handsome, flamboyant Kim Sigler, who had risen to fame as a special prosecutor uncovering corruption in certain state governmental circles, was elected governor, leading the Republicans to a thunderous victory over a disorganized Democratic Party. But by April, 1948, the flashy-dressed Sigler, shown here between Mrs. Walter O. Briggs, Sr., and her husband, owner of the Detroit Tigers, at the opening of the baseball season in Detroit, was in serious trouble with many of his fellow party members who were unhappy with the unorthodox and often autocratic manner in which he had operated as governor. Meanwhile, some state Democrats were organizing to turn the tables on the GOP to a degree that had never been accomplished in Michigan since the founding of the Republican Party at Jackson in 1854.

The shape of things to come began to appear on Labor Day, September 6, 1948, when President Harry S. Truman kicked off his campaign for reelection with a rousing speech, broadcast nationwide, in Detroit's historic Cadillac Square. As he looked out from the podium, Truman was greatly encouraged over the prospects for the success of his campaign when he saw the size of the crowd, estimated at over one hundred thousand, pushing against the police-guarded fence and filling the square and the surrounding thoroughfares almost as far as the eye could see.

Behind Truman on the platform, which was built on the steps of City Hall, was a large group of officials and guests who were of greater interest to Michigan political observers than almost anything the President might say. Seated in the second row, sporting a bow tie that would become his most recognizable trademark, was Gerhard Mennen Williams, one of three Democrats seeking the party's nomination for governor in the upcoming primary. On Williams' right was August Scholle, president of the Michigan CIO Council, and the president of the United Automobile Workers, Walter Reuther, conspicuous in his sport shirt, open at the neck. The ability of these two labor leaders, supporters of Williams, to deliver the vote of their union members would largely determine the fate of Williams in the primary and the success or failure of the Democratic ticket in November. It had been the failure of the Democratic Party in Michigan to take advantage of the predominantly Democratic political leanings of organized labor that accounted for the party's lack of success since the depression.

230

Most of the political forecasters in September predicted that 1948 was going to be a Republican year in the country. This was good news for Thomas E. Dewey, the governor of New York, who was once again, as he had been four years earlier, the Republican nominee for President. In Dewey's birthplace, Owosso, Michigan, the approach of election day aroused great excitement and anticipation among the many who remembered the boy who had grown up in that Shiawassee County town, and who had then gone on to the University of Michigan and to New York, where, in the late 1930's, he achieved national fame as a crusading, crime-busting district attorney. A victory celebration was planned for Owosso's native son, and posters were printed for the occasion. But then came the news that few except Harry Truman had expected — Thomas E. Dewey had lost the election! Once again, as in 1944, the honor of seeing a native son in the White House eluded Owosso, as it has all other Michigan communities.

Courtesy: Michigan Historical Commission

The state election results in 1948 were almost as surprising as those from across the nation, for, despite the fact that Dewey ran ahead of Truman in Michigan, the incumbent Republican Governor Sigler lost his bid for reelection by over 160,000 votes to his Democratic opponent G. Mennen Williams. Although many factors were involved, Williams himself deserved much of the credit for his triumph. The thirty-seven-year-old Detroiter was heir to part of the Mennen soap fortune, hence his nickname of "Soapy," bestowed on him when he was a boy. Williams had been educated in private schools, had gone on to graduate from Princeton and the University of Michigan

Courtesy: Michigan Historical Collections

Law School, and eventually became a partner in a successful Detroit law firm. Despite his evident upper-class social background, however, Williams quickly established himself as a political campaigner with an ability to be at home with any group or individual that has rarely if ever been equaled in Michigan politics. The sight of Williams, the governor, taking off his coat and calling a square dance or taking part in a polka party now became a familiar one throughout the state for many years. Some might wince at these actions, but they helped Williams to establish a rapport with the common people that was absolutely essential if he was to win support for the liberal-humanitarian programs he advocated.

In 1952, Williams, who had been reelected two years earlier by a thin 1,200-vote margin over former governor Harry Kelly, hoped for help from the Democratic presidential candidate Adlai Stevenson, not only to bring Williams through to a third term as governor but also to get more Democrats into the legislature, where strong Republican majorities were still able to block any of Williams' proposals they did not favor. At Flint, Bill Gallagher of the Flint *Journal* took one of the most memorable news pictures of the decade when he captured Williams and Stevenson deep in thought, the well-worn shoe of Stevenson's right foot testifying to the amount of walking a candidate had to do even in the motorized era of the mid-twentieth century. Gallagher's Pulitzer Prize-winning photograph, reproduced in newspapers and magazines throughout the nation, made a hole in the sole quite fashionable among many politicians.

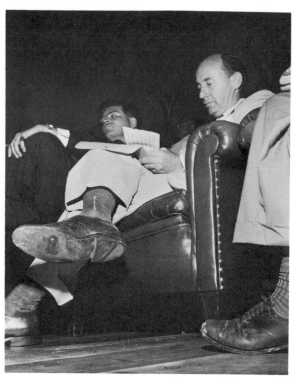

Courtesy: Flint Journal

Stevenson, although he would have been a strong and attractive candidate in normal times, could provide no effective help in the abnormal year of 1952 when the Republicans had as their candidate the superhero of World War II, Dwight D. Eisenhower. Here in Detroit on June 14, Eisenhower, with Councilman Louis C. Miriani (in the dark suit) and James B. Webber, Jr., head of the J. L. Hudson Department Store, flashed his million-dollar grin as he sought support in the preconvention campaigning. Led by the Flint auto dealer Arthur Summerfield, Michigan Republicans played a key role in the successful Eisenhower drive for the White House, and they were rewarded with more top spots in the new Republican administration than any President had ever given to Michigan residents in the past.

Courtesy: Detroit News

Although Eisenhower carried Michigan by over 300,000 votes in 1952, Williams won reelection by over eight thousand votes. Two years later, Williams sought an unprecedented fourth term in office, and although President Eisenhower appeared in the state late in October, 1954, to try to bolster the Republican state ticket, Williams won once again, this time easily by a margin of a quarter of a million votes.

Williams in the general election of 1954 for the first time carried into office all the other Democratic candidates for state administrative offices. Governor and Mrs. Williams, Lieutenant-Governor and Mrs. Philip A. Hart, Secretary of State and Mrs. James M. Hare, and Attorney General and Mrs. Thomas M. Kavanaugh were understandably elated as they took part in the Grand March at the Inaugural Ball in Detroit's Masonic Auditorium on January 1, 1955.

When Williams and his fellow Democrats took over their offices in the State Capitol in January, 1955, they had a greater degree of control over state administrative offices than the Democrats had had since the 1930's; and before the decade was out, the party's control had extended to all administrative departments and to Michigan's two seats in the United States Senate, something unheard of in over a century. But the lights that burned in the portions of the Capitol occupied by the two houses of the state legislature during the long, cold winter sessions were still controlled by Republican majorities.

233

The elements that combined to carry the Democrats to victory are all represented by the figures in the foreground of this picture, taken at the 1956 Democratic National Convention. On the left is Mildred M. Jeffrey of Detroit, an official of the UAW, which supplied the party with its largest bloc of votes. Next to her was Lieutenant-Governor Philip Hart of the Detroit suburb of Birmingham, who, like Williams, was a lawyer and had great appeal to the liberal-intellectual members of the party and, through his marriage to Jane Briggs, had entrée to the most socially acceptable circles in the Detroit area. On Hart's left was the master politician, Neil Staebler of Ann Arbor, state party chairman, who had worked to build up the alliance of labor and intellectual forces. Finally, there was Williams who, by being able to appeal to both workingman and

Courtesy: Michigan Historical Collections

intellectual, despite the often differing interests of these groups, was able to hold the coalition together and lead it to victory for twelve years. The importance of his contribution became evident in the following decade when he no longer headed the party's state ticket and the coalition came apart at the seams.

Williams did not run for reelection in 1960. Whatever hopes he and his followers had had that he might gain the Democratic Party's presidential nomination had been dashed by his failure to overcome the opposition of the Republicans to his state legislative proposals. Instead, the youthful figure of John F. Kennedy appeared on the campaign trail here in Detroit and elsewhere in the state as the Democratic presidential nominee. On the right is John B. Swainson, who had won the Democratic gubernatorial nomination, but only after a bitter primary fight. (On the left of Kennedy is Congressman Harold M. Ryan, Detroit Democrat, while Michigan's only Negro Congressman at this time, Charles C. Diggs, Jr., also of Detroit, is partially visible behind Kennedy.)

Courtesy: Detroit News

234

Courtesy: Ann Arbor News

On the steps of the Michigan Union at the University of Michigan in Ann Arbor, Kennedy addressed a crowd of devoted followers who had waited until 2 A.M., October 14, when his scheduled arrival had been delayed by inclement weather and the pressures of campaigning. Indicative of the key importance attached to Michigan, with its big bloc of twenty electoral votes, seventh largest in the union, Kennedy used this occasion to make a major campaign announcement, promising to establish a Peace Corps, something that could be expected to appeal to the idealistic young people in his audience and across the country. Michigan's presence in Kennedy's column when the votes were counted was a vital contribution to his narrow victory margin, but many Michigan Democrats were bitterly disappointed when G. Mennen Williams was rewarded for his support of the Kennedy ticket not with a cabinet post but with an appointment of decidedly secondary importance.

Michigan voters continued to cast their votes by large majorities for the subsequent Democratic presidential candidates of the 1960's. The hands reaching out to Lyndon B. Johnson when he campaigned in Detroit in September, 1964, were evidence of the support that would enable him to carry Michigan by a fantastic two-to-one ratio in his landslide victory that year over the Republican presidential candidate Barry Goldwater.

Courtesy: Detroit News

Four years later, despite intensive campaigning by Richard M. Nixon, shown here arriving at Wayne County's Metropolitan Airport on September 20, 1968, Michigan voters still gave their support, although by a much reduced margin, to the losing Democratic presidential candidate Hubert H. Humphrey.

Courtesy: Detroit News

Meanwhile, major changes in Michigan's governmental structure resulted from the work of a convention that drafted a new state constitution in 1961-62. Under the leadership of convention president Stephen S. Nisbet (third from right, seated), a distinguished group of leaders from public and private sectors put together the first wide-ranging constitutional revision since 1850.

Courtesy: Michigan Historical Collections

Courtesy: Detroit *News*

Another result of the Constitutional Convention was the role it played in transforming the automobile executive George W. Romney into the major political force in Michigan in the sixties. The independent-minded Michigan voter turned to Romney and elected him governor in 1962 over the incumbent chief executive John Swainson. At his inauguration on January 2, 1963, Romney radiated the vigor and dynamism that one expected of a successful industrialist. These qualities helped him as he successfully championed adoption of the new constitution in 1963 and went on to secure reelection as governor in 1964 and 1966, proving to be as effective a vote-getter for the Republicans as Williams had been for the Democrats in the previous decade.

Courtesy: Michigan Historical Collections

The sight of Governor Romney in his shirt sleeves, as here when he was talking with Michigan National Guard officers at Grayling, became a familiar one now, adding perhaps the same common touch that Williams had sought to achieve with his bow tie and his calling of square dances.

237

A decided asset to Romney in his campaigning was his charming and articulate wife, Lenore, photographed here by Tony Spina, chief photographer of the Detroit *Free Press,* as she walked down the drive of the Romneys' Bloomfield Hills home. Had Mrs. Romney been able to see into the future and discern the enormous problems that lay ahead for her and her husband in their new political career, it is conceivable that she would have persuaded him to stay in the business world where the strains might not have been as great as those under which political leaders of Michigan in the last half of the twentieth century had to labor.

Courtesy: Michigan Historical Collections

The scene in Detroit's huge new Cobo Hall in October, 1960, was symbolic of much that contributed strength to Michigan as its people moved through the troubled and complex years of the last half of the twentieth century. Hordes of well-dressed people — 1,403,872 of them — came to examine the new models and other exhibits displayed at the National Automobile show, which was held for the first time not only in the Motor City but for the first time anywhere outside of New York. Times were good. The automobile industry had come

Courtesy: Automobile Manufacturers Association

through the slump that had hit the American economy in the latter part of the fifties. Ahead for the industry and for Michigan was a period of prosperity whose length had never been equaled in any previous era.

Cobo Hall, a portion of which is shown here on the left at the water's edge, was itself a monument to the fantastic postwar building boom that left few areas of the state untouched and pumped billions of dollars into the coffers of the construction industry. The enormous size of the building (one room alone had 300,000 square feet of exhibit space) was matched by the equally enormous cost ($54,000,000)

Courtesy: Michigan Tourist Council

of the structure, which was named after Albert Cobo, mayor of Detroit during much of the fifties. The city hoped to regain the money by the convention business, which the hall was expected to generate. A new Pontchartrain Hotel (the tall, dark building just to the right of Cobo Hall in this picture) and the Michigan Consolidated Gas Building (the rectangular skyscraper overlooking the river at the right) were but two of the other new additions in this period that brightened the formerly drab Detroit waterfront.

240

Courtesy: Michigan Historical Commission

The architectural style of a great many of the institutional, governmental, and commercial buildings erected in this era conformed to what the layman somewhat inadequately described as modernistic. The sharp contrast with the prevailing styles of a period as recent as the 1920's is dramatically revealed in the polished-granite walls of the South Wing of the Detroit Institute of Arts, opened in 1966, in which are mirrored the classic lines of the original building, dating from 1927. Strange as this marriage of two different styles might appear, at least no one in the future should have much difficulty in recognizing the difference in the ages of these two sections of the museum.

The trend away from the classical models favored by Michigan's earlier architects to the contemporary styles stemming from the work of such architects as Frank Lloyd Wright was certainly aided by the acclaim given to the work of Michigan's most distinguished native-born architect, Alden Dow, the youngest son of the founder of the Dow Chemical Company. Young Dow was a student of the great Wright, and the influence of the master is clearly evident in the numerous buildings Dow has designed for his hometown of Midland, buildings that have given this city some of the same architectural distinction that Marshall's many fine examples of nineteenth-century styles have bestowed upon that small southern Michigan city. Dow's early interest in residential house design, such as his own home at 315 Post Street in Midland, built in 1935, led to his being awarded the *Diplome de Grand Prix* for residential architecture at the Paris Exposition of 1937.

Courtesy: Balthazar Korab

Although Dow was not successful in turning most residential home builders away from their preference for the tried-and-true designs of the past, the several churches he designed in Midland, such as the First Methodist Church, provided striking examples of new designs that undoubtedly helped to account for the surprisingly widespread move away from the traditional architectural forms by religious organizations planning new sanctuaries.

Courtesy: Bill Hedrich, Hedrich-Blessing

Courtesy: City of Ann Arbor

Although most of Dow's work is associated with Midland, the city of Ann Arbor, where he attended the University of Michigan in the 1920's, is the site of some of his most recent work, including the $2,500,000 city hall, completed in 1963. It is a rare example of a governmental building in Michigan that departs from the more conventional designs. "Bold" was a term used to describe the exterior, which looms up over the aging nineteenth-century homes and commercial buildings in this section of the city, one of the oldest in Ann Arbor, and one of the most interesting.

More in keeping with traditional government-building styles were the massive state structures that arose in the middle sixties in Lansing. The expansion of state governmental activities beginning with the Depression years had long since made it impossible to house all the numerous departments, commissions, and agencies in the State Capitol and in the office building constructed in the twenties. A Capitol Development Plan began to emerge in the 1940's as state and city officials sought to establish a definite area in which new quarters for state employees could be built. In the sixties, Governor Romney and Democratic leaders of the legislature joined forces to launch a huge public-building program. In a four-block area west of the Capitol a gigantic hole was dug for a two-story underground parking facility, which, when completed, would hold two thousand cars, more than could be parked solidly on both sides of Michigan Avenue from the Capitol in downtown Lansing clear out to the main entrance to the Michigan State campus in downtown East Lansing.

Courtesy: State Building Division

On top of the underground garage rose the framework of a seven-story building (in the foreground) to house a number of different agencies, a four-story, nearly two-block-long building to house the State Highway Department (in the background), and another four-story State Treasury building (in the area to the right of that shown in this photograph).

By the late summer of 1968, this phase of the Capitol Development was virtually completed, with the three new buildings finished, along with a fourth in the same area, the Stevens T. Mason Building, which had been erected a decade and a half earlier. Still on the drawing boards of Smith, Hinchman, and Grylls, architects for the project, were plans for a Supreme Court building, other office buildings, and a new Capitol, to replace the ninety-year-old domed Capitol that sits in the center of the Capitol grounds. The design of the proposed new Capitol caused howls of protest from many who considered it inappropriate, if not unsightly, while pained cries came from those who were distressed at the thought of the historic building being removed.

Nostalgia had little place in this age of rapid growth, however, and so it was a virtual certainty that the State Capitol would shortly give way to a new, larger, and more efficient structure, just as the Lansing City Hall Annex building, across Capitol Avenue, with its arches and beautifully constructed tower, was replaced in 1959 by the glistening glass and aluminum facade of a new City Hall.

243

It was the exception in this period in Michigan, as throughout the country, when a historic building that stood in the way of progress was saved from destruction. A notable exception saw Mariners' Church, which had been built by the Buffalo architect Calvin N. Otis in 1849, moved, at great expense, from Woodward Avenue and Woodbridge Street in Detroit to Jefferson Avenue and Randolph Street in the new Civic Center near the waterfront. Even here, however, it was not enough to leave the building as it had been originally planned. Alterations were made, and a tower was added, presumably to make it look more like a church.

In addition to his architectural work for the Cranbrook educational complex, Saarinen also headed the Cranbrook Academy of Art, whose arcade, shown here, he completed in 1940. Under his leadership the school became one of the leading training grounds not only for architects but for artists and craftsmen as well.

Michigan's most important architectural influence in the middle decades of the twentieth century emanated from Bloomfield Hills, where in the twenties George Gough Booth, publisher of the Detroit *News,* and his wife, Ellen Scripps Booth, gave over $20,000,000 to establish and endow the several educational institutions that together became known as Cranbrook. They commissioned a noted Finnish architect, Eliel Saarinen, to design the buildings for these schools. Saarinen's work over the next two decades gave Cranbrook some of the most widely acclaimed examples of modern architecture in the entire country. His plan for the Kingswood School for girls is regarded by many as his finest work.

The fountain figures in front of the Academy
of Art are by Carl Milles, the Swedish
sculptor, whose work as head of the school's
department of sculpture in the thirties and
forties complemented that of the Finn,
Saarinen, in the field of architecture.

Eliel Saarinen died in 1950 at a time when
work on what would have been his crowning
achievement, the General Motors Technical
Center in Warren, was only beginning. The
project, which had entered the planning
stage as early as 1945, was carried to its
magnificent conclusion in 1956 by
Saarinen's son Eero, Cranbrook's most
distinguished graduate in architecture.
Behind the jets of the water curtain can
be seen the administration and studio
buildings at the Center, with the styling
auditorium, a dome sheathed in aluminum,
on the right. The clean, modern lines of
the buildings are a fitting
monument to Alfred P. Sloan, Jr., the
long-time head of General Motors who
conceived the idea of the Center, just as
the more grandiose General Motors Building
in Detroit was an appropriate capstone to
the earlier administration of
William C. Durant.

Aside from the General Motors Technical Center, most of Eero Saarinen's work before his untimely
death in 1961 was done outside of Michigan. Meanwhile, a major new architect had emerged in
Michigan, Minoru Yamasaki, a native of Seattle, Washington, who was employed by the Detroit
architectural firm of Smith, Hinchman, and Grylls before establishing his own firm in the 1950's.
Yamasaki developed the site plan for the new campus of the rapidly expanding Wayne State University,
and it was here in 1958 that the general public first became aware of this architect through his McGregor
Memorial Community Conference Center. "Jewellike" was a term frequently used to describe the
structure, one in which Yamasaki obviously drew upon his Oriental heritage, especially his close study
of the Taj Mahal, in much the same way that earlier architects such as Albert Kahn had drawn inspiration
from architectural masterpieces of the Western world.

Other buildings in the Detroit area, such as the School of Education building at Wayne and the superb Reynolds Metals Building at 16200 Northland Drive in Southfield reflected Yamasaki's belief that "the social function of the architect is to create a work of art." The decorative features, which were so characteristic of Yamasaki's work in the mid-twentieth century, marked something of a return to the style of the Victorian period, when aesthetic, not practical considerations dictated much of the ornamentation for which the Victorian buildings are noted.

Yamasaki's work at Wayne State University was an outgrowth of the postwar boom in college enrollments which transformed Wayne from a comparatively small city-supported school into a huge university, which the state took over in 1956 when Detroit's resources were no longer adequate to provide for it. Somewhat the same

transformation occurred at East Lansing, where the main campus of Michigan State College, as shown here in this photograph taken just after World War II, lay between Michigan Avenue on the right and the Red Cedar River on the left. These facilities proved entirely insufficient to accommodate a student body that numbered sixteen thousand by 1949, compared with only seven thousand in 1940. Temporary classroom and housing units, some of which can be seen in the upper left-hand corner, were hastily erected to deal with the overflow from across the river. Initially, the increase at Michigan State and other colleges was due largely to war veterans whose education was financed by the government. But with an ever-increasing population and with prosperous times that made it possible for more families to afford the cost of a college education, it was inevitable that college enrollments would continue to spiral upwards.

The growth of Michigan State was only partly the result of the general postwar increase in enrollments. The process of reorganization and change in the curriculum that had earlier been instituted was now carried on at a greatly accelerated pace under the direction of Dr. John A. Hannah, a Grand Rapids native who had been appointed secretary of the school's governing board in 1935 and in 1941 was named president. Although Hannah himself was an agricultural scientist, he, more than anyone else, was responsible for changing the image of the institution from that of a "cow college" to that of a highly respected, broadly based university. The expanded course offerings in turn attracted large numbers of students with far more diversified interests than those who had attended the old Michigan Agricultural College.

Courtesy: Michigan State University

Fortunately, Michigan State could easily expand and provide the new facilities needed to house its many new academic departments and colleges and its enlarged student body by moving from the old campus, shown here at the left center, across the Red Cedar River into land formerly used for experimental farms and related activities. Fall enrollment at this East Lansing campus reached 38,758 in 1968. A university-operated bus service had become necessary to transport the students around the vast, sprawling campus.

Courtesy: Abrams Aerial Survey Corporation

Courtesy: Michigan State University

Courtesy: Michigan State University

Rightly or wrongly, the symbol of Michigan State's advancement to the status of a full-scale university, a rank formally bestowed on it in 1955 during the observance of its centennial, was the school's emergence in the 1950's as a major athletic power. Admitted to membership in the Big Ten in 1949, Michigan State's teams, especially football, now consistently outshone those of its fellow conference member, the University of Michigan. In one of the most famous football games of the period, billed as "the game of the century," the MSU Spartans and the Irish of Notre Dame, both undefeated and ranked as the two best teams in the nation, battled to a 10-10 deadlock before an overflow crowd of 80,011 spectators in Spartan Stadium on November 19, 1966. At the game's end, supporters of both teams insisted that their school was number one in the nation, despite what the scoreboard said.

Courtesy: Michigan Historical Commission

Meanwhile, the University of Michigan, which viewed the growth of its sister state institution in East Lansing with decidedly restrained enthusiasm, was not content to rest on its laurels. Its football stadium, already the largest university-owned facility of its kind in the country when this aerial photograph was taken in the early fifties, was enlarged to cram in a few more fans and increase its seating capacity to over one hundred thousand, although during the fifties and sixties the stadium was usually not filled to capacity during the half-dozen times a year it was used.

Courtesy: University of Michigan News Service

Having long since outgrown the original forty-acre tract that had been donated in 1837 as the site for its campus, the University of Michigan in the fifties began the development of its North Campus on land north of the Huron River, well outside the developed areas of Ann Arbor where land prices made expansion of the original campus extremely costly. Here an entirely new educational complex arose in beautifully landscaped surroundings. Although many of the buildings housed specialized research projects in atomic energy and related scientific activities, the humanities were not excluded. In the foreground at the bottom of this view is the new home of the School of Music, designed by Eero Saarinen's architectural firm and completed in 1965, four years after his death.

In this period, the changes that occurred at the four regional teachers colleges were so great as to make these institutions almost unrecognizable to those who had known them in the prewar years. Not only did student enrollment increase but also the number of course offerings rose as the decision was made to give more attention to other areas of study beyond the teacher-training programs for which the schools were originally established. This decision was formally recognized by name changes that advanced each of the four institutions to the rank of a "university." Western Michigan University in Kalamazoo, the youngest of the four schools, grew the fastest. An entirely new campus was developed, part of which is shown in this aerial photograph taken in the fall of 1968. The curriculum, too, was expanded at a rate that indicated Western was determined to become a university in fact as well as in name, and to move up into the upper echelon previously reserved for the Big Three: Michigan, Michigan State, and Wayne.

Courtesy: Western Michigan University Archives

Courtesy: Adrian College

Courtesy: Adrian College

During these years of enormous growth in the state-supported colleges and universities, Michigan's small private colleges sometimes seemed in danger of being completely overwhelmed, as their sources of income did not keep pace with the rising costs of education. Under vigorous leadership, however, and eventually with a certain amount of governmental help, direct and indirect, some of these schools managed not only to survive but to make remarkable progress. Adrian College, although one of the state's oldest institutions of higher education, had always been operated on a shoestring, a distant second in this regard to its wealthier sister Methodist school, Albion College. But in the late fifties, under a new president, Dr. John H. Dawson, and with a number of substantial gifts of money, particularly from the Tecumseh industrialist Ray Herrick, an ambitious building program was launched. Here a new social science classroom building, Jones Hall, begins to take shape next to the newly completed Peelle Science Building.

By the time this aerial view of Adrian's greatly enlarged campus was taken in 1967, enrollment had risen from 295 full-time students in 1955 to 1,378 full-time students in 1966-67. These students lived and attended classes in surroundings composed almost entirely of new buildings, numbering more than twenty-five since 1957, leaving little in the way of physical evidence to suggest that the college was nearly a century and a quarter old.

Courtesy: Michigan Education Association

In the area of elementary and secondary education, great advances were made, but at the same time great problems were encountered. A determined effort by the state to see that every school district must offer instruction from kindergarten through twelfth grade led to the consolidation of many hundreds of small rural districts with neighboring city and town districts. Sentimentalists might cry out, but conditions such as these that existed in a Calhoun County rural school during the administration of President John F. Kennedy in the last half of the twentieth century made the old one-room schoolhouse seem somewhat less than the romantic, idyllic educational setting that its defenders had made it out to be in the nineteenth century.

250

Courtesy: Michigan Education Association

The population explosion resulting from the bumper crop of babies during the war years and the immediate postwar period plus the development of enlarged, consolidated districts resulted in sharply increased school enrollments that overtaxed existing facilities. As a stop-gap measure, temporary classrooms were put up to handle the overflow until the problem could be dealt with on a more permanent basis. The results, as in the case of this class, meeting in one such temporary structure in Niles in 1961, were frequently unsatisfactory, as was also true of an alternative measure, which involved holding half-day sessions in order to accommodate twice the number of students.

The ultimate solution was to construct new, enlarged school facilities, as was done here at St. Ignace, whose new high school bore a name that recalled the French period of this historic Upper Peninsula community's development. The new building had been erected on the outskirts of town, with the increased classroom space that was needed and also with far more ample space for parking the buses and cars that were required to transport the students from throughout the expanded school district than could have been made available at the older school site in the center of town.

Courtesy: St. Ignace School District

251

The Weather
Cloudy, colder tonight; cold, flurries Friday

134th Year, No. 329

THE ANN ARBOR NEWS

Ann Arbor, Michigan, Thursday, December 19, 1968 ★ ★ ★ 56 Pages

10 Cents A Copy
Newsboy Delivered 60 cents per week
Motor Delivered 65 cents per week

City, County School Issues Lose

Indian Carried Off Blocked Bridge

Bridge Blockaded In Indian Uprising

MASSENA, N. Y. (AP) — All but three of 48 Mohawk Indians arrested after a two-hour uprising that blocked the international bridge linking the United States and Canada were released on bond early today.

A spokesman for the Cornwall City Jail said three persons remained in jail on charges stemming with the shouting, shoving demonstration Wednesday that blocked the international bridge for two hours in protest of Canada's failure to live up to the 1794 Jay Treaty.

Cornwall Police said two shots from a hunting rifle slammed into the Canadian Customs House on the St. Regis Reservation, home of the protesting Mohawk Indians.

The Indians had fielded some 100 demonstrators for Wednesday's blockade.

The bridge was quiet early today.

Ernest Benedict, the craggy-faced, black-haired chief of the Indians, said there would be no repeat blockade.

"It is not the Indian way, to be arrested," Benedict said.

Canadian Police, unarmed, waded through a wall of angry Mohawks Wednesday and cleared away 25 automobiles the Mohawks had brought up to blockade the bridge.

There was no one hurt in the shots at the customs house. Cornwall police officers said they had no suspects.

Benedict spoke to his tribesmen late Wednesday, making it clear that he was against further demonstrations against the Canadians, who drew the Indians' lre three weeks ago with the imposition of customs duties. The Mohawks, who live on both the Canadian and American sides of the bridge, contend the 1794 Jay Treaty guarantees them free passage.

Pueblo Release Formula Found?

NEW YORK (AP)—A formula which might permit the early release of the 82 captive crewmen of the U. S. intelligence ship Pueblo appears to have been found in the secret talks between the United States and North Korea at Panmunjom, The New York Times said today.

The Seoul newspaper Kyunghyang Shinmoon reported that U. S. and North Korean representatives met at Panmunjom Thursday to discuss procedural matters in connection with the return of the Americans held by North Korea since last Jan. 23. Both the Times and the Seoul paper indicated that release of the Pueblo's crew was only a matter of time.

"A draft of a proposed public statement is believed to have been worked out by negotiators," the Times said. "This draft is understood now to have been referred back to the two governments for approval, along with an agreed timetable for the prisoners' release."

Officials in Washington maintained silence, but no official denial was issued as has been the case with similar reports earlier.

Earlier, a spokesman for U. S. forces in South Korea would neither confirm nor deny a story in the Boston Herald-Traveler that the Pueblo crew might be released during the Christmas holidays.

Giant Nuclear Test Jars Nevada Desert

PAHUTE MESA, Nev. (AP)—A hydrogen type nuclear device with the wallop of a million tons of TNT heaved a mesa top momentarily heavenward today and sent oceanlike waves rippling over the Nevada desert.

A great cloud of dust spurted high above the sabe and sand.

And newsmen, allowed to watch a major underground test for the first time from a vantage point but 12 miles away, felt the ground heave beneath them "like the motion of a bouncing boat."

The blast, one of the mightiest yet in the United States, went on despite protests to the Atomic Energy Commission from some sicentists, labor leaders and pacifist groups.

And, as the AEC predicted, it apparently caused little if any off site harm.

In the gambling town of Las Vegas, 105 miles from the explosion 4,600 feet under 6,200-foot-high Pahute Mesa, shock waves swayed tall buildings perceptibly.

At Panaca, Nev., a bit less than 200 miles away, school superintendent Preston Price, gave this description: "I was sitting in the office and desks and furniture began moving back and forth. Coat hangers on racks were rattling. . . . We could feel the tremor for nearly a minute."

Shock waves also were felt at the mining hamlet of Tonopah, 70 miles away, but weakly. At St. George, Utah, where some past blasts have been felt, authorities said they had no reports on this one.

Norman Thomas Dies

HUNTINGTON, N.Y. (AP) — Norman Thomas, six times Socialist candidate for

Herbert Hoover to Harry S. Truman and criticized every one since.

By Jan Stucker
(News Education Reporter)

Nearly 13,000 Washtenaw County voters went to the polls yesterday to defeat all five millage and bonding propositions offered by the Ann Arbor School District and the Washtenaw Intermediate School District.

The one-mill proposal and $5 million bonding proposition to finance a county-wide vocational education facility were rather narrowly defeated in the Ann Arbor School District by some 600 votes.

In the nine out-county districts, however, the Washtenaw Intermediate School District's proposals were rejected by a 3-to-1 margin.

Nick A. Ianni, superintendent of the Intermediate School District, said this was the first time, to his knowledge, that a county-wide educational proposal has failed in the county.

Proposal I of the Ann Arbor School District's three-part, $9.5 million bonding issue — which would have provided funds for school construction and renovations — was rejected by a 450-vote margin, 4,230 "no" votes to 3,780 "yes" votes.

This was the closest race of the three propositions.

Proposal I was approved in Precincts 1, 2, 3 and 6 — Jones, Angell, Burns Park and Wines schools, respectively.

Proposal II, which asked for funds to finance school services and administration facilities, was soundly beaten by more than 2,300 votes — 5,114 "no" votes to 2,779 "yes" votes. It lost in all seven Ann Arbor precincts.

Proposal III, which requested funds for an addition to Ann Arbor's main public library, was turned down by 698 votes — 4,313 "no" votes to 3,615 "yes" votes.

Proposal III won in Precincts 2, 3 and 6 — Angell, Burns Park and Wines schools, respectively.

Yesterday's election marked the second time in less than a year that an Ann Arbor School District bonding issue has gone down to defeat.

Last Jan. 8, a $15,525,000 bonding issue for school construction was rebuffed by a nearly 2-to-1 margin.

Both defeated bonding issues asked for funds to construct a fifth junior high school in northeast Ann Arbor. Last year's bonding proposal requested money to build a third senior high school — a request deleted from yesterday's proposals.

Joseph R. Julin, president of the Ann Arbor Board of Education, termed the results of yesterday's defeat "a very bad situation."

"Unfortunately, it is not possible to vote the need for space away," Julin said. "The delay in meeting this need will be costly, both in dollar terms and in the crowded conditions students must accept as good enough for now and the foreseeable future. It is the right of the voter to substitute his judgment for that of the Board of Education. This he has done.

"We will do everything possible to make the best of a very bad situation."

School Supt. W. Scott Westerman Jr. declined to comment on the election and said he and the Ann Arbor trustees will discuss future building plans at today's school board meeting. The session begins at 7:30 p.m. at the school board offices, 1220 Wells.

The Ann Arbor Education Association (AAEA) released a statement this morning, saying its members were "deeply disturbed" at the defeat of all five bonding and millage proposals.

"These are not issues which directly affect teachers . . ." the AAEA said. "Our concern is with children and with the impact on them of the loss."

Predicting that the failure of Ann Arbor School District voters to approve the bonds for construction of new school facilities "may shortly lead to split sessions in the junior high schools," the AAEA urged that tax reforms be implemented immediately. (School officials up to the present time have not mentioned the possibility of split shifts at the junior highs).

"The AAEA is in full sympathy with the plight of every person paying taxes in Ann Arbor, both property owners and renters," the statement said. "The growing number of defeated bonding and millage proposals serves to point up the desperate need for tax reform in the state and for increased federal support of education . . . Reform is needed now.

"New and bold measures for the financing of schools must be found," the AAEA said. "The time for searching is already past. Action is needed now."

The total vote turnout was about 5,000 below school officials expectations.

Voter turnout in the Ann Arbor School District was considered average, with about 20 per cent of all registered voters, or 8,363 persons, going to the polls.

In the out-county districts, however, voting was extremely light, with only 4,568 voters casting their ballots. School officials had expected about 8,000 out-county votes.

Nearly 14 per cent of all registered voters in Washtenaw County went to the polls yesterday. Not all persons could vote, however.

Only property owners were allowed to vote on the Ann Arbor School District's bond issue, as well as on Proposition II of the Intermediate School District's issue.

Ianni told The News this morning that he and his staff are naturally "disappointed" at the results of yesterday's referendum, but he indicated the Intermediate School District will return to the voters on the vocational school issue at a later date.

Ianni's statement said, in part: "Naturally, we are disappointed with the results of yesterday's referendum, but we are not totally discouraged. This service for our young people is too important to their well-being and to the benefit of our total community to just quit now. We would like to think that once more we have been victimized by circumstances not of our own choosing.

"'It appears," Ianni continued, "that at least 13 per cent of the registered voters of the Intermediate School District yesterday were saying — 'We don't care how meritorious an educational service it might be. We're just darned good and tired of additional taxes, especially property taxes.'

"In the immediate months ahead, we will determine through discussion of our local school people when we shall try again. In the meantime, we shall work in other directions for changes as to the way educational services are being financed . . ."

The final, county-wide tally on Proposal I of the Intermediate School District, which asked permission to levy a one-mill tax to finance the vocational school, was 4,960 "yes" votes to 7,842 "no" votes.

The total figures on Proposal II, which requested bonding authority to construct the vocational school, were 4,667 "yes" votes to 7,689 "no" votes.

The Intermediate School District's proposals were approved in three Ann Arbor precincts—Precinct 2, Angell School, Precinct 3, Burns Park School, and Precinct 6, Wines School. But they lost heavily in all nine out-county school districts.

(Story on Whitmore Lake school election on page 29.)

Reader's Guide

Classified	49-55	Sports	30-34
Comics	46, 47	Theaters	40-42
Deaths	50	Vital Statistics	48
Editorials	4	Weather	3
Local	29	Women	23-27
Markets	48		
Radio, TV	47		

SHOPPING DAYS 'TIL CHRISTMAS

U.S. Aide Denies Bombing Threat

PARIS (AP) — The U.S. delegation announced tonight it has advised North Vietnam any attack on Saigon will jeopardize talks to end the Vietnam war.

An American delegation official emphasized no threats have been directed at the North Vietnamese on the possible resumption of U.S. bombing of the Communist North.

This appeared in conflict with a Hanoi delegation statement issued after a no-progress, two-hour private U.S.-North Vietnamese session on the deadlock over the delayed peace conference.

The North Vietnamese said the United States declared any Viet Cong attack on Saigon could cause a resumption of the bombing of the North.

In a related development, Cambodia announced today that it is releasing 12 American soldiers captured in the past year, and the Viet Cong offered to free three U.S. troops it holds and possibly more.

Prince Norodom Sihanouk, the Cambodian chief of state, told a news conference in Phnom Penh he was freeing 11 American soldiers and a South Vietnamese captured last July when their river boat strayed into Cambodian waters and an American helicopter crewman captured last month.

A Viet Cong spokesman in Paris said the three soldiers it is offering to release are Thomas Nelson Jones, Donald L. Smith and James W. Brigham.

The U.S. and South Vietnamese commands in Saigon announced, meanwhile, that American, South Vietnamese and enemy casualties all increased last week although no major sustained ground fighting was reported. The U.S. Command also reported four sharp skirmishes Wednesday in which it said American forces killed 131 enemy troops.

Sihanouk told the news conference he was releasing his prisoners so they can spend Christmas with their families.

Sihanouk called another news conference two hours later to announce he had received a "cordial" message from President Johnson. He said the President told him the release of the prisoners would contribute to an improvement in relations between their two countries.

In his announcement that he was freeing the prisoners the prince complained that Washington had fulfilled none of the conditions he set for the release, and especially that Johnson had not acceded to his request for a personal letter saying efforts would be made to stop violation of Cambodian territory by U.S. and South Vietnamese troops.

The release of three Americans held prisoner by the Viet Cong was made contingent on a Christmas Day battlefield meeting between U.S. and Viet Cong delegations to arrange the transfer of the men. The proposal was made in a radio broadcast by the National Liberation Front, the political arm of the Viet Cong.

A North Vietnamese communique released in Paris said Vance called today's session and that he repeated "old American propositions concerning the conference table, the order of speakers according to the U.S. conception of the conference as two-sided."

Vance "declared that if this happens, 'It would create a situation such that it would be impossible to carry on serious talks and to continue the halt in bombing of North Vietnam,'" the North Vietnamese said.

In its weekly casualty report, U. S. Command said 222 Americans were killed in action and 1,199 were wounded. The week before 192 Americans were reported killed and 1,110 wounded.

South Vietnamese headquarters reported 190 government soldiers killed and 815 wounded last week. The previous week the toll of government troops was 150 killed and 811 wounded.

The two allied commands reported 2,059 enemy killed last week, compared with 1,715 reported last Thursday for the week before.

Alert Police Gum Up Coed Ransom Attempt

MIAMI, Fla. (AP) — Police accidentally broke up an attempt to ransom kidnaped coed Barbara Jane Mackle today when they stumbled on two men who had fished a suitcase stuffed with an estimated $500,000 out of Biscayne Bay.

Unaware that the girl's father, home building millionaire Robert Mackle, had placed the money in the bay upon instructions from the kidnapers, the officers chased the men they saw emerge from a jungle area adjoining the water.

But the men, one described as stocky and about 40 years old with dark hair and the other as handsome and 25, dropped the suitcase full of money and fled.

The officers, one a Dade County deputy and the other a Miami policeman, exchanged shots with one of the men, who they said was armed with a carbine.

Authorities later said Mackle personally placed the suitcase in the bay just before dawn. The men made the pickup, just yards from a causeway leading to Key Biscayne, in a small motorboat stolen several hours earlier.

Authorities denied rumors that Barbara had been returned to her family.

Asked about the rumor, Acting Police Chief Charles Price said, "we certainly couldn't make any statement right now because a girl's life is still in danger."

Mackle, who made a fortune as a Florida land developer, said shortly after the money was found that his daughter had not been released.

Barbara was kidnaped from an Atlanta motel room early Tuesday.

Mackle, through Fred Frohbose, chief of the Miami FBI, issued a statement saying he wanted the kidnapers to know he had nothing to do with the recovery.

Frohbose said Mackle "will do anything the kidnapers say to obtain the release" of Barbara Jane, 20.

One of the men, wearing a skin diving wet suit, recovered the money from the water. Then the twelve foot outboard boat with the name "Whaler," painted on it put ashore in an expensive residential area just south of downtown Miami.

At about six a.m., Dade County Deputy Sheriff Paul S. Self and Miami policeman William Sweeney were sitting in their cars talking near the Brickell Avenue area.

"I saw this car that just didn't belong there," Self said.

Self and Sweeney said they saw two men walking to the car, which had Massachusetts license tags, from the direction of the water. One carried a duffel bag and the other the suitcase.

When the police approached the men, they ran, dropping the suitcase and duffel bag but hanging on to a carbine from which several shots were fired, Self said.

After the men escaped, the police found the suitcase was crammed with money and the duffel bag contained the wet-suit, frogman's fins, and a underwater face mask.

At the shore line the police found the abandoned boat.

Using helicopters and dogs, police combed a jungle area near Biscayne Bay where the two men were first spotted as they ran toward their car. The search flushed an unidentified hermit, about 55, who was taken into custody for questioning.

Police said the hermit, whom neighbors said had lived in the lush undergrowth for years living mostly on coconuts, had $500 in his possession.

"My first concern and the father's concern is the girl's safety," said Fox.

Patrolman Self said he had been unaware that an effort was underway to ransom the kidnaped girl. When Fox was asked if the FBI knew in advance or had told local police about the ransom, he said, "We'd prefer not to comment on that."

"As far as our men are concerned that's one of these things that won't happen again in a thousand years—they were just in the right place at the wrong time," said a Miami police official.

Marvin Mathes, about 35, caretaker of the estate—part of the city park system—where the boat landed, said a man and a woman driving a car similar to the one police described as a blue Volvo visited him Wednesday.

The visitors asked what time the park closed and whether they could bring a boat or swim in the area, Mathes said.

Courtesy: Ann Arbor News

By the sixties, not only enrollments but also construction costs and other school expenses were spiraling upwards. Even in such comparatively wealthy school districts as Ann Arbor, strong voter resistance developed to repeated requests from school boards for millage increases to finance new buildings and services. As more and more such requests were turned down at the polls, it became obvious that the old reliance on property taxes to finance school operations would have to be supplemented or replaced by revenue from other sources.

Courtesy: Michigan Historical Commission

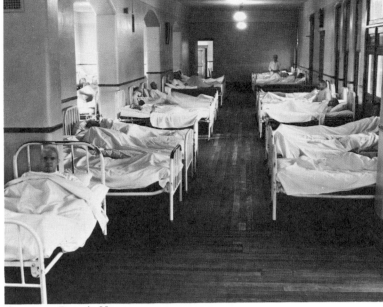

Courtesy: Detroit News

But schools were not the only public facilities to be affected by the problem of overcrowding and the need for more and more money to overcome the difficulty. The state-operated mental hospitals, such as this one at Traverse City, established in 1881, some thirty years after Michigan had first recognized that the care of the mentally ill was a proper concern of the state government, were taxed far beyond their capacity in this period. The incidence of mental illness rose, and admission to a mental institution came to be regarded as less of a social disgrace than formerly — factors that helped to account for the ever-lengthening patient lists.

At the Pontiac State Hospital, which was, next to Kalamazoo's, the state's oldest mental institution, beds for patients in 1950 were set up in every available space. In the small area shown here, normally used as a day room, at least twenty-one patients can be counted. Although the Department of Mental Health was the largest state agency in terms of employees and one of the largest in terms of appropriations, it was not nearly up to the task of caring for all those who needed treatment.

Courtesy: Michigan State Highway Department

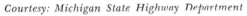

The largest of all the state departments in terms of money spent in this period was the Highway Department, which was faced with the headache of what to do with all the cars Michigan's automobile plants turned out. The result was the mid-twentieth-century phenomenon of bumper-to-bumper traffic at rush hours and hazardous driving conditions at almost all times on roads that had been built to handle far fewer vehicles.

253

In an effort to eliminate some of this inconvenience and to make travel by car both faster and safer, the highway department launched a massive construction program to develop a system of urban and rural expressways — divided highways with no traffic lights or grade crossings. Although much of the enormous cost of this program was borne by the federal government, the cost to the state and local units of government mounted into the hundreds of millions of dollars. Here work on the John Lodge Expressway in Detroit is in its early stages in June, 1952, with blocks and blocks of buildings being ripped out to make the access between the northwestern areas of the city and downtown easier.

Courtesy: Michigan State Highway Department

Courtesy: Michigan State Highway Department

This aerial photo, taken in July, 1957, shows the bewildering pattern of overpasses and underpasses that had to be constructed when the Lodge Expressway intersected the Edsel Ford Expressway, the extension into mid-town Detroit of the old Willow Run Expressway that had been built during World War II. But impressive as these broad ribbons of concrete were, they still were not enough to handle the flood of cars, buses, and trucks that clogged these expressways in the early-morning and late-afternoon hours and slowed traffic to a snail's pace Monday through Friday.

Although practical rather than aesthetic considerations came first in the construction of expressways, the motorist who was able to speed through Grand Rapids on the I-296 Expressway, completed in the mid-1960's, was at the same time treated to a magnificent view of the city, which he could not have obtained from the standard city streets, hemmed in by buildings, traffic signals and signs, and billboards.

Michigan's continuing industrial and urban growth now brought other problems to the forefront. Industrial waste, such as can be seen at this plant in Wyandotte, was dumped into the Detroit River in ever-growing quantities and together with other contaminants threatened one of the area's greatest assets, its water.

Courtesy: Monroe *Evening News*

The combination of pollutants carried down from the Detroit River, together with waste from other large population centers around Lake Erie, turned that great body of once fresh water into a cesspool. As Michigan and Ohio continued to squabble over the location of their boundary in Lake Erie and over possession of Michigan's Lost Peninsula, shown here looking south, isolated from the rest of Michigan by the state boundary that cuts across the narrow neck of the peninsula at the top of this picture, these waters had become far less of a prize than they once had been.

Courtesy:

Michigan Department of Conservation

But the Detroit River and Lake Erie, although the most publicized victims of water pollution, were unfortunately not the only examples of the advances this scourge of a densely populated urban society had made in Michigan. Across southern Michigan signs such as this one on the banks of the Red Cedar River near the state's capital told their grim story, one that had been told many times before in Michigan's history — of man's misuse of the resources that nature has granted to him.

Courtesy: Michigan Department of Conservation

Although the water supplies of southern Michigan could be and were treated to make them safe for human consumption, there was little that could be done to treat the air one breathed once it had been polluted by smoke and fumes from industrial plants, such as this one in the Detroit area, the exhaust from heavy city automobile traffic, or the hundred and one other sources of air pollution.

Here children at the High Street Elementary School in Lansing are silhouetted against a window that has been taped shut in an effort to keep out the fumes that are filling the air on the other side of the glass panes. In this period, efforts were being made by federal, state, local, and private agencies to fight and control air and water pollution, but success, if it was to be achieved, would depend on a far greater degree of cooperation from those responsible for the creation of these pollutants and on much larger sums of money than these efforts had thus far received.

Relief from polluted air was still available in outstate Michigan, however, where peaceful farm scenes such as this one, free of smog, awaited the gasping city dweller.

And in the vast reaches of northern Michigan, the problem of water pollution, too, seemed remote. Experts might say No, but to the average traveler, Walloon Lake, in the center of this picture, just beyond US-131 leading into Petoskey, looked as fresh and clear in the 1960's as it must have looked in Ernest Hemingway's day, fifty years earlier, while the air had that special pure quality that had made this region a haven for hay-fever sufferers as far back as the 1870's.

257

Courtesy: Michigan State Highway Department

Access to Michigan's great out-of-doors region was made easier as the highway program of the late fifties and sixties extended the state's system of expressways into the upper part of the lower peninsula. By 1963, when this stretch of I-75 between Gaylord and Indian River was selected by a national organization as America's most scenic freeway, it was possible to drive from the Ohio border to the Straits of Mackinac entirely on divided highways, without a traffic signal to slow the motorist's progress.

The waters of the Straits of Mackinac had presented a formidable barrier to easy travel between Michigan's two peninsulas since the first men arrived in this area thousands of years ago. Railroad ferries had begun to close the gap in the 1880's, and in 1923, in response to the demands of automobile owners, the State Highway Department initiated a ferry service for cars. The largest of these state car ferries was the *Vacationland,* shown here, which was built at a cost of some $5,000,000. The trip across the straits aboard these ferries was a pleasant break in a long, tiring trip for those who were driving through the state. But as roads in the north improved and traffic increased, the lines of cars waiting to board the ferries at Mackinaw City and St. Ignace grew longer, and the cries for a better transportation link between the peninsulas became louder.

At last, in the 1950's, the dream of a bridge across the historic waters of the straits became a reality. Governor Williams, who had promised in his initial campaign of 1948 to revive the idea of a bridge, joined with interested citizens to fight for the Mackinac Bridge Authority, which would be given the responsibility for this project. Their efforts succeeded, and approximately $100,000,000 in revenue bonds were sold in 1953 to finance the span. Construction began in 1954. By the summer of 1956, when this photograph was taken, the bridge was beginning to take visible shape. Mackinaw City, at the tip of the lower peninsula, is in the foreground. The cleared area at the water's edge, a little to the left of the bridge, is the site of the old French and British fort that stood guard over this strategic waterway in the eighteenth century.

Courtesy: Michigan Historical Commission

Courtesy: Michigan Historical Commission

On November 1, 1957, three and a half years after the ground-breaking ceremonies, the bridge was opened to traffic. This aerial view was taken to the west of the main spans. The bit of land at the top is the Upper Peninsula shore of the Straits of Mackinac. As many as six thousand cars could now drive over these waters each hour, compared with about 470 cars an hour on the now discontinued auto-ferry service. A physical tie had been cemented between two land masses which nature had decreed should be separate but which man had decided should be joined together.

"Big Mac" or "Mighty Mac," as the publicists and the public immediately nicknamed the bridge, now became one of the major attractions of the Great Lakes area? Designed by the famous New York bridge designer David B. Steinman, who had just finished the reconstruction of the Brooklyn Bridge, the Mackinac Bridge was now called, by some people, the world's longest suspension bridge. Although New York's

Verrazano-Narrows Bridge and San Francisco's Golden Gate Bridge both have a longer suspension span, the Mackinac Bridge is the longest overall, with a measurement of 8,614 feet between the cable anchorages on either end. Total length of the bridge, including the approaches, is about five miles. A popular time to view the bridge is at night when it is outlined by innumerable lights. This photograph was taken from a point atop the bluff that rises up from the Lake Michigan shore of the Upper Peninsula, west of the bridge approaches.

259

Early in the 1960's at Sault Ste. Marie, the new International Bridge, with its graceful, swooping configurations, was completed across the St. Mary's River to Sault Ste. Marie, Ontario, eliminating still another natural barrier to the free and easy flow of motor traffic in the northern Great Lakes.

Courtesy: Michigan Tourist Council

The enormous sums invested in the improvement of Michigan's highway system began to be repaid as more and more tourists took advantage of the new roads and bridges to enjoy the state's many natural recreational opportunities. West of St. Ignace, US-2 runs for many miles along the very edge of Lake Michigan's waters, providing some very serious problems to road crews who have to cope with the shifting, soft sands of this shoreline, but also providing a breathtaking panoramic view to the motorists or to those who prefer to leave the driving to others.

Courtesy: Michigan Historical Commission

Tourism had been an important business in Michigan for many years, and as early as the 1920's state and county road departments, in addition to trying to keep up with the demand for better roads, had pioneered in providing additional facilities aimed at the tourist. Many small roadside parks were built, such as this one along US-31, south of Ludington, offering the weary motorist and his family the chance to stop and rest in pleasant surroundings within a few feet of the highway.

Courtesy: Michigan Historical Commission

Since the mid-nineteenth century, historic Mackinac Island had been the central attraction for visitors to northern Michigan. A century later hundreds of thousands of people poured onto the island during the short summer season. Although the commercial attractions that hug the shoreline of the island's harbor are privately owned, most of the island is owned by the state, which has preserved it as Michigan's oldest state park, since this land was transferred to the state in 1895 by the federal government, under whose supervision Mackinac Island had been one of the first two national parks in the country.

Courtesy: Michigan Historical Commission

261

Courtesy: Michigan Historical Commission

Mackinac Island has remained unique as the one area in the state that is open to the public but from which automobiles are barred. After World War I, the state began to develop a network of other parks into which the motoring public was free to drive. The most popular of these were those located along Lake Michigan. By mid-century, a million people and more were visiting Grand Haven State Park each summer, and similar numbers were using parks at Holland, Muskegon, Ludington, and other west Michigan areas where the magnificent white-sand beaches lent an aura of truth to the claims of those who called this the Riviera of mid-America.

Courtesy: Michigan Department of Conservation

In an earlier era, visitors had spent most of their time at resort hotels, but with the greater mobility provided by the automobile, camping became popular with young and old as a way of taking advantage of that mobility to see and do far more things than had been possible for the resorter who was confined to one place. Campgrounds at places such as Porcupine Mountains State Park, where this elderly man has parked his trailer, could not accommodate all those who wanted to get in during the height of the season.

For the noncamping tourists, however, increasingly elaborate motel and hotel facilities were built as the volume of business increased with the improvement of highways leading north. The change was particularly notable in the Upper Peninsula, where the older tourist-cabin accommodations gave way to more modern establishments, such as Dettman's Motel at St. Ignace, to meet the needs and the desires of the multitudes who now streamed over the bridges at the Straits of Mackinac and at Sault Ste. Marie.

Courtesy: Upper Michigan Tourist Association

262

Courtesy: Michigan Historical Commission

Michigan's attractions for the tourist included some that were old and others that were new, at least in the way in which they were now developed. Probably the greatest number of people, both residents of the state and visitors, gained the greatest pleasure from the almost unlimited opportunities Michigan offered for various kinds of water activities. Whether it was at a municipally-operated beach, such as this one at Menominee, or in county, regional, or state parks, there were few areas in Michigan where one was unable to enjoy the pleasures of swimming and frolicking in the water on a warm, sunny day.

The departure of the Class C boats from Port Huron in the summer of 1958, with the Blue-Water Bridge visible in the background behind the cluster of masts and wind-filled sails, marked the start of the annual Port Huron-to-Mackinac race, which, together with the older Chicago-to-Mackinac race, has been the great sailing regatta on the Great Lakes since the mid-twenties. Although those who took part in these races hardly typified the average tourist and vacationer, the races themselves helped to highlight the great potential Michigan's lakes and waterways have for the boating enthusiast.

Courtesy: Detroit News

Until 1967, the Georgian Bay line had carried on a century-old tradition with its tours through the Great Lakes. But the end of this pleasant mode of relaxation was foretold by the numbers of small boats that were tied up in the Michigan ports where the *North American* docked. In the 1950's and the 1960's, public agencies spent many millions of dollars to build new docks and marinas and otherwise to improve harbor facilities for the benefit of private boat owners, individuals whose numbers had totaled only a few thousand in the pre-World War II days, but now came to be numbered in the hundreds of thousands.

Courtesy: Michigan Historical Commission

Courtesy: Michigan Tourist Council

To many communities, such as Saugatuck, at the mouth of the Kalamazoo River, tourism now became the main source of income. Waters that had once been used by commercial fishing boats and lumber schooners were now the domain of yachts and sight-seeing boats, such as the *Island Queen*. The bulk of the visitors to Saugatuck found so many things to do in the shops and restaurants and bars of the village, however, that they rarely, if ever, got their feet wet in a state that billed itself as the "Water Wonderland."

Up the Lake Michigan shore from Saugatuck, the village of Leland in the mid-twentieth century was one of the few places left in Michigan where one could see the old-time commercial fishing activities still being carried on. The picturesquesness of the scene, so suggestive of another day and another world, made the fishermen's dock at Leland a favorite hangout for the artist, the photographer, and the just-plain-curious visitor.

Courtesy: Michigan Historical Commission

Courtesy: Michigan Historical Commission

Scenes such as this, where there is standing room only on the dock at East Tawas State Park, as men, women, and children brave the cold while they wait for a tug on their lines, testified to the undiminished popularity of the sport of fishing in Michigan during these same years that saw a decline in commercial fishing.

264

In the 1960's, the Michigan Department of Conservation (renamed the Department of Natural Resources in 1968), and other governmenal agencies, had begun to win the battle against the lamprey eel, a major cause of the sharp decline in lake fish. Coho and other types of salmon were introduced, none of which were native to the Great Lakes area. The success that was achieved in getting these fish to live, thrive, and breed in Michigan's lakes and rivers far exceeded the department's expectations. Here at the fish hatchery at Honor on the Platte River, the waters below the dam are darkened by thousands of young salmon.

By 1967 and 1968, hordes of people were descending on western Michigan, attracted by the lure of the big Michigan salmon, which were now flourishing and rapidly spreading into other areas of the upper Great Lakes. Happy faces such as those of these fishermen were a common sight as sportsmen experienced the thrill of catching a fish that no one, since the days of the prehistoric Indian fishermen, had ever seen, let alone caught, in these waters. But the program was not without its headaches. There were those who contended that the salmon would drive out many native fish. Some of the fishermen, in their greed, were heedless of some of the basic principles of the conservationist and sportsman. When commercial fishermen were allowed to harvest some of the enormous annual surplus of salmon, sports fishermen let out howls of protest. Time would tell whether the decision to introduce the Coho salmon would be acclaimed in the long run as a beneficial action or whether it would be ranked with Michigan's decision in 1877 to bring in the carp, an alien fish that shortly was regarded in the state as a nuisance.

Courtesy: Michigan Historical Commission

To the naturalist and to the devotee of that popular twentieth-century pastime, bird watching, the sight of a flock of wild fowl circling in the air along Michigan's rocky Lake Huron shore was sufficient motive to come to such areas, while since time immemorial these same birds had served to attract hunters and sportsmen for an entirely different motive.

Courtesy: Michigan Historical Commission

Courtesy: Michigan Historical Commission

But year in and year out, no other member of Michigan's wildlife family could equal the attention that was received by the state's deer. Half a million licensed hunters, plus uncounted thousands of others who went along simply for the fun and revelry, descended upon northern Michigan each fall. In the case of no other animal or bird or fish was there the same kind of anticipation, which built up as the opening day of the brief deer-hunting season approached. For those who were truly hooked on this particular kind of hunting, failure to get a buck (or doe, when this was permissible) only provided added incentive to go out again the following year.

The most remarkable tourist development in the mid-twentieth century was the manner in which Michigan's northerly geographical location was used to attract great numbers of tourists in the winter to a state that had once been regarded as solely a place for summer vacations. To those in charge of keeping the state's streets and highways open, winter snows were hardly welcome. An unusually hard winter could easily run the department's maintenance budget into the red for the entire year.

Courtesy: Michigan State Highway Department

For the author's father, a powerful two-hundred-pound six-footer, and for many others like him, there was nothing glamorous about the 150 or so inches of snow that fell upon Ironwood and other northern Michigan towns each winter. For him it meant many hours of back-breaking labor to shovel the walks, the driveway, the roof, when the accumulated snow became dangerously heavy, and in some cases to clear the drifted snow away from downstairs windows to let in some light. In one memorable storm in the late 1930's, Ironwood merchants actually had to tunnel through the piles of snow to provide access to their stores.

Courtesy: Michigan Histroical Commission

The numbers of people who looked upon the first snows as signaling the start of another winter sports season, however, mushroomed in the middle decades of the century. The sport of ski jumping, which had begun to develop in Michigan in the late 1880's, gained increasing popularity, with large numbers of fans turning out in the cold and snow to watch the jumpers perform their daring deeds on such occasions as this one on February 28, 1947, when the National Ski Jumping championships were held at Ishpeming on what is ominously called Suicide Hill. Even longer, record-breaking leaps were possible from the Pine Mountain Ski Jump in Iron Mountain.

268

But ski jumping is essentially a spectator sport, except for the expert. It was the interest that developed in skiing down a slope, a sport that required far less skill and seemed to involve much less risk, that led to the boom that began to develop in the 1930's and exploded in the years after World War II. Michigan now became the leading center in the Middle West for those who wished to participate in this popular new activity, and millions of dollars were sunk into elaborate facilities, such as this one at Boyne Mountain, that catered to these wishes.

Meanwhile, additional attractions had been developed to draw other visitors to the state who might not be interested in fishing or hunting or skiing. In the late 1920's, Henry Ford had opened a great outdoor museum at Dearborn, which he called Greenfield Village. Here, through such things as an old nineteenth-century train, buildings from that era, which he had moved to this site, and a variety of other means, Ford sought to preserve something of the atmosphere and environment in which he had grown up, before the automobile had changed that older way of life. Greenfield Village, together with the more conventional Henry Ford Museum adjoining the village, was one of Ford's better ideas. By the 1960's, more than a million visitors a year were paying to visit what had become one of America's major historical attractions.

Courtesy: Michigan Historical Commission

Still more variety was added with the increasing popularity in the 1950's and 1960's of summer theaters. Numerous such ventures, such as the Cherry County Playhouse in Traverse City (in what is actually Grand Traverse County, in the heart of an area famous for its cherries), offered the public live stage performances, frequently with such name actors as Edward Everett Horton. Nothing like this had been seen in Michigan since the heyday of the opera house in the 1890's.

Not all of these theatrical endeavors had a happy ending. In 1966, hoping to emulate the success of Stratford, Ontario, in staging annual Shakespeare

Courtesy: Michigan Historical Commission

festivals, a group of Ypsilanti citizens and others organized a Greek Theatre and performed two of the classics of Greek drama throughout the summer in Eastern Michigan University's baseball stadium. The idea made some sense, since Ypsilanti had been named after a hero of the Greek War of Independence and the city contained some fine examples of the classical style of architecture that had been influenced by ancient Greek models. In addition, the casts were excellent, featuring the great Bert Lahr (in the striped shirt) in one of his last public performances as the star of one of the plays, and the famous tragedian, Judith Anderson, in the other. The critics, who came from as far away as New York, wrote favorable and even rave notices. But the results were disastrous. Enough people simply were not interested in what the Greek playwrights had to say. The season ended with the company being hundreds of thousands of dollars in the red. The hopes for a second season of Greek drama in Ypsilanti had to be shelved, perhaps permanently.

270

More fortunate in its outcome was the Meadow Brook Music Festival, an outdoor event begun in the summer of 1964 on the campus of Oakland University at Rochester. Here in the Baldwin Pavilion thousands of music-lovers from the metropolitan Detroit area assembled for one of the numerous concerts by the Detroit Symphony and other nationally known artists and musical organizations that were held annually, joining the long-established summer music program at Interlochen and providing Michigan with an impressive lineup of cultural events during the busy summer months.

Courtesy: Meadow Brook Music Festival

But for many people, Michigan's foremost attraction remained its natural beauty. Great concern was voiced by this group that commercial developments intended to lure more tourist dollars to the state might ultimately destroy that which so many tourists were seeking, particularly in northern Michigan — the opportunity to get back to nature untarnished by mankind's embellishments. Such an area was Isle Royale, that remote portion of Michigan in northern Lake Superior that is so far removed from the Upper Peninsula. Some assurances that this area, with its rugged coastlines and its herd of moose, long since extinct in mainland Michigan, would be preserved in its raw wilderness state came in 1940 when Isle Royale became a national park.

Courtesy: Michigan Historical Commission

Courtesy: Michigan Historical Commission

271

Courtesy: U. S. Forest Service

Courtesy: U. S. Forest Service

Another major step in preserving Michigan's surviving wilderness was taken when the Sylvania Recreation Area, a huge tract of forests and lakes in the extreme western part of the Upper Peninsula, formerly owned by the Fisher brothers of General Motors' Fisher Body Division, was obtained by the United States Forest Service and dedicated on September 22, 1967, by Mrs. Lyndon B. Johnson, together with the wife of Vice President Hubert H. Humphrey and Secretary of Agriculture Orville Freeman. In the 1960's, Congress also took action to preserve the unique Pictured Rock area near Munising in the Upper Peninsula, but similar efforts to save the Sleeping Bear Dunes area in lower Michigan from further despoilment were blocked by the opposition of some of the private interests in that region who felt they would be adversely affected by such a measure.

The development of the Sylvania Recreation Area, together with the overall increase in tourist business, came at an opportune moment for that western Upper Peninsula region that was hard hit by the decline of what had been the backbone of its economy, the mining industry. On January 29, 1966, in fact, an era officially ended when the Peterson Mine, near Bessemer in Gogebic County, ceased operations. The last shift of fifty miners paused in their work down in the mine, opened their lunch pails, and glumly ate their last meal on this job, staring at the camera through their safety glasses.

Courtesy: Ironwood **Daily Globe**

Courtesy: Ironwood **Daily Globe**

Courtesy: Ironwood **Daily Globe**

At seven in the morning, the men came up out of the mine, changed out of their work clothes, closed their lockers, and went home. The last iron mine to be operated on the Gogebic Iron Range was out of business. Its closing brought an end to mining activities that had begun in 1884 and had resulted in shipments of well over 300,000,000 tons of iron ore from some sixty-five mines. Much ore still remained deep beneath the surface, but the cost of mining it had become too great. All that remained now were abandoned mines — the Norrie, Aurora, Eureka, Sunday Lake, Geneva, Tilden, Newport, Colby — beautiful names that had once spelled economic prosperity but now evoked only memories while they underscored the bleak economic prospects of the 1960's.

273

Although the mining areas of the Upper Peninsula all suffered a period of declining fortunes compared with their boom years at the beginning of the century, there were encouraging developments that portended better days ahead. In the mid-fifties, the town of White Pine emerged from the forests of Ontonagon County as the Copper Range Company developed the White Pine copper mine (marked by the towering smokestack), with the aid of a loan of $56,000,000 from the federal government.

The White Pine Mine was a great success. Tapping an enormous body of copper ore that would reportedly take decades to exhaust, the mine gave employment to hundreds of men, many of them experienced miners who had been without work since the closing of other mines. Using new methods of treating low-grade ores it had previously been uneconomical to mine, the White Pine Mine's output was chiefly responsible for boosting Michigan's copper production from about 20,000,000 pounds annually in the decade 1945-1955, a tenth of the production figures reached forty years earlier, to about 120,000,000 pounds annually in the following decade.

274

Courtesy: Michigan Department of Conservation

At the same time that new hope was coming to the Copper Country, developments at the Humboldt Mine near Ishpeming sparked a similar regeneration of the mining industry on the Marquette Iron Range. Through the beneficiation process, low-grade iron ores, which could not be mined and shipped profitably through conventional mining methods, were now processed and the iron in the ore concentrated in tiny pellets, easy to ship and easy to use in the iron and steel mills. The beneficiation plant set up in 1954 by the Cleveland-Cliffs Iron Company at the Humboldt mine, at nearly the same site where Thomas Edison had experimented with a similar process some sixty-five years earlier, was followed by four other plants, which by 1968 were producing nearly ten million tons of pellets a year. In the sixties, beneficiation also began to be applied to low-yield ores on the Menominee Iron Range but no success had been achieved in adapting these techniques to handle the particular kind of ores found on the Gogebic Iron Range, the only one of these districts where mining by any method had ceased entirely.

Courtesy: Michigan Department of Conservation

275

The changes that were remolding the tourist and mining industries found their counterpart in all aspects of life in the mid-twentieth century. Steam locomotives, such as this one rounding the curve approaching Fenton in 1960, passed from the scene, except for a few that were operated over short lines as tourist attractions.

Not only had steam locomotives disappeared from the railroad industry, but most of the passengers who had formerly made use of the railroad were taking airplanes when they wished to go farther than they cared to drive in their automobile. A huge new airport, serving the metropolitan areas of southeastern Michigan, was built by Wayne County. Metropolitan Airport, as it was called, was located just off the I-94 Expressway, considerably closer to Detroit than the Willow Run Airport, which had served as the terminal in this area in the years right after World War II.

276

Changes in the transportation field were matched in such other areas as the power industry. At Big Rock Point on the shores of Lake Michigan, near Charlevoix, the Consumers Power Company in 1960 began the construction of a $27,000,000 new power plant to provide electricity for its customers in northern Michigan.

But this was no ordinary power plant. It was, when completed in 1962, the world's first high-power density boiling water reactor for generating electricity. Put in simple terms, the Big Rock Point plant generated power through use of nuclear energy. A red-letter day in the construction schedule was that day in 1961 when the reactor vessel, in which the nuclear fuel would be contained, was lifted into place. When the button was pressed at 2:30 P.M., September 27, 1962, starting a controlled chain reaction, Michigan entered a new phase of the atomic age.

277

Courtesy: Detroit Edison Company

In the same period, the Enrico Fermi Atomic Power Plant was built on Lake Erie, near Monroe, by a specially formed company that represented Detroit Edison, Consumers Power, and eighteen other electric power and industrial companies. Primarily an experimental operation designed, in its initial stages, at least, to enable engineers and scientists to solve some of the technical problems inherent in the generation of power by nuclear action, the Fermi Plant was from the outset the center of controversy, as many individuals and organizations protested its location so near the heart of the most heavily populated area of Michigan. Despite the assurances of the experts who declared that a nuclear power plant was perfectly safe and that its operations should not be confused with a nuclear bomb, there remained those who feared that another menace hung over an area already beset by more problems than it could handle.

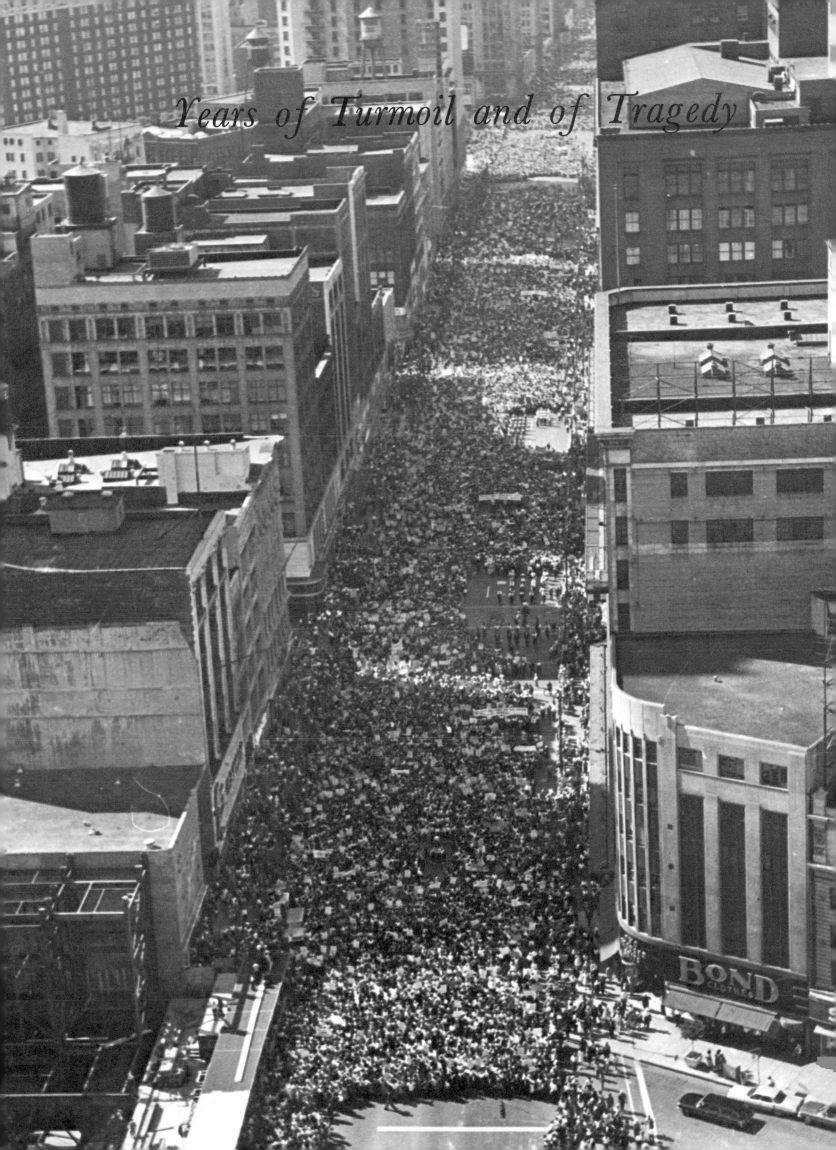

It was in the cities, where most of the residents of Michigan now lived, that the most critical problems had developed by the last half of the twentieth century. The heart of any city is its business district. Here, as in the case of downtown Grand Rapids, were the department stores, the hotels, the office buildings, and the other buildings around which a city's life had traditionally revolved.

But as the cities grew in size and spread out, and everyone began to drive his own car to get about in the city, traffic in the downtown areas became increasingly congested and more and more people came to look upon the shopping trip downtown as a chore rather than a pleasure. Kalamazoo in 1959 pioneered in trying to do something about this particular problem by removing motor traffic entirely from several blocks of the main street through the heart of the business area. Pavements were ripped up, and a series of malls were built. Motor traffic was rerouted, new parking areas were provided, and the shopper on foot was free to wander back and forth across the mall between stores.

But in most cases, as the residential areas spread farther and farther out from the central business district, the merchants followed their customers into the suburbs. In the early fifties, the J. L. Hudson Company of Detroit built the huge Northland Shopping Center, just north of Eight-Mile Road,

which marks the northern city limits of Detroit as well as the dividing line between Wayne County and Oakland County. The large Hudson store in the center of the complex is flanked on three sides by one-story buildings containing a multitude of smaller shops that cater to virtually every conceivable need of the shopper. Radiating out from the stores are carefully arranged parking lots, provided free of charge. Beyond Northland in this aerial photograph can be seen thousands and thousands of acres of suburban homes, acres which once had been farmland and which now were incorporated into a flock of new cities that emerged in these years. These new cities had larger populations than most of Michigan's older cities that had been established a century earlier, but to a very large extent the income of the residents of these new communities was still dependent on jobs they held in Detroit.

Although Detroit's central, downtown business district continued to attract great numbers of people who needed the services found there that were not available even at Northland, the contrast between the sleek new shopping areas and many of Detroit's business areas, such as this one along Grand River Avenue near 14th Street, was graphic evidence of the decay that infected much of the city as tax-paying residents and businesses moved to the suburbs.

Evidence of decay was everywhere. At the corner of Third Street and Temple, just a short walk away from one of Detroit's showplaces, the Masonic Auditorium, this once proud home, photographed in 1965, was nothing but a large and picturesque billboard.

Slums were visible throughout the city — dilapidated, unpainted houses, littered streets — constituting veritable breeding grounds of trouble for the hapless residents of these areas as well as for the city and the state.

Courtesy: Detroit News

Slum-clearance programs, which had begun during the Depression years, helped a little. One of the most ambitious was the Jeffries Project, which consisted of a group of modern apartment buildings erected in the fifties along the John Lodge Expressway. These public-housing units gave many low-income families new hope to replace some of that which they had lost during long years of slum life.

But in other cases, blocks of slum housing were bulldozed and were replaced by luxury high-rise apartments — apartments that brought back into the city an affluent element that was much needed, but did little to benefit the displaced slum families. Lafayette Towers, designed by the great architect Ludwig Mies van der Rohe, was hailed as symbolic of the rebirth of downtown Detroit as a place to live as well as to work. In this photograph, taken October 3, 1968, the shack in the foreground, designer unknown, was symbolic of something quite different.

Courtesy: Detroit News

282

By the mid-sixties, one-third of Detroit's population was Negro, twice the proportion that had existed in 1950. Those who were living at or near the poverty level in the slums of Detroit, however, contained a far greater number of Negroes than the one-to-three ratio for the entire population would have indicated. There were, of course, plenty of examples of Negroes who had risen out of the ghetto and become as successful in their particular profession as anyone else. Willie Horton followed in the footsteps of such earlier Detroit Negroes as Eddie Tolan and Joe Louis to cash in on his athletic talents. In the postwar years, the doors of organized baseball, previously barred to the Negro, were opened, and although the Detroit Tigers were one of the last major-league teams to lower the color barrier, by the mid-sixties they had in the young, husky Horton, shown here cracking out a double at Tiger Stadium in the fateful summer of 1967, one of the most promising hitters in the big leagues and one of the most popular players with his home-town fans. By 1969 he was earning $65,000 a year, a far cry from the income his family had had a few years earlier.

Detroit Negroes also began to achieve success in the field of entertainment. In 1959, using $700 he had borrowed from a credit union, a young Detroit Negro, Berry Gordy, Jr., established Motown Records. Within little more than a half-decade, Gordy's company was at the top as seller of popular records, all of them featuring the distinctive "Motown Sound" and grossing $30,000,000 annually. Among the many Detroit Negro performers whom Gordy promoted, none were more successful than the Supremes, three young girls who in the mid-sixties were the foremost female singing group in the country. In less than two and a half years they had nine gold records, each symbolic of sales of at least a million copies. They were stars of national television shows, and they could not accept all the offers they received to perform in nightclubs, such as Detroit's Roostertail, where this picture was taken in 1966.

283

The somewhat special fields of sports and music were not the only fields in which Detroit and Michigan Negroes now began to make their mark. When Detroit observed its 250th birthday in 1951, few dignitaries who participated in the ceremonies were as famous as Ralph J. Bunche (second from the right in the front row), the recipient of the 1950 Nobel Peace Prize for his work as a United Nations negotiator who had succeeded in 1949 in ending the Arab-Israeli War. Bunche had been born in Detroit on August 7, 1904, at a time when Negroes in such professions as medicine, law, or education were almost nonexistent in that city. Nevertheless, Bunche went forth to graduate from the University of California in 1927, and to go on to Harvard, where he received his Ph.D. in political science in 1934. While on the faculty at Howard University, Bunche became well known in the thirties for his research in the areas of race relations and colonial administration. Following service with the Office of Strategic Services and the State Department during World War II, Bunche began his work with the United Nations organization in 1945, work that would soon gain him world-wide attention.

In Michigan itself, few individuals in the 1950's and 1960's had as distinguished a record of public service as Otis M. Smith, a Negro from Tennessee who had come to Michigan to practice law in Flint and after rapid advancement in that city was named chairman of the Michigan Public Service Commission in 1957. Two years later Governor Williams appointed Smith to the position of state Auditor General. After being elected to a full term in this office in 1960, Smith in 1961 was named by Governor Swainson to fill a vacancy on the state Supreme Court, a position to which Smith was elected for a full term in 1962. Later, in 1968, after leaving the court, Smith was appointed by Governor Romney to serve as a regent of the University of Michigan. In each instance, Otis Smith was the first Negro to hold these state offices. The fact that a talented Negro had been accorded these honors by three governors, representing both major parties, and by a majority of the voters of the state may have made it easier for other Negroes with similar abilities to gain more high offices in the future.

Willie Horton, the Supremes, Ralph Bunche, and Otis Smith were still the exceptions, however. Although Michigan's Negroes had made great advances in the first half of the twentieth century, the goals of achieving opportunities and treatment for the Negro equal to those accorded the whites were still a long way from being reached. Dewey Crosby was far more typical of Michigan Negroes than the handful of those who, like Joe Louis, became household names. The famed photographer David E. Scherman captured Crosby in the early fifties hard at work in the foundry at the Ford Rouge plant. Facing the white heat of the electric furnace, Crosby skims the slag from the molten iron, using a wooden two-by-four. Most whites, too, like Crosby, lived a life of relative anonymity in comparison with the illustrious few, but there was a difference. As hard as he might work, and as capable as he might be, there were still many jobs in many companies that were open to whites but not to Negroes. During the prosperous years of the fifties and sixties, the average Negro's income increased, but at a rate far below that of the average white man's income.

Courtesy: Ford Motor Company

It was certainly true that attitudes had changed since the early 1940's when white automobile workers in Detroit went on strike to protest the hiring of a few Negro employees or when other whites rioted to prevent Negro families from being permitted to live in public-housing developments. But despite what Detroit's leaders might say about the improvements in that city's racial relationships since the tragic days of 1943, deep divisions still existed, even if they were carefully hidden, as were these crude sentiments, scrawled on the rear of an upholstering shop in 1962. *Courtesy: Detroit News*

Courtesy: Detroit News

Then in the 1960's, out of the frustration at the slow progress that had been made in attaining the objectives Negro and many white leaders had been advocating for so many years, a new attitude was born among Negroes in Michigan and throughout the land. Demonstrations were held to show the determination of the Negro to break the barriers that had for so long held him back. One of the most massive of these held anywhere in the country was a "Walk to Freedom," called by an organization of Detroit Negro groups on June 23, 1963, the twentieth anniversary of that city's World War II race riot. National Negro leaders, including Dr. Martin Luther King (to the right of the policeman), led the march down Woodward Avenue.

Courtesy: Detroit News

Official estimates placed at 125,000 the number of marchers who filled the street and sidewalks as far as the observer could see out Woodward from the First National Bank building. Nothing like it had been seen before, and the sight undoubtedly struck terror into the hearts of many white racists. But at Cobo Hall, Martin Luther King told the fifteen thousand who assembled in the convention arena at the conclusion of the march that the events of the day had been "a magnificent demonstration of our commitment to non-violence." Dr. King concluded his speech with remarks virtually the same as those he expressed two months later following another great demonstration at Washington. He said he had had a dream, a dream of Negroes and whites "walking together hand in hand, free at last, free at last, free at last."

286

Other Negro leaders came to Detroit in these years, including Malcolm X, who, as Malcolm Little, had spent several years as a boy in the Lansing area. The manner in which his family had been treated at that time went a long way toward turning him into the militant Negro leader he had become in the early sixties. First as the second most powerful figure in the Black Muslim movement, the position he held when this picture was taken when he addressed a rally in Detroit's Olympic Stadium in 1962, and later as the head of a separate organization, Malcolm X had a far different message to bring than did Dr. King. Instead of the traditional integrationist approach, achieved through nonviolent means, Malcolm X preached black nationalism, with the black man seeking to gain what belonged to him by his own efforts and by whatever means were necessary.

Courtesy: Marquette Mining Journal

Courtesy: Detroit News

Although most people, Negro and white, hoped that the nonviolent approach advocated by the Rev. Martin Luther King would continue to prevail over what was generally interpreted, rightly or wrongly, as the appeal to violent methods put forth by Malcolm X, ultimately it appeared certain that historians of the future would look back upon the decade of the sixties as a period of violent upheavals. The pattern began to emerge in 1963 when readers of the Marquette *Mining Journal,* who might not have already heard the terrible news on their radio or television set, saw the headline in their afternoon paper that told them of the violent death of their President. Within five years both Martin Luther King and Malcolm X would meet their deaths in the same shocking manner.

To the young people who had been caught up in the magic of the Kennedy oratory on the steps of the Michigan Union in the fall of 1960, the assassination of their idol served to bring out into the open the vague feelings many of them had had of alienation from the goals and ideals of what now was called "the Establishment." Basically white in makeup, the student demonstrations of the sixties were sometimes, as in the case of this one at the University of Michigan in 1967, nonviolent, using techniques developed by Dr. King, but with increasing overtones of other methods of approach as the decade wore on. The well-publicized "generation gap" was nowhere more poignantly illustrated than in this scene where Dean William Haber leans against a desk, his chin resting on his hand, listening to one of the leaders of the student rebels standing in front of the desk, Haber's own son.

The violent death of President Kennedy, who had given millions of Negroes greater hopes for the future, helped to trigger expressions of Negro frustration far different from those led earlier by Martin Luther King and, once again, Detroit led the way. In the early morning hours of Sunday, July 23, 1967, Detroit police raided a Negro blind-pig establishment on the second floor of the building occupied by the Economy Printing Company (whose sign is partially visible in this photograph) on Twelfth Street near Clairmont. Despite the belief that was widespread among community leaders in the city, both black and white, that a system of communication between all elements in Detroit had been developed that would make it impossible for another event to occur such as had occurred twenty-four years earlier, within hours residents of this Negro section were rioting and looting in open defiance of the authorities, including some of the most prominent Negro leaders.

Courtesy: Burton Historical Collection

Although much of what happened during the next several days defied logical explanation, much of the looting in the Negro inner-city area was the result of long-held resentments against white-owned businesses. Here a loan company, a favorite target, has been broken into and looters calmly leave with their spoils.

Courtesy: Burton Historical Collection

As the frenzy of looting spread, however, the looters became less discriminating, and Negro business owners frantically sought to stave off attacks by putting up signs such as this one. The term "Soul," which replaced the word "Colored" that Negro merchants had scrawled on their windows during the riot of 1943, was in itself not only a new term used by the Negro to refer to himself and members of his race but was at the same time indicative of a far different attitude.

Courtesy: Burton Historical Collection

The looting was accompanied by fire bombings, which were so widespread that the fire department was unable to deal with all of them. When firemen were attacked by rioters and police were unable to protect them, fire-fighting equipment had to be withdrawn from some areas and the fires allowed to rage until they had burned themselves out, leaving blocks of devastation, such as this one, which observers at the time frequently compared with scenes of bombed-out cities in Europe during World War II.

When city authorities could not deal with the riot, the State Police and then Michigan National Guard units were called in. Finally, on the second day, after the same kind of agonizing and maneuvering that had accompanied the same decision in 1943, federal troops were called in who quickly gained control of the situation, but not before at least forty-two persons, nine of them white, had lost their lives, thousands had been injured, over four thousand arrested, and a tremendous amount of property destroyed (although the estimate of losses given out at the time was subsequently shown to have been grossly exaggerated). Significantly, the forces that quelled the riot and protected the crews who restored public services in the riot-torn areas were composed of both Negroes and whites.

Detroit, as it had so often been in the twentieth century, was once again the center of world-wide attention as reporters for newspapers, television, and radio flocked into the city to cover the big story. At press conferences, such as this one, they sought answers to the many questions that had arisen regarding the origins of the riot and how it had been handled by Cyrus Vance, special representative of President Johnson (seated in the middle), Governor Romney, and Detroit Mayor Jerome Cavanagh. Satisfactory answers might never be obtained in some cases, but there could be no doubt that the events in Detroit and the controversy over how these men had dealt with them proved to be a serious blow to the future political hopes of Romney, Cavanagh, and Vance's boss.

The rioting and violence of the summer of 1967 was not confined in Michigan to Detroit. Similar occurrences, on a scale somewhat proportionate to the size of the Negro population in the communities involved, broke out in Pontiac, Flint, Lansing, and Grand Rapids. Months later, a young boy in Grand Rapids walked by a building that had been damaged the previous summer and was still unrepaired while riot debris still littered the curb.

In the postriot period, Michigan Negroes began to evidence increased militancy, demanding action in many areas, especially in the area of education. Here a Grand Rapids Negro leader talks with a group of white teachers at the troubled South High School, located in a predominantly Negro section of the city. Student boycotts and other actions were taken to voice the dissatisfaction of many blacks with the kind of education they were receiving. The Negro leader's dress emphasizes the reawakening interest of many Negroes in their African background and heritage, an interest they now felt should be more evident in the courses that were taught in the schools.

Courtesy: Michigan Education Association

The exact degree to which the sentiments expressed on this page from a Detroit black militant paper reflected those of that city's Negro community in general was not readily determinable. But there could be no doubt that there had been a marked swing to increased militancy, a militancy that often seemed to reject the very goals for which Negroes had been fighting in the past, and to brand all those who still held with these established objectives as "Uncle Toms" in the case of Negroes, or "racists" in the case of whites who supported the same principles.

Inner City Voice, June, 1968

CAPON CORNER

Some trifling "Kneegrow" woman appeared on that job opportunity television program with the most notorious Tom in town, namely Francis the gay one and stated that she was the only negro woman in her business and she felt good about it.

The ad in the local Uncle Tom nespaper in support of Hubert Humphrey in which their names were listed looked like a who's who of Uncle Tomdom in Detroit

A nigger Policeman came by our office and tried to impress one of the sisters on the staff with the fact that he had gotten a medal for marksmanship during the July Rebellion in Detroit. It seems that the whitey's are not the only ones crazy on the police force. In checking on him we found that this fool was almost sent to the nut house last summer but, turned informer for the police and was subsequently reward-ed with a gun and uniform.

WHAT WE WANT NOW!   # WHAT WE BELIEVE

WHAT WE WANT

1. WE WANT FREEDOM. WE WANT POWER TO DETERMINE THE DESTINY OF OUR BLACK COMMUNITY.
2. WE WANT FULL EMPLOYMENT FOR OUR PEOPLE.
3. WE WANT AN END TO THE ROBBERY BY THE WHITE MAN OF OUR BLACK COMM-UNITY.
4. WE WANT DECENT HOUSING, FIT FOR SHELTER OF HUMAN BEINGS.
5. WE WANT EDUCATION FOR OUR PEOPLE THAT EXPOSES THE TRUE NATURE OF THIS DECADENT AMERICAN SOCIETY. WE WANT EDUCATION THAT TEACHES US OUR TRUE HISTORY AND OUR ROLE IN THE PRESENT DAY SOCIETY.
6. WE WANT ALL BLACK MEN TO BE EXEMPT FROM MILITARY SERVICE.
7. WE WANT AN IMMEDIATE END TO POLICE BRUTALITY AND MURDER OF BLACK PEOPLE.
8. WE WANT FREEDOM FOR ALL BLACK MEN HELD IN FEDERAL, STATE, COUNTY, AND CITY PRISONS AND JAILS.
9. WE WANT ALL BLACK PEOPLE WHEN BROUGHT TO TRIAL TO BE TRIED IN COURT BY A JURY OF THEIR PEER GROUP OR PEOPLE FROM THEIR BLACK COMM-UNITIES AS DEFINED BY THE CONSTITUTION OF THE UNITED STATES.
10. WE WANT LAND, BREAD, HOUSING, EDUCATION, CLOTHING, JUSTICE AND PEACE.

WHAT WE BELIEVE

1. WE BELIEVE THAT BLACK PEOPLE WILL NOT BE FREE UNTIL WE ARE ABLE TO DETERMINE OUR DESTINY.

2. WE BELIEVE THAT THE FEDERAL GOVERNMENT IS RESPONSIBLE AND OBLIGATED TO GIVE EVERY MAN EMPLOYMENT OR A GUARANTEED INCOME. WE BELIEVE THAT IF THE WHITE AMERICAN BUSINESS MEN WILL NOT GIVE FULL EMPLOYMENT, THEN THE MEANS OF PRODUCTION SHOULD BE TAKEN FROM THE BUSINESS MEN AND PLACED IN THE COMMUNITY SO THAT THE PEOPLE OF THE COMMUNITY CAN ORGAN-IZE AND EMPLOY ALL OF ITS PEOPLE AND GIVE A HIGH STANDARD OF LIVING.

3. WE BELIEVE THAT THIS RACIST GOVERNMENT HAS ROBBED US AND NOW WE ARE DEMANDING THE OVERDUE DEBT OF FORTY ACRES AND TWO MULES. FORTY ACRES AND TWO MULES WAS PROMISED 100 YEARS AGO AS RETRIBUTION FOR SLAVE LABOR AND MASS MURDER OF BLACK PEOPLE. WE WILL ACCEPT THE PAY-MENT IN CURRENCY WHICH WILL BE DISTRIBUTED TO OUR MANY COMMUNITIES. THE GERMANS ARE NOW AIDING THE JEWS IN ISRAEL FOR THE GENOCIDE OF THE JEWISH PEOPLE. THE GERMANS MURDERED 6,000,000 JEWS. THE AMERICAN RACIST HAS TAKEN PART IN THE SLAUGHTER OF OVER 50,000,000 BLACK PEOPLE; THEREFORE, WE FEEL THAT THIS IS A MODEST DEMAND THAT WE MAKE.

4. WE BELIEVE THAT IF THE WHITE LANDLORDS WILL NOT GIVE DECENT HOUS-ING TO OUR BLACK COMMUNITY, THEN THE HOUSING AND THE LAND SHOULD BE MADE INTO COOPERATIVES SO THAT OUR COMMUNITY, WITH GOVERNMENT AID, CAN BUILD AND MAKE DECENT HOUSING FOR ITS PEOPLE.

5. WE BELIEVE IN AN EDUCATIONAL SYSTEM THAT WILL GIVE TO OUR PEOPLE A KNOWLEDGE OF SELF. IF A MAN DOES NOT HAVE KNOWLEDGE OF HIMSELF AND HIS POSITION IN SOCIETY AND THE WORLD, THEN HE HAS LITTLE CHANCE TO RELATE TO ANYTHING ELSE.

6. WE BELIEVE THAT BLACK PEOPLE SHOULD NOT BE FORCED TO FIGHT IN THE MILITARY SERVICE TO DEFEND A RACIST GOVERNMENT THAT DOES NOT PROTECT US. WE WILL NOT FIGHT AND KILL OTHER PEOPLE OF COLOR IN THE WORLD WHO, LIKE BLACK PEOPLE, ARE BEING VICTIMIZED BY THE WHITE RACIST GOVERNMENT OF AMERICA. WE WILL PROTECT OURSELVES FROM THE FORCE AND VIOLENCE OF THE RACIST POLICE AND THE RACIST MILITARY, BY WHATEVER MEANS NECESSARY.

7. WE BELIEVE WE CAN END POLICE BRUTALITY IN OUR BLACK COMMUNITY BY ORGANIZING BLACK SELF DEFENSE GROUPS THAT ARE DEDICATED TO DEFENDING OUR BLACK COMMUNITY FROM RACIST POLICE OPPRESSION AND BRUTALITY. THE SECOND AMENDMENT OF THE CONSTITUTION OF THE UNITED STATES GIVES US A RIGHT TO BEAR ARMS. WE THEREFORE BELIEVE THAT ALL BLACK PEOPLE SHOULD ARM THEMSELVES FOR SELF DEFENSE.

8. WE BELIEVE THAT ALL BLACK PEOPLE SHOULD BE RELEASED FROM THE MANY JAILS AND PRISONS BECAUSE THEY HAVE NOT RECEIVED A FAIR AND IMPARTIAL TRIAL.

9. WE BELIEVE THAT THE COURTS SHOULD FOLLOW THE UNITED STATES CON-STITUTION SO THAT BLACK PEOPLE WILL RECEIVE FAIR TRIALS. THE 14TH AMENDMENT OF THE U.S. CONSTITUTION GIVES A MAN A RIGHT TO BE TRIED BY HIS PEER GROUP. A PEER IS A PERSON FROM A SIMILAR ECONOMIC, SOCIAL, RELIGIOUS, GEOGRAPHICAL, ENVIRONMENTAL, HISTORICAL AND RACIAL BACK-GROUND. TO DO THIS THE COURT WILL BE FORCED TO SELECT A JURY FROM THE BLACK COMMUNITY FROM WHICH THE BLACK DEFENDANT CAME. WE HAVE BEEN, AND ARE BEING TRIED BY ALL WHITE JURIES THAT HAVE NO UNDERSTANDING OF THE "AVERAGE REASONING MAN" OF THE BLACK COMMUNITY.

10. WHEN IN THE COURSE OF HUMAN EVENTS, IT BECOMES NECESSARY FOR ONE PEOPLE TO DISSOLVE THE POLITICAL BONDS WHICH HAVE CONNECTED THEM WITH ANOTHER, AND TO ASSUME AMONG THE POWERS OF THE EARTH, THE SEPARATE AND EQUAL STATION TO WHICH THE LAWS OF NATURE AND NATURE'S GOD ENTITLE THEM, A DECENT RESPECT TO THE OPINIONS OF MANKIND REQUIRES THAT THEY SHOULD DECLARE THE CAUSES WHICH IMPEL THEM TO SEPARATION. WE HOLD THESE TRUTHS TO BE SELF-EVIDENT, THAT ALL MEN ARE CREATED EQUAL, THAT THEY ARE ENDOWED BY THEIR CREATOR WITH CERTAIN INALIENABLE RIGHTS, THAT AMONG THESE ARE LIFE, LIBERTY AND THE PURSUIT OF HAPPINESS. THAT AMONG THESE ARE LIFE, LIBERTY AND THE PURSUIT OF HAPPINESS. THAT TO SECURE THESE RIGHTS, GOVERNMENTS ARE INSTITUTED AMONG MEN, DERIVING THEIR JUST POWERS FROM THE CONSENT OF THE GOVERNED, – THAT WHENEVER ANY FORM OF GOVERNMENT BECOMES DESTRUCTIVE OF THESE ENDS, IT IS THE RIGHT OF PEOPLE TO ALTER OR TO ABOLISH IT, AND TO INSTITUTE NEW GOVERNMENT, LAYING ITS FOUNDATION ON SUCH PRINCIPLES AND ORGANIZING ITS POWERS IN SUCH FORM AS TO THEM SHALL SEEM MOST LIKELY TO EFFECT THEIR SAFETY AND HAPPINESS.

PRUDENCE, INDEED, WILL DICTATE THAT GOVERNMENTS LONG ESTABLISHED SHOULD NOT BE CHANGED FOR LIGHT AND TRANSIENT CAUSES; AND ACCORDINGLY ALL EXPERIENCE HATH SHEWN, THAT MANKIND ARE MORE DISPOSED TO SUFFER, WHILE EVILS ARE SUFFERABLE, THAN TO RIGHT THEMSELVES BY ABOLISHING THE FORMS TO WHICH THEY ARE ACCUSTOMED. BUT WHEN A LONG TRAIN OF ABUSES AND USURPATIONS, PURSUING INVARIABLY THE SAME OBJECT, EVINCES A DESIGN TO REDUCE THEM UNDER ABSOLUTE DESPOTISM, IT IS THEIR RIGHT, IT IS THEIR DUTY, TO THROW OFF SUCH GOVERNMENT, AND TO PROVIDE NEW GUARDS FOR THEIR FUTURE SECURITY.

GUNS BABY GUNS

Human misery, caused by racial differences, was not confined entirely to Michigan's cities. In northern Michigan, where many of the state's Indians still lived, members of the once proud and mighty Potawatomi tribe were living in the most abject squalor on the Hannahville Reservation in Menominee County — off the heavily traveled main routes, forgotten by nearly everyone, eking out some income from the sale of handwoven baskets that were made beneath a sign that proclaimed: "What a Friend We Have in Jesus."

Courtesy: Detroit News

To some, the events of the sixties and the conditions that created them left little hope for the future, and only one who was completely insensitive to what was going on or who was an incurable optimist would deny that Michigan, as a community of human beings living side by side, was in the most critical period of its entire history. A glimmer of hope emerged from an unlikely source in the summer and fall of 1968 as Detroit's baseball team, composed of both white and Negro players, fought its way to the team's first American League championship since 1945. Playing before what was by far the largest number of fans ever to turn out during a season at Tiger Stadium, many of the players felt an added pressure in representing a city that had suffered so much and which they felt they had let down the previous year when they had muffed an earlier opportunity to win the pennant. In the World Series against the St. Louis Cardinals, the Tigers fell behind by what seemed, even to their staunchest supporters, a hopeless margin. But they battled back and miraculously emerged as World Champions. This was the scene at the conclusion of the seventh and decisive game in St. Louis on October 10, as catcher Bill Freehan joyfully lifts the winning pitcher, Mickey Lolich, off his feet, and second baseman Dick McAuliffe rushes over to join in the congratulations.

In Detroit and throughout Michigan, wild celebrations followed the Tiger victory, as Detroit became the champion of the baseball world again, as had happened eighty-one years earlier, as a result of defeating St. Louis. Thousands of fans came out to Metropolitan Airport on the night of October 10 to welcome their team back home. They broke through the gates and flooded the landing field, forcing airline officials for several hours to delay or reroute Detroit-bound planes, including the one carrying the Tigers, which landed instead at Willow Run Airport. The throng on the field was composed mostly of young people, most of them white, but with a scattering of Negroes. The thought must have occurred to some that if a baseball team could generate this kind of community spirit among so many people, who cheered or booed a player because of how he performed on the field and not because of the color of his skin, why could not the same spirit prevail on other levels of activity in the same community.

Courtesy: Detroit News

293

Courtesy: Michigan Historical Commission

In front of the City-County Building in downtown Detroit stands this figure by the Michigan sculptor Marshall Fredericks. It represents "The Spirit of Detroit," with the symbolism the artist intended being explained in the inscription placed near the base of the statue. In the late 1960's, the spirit of Detroit was frequently very low, and its spiritual depression affected the rest of the state as much as the depressed condition of the Motor City's economy in an earlier time had been reflected in economic conditions in the outstate areas. But just as Detroit and Michigan had survived that challenge, and just as Detroit had arisen anew from the ashes of the fire of 1805, as expressed in the motto inscribed on the city's coat of arms on the wall behind the statue, so now there are those who have confidence that Michigan will survive this latest and greatest crisis and emerge strengthened by the process of reevaluation, which these years of turmoil have forced upon its citizens.

INDEX

For convenience in reference, the major headings "Automobiles, *companies,*" and "Automobiles, *individual makes,*" have been used.

296

ACKNOWLEDGMENTS

Again, as in the case of the first volume of this history, it is a pleasure to acknowledge my indebtedness to the many individuals and organizations who helped me find the pictorial materials for this book. As was also true in Volume I, I relied heaviest upon the staff and the resources of the Michigan Historical Commission in Lansing. To Dr. Harry Kelsey and the members of his staff, especially Dennis Bodem, Donald Chaput, Kaye Averitt, Geneva Kebler, Mrs. Elizabeth Rademacher, and Steven B. Zamiara, I offer my gratitude for the assistance they supplied at all times during the project.

In addition, the following individuals and organizations provided assistance for which I am likewise grateful.

Adrian College, Adrian: Darrell H. Pollard and Ray Laakaniemi.
Alden B. Dow Associates, Inc., Midland: Robert A. Paulsen.
Ann Arbor *News:* Arthur Gallagher and Eck Stanger.
Automobile Manufacturers Association, Detroit: Robert C. Lusk.
Automotive History Collection, Detroit Public Library: James Bradley.
Bacon Memorial Public Library, Wyandotte: Mrs. Joseph C. DeWindt.
Baird, Willard, Lansing *State Journal.*
Bolt, Jack, Lansing *State Journal.*
Brown Brothers, New York City.
Burton Historical Collection, Detroit Public Library: James M. Babcock and Mrs. Bernice Sprenger.
Chicago *Tribune:* Harold F. Grumhaus.
Chrysler Historical Collection, Chrysler Corporation, Detroit: C. C. Lockwood.
Clarke Historical Library, Central Michigan University, Mt. Pleasant: John Cumming and Alexander Vittands.
Consumers Power Company, Jackson: Jack Dyer.
Cranbrook, Bloomfield Hills: Robert Hatt and Margaret Russell.
Crooks Studio, Flint: Kenneth Wallace.
Detroit Edison Company: Fred Steiner and Walter Doyle, Jr.
Detroit Historical Commission: Henry Brown and Lynda Heaton.
Detroit Lions: Elliott Trumbull.
Detroit *News:* Mrs. Ruth Braun and Ludean Earnest.
Detroit Public Library: Lawrence Brown of the Music and Fine Arts Division. (See also Automotive History Collection and Burton Historical Collection.)
Detroit Urban League: Francis A. Kornegay.
Eastern Michigan University, Ypsilanti: Mrs. Linda Chew and Walter Wager of the Audio-Visual Department, who made the photographic copies of most of the advertisements used in this book; Mrs. May T. Suzuki and Margaret A. Eide of the Library.
Flint *Journal:* Roland L. Martin and W. D. Chase.
Ford Archives, Dearborn: Henry E. Edmunds and Win Sears.
Ford Motor Company, Dearborn: Hal Stopchinski of the Photographic Department.
General Motors Corporation, Detroit: Maurice Wyss.
Grand Rapids *Press:* David Osborne.
Grand Rapids Public Museum: Dorothy E. Jaqua.
Henry Ford Museum, Dearborn: John S. Still.
Hagelthorn, E. G., Ford Motor Company, Dearborn.
Hidde, Doris, Flint Public Library.
Humberstone, Jordan, Ann Arbor.
Ironwood *Daily Globe:* Edwin Johnson.
Kalamazoo County Chamber of Commerce: John F. Hall.

Kalamazoo *Gazette:* Daniel M. Ryan.
Kellogg Company, Battle Creek: A. F. Finlay and Deryl Fleming.
Ketten, Tom, Sr., Belleville.
Kilborn, Harriet, Petoskey.
Klima, Joseph, Jr., Detroit Institute of Arts, who made the photographic copies of the materials credited to the Detroit Public Library, Automotive History Collection, and Burton Historical Collection.
Korab, Balthazar, Troy.
Lemmer, Victor F., Ironwood.
Manning, Bud, Manning Bros. Commercial Photographers, Highland Park.
Marquette *Mining Journal:* Kenneth S. Lowe.
Michigan Bell Telephone Company, Detroit: Sid Schroeder.
Michigan Department of Conservation, Lansing: John Gray, Russell McKee, and Mrs. Orpha Charles.
Michigan Department of Education, Lansing: Ira Polley and Dale Arnold.
Michigan Department of State Highways, Lansing: Ed Boucher.
Michigan Education Association, East Lansing: Elwood W. Landis.
Michigan Historical Collections, University of Michigan, Ann Arbor: Robert M. Warner and the members of his staff, especially Ida Brown, Tom Powers, Mrs. Janice Earle, and Mary Jo Pugh.
Michigan National Bank, Lansing: Howard J. Stoddard and Robert A. Fisher.
Michigan State University, East Lansing: William H. Combs of the Historical Collections.
Michigan Tourist Council, Lansing: John Boughton and John Maters.
Micro-Photo Division, Bell and Howell, Wooster, Ohio: Jess Box.
Middleton, Arthur, Battle Creek *Enquirer and News.*
Monroe *Evening News:* Roy Hamlin.
National Park Service, Washington, D. C.: Jerry L. Rogers.
Netherlands Information Service, Holland: George Cook.
Niemeyer, Glenn A., Grand Valley State College.
Nye, Russel B., Michigan State University.
Pierrot, George F., Detroit.
Rich, Philip T., Midland *Daily News.*
St. Ignace Chamber of Commerce: Mrs. Norma Hedrick.
St. Ignace School District: Lee A. Richlen.
Schwarz, Richard W., Andrews University.
Smithsonian Institution, Washington, D. C.: Peter C. Welsh.
Soini, Paul D., Bad Axe.
State Building Division, Bureau of the Budget, Lansing: Adrian N. Langius.
Stross, Allen, Detroit.

Transportation Library, University of Michigan, Ann Arbor: Robert T. Freese, Sharon Hafeman.

University of Michigan, Ann Arbor: Fred Anderegg and Mrs. Carmen Krasteff of Photographic Services, through whose efforts photographic copies were made of the items credited to the Michigan Historical Collections and of a number of the other illustrations; Bob McFarland of Sports Information. (See also Michigan Historical Collections, Transportation Library, and William L. Clements Library.)

Upper Michigan Tourist Association, Iron Mountain: Kenneth Dorman and Mrs. Dorothy Lodge.

Wayne State University, Detroit: Philip P. Mason and Warner W. Pflug of the Labor History Archives; Charles A. Lewis of University Relations.

Wells, Carlton F., Ann Arbor.

Western Michigan University, Kalamazoo: Wayne C. Mann of the Archives; Arthur O'Connor of University Information; and Willis F. Dunbar.

Wide World Photos, Inc., New York City.

William L. Clements Library, University of Michigan, Ann Arbor: Nathan Shipton.

Sometimes, although unfortunately not in all cases, the agencies whose pictures I have used have indicated where they originally obtained these photographs. I have given this information below, together with information regarding the origins of certain other illustrations.

P. 18, lower left: Port Huron Chamber of Commerce. P. 20, all pictures: Al Barnes. P. 21, middle: Adrian *Daily Telegram*. P. 22, bottom: Al Barnes. P. 23, upper left, upper right, lower left: Music and Fine Arts Division. Lower right: Michigan Historical Collections. P. 24, middle: Detroit *News*. P. 32, both pictures: Al Barnes. P. 33, bottom: Al Barnes. P. 34, bottom: Vaughan Lake. P. 35, top: Mrs. Vena Spencer Lett. Bottom: National Archives. P. 37, lower left: Paul Steketee and Sons. Lower right: Detroit Edison Company. P. 43, top: George Wiskemann. Middle: Marquette County Historical Society. P. 44, Mrs. Athol Gamble. P. 48, bottom: Al Barnes. P. 54, top: Harvey Croze, photographer. Bottom: Michigan National Guard. P. 59, top: Saginaw Chamber of Commerce. Middle: Alma Chamber of Commerce. Bottom: Shiawassee *News*. P. 60, upper left: Burton Historical Collection. Lower right: Ferry-Morse Seed Company. P. 61, bottom: Hastings *Banner*. P. 68, lower left and right: Michigan Department of Conservation. P. 69, upper left and right: Michigan Department of Conservation. Lower right: Michigan Tourist Council. P. 70, upper left: Packaging Corporation of America. Center right: Michigan Tourist Council. P. 71, bottom: Library of Congress. P. 73, upper left: Vaughan Lake. P. 76, center left and bottom: John Widdicomb Company. P. 78, upper right: Marquette County Historical Society. P. 79, upper right: Detroit *News*. Lower left: Michigan Tourist Council. P. 80, upper left and right: Curran Russell. Lower left: International Salt Company. Lower right: Ferde Beltz Studio. P. 81, upper left and right: United States Steel Corporation. Lower left: Abrams Aerial Survey. Lower right: Michigan Tourist Council. P. 82, lower left: Detroit Edison Company. P. 83, all pictures: Esther R. Railton. P. 84, top and center: Dow Chemical Company. Bottom: Wyandotte Chemicals Corporation. P. 85, upper left: Burton Historical Collection. P. 86, lower left: Burton Historical Collection. P. 87, top: Great Lakes Steel Corporation. P. 99, top: Ford Motor Company. P. 107, middle: Ford Archives. P. 121, top: Library of Congress. P. 122, top: Ford Archives. P. 130, middle: Marquette County Historical Society. P. 131, top: Automobile Manufacturers Association. Bottom: Adrian *Daily Telegram*. P. 133, bottom: Bureau of Public Roads. P. 146, top: Detroit *News*. P. 151, top: Transportation Library. P. 156, bottom: Verne Hohl Studios. P. 159, lower left and right: Music and Fine Arts Division. P. 161, top: Holland Tulip Time Festival. P. 163, bottom: Farmers and Manufacturers Beet Sugar Association. P. 167, lower left: Michigan Department of Conservation. Lower right: Michigan Tourist Council. P. 174, bottom: Manning Brothers, photographers. P. 175, top: J. L. Hudson Company. P. 185, upper right: Linn Photo. P. 197, middle: National Archives. Bottom: Mason County Historical Society. P. 198, top: National Archives. P. 201, upper left: Sports Information Office. P. 205, bottom: Marquette County Historical Society. P. 206, Marquette County Historical Society. P. 208, top: Labor History Archives. P. 209, upper right: Labor History Archives. P. 213, middle: General Motors Corporation. P. 218, top: Albert Kahn Associated Architects and Engineers. P. 219, bottom: Ford Archives. P. 226, bottom: Labor History Archives. P. 228, top: General Motors Corporation. P. 233, bottom: Michigan Tourist Council. P. 241, top: Lens-Art Photo. P. 242, top: photo furnished by Alden Dow Associates. Bottom: Michigan State Highway Department. P. 243, top and middle: Michigan State Highway Department. P. 245, upper left: Michigan Tourist Council. Upper right: General Motors Photographic. Bottom: Allen Stross. P. 246, upper right: Reynolds Metals Company. P. 247, bottom: photo furnished by Michigan State University. P. 248, bottom: University of Michigan. P. 251, bottom: Mackinac Bridge Authority. P. 253, upper left: Traverse City Chamber of Commerce. P. 258, lower left: Michigan Tourist Council. Lower right: Mickey Duggan, photographer, and Carl Nordberg. P. 259, both pictures: Mackinac Bridge Authority. P. 260, bottom: Michigan Tourist Council. P. 261, top: West Michigan Tourist Association. Bottom: Virgil D. Haynes. P. 262, top: Michigan Tourist Council. P. 263, top: Menominee Chamber of Commerce. Bottom: Virgil D. Haynes. P. 264, middle: Michigan Tourist Council. Bottom: Tawas City Chamber of Commerce. P. 266, both pictures: Michigan Tourist Council. P. 267, top: East Michigan Tourist Association. P. 268, bottom: Detroit *News*. P. 270, bottom: Jim Galbraith, photographer. P. 271, lower left: Michigan Tourist Council. Lower right: Michigan Department of Conservation. P. 272, both pictures: photos furnished by Victor F. Lemmer. P. 273, all pictures: photos furnished by Victor F. Lemmer. P. 276, top: Wayne Schieber, photographer. P. 280, bottom: York Photographic Studios. P. 292, all pictures: Victor Lundgren, photographer. P. 294, Michigan Tourist Council.